Today We Celebrate

Today We Celebrate

The saints and their message for us

Gerard MacGinty OSB

Collins

Collins Liturgical Publications
8 Grafton Street, London W1X 3LA

Distributed in Ireland by
Educational Company of Ireland
21 Talbot Street, Dublin 1

Collins Liturgical Australia
PO Box 3023, Sydney 2001

Nihil obstat Anton Cowan *censor*
Imprimatur Ralph Brown VG

Westminster 17 October, 1985
Feast of St Ignatius of Antioch

The Nihil obstat and Imprimatur are a declaration that a book or pamphlet is considered to be free from doctrinal or moral error. It is not implied that those who have granted the Nihil obstat and Imprimatur agree with the contents, opinions or statements expressed.

Typographical design by Yvonne Dedman
Typeset by John Swain and Son (Glasgow) Limited
Made and printed in Great Britain by The Bath Press

Contents

Acknowledgements

Every effort has been made to trace the copyright owners of material included in this book. However, the author and publisher would be grateful if any omissions in these acknowledgements could be brought to their attention, for correction in future editions. The publishers are grateful for permission to reprint the following material:

America: National Catholic Weekly Review for *A Homily* by Fr. Delp SJ.

Anthony Clarke Books for *St John Fisher* by E. E. Reynolds.

The Catholic University of America Press for extracts from the *Fathers of the Church* series.

Cistercian Publications Inc. for *Bernard of Clairvaux: Five Books on Consideration* tr. John D. Anderson and Elizabeth T. Kennan; *Magnificat: Homilies in Praise of the Blessed Virgin Mary* tr. Grace Perigo.

Wm. Collins Sons & Co., Harvill Press for *The Life of St Catherine of Siena* tr. George Lamb.

Darton Longman & Todd Ltd. for *Day by Day with St Matthew's Gospel* by R. Gutzwiller; *St Margaret Mary, her Autobiography* tr. Vincent Kerns.

Dominican Publications, Dublin and Passionist Fathers for *In This Sign: The Spirituality of St Paul of the Cross* by Martin Bielas CP.

Dublin Institute for Advanced Studies for *Sancti Columbani Opera* tr. G. S. M. Walker in the *Series Scriptores Latini Hiberniae* (Dublin 1957).

Faber and Faber Ltd. for *Selected Writings on the Spiritual Life* by St Peter Damian (translated and introduced by Patricia McNulty).

David Farmer for *The Monk of Farne* by a Benedictine of Stanbrook.

Gill and Macmillan Ltd. for *St John of God* by Norbert McMahon; *St John Eudes: A Spiritual Portrait* tr. P. Herambourg; *A Letter from Jesus Christ by John of Landsberg* ed. John Griffiths.

Hodder & Stoughton for *Searching for God* by Cardinal Basil Hume.

Longman's for *St Briget of Sweden II* tr. Ingeborg Lund.

Macmillan Publishing Co. Inc. New York for *Early Christian Fathers* by Cyril Richardson.

A. R. Mowbray & Co. Ltd. for *The Steps of Humility* tr. G. Webb and A. Walker; *The Ladder of Monks and Twelve Meditations* tr. E. Colledge OSA and J. Walsh SJ.

Oxford University Press for *Documents of the Christian Church* ed. H. Bettenson; *Theological Texts* ed. Thomas Gilby OP; *Adomnan's Life of Columba* by A. O. and M. O. Anderson.

Paulist Newman Press for *Letters of Paulinus of Nola 2* tr. P. G. Walsh. Paulist Newman Press and SPCK for *Francis and Clare, The Complete Works* tr. R. J. Armstrong OFM and C. M. Brady OFM.

Penguin Books Ltd. for *St Augustine: Confessions* tr. R. S. Pine-Coffin; *The Prayers and Meditations of St Anselm* tr. Sister Benedicta Ward; *Early Christian Writings: The Apostolic Fathers* tr. Maxwell Staniforth.

Terry Shand for *Heart of Saints* by Francis W. Johnson.

SPCK for *Lactantis' Epitome of the Divine Institutions* tr. E. H. Blakeney.

St Anthony's Guild Press for *The Breviloquium IV* tr. Jose de Vinck.

The Trustees for Roman Catholic Purposes for *Life of St Camillus of Lellis* by C. C. Martindale SJ and for *Francis Xavier* and *St Peter Canisius* by Father James Brodrick SJ.

Verlag Herder GmbH & Co Kg for *Mary, Mother of the Lord* by Karl Rahner.

A. P. Watt Ltd. and the Estate of Ronald Knox for *Sermon on the English Martyrs* from *Occasional Sermons* by Mgr. Ronald Knox.

Winston Seabury Press for *The Life and Writings of the Historical St Patrick* by R. P. C. Hanson.

Non nobis, Domine, non nobis
sed nomini tuo da gloriam

Preface

I warmly welcome *Today We Celebrate* compiled by Father Gerard MacGinty OSB, a monk of Glenstal. It is encouraging to find Glenstal Abbey continuing its quiet but essential work in the liturgical apostolate in Ireland.

In this book Father MacGinty gives us a short biographical note on each saint in the General Calendar of the Roman Missal, and this is followed by a reading from the saint's own writings, where such exist, or from the biographer of the saint or some writing relating to the saint's character and work.

All this is very timely because the saints are in danger of being marginalized in liturgical celebrations and in the lived experience of Christians. The dropping of certain saints from the Roman Calendar in recent years has been wrongly interpreted as a down-grading of the saints in liturgical celebrations and in Christian life. This is not so. The Church wants to broaden, not narrow, our Christian experience by directing our attention to those who gave heroic witness to holiness in all ages and in all walks of life. The memory of all of us should encompass not only the essential truths of faith but also familiarity with the varied lives of those who demonstrated generosity and nobility in living that faith.

In the past the biographers of the saints may not have served their subjects well: by presenting people larger than life they made it difficult for us to identify with them. Father MacGinty wisely allows the saints to speak for themselves. May their message as presented here find many attentive listeners.

✠ *Michael A. Harty*
Bishop of Killaloe

Prefatory Note

This book has been prepared with the intention of helping those who follow the General Calendar of the Roman Missal to celebrate with some degree of understanding and devotion those saints' days contained in the Proper of Saints. The book itself was undertaken at the suggestion of Mrs Sue Chapman of Collins Liturgical Publications. Now that it is completed I can say that I enjoyed doing the work, but still wonder at my own temerity in accepting to do it in the first place!

The matter is treated as follows: First, a general introduction explains the position of the saints in God's plan and their relationship with us. This is set out almost exclusively in the words of the Second Vatican Council. Then the meaning of such concepts as 'martyr', etc., and the nature of christian holiness are dealt with, followed by a note on the celebration of saints' days. The Introduction concludes with an important cautionary note. In the main section of the book that follows, the celebrations are presented one by one, beginning with 2 January. Each has a short historical introduction and commentary, followed by a reading from the saint's own writings, where such exist or are meaningful today, or from christian tradition relating in some way to what is being celebrated.

My choice of readings has been governed by a desire to help contemporaries appreciate something of the teaching or the witness of the saints, and not necessarily to present what is most typical of the saint being celebrated (see p. 26 below). It is important to note that the spirit in which the various choices was made was 'contemplative'. That is to say, the readings aim to fill a spiritual need by providing food for thought and reflection and thus leading the reader to enrich and deepen his or her prayer life. In this sense, and because the readings follow the Church's General Calendar, *Today We Celebrate* may become a useful companion to the Divine Office and daily Mass. Finally, it should be noted that in various texts, where the sense permitted it, an attempt has been made to universalize the language, in this way slightly modifying the original. This has been done to avoid offending the susceptibilities of certain readers.

Most of the books I used are from the monastery library, but I have to thank others who facilitated me with access to texts I could not come by here, in particular The Reverend Librarian SJ of the Milltown Institute, Dublin, The Reverend Librarian OP, St Mary's Priory, Tallaght, and others who helped me by the gift or loan of books, or by making enquiries for me.

Lastly I must thank my confrere, Fr Christopher Dillon, for casting an eye over my few translations from Greek. In all events the responsibility for any errors remains mine.

Saint Columba's Day 1985   *Gerard MacGinty OSB*
                                        Glenstal Abbey, Ireland

Introduction   Today We Celebrate

The Church offers her worship to God day by day. The days build into weeks, the weeks into years. The first day of the week, the Lord's Day or Sunday, is marked since apostolic times by the celebration of the Easter mystery and is the original feast day. Upon this weekly recalling of the Lord's death and resurrection, which is ours too by virtue of baptism, is superimposed a yearly cycle beginning with Advent. Advent prepares for the coming of the Lord, not just at the first Christmas or in the Christmas mystery but finally at the end of time. Lent prepares for the solemn celebration of the Easter mystery in a particular way, and Eastertide dwells especially on the joy of our new life in the Risen Christ and looks to the coming of the Spirit, already in that Spirit, before returning to the weekly routine of the Sundays in 'Ordinary Time'.

Another round of celebrations, following the slightly different rhythm of the calendar year, is that of the Saints' Days. These are the occasions for calling to mind those who have gone before us in the christian life and have been judged to have excelled in the living of that life. It is with this particular round that we are now concerned — that those who pray may be helped to pray with understanding (cf 1 Cor 14:15).

The Church and the Saints

The saints are God's gift to his Church which, in turn, proposes them to us for our celebration and inspiration. Since it is in the Church that we recall the saints, we cannot do better than look to its teaching on the relationships between ourselves, as the Church on earth, and those who have passed from this mortal life to constitute the Church in heaven. We find this teaching in the Second Vatican Council's *Dogmatic Constitution on The Church,* chapter 7 'The Eschatological Nature of the Pilgrim Church and her Union with the Heavenly Church' (nn. 48-51). The text of the chapter is here given in full.

48 The Church, to which we are all called in Christ Jesus, and in which we acquire sanctity through the grace of God, will attain her full perfection only in the glory of heaven. Then will come the time

of the restoration of all things (Acts 3:21). Then the human race as well as the entire world, which is intimately related to humankind and achieves its purpose through humankind, will be perfectly re-established in Christ (cf Eph 1:10; Col 1:20; 2 Pet 3:10-13).

Christ, having been lifted up from the earth, is drawing all people to himself (Jn 12:32, Greek text). Rising from the dead (cf Rom 6:9), he sent his life-giving Spirit upon his disciples and through this Spirit has established his body, the Church, as the universal sacrament of salvation. Sitting at the right hand of the Father, he is continually active in the world, leading men and women to the Church, and through her joining them more closely to himself and making them partakers of his glorious life by nourishing them with his own body and blood.

Therefore, the promised restoration which we are awaiting has already begun in Christ, is carried forward in the mission of the Holy Spirit, and through him continues in the Church. There we learn through faith the meaning, too, of our temporal life, as we perform, with hope of good things to come, the task committed to us in this world by the Father, and work out our salvation (cf Phil 2:12).

The final age of the world has already come upon us (cf 1 Cor 10:11). The renovation of the world has been irrevocably decreed and in this age is already anticipated in some real way. For even now on this earth the Church is marked with a genuine though imperfect holiness. However, until there is a new heaven and a new earth where justice dwells (cf 2 Pet 3:13), the pilgrim Church in her sacraments and institutions, which pertain to this present time, takes on the appearance of this passing world. She herself dwells among creatures who groan and travail in pain until now and await the revelation of the sons of God (cf Rom 8:19-22).

Joined with Christ in the Church and signed with the Holy Spirit 'who is the pledge of our inheritance' (Eph 1:14), we are truly called children of God and such we are (cf 1 Jn 3:1). But we have not yet appeared with Christ in the state of glory (cf Col 3:4), in which we shall be like to God, since we shall see him as he is (cf 1 Jn 3:2). Therefore 'while we are in the body, we are exiled from the Lord' (2 Cor 5:6), and having the first fruits of the Spirit we groan within ourselves (cf Rom 8:23) and desire to be with Christ (cf Phil 1:23). A common love urges us to live more for him, who died for us and rose again (cf 2 Cor 5:15). We strive therefore to please the Lord in all things (cf 2 Cor 5:9). We put on the armour of God that we may be able to stand against the wiles of the devil and resist on the evil day (cf Eph 6:11-13).

Since we know not the day nor the hour, on our Lord's advice we must constantly stand guard. Thus when we have finished the one and only course of our earthly life (cf Heb 9:27) we may merit to enter into the marriage feast with him and to be numbered among the blessed (cf Mt 25:31-46). Thus we may not be commanded to go into eternal fire (cf Mt 25:41) like the wicked and slothful servant (cf Mt 25:26), into the exterior darkness where 'there will be the weeping and the gnashing of teeth' (Mt 22:13; 25:30). For before we reign with the glorious Christ, all of us will be made manifest 'before the tribunal of Christ, so that each one may receive what he has won through the body, according to his works, whether good or evil' (2 Cor 5:10). At the end of the world, 'they who have done good shall come forth unto resurrection of life; but who have done evil unto resurrection of judgment' (Jn 5:29; cf Mt 25:46).

We reckon therefore that 'the sufferings of the present time are not worthy to be compared with the glory to come that will be revealed in us' (Rom 8:18; cf 2 Tim 2:11-12). Strong in faith we look for 'the blessed hope and glorious coming of our great God and saviour, Jesus Christ' (Tit 2:13) 'who will refashion the body of our lowliness, conforming it to the body of his glory' (Phil 3:21) and who will come 'to be glorified in his saints, and to be marvelled at in all those who have believed' (2 Thess 1:10).

49 When the Lord comes in his majesty, and all the angels with him (cf Mt 25:31), death will be destroyed and all things will be subject to him (cf 1 Cor 15:26-27). Meanwhile some of his disciples are exiles on earth. Some have finished with this life and are being purified. Others are in glory, beholding 'clearly God himself triune and one, as he is'.

But in various ways and degrees we all partake in the same love

15

for God and neighbour, and all sing the same hymn of glory to our God. For all who belong to Christ, having his Spirit, form one Church and cleave together in him (cf Eph 4:16). Therefore the union of the wayfarers with the brethren who have gone to sleep in the peace of Christ is not in the least interrupted. On the contrary, according to the perennial faith of the Church, it is strengthened through the exchanging of spiritual goods.

For by reason of the fact that those in heaven are more closely united with Christ, they establish the whole Church more firmly in holiness, lend nobility to the worship which the Church offers on earth to God, and in many ways contribute to its greater upbuilding (cf 1 Cor 12:12-27). For after they have been received into their heavenly home and are present to the Lord (cf 2 Cor 5:8), through him and in him, they do not cease to intercede with the Father for us. Rather, they show forth the merits which they won on earth through the one mediator between God and man, Christ Jesus (cf 1 Tim 2:5). There they served God in all things and filled up in their flesh whatever was lacking of the sufferings of Christ on behalf of his body which is the Church (cf Col 1:24). Thus by their brotherly interest our weakness is very greatly strengthened.

50 Very much aware of the bonds linking the whole Mystical Body of Jesus Christ, the pilgrim Church from the very first ages of the christian religion has cultivated with great piety the memory of the dead. Because it is 'a holy and wholesome thought to pray for the dead that they may be loosed from sins' (2 Mach 12:46), she has also offered prayers for them.

The Church has always believed that the apostles, and Christ's martyrs who had given the supreme witness of faith and charity by the shedding of their blood, are quite closely joined with us in Christ. She has always venerated them with special devotion, together with the Blessed Virgin Mary and the holy angels. The Church too has devoutly implored the aid of their intercession. To these were soon added those who had imitated Christ's virginity and poverty more exactly, and finally others whom the outstanding practice of the christian virtues and the divine charisms recommended to the pious devotion and imitation of the faithful.

For when we look at the lives of those who have faithfully followed Christ, we are inspired with a new reason for seeking the city which is to come (Heb 13:14; 11:10). At the same time we are shown a most safe path by which, among the vicissitudes of this world and in keeping with the state in life and condition proper to each of us, we will be able to arrive at perfect union with Christ, that is, holiness. In the lives of those who shared in our humanity and yet were transformed into especially successful images of Christ (cf 2 Cor 3:18), God vividly manifests to all people his presence and his face. He speaks to us in them, and gives us a sign of his kingdom, to which we are powerfully drawn, surrounded as we are by so many witnesses (cf Heb 12:1), and having such an argument for the truth of the gospel.

Now, it is not only by the title of example that we cherish the memory of those in heaven. We do so still more in order that the union of the whole Church may be strengthened in the Spirit by the practice of fraternal charity (cf Eph 4:1-6). For just as christian communion among wayfarers brings us closer to Christ, so our companionship with the saints joins us to Christ, from whom as from their fountain and head issue every grace and the life of God's People itself.

It is supremely fitting, therefore, that we love those friends and fellow heirs of Jesus Christ, who are also our brothers and extraordinary benefactors, that we render due thanks to God for them and 'suppliantly invoke them and have recourse to their prayers, their power and help in obtaining benefits from God through his Son, Jesus Christ, our Lord, who is our sole redeemer and saviour'. For by its very nature every genuine testimony of love which we show to those in heaven tends toward and terminates in Christ, who is the 'crown of all saints'. Through him it tends toward and terminates in God, who is wonderful in his saints and is magnified in them.

Our union with the Church in heaven is put into effect in its noblest manner when with common rejoicing we celebrate together the praise of the divine Majesty. Then all those from every tribe and tongue and people and nation (cf Apoc 5:9) who have been redeemed by the blood of Christ and gathered together

17

into one Church, with one song of praise magnify the one and triune God. Such is especially the case in the sacred liturgy, where the power of the Holy Spirit acts upon us through sacramental signs. Celebrating the eucharistic sacrifice, therefore, we are most closely united to the worshipping Church in heaven as we join with and venerate the memory first of all of the glorious ever-Virgin Mary, of the Blessed Joseph and the blessed apostles and martyrs, and of all the saints.

51 This most sacred Synod accepts with great devotion the venerable faith of our ancestors regarding this vital fellowship with our brethren who are in heavenly glory or who are still being purified after death. It proposes again the decrees of the Second Council of Nicea, the Council of Florence and the Council of Trent. And at the same time, as part of its own pastoral solicitude, this Synod urges all concerned to work hard to prevent or correct any abuses, excesses, or defects which may have crept in here and there, and to restore all things to a more ample praise of Christ and of God.

Let the faithful be taught, therefore, that the authentic cult of the saints consists not so much in the multiplying of external acts, but rather in the intensity of our active love. By such love, for our own greater good and that of the Church, we seek from the saints 'example in their way of life, fellowship in their communion, and aid by their intercession'. At the same time, let the people be instructed that our communion with those in heaven, provided that it is understood in the more adequate light of faith, in no way weakens, but conversely, more thoroughly enriches the supreme worship we give to God the Father, through Christ, in the Spirit.

For as long as all of us, who are sons of God and comprise one family in Christ (cf Heb 3:6), remain in communion with one another in mutual charity and in one praise of the most Holy Trinity, we are responding to the deepest vocation of the Church and partaking in a foretaste of the liturgy of consummate glory. For when Christ shall appear and the glorious resurrection of the dead takes place, the splendour of God will brighten the heavenly city and the Lamb will be its lamp (cf Apoc 21:23). Then in the supreme happiness of charity the whole Church of the saints will adore God and 'the Lamb who was slain' (Apoc 5:12), proclaiming with one voice: 'To him who sits upon the throne, and to the Lamb, blessing and honour and glory and dominion, forever and ever' (Apoc 5:13-14).*

Martyrs and Martyrdom

To understand better the various references to martyrs and saints something must be said about martyrs and martyrdom and about christian holiness.

Martyr is a Greek word meaning 'a witness'. In the New Testament it is used in this primary sense (e.g. Mt 18:16; 26:65; Mk 14:63; 2 Cor 13:1; 1 Tim 5:19; Heb 10:28; Acts 7:58), but it also has further uses, for underlying the notion is the *authority* of the one who witnesses. So God can be called as witness (Rom 1:19; Phil 1:8; 1 Thess 2:5, 10; 1 Tim 6:12; 2 Tim 2:2). Then in the Apocalypse Jesus himself is called 'the witness' (1:5; 3:14). A further development from this in the New Testament is the use of the word to mean those who preach Christ. This is a usage of the Acts of the Apostles (1:8, 22; 2:32; 3:15; 5:32; 10:39, 40-41; 13:31; 22:15; 26:16; and see also, 1 Pet 5:1; Apoc 11:3) the general sense of which is that of bearing witness to the events of Christ's life, to his sufferings, and particularly to *his rising from the dead*. Manifestly this witness must be borne before others. A last use in the New Testament is the applying of the term to those *who died as a consequence of this witness*; so Stephen (Acts 22:20), and others unnamed (Apoc 2:13; 17:6). The emphasis is on their witnessing.

Then a change took place. We do not know how. By the latter half of the second century of the christian era, at least, the word *martyr* had taken on the technical meaning of one who had witnessed to Christ by the shedding of his or her blood, and it is this meaning which the word retains down to our day. We can understand the sense of the development, although we are ignorant of its precise mechanics. The undergoing of death for Christ's sake was a witness-ing, and a supreme witnessing, to the truth of his resurrection, for it is in his resurrection that we have the assurance of our new life in him. It would be helpful to read chapter 8 of the Letter to the Romans

---

* From *The Documents of Vatican II*, General Editor: Walter M. Abbott SJ, Geoffrey Chapman, London–Dublin 1966, pp 78-85.

in this context, but the ideal which inspired the martyrs is to be found elsewhere in the New Testament as well. Knowing the sense of the development we also know that it was occasioned by persecution.

Persecution had different origins, in the first place coming from the Jewish authorities, whether religious or secular, then later from the Roman Empire.

The New Testament gives us some details of the persecution of which the 'martyr' St Stephen was a victim (Acts 6:9-15; 7:55-8:3), and of the later one in which James, son of Zebedee, perished (Acts 12:2). James, the brother of Jesus, died in similar circumstances some time after the son of Zebedee. Stephen was stoned for what was judged blasphemy; James was slain by Herod, possibly to gain favour with the Jewish authorities.

The Roman authorities initially regarded Christianity as a Jewish sect, and so gave it the toleration accorded to Judaism as a 'lawful religion' within the empire. The first break with this position was under *Nero* (emperor 54-68 AD), who, towards the latter half of his reign, savagely persecuted the Christians in Rome itself — St Peter suffered in this persecution. Nero's action would seem to have been purely personal. Towards the end of the century, however, Christianity came to be seen as distinct from Judaism, and persecution flared under *Domitian* (emperor 81-96 AD). The stage was set for subsequent persecutions.

Under Domitian's successor, *Trajan,* the lines of policy were set down which were to endure for about a hundred and fifty years. In a reply to one of his governors he stated: (i) Christians denounced and convicted as such were to be punished; (ii) those who renounced their faith and offered sacrifices to the gods were to be set free; and (iii) anonymous denunciations were to be ignored.

In the middle of the third century a change of policy took place, under *Decius* first and then *Valerian*. Both sought to weed out Christianity. Everyone was ordered to offer sacrifice in 249-250 and again in 257-258. A lull followed, but the most savage persecution took place in the period 303-324. This persecution did not affect all parts of the empire equally, and was bound up with wars between the rival aspirants to the imperial throne. In 324 toleration was granted to Christians in all parts of the empire by *Constantine.*

The cult of the martyrs

Polycarp, bishop of Smyrna, was martyred in 156 AD. We are very well informed about his death by contemporary letters which have come down to us. We find him hailed as a 'martyr', we find as well that the anniversary of his martyrdom, styled his 'birthday', was, and was to be, celebrated, and that value was placed upon his relics. These features were to remain attached to the cult of the martyrs.

By the next, that is the third century, at least, the annual celebration of the martyr's 'birthday' involved the celebration of the eucharist: 'to praise and thank the Lord and to encourage the worshipper' (St Cyprian).

With the peace of Constantine, churches were built over the martyrs' tombs and the relics of the martyrs were eagerly gathered to give holiness to a place which had no martyrs. The celebration of the martyrs' 'birthdays' spread from church to church. Some martyrs enjoyed immense popularity and their legends grew in proportion, a situation which was inclined to get out of hand and required episcopal intervention at times; the controlling of the cult of the martyrs was the beginning of the process of canonization.

Martyrdom in later times

After Constantine we do not find persecution of Christians, as such, in most parts of Europe. There were martyrs, however. Sometimes ascetics living on their own were murdered by suspicious and ignorant heathens or semi-heathens; sometimes missionaries or groups of missionaries were slain in heathen reaction, e.g. St Boniface and his companions. The rise and expansion of Islam brought its quota of martyrs, although the Koran taught explicitly that Jews and Christians were not to be molested. Quite apart from Islam there were periodic mixed politico-religious upheavals which led some to martyrdom.

In the Reformation period the state became once more a persecutor in the interests of the 'lawful' form of religious worship. It is then that we find martyrs such as St John Fisher, St Thomas More, St Oliver Plunkett and many others. These were really martyrs for conscience and, as such, there were martyrs on both sides of the religious divide. It was a sad period for Christianity.

In the same epoch there were those who died as martyrs for their Christianity, of whom the martyrs of Japan are the best known.

The French Revolution and the virulent anti-clericalism of various totalitarian regimes of more recent times have also resulted in martyrs. In our own day such bloody persecution would seem temporarily halted, but in many parts of the world there are still those who one way or another suffer for their faith in Christ and their loyalty to his teaching, though their persecutors invent other charges.

Christian Holiness

For a short time holiness was practically identified with martyrdom, yet in the earliest period some had been venerated as saints who were not martyrs, e.g. St John the Evangelist (though in his case legend had to make him one who was 'miraculously preserved') and particularly the Blessed Virgin Mary.

From the fourth century on many were revered as saints who in no way could be considered as 'martyrs'; to this day we venerate St Anthony of Egypt, St Basil of Caesarea and many others. The recognition of sanctity was very much a popular act and the concern of the local church under its bishop. We have only to think of the great Fathers of the Church, the early monastic saints, the evangelizers such as Martin in Gaul, Patrick in Ireland and many others. These were all individuals who made their mark upon their times and were recognized as faithful witnesses to Christ, though they did not shed their blood for him. To them was given the title of 'confessor', a title given in the era of persecution to those who were imprisoned for their faith but not put to death. Strangely, among women, the corresponding titles were 'virgin' or 'widow', as if a married woman whose husband outlived her could not attain recognisable sanctity. In fact some married women were venerated as saints, but they were very exceptional. We have here an example of social values prevailing over religious ones.

The revitalised papacy of the eleventh century began to exercise a control over the recognition of saints and their cult. Within a few centuries this control developed into the canonization process which has lasted down to our own times. In the new Code of Canon Law a greater degree of responsibility has been returned to the local church and its ordinary.

The nature of christian holiness

God — Father, Son and Holy Spirit — is 'alone holy' (Vatican II, *on The Church*, n.39), but this holiness is communicated to the Church, the bride of Christ. Each and every one of the baptized is a child of God, a sharer in the divine nature, and, consequently, in their turn holy (*ib.*, n.40). The holiness we are discussing here, however, is not the fundamental holiness which is our common birthright as Christians, but *that achieved perfection of christian love to which we are all called* but, in the common judgment of men, *to which only a few attain in this life*. In nn.40-43 of Vatican II's *Dogmatic Constitution on The Church* the call of every christian to perfect love is outlined. Here I content myself by citing the first four paragraphs of n.42 to set out the pattern of perfect love:

> 42 'God is love, and he who abides in love abides in God, and God in him' (1 Jn 4:16). God pours out his love into our hearts through the Holy Spirit, who has been given to us (cf Rom 5:5). Thus the first and most necessary gift is that charity by which we love God above all things and our neighbour because of God. If that love, as good seed, is to grow and bring forth fruit in the soul, each one of the faithful must willingly hear the Word of God and with the help of his grace act to fulfil his will.
>
> Each must share frequently in the sacraments, the eucharist especially, and in liturgical rites. Each must apply himself constantly to prayer, self-denial, active brotherly service, and the exercise of all the virtues. For charity, as the bond of perfection and the fulfilment of the law (cf Col 3:14; Rom 13:10), rules over all the means of attaining holiness, gives life to them, and makes them work. Hence it is the love of God and of neighbour which points out the true disciple of Christ.
>
> Since Jesus, the Son of God, manifested his charity by laying down his life for us, no one has greater love than he who lays down his life for Christ and his brothers (cf 1 Jn 3:16; Jn 15:13). From the earliest times, then, some Christians have been called upon — and

some will always be called upon — to give this supreme testimony of love to all men, but especially to persecutors. The Church, therefore, considers martyrdom as an exceptional gift and as the highest proof of love.

By martyrdom a disciple is transformed into an image of his Master, who freely accepted death on behalf of the world's salvation; he perfects that image even to the shedding of blood. Though few are presented with such an opportunity, nevertheless all must be prepared to confess Christ before men, and to follow him along the way of the cross through the persecutions which the Church will never fail to suffer.*

* *The Documents of Vatican II* , *(op cit)* pp 70-71.

The cult of the saints — *saints and ourselves*

It has been suggested that in the Middle Ages the emphasis on the saints as models was lost sight of, and that they were venerated especially as *helpers* or *intercessors* before God. This is perhaps true, at least in part. In a measure it was a consequence of presenting the saints as not only perfect in love but perfect in every respect, so that sanctity itself became almost unattainable. The saints were miracles of grace and, as such, scarcely models.

It required saints and teachers of the calibre of St Francis de Sales and St Theresa of Avila to restore true perspectives. A similar function was fulfilled in more recent times and in very concrete form by St Thérèse of Lisieux and St Bernardette Soubirous.

We celebrate the saints to praise and thank God for the triumph of Christ's paschal mystery in them, and to obtain courage and inspiration for ourselves in the living of our christian lives. If some or other saint seems very distant from us or our problems, this can serve as a source of patience and tolerance — the understanding that there are many different ways of going to God. It should bring home to us the truth that none of us possesses a monopoly of *the* truth.

The calendar and norms for the celebration of saints' days

There is a psychological problem. 'Celebration' carries with it a certain air of festivity. We celebrate some triumph, some achievement, and this usually when we are personally concerned in some way or other. There can be national rejoicing or celebration, but it can tend to be rather forced. At the beginning of the Church's history, with a few exceptions, celebration was confined to local martyrs, and then to other saints — those, in fact, in whom and through whom God spoke to the local church.

In the Calendar of the Universal Church as put before us since Vatican II, regard is had for these realities. Few saints' days are ranked higher than *memorial days*. The intention is that local calendars should develop and stress the celebration of those saints who mean most to the local church. Only those saints' days are included in the General Calendar of the Roman Church which are judged of universal significance. Inevitably the choice of this or that saint will not please everyone. For ourselves we can try to understand why the choice was made!

The ranking of saints' days

Some very few saints' days are celebrated as *solemnities*. Apart from the Blessed Virgin (the Solemnity of Mary, her Assumption and Immaculate Conception), only St Joseph, St John the Baptist, Saints Peter and Paul, and All Saints are given this rank in the General Calendar (the Annunciation is a solemnity, but of the *Lord*). Outside of Advent, Lent and Eastertide a solemnity will replace a Sunday.

In particular calendars there may be one or two other solemnities.

A lesser rank of liturgical day is the *feast*. The feast is celebrated within the limits of the natural day, and only a *feast of the Lord* would replace a Sunday of Ordinary Time. Among the saints' days it is most frequently the apostles' days which rank as feasts.

Finally there are *memorial days*. Where *memorial* appears after the entry of a saint in the calendar* it is to be understood that, unless displaced by some feast or solemnity, a Sunday, or a weekday in certain seasons, the memorial in question is to be celebrated universally. Where there is no entry after the saint's name in the calendar then the celebration is understood to be *optional*. There may be two *optional*

---

* The reference is to the calendar as in the Roman Missal. In this work the rank of the celebration is always made explicit.

memorials assigned to the same day; then one or other may be chosen, or again, neither.

It should be remembered that there are certain special weekdays. The octaves of Easter and Christmas are governed by their own special rules. Ash Wednesday and the days of Holy Week, from Monday to Thursday inclusive, are preferred to all other celebrations. Then the weekdays of Advent from 17 December to 24 December inclusive and all the weekdays of Lent take precedence over *obligatory memorials.*

Readings at Mass

In the second, revised edition of the Mass Lectionary, readings are provided for each saint's day, irrespective of rank. The normal preference on *memorial days* should be for the readings provided for the weekday of ordinary time, unless the readings given under the memorial are marked *proper* to the day. Local conditions and/or special devotion may, however, suggest or favour the use of the readings given under the saint's day. Manifestly where a memorial in the General Calendar is celebrated at a higher rank in a particular calendar then the readings of the saint are to be used.

A Cautionary Note

In the following pages I have taken extracts from sermons, letters, writings; I have chosen texts or observations which I judge may be of use to the men and women of today. This is a dangerous proceeding, particularly if it be assumed that this presents the 'whole' saint. This is quite simply not the case. The reading is only a shaft of light drawn from them or shining on them, to help us on our way through life. Other things in one or other saint might repel us or, at least, some of us.

I have drawn on the writings of John Henry Newman in compiling this book. It is, perhaps, only fair that I give here an extensive quotation from him, something he wrote in part explanation of why he never did write a life of St Philip Neri. I think he states what is a universal truth.

While I dwell on particular paragraphs of his process, if he does rise out at all from the letter of the documents on our persevering

26

meditation, he rises, according to the subject matter before us, a different man. He is four or five different persons at once to me, according as I am engaged in this or that detached incident of his life; or, in other words, I have not got the real man before me at all. Philip is away, lived three centuries ago; I have never seen him; I wish to be as though I had seen him; the spiritual reading to which I have given myself, profitable as it is, does not tend to make us see him as a particular person or a living individual. Nor is this all. Let it be recollected that no acts have a definite value in themselves, but are estimated by their circumstances. A thing may be neither right nor wrong in itself, yet must be either the one or the other in the individual in whom we find it. Of few deeds comparatively out of the multitude that have been done, could we surely pronounce, a saint did, or no saint ever did this. And the deeds of one saint are not the deeds of another saint; and what is saintly in one might be a sin in another. There are acts certainly which in any one would be sins; but acts in general are to be praised or blamed by the occasion, the time, the person, the place, the manner, the object, and the bearing. To do justice to a saint's acts, we must know the saint himself. It is the absence commonly, often unavoidably, of this knowledge, which obliges us to resolve so many of their deeds into particular inspirations, a term which means (nothing else than to imply) that what in itself may be of a doubtful or invidious character is nevertheless right in the individual who does it. Nor do we merely lose the impressiveness and truthfulness of the particular passages of a life, by not realizing it as a whole. It may lose in edification. It is no human curiosity which makes us desire to know the age at which certain virtues were acquired, certain temptations overcome, certain gifts gained, certain works achieved, certain miracles wrought; all which are unaccounted for, if the mere facts are barely related as in the process. Spiritual readings are properly limited to spiritual subjects; but a saint's life may often have in it things not directly and immediately spiritual. To find a saint sitting down to cards, or reading a heathen author, or listening to music, or taking snuff, is often a relief and an encouragement to the reader, as convincing him that grace does not supersede nature, and that he is reading of a child of Adam and his own brother; and he is drawn up to his pattern and guide while he sees that pattern can descend to him; whereas that shadowy paper-saint, as I may call it, bloodless, ideality which may be set up in the mind from the exclusive perusal of a roll of unconnected details, may, from the weakness of our hearts, chill us unduly, lead us to shrink from the saints and to despond about ourselves. And then what professes and promises to be the most edifying mode of studying them may in the event prove to be the least.

The lights and shades of the saintly character, of the individual saint are necessary for understanding what a saint is. To enter into the meaning and the beauty of St Philip's life, I must compare together what he did when he was young and when he was old, when he was obscure and when he was an apostle.

J.H. Newman, 'Oratory Papers',
no. 17 in P. Murray, *Newman the Oratorian*,
Gill & Macmillan, Dublin 1969, pp 258-9.

Saints of the General Roman Calendar

When we have entered the holy dwelling, whose dimensions are vaster than those of the universe, and have become members of the Mystical Body — we have at our disposal for loving, understanding and serving God not only our own powers but everything from the blessed Virgin in the summit of heaven down to the poor African leper who, bell in hand, whispers the responses of the Mass through a mouth half eaten away. The whole of creation, visible and invisible, all history, all the past, the present and the future, all the treasure of the saints, multiplied by grace — all that is at our disposal as an extension of ourselves, a mighty instrument. All the saints and the angels belong to us.

We can use the intelligence of St Thomas, the right arm of St Michael, the hearts of Joan of Arc and Catherine of Siena, and all the hidden resources which have only to be touched to be set in action. Everything of the good, the great and the beautiful from one end of the earth to the other — everything which *begets* sanctity (as a doctor says of a patient that he has *got* a fever) — it is as if all that were our work. The heroism of the missionary, the inspiration of the Doctors of the Church, the generosity of the martyrs, the genius of the artists, the burning prayer of the Poor Clares and Carmelites — it is as if all that were ourselves; it is ourselves. All that is one with us, from the North to the South, from the Alpha to the Omega, from the Orient to the Occident; we clothe ourselves in it, we set it in motion. All that is in the orchestral activity by which we are at one and the same time revealed and made as nothing.

In the core of the vast gathering of Christianity there is to be found the equivalent of all that which, in the individual body, is entrusted to the choir of cells — nourishment, respiration, circulation, elimination, appetite. The Church transposes, and paints outside us on a vast scale, all that is in us almost without our knowing it. Our brief and blind impulses are wedded, taken up again, interpreted, developed, by vast stellar movements. Outside ourselves we can decipher at astronomic distances the text written on a microscopic scale in the further depths of the heart.

Paul Claudel

2 January
Saints Basil the Great and Gregory Nazianzen,
bishops and doctors of the Church
MEMORIAL

St Basil died on 1 January in the year 379; St Gregory on the 25 of the month, about ten or eleven years later. Both were born in Cappadocia in 330. Basil, though he came from a deeply christian family, was only baptized when in his late twenties. He resolved from that moment to give himself wholly to God. He established a form of the ascetic life lived in common and his subsequent writings on his ideal formed the tradition of Byzantine monasticism, and, in translation (?), influenced St Benedict. Made bishop of Caesarea, he was instrumental in winning over most of Asia Minor and Western Syria to the faith of Nicaea, and is viewed as one of the great fathers of the Church.

He was a man of wide culture as the reading given indicates. His vision of God was not tied to the world he could see. Long before the space age, Basil states that God could have made an infinity of worlds; he would set no limits to his creative power.

In other respects he was very rigid and one-sided, rather too touchy, yet truly holy.

Gregory's life story relates to that of Basil, whom he had met when a student in Athens. Relations between the two became strained at times, as Basil wanted to use Gregory as a tool in his own ecclesiastical politics. Basil's intentions were laudable enough, but he showed little respect for Gregory as a person who was torn between loyalty to his father and an over-demanding friend. . . .

For a time Gregory was bishop of Constantinople, but resigned in the interests of Church peace. He ended his days in austere retreat.

Gregory's clear mind, love of tradition and mastery of rhetoric, made him one of the ablest exponents of Catholic teaching against the fourth century heretics. The force and orthodoxy of his teaching earned for him the title of 'the divine'. A reading from his Second Theological Discourse is given below.

Saint Basil

'In the beginning God created the heaven and the earth.' I stop struck with admiration at this thought. What shall I first say? Where shall I begin my story? Shall I show forth the vanity of the gentiles? Shall I exalt the truth of our faith? The philosophers of Greece have made much ado to explain nature, and not one of their systems has remained firm and unshaken, each being overturned by its successor. It is vain to refute them; they are sufficient in themselves to destroy one another. Those who were too ignorant to rise to a knowledge of a God, could not allow that an intelligent cause presided at the birth of the universe; a primary error that involved them in sad consequences. Some had recourse to material principles and attributed the origin of the universe to the elements of the world. Others imagined that atoms, and indivisible bodies, molecules and ducts, form, by their union, the nature of the visible world. Atoms reuniting or separating, produce births and deaths and the most durable bodies only owe their consistency to the strength of their mutual adhesion: a true spider's web woven by these writers who give to heaven, to earth, and to sea so weak an origin and so little consistency! It is because they knew not how to say 'In the beginning God created the heaven and the earth'. Deceived by their inherent atheism it appeared to them that nothing governed or ruled the universe, and that all was given up to chance. To guard us against this error the writer on the creation, from the very first words, enlightens our understanding with the name of God; 'In the beginning God created.' What a glorious order! He first establishes a beginning, so that it might not be supposed that the world never had a beginning. Then he adds 'created' to show that that which was made was a very small part of the power of the Creator. In the same way that the potter, after having made with equal pains a great number of vessels, has not exhausted either his art or his talent; thus the maker of the universe, whose creative power, far from being bounded by one world, could extend to the infinite, needed only the impulse of his will to bring the immensities of the visible world into being. If then the world has a beginning, and if it has been created, enquire who gave it this beginning, and who was the Creator: or rather, in the fear that human reasonings may make you wander from the truth, Moses has anticipated enquiry by engraving in our hearts, as a seal and a safeguard, the awful name of God: 'In the beginning God created' — It is he, beneficient nature, goodness without measure, a worthy object of love for all beings endowed with reason, the beauty the most to be desired, the origin of all that exists, the source of life, intellectual light, impenetrable wisdom, it is he who 'in the beginning created heaven and earth'.

St Basil of Caesarea, *The Hexaemeron, n 2*

Saint Gregory Nazianzen

God is beyond our understanding, though we know that he 'is'

(What concerns us is that) it is not only the peace of God which 'surpasses all understanding' and mastering. It is not those things stored up in promise for the just, which have neither been seen by the eyes, nor heard by the ears, nor, except to a small extent, have been contemplated by the mind; nor is it the accurate knowledge of creation. For, when you hear the words, 'I *will* consider the heavens, the work of your hands, the moon and the stars, . . .' and the order prevailing in them, I would have you know that you have only a shadow even of the knowledge of creation. It is not as if the inspired writer were seeing now, but when he *will* be seeing. But that incomprehensible and illimitable nature, which is above the heavens, the moon and stars and from which they are, is much beyond them; not, I mean, that it 'is', but just 'what' it is. For our preaching is not empty, nor is our faith foolish, nor do we proclaim that God is not. We would not indeed, have you take our reasonable statement as a starting point for a quibbling denial of God, and our confession of ignorance for putting yourself above us. For it is one thing to be persuaded of the existence of a thing, and quite another to know what it is.

Now our eyes and the law of nature teach us that God exists and that he is the creative cause of all things, maintaining them in harmony: our eyes — because they fall on visible things, and see them beautifully stable and journeying, and immovably, if I may say such a thing, moving and being carried along; the law of our nature — because through these visible things, it reasons back to their author. For how could this universe have come into being or been put together, unless God had called it into existence, and held it together? For everyone who sees a beautifully made lyre, and considers the skill with which it has been fitted together and arranged, or who hears its melody, would think of no one but the maker or the player of the lyre, and will pass to him in thought, although he may not be acquainted with him by sight. To us, in this way, that which made and moves and sustains all created things is evident even though he be not comprehended by our intellect. And he is very wanting in sense who will not willingly go so far in following natural proofs; but this is not to identify God with what we have imagined or hammered out for ourselves, or reason has sketched for us. If ever anyone in any degree has attained to an understanding of him, what proof is there of the fact? Who has reached the limit of wisdom in this way? Who has been deemed worthy of so great a grace? Who has opened the mouth of his mind and drawn in the Spirit, so that moved by him who searches and knows all things even the deep things of God, to take hold of God in the Spirit, no longer needs to advance, since he already possesses the ultimate object of desire, and that to which all a high-minded man's life and intelligence hastens?

St Gregory Nazianzen, *Theological Discourse 2*, cc 5, 6

7 January
Saint Raymond of Penyafort, *priest*
OPTIONAL MEMORIAL

St Raymond died in 1275. He was born near Barcelona and entered the service of the Church. Later he joined the Order of Preachers, the Dominicans, and became in time their Master General. He was an outstanding student of Church law, and was remarkable for his wisdom and balance. On the pastoral level his *Summary of Cases*, marked with those same qualities, was of considerable importance through the Middle Ages as a practical guide for the administration of the sacrament of penance. He died at Barcelona on 6 January. St Raymond was canonized in 1601.

He was not one of the most dramatic of saints, but rather a quiet and balanced scholar with a great love of souls. The Church needs all sorts of men and women to build it up and sustain it in life. Perhaps some of those who do most in this regard are among the least known and appreciated by their fellow Christians on earth.

The reading is taken from the Introduction to the Rite of Penance in our renewed liturgy, continuing, in some way, the legacy of St Raymond.

Through the sign of absolution God grants pardon to the sinner who in sacramental confession manifests his change of heart to the Church's minister, and thus the sacrament of penance is completed. In God's design the humanity and loving kindness of our Saviour have visibly appeared to us, and God uses visible signs to give salvation and to renew the broken covenant.

In the sacrament of penance the Father receives the repentant son who comes back to him, Christ places the lost sheep on his shoulders and brings it back to the sheepfold, and the Holy Spirit sanctifies this temple of God again or lives more fully within it. This is finally expressed in a renewed and more fervent sharing of the Lord's table, and there is great joy at the banquet of God's Church over the son who has returned from afar.

Just as the wound of sin is varied and multiple in the life of individuals and of the community, so too the healing which penance provides is varied. Those who by grave sin have withdrawn from the communion of love with God are called back in the sacrament of penance to the life they have lost. And those who through daily weakness fall into venial sins draw strength from a repeated celebration of penance to gain the full freedom of the children of God.

To obtain the saving remedy of the sacrament of penance, according to the plan of our merciful God, the faithful must confess to a priest each and every grave sin which they remember upon examination of their conscience.

Moreover, frequent and careful celebration of this sacrament is also very useful as a remedy for venial sins. This is not a mere ritual repetition or psychological exercise, but a serious striving to perfect the grace of baptism so that, as we bear in our body the death of Jesus Christ, his life may be seen in us ever more clearly. In confession of this kind, penitents who accuse themselves of venial faults should try to conform more closely to Christ and to follow the voice of the Spirit more attentively.

In order that this sacrament of healing may truly achieve its purpose among Christ's faithful, it must take root in their whole lives and move them to more fervent service of God and neighbour.

The celebration of this sacrament is thus always an act in which the Church proclaims its faith, gives thanks to God for the freedom with which Christ has made us free, and offers its life as a spiritual sacrifice in praise of God's glory, as it hastens to meet the Lord Jesus.

The whole Church, as a priestly people, acts in different ways in the work of reconciliation which has been entrusted to it by the Lord. Not only does the Church call sinners to repentance by preaching the word of God, but it also intercedes for them and helps penitents with

maternal care and solicitude to acknowledge and admit their sins and
so obtain the mercy of God who alone can forgive sins. Furthermore,
the Church becomes the instrument of the conversion and absolution of the penitent through the ministry entrusted by Christ to the
apostles and their successors.

The Rite of Penitence, Introduction, nn 6 d, 7, 8

13 January
Saint Hilary, *bishop and doctor of the Church*
OPTIONAL MEMORIAL

A native of Gaul, Hilary was led through the study of philosophy to Christianity. He was made bishop of Poitiers about the year 350. He was exiled for his
defence of the true faith by the Arian Emperor Constantius (*not* Constan*tine*).
Hilary was allowed to return to his diocese in 360, and died there about 368.
He was declared a doctor of the Church only in 1851.

Hilary's writings are of considerable importance in the history of the conflict with the Arians. He knew Greek very well indeed, and would seem to
have been one of the few Latins who really understood what the Greeks were
talking about and discussing. Perhaps as a consequence of this familiarity
with Greek, his Latin style is difficult, as that of St Ambrose tends to be.
St Hilary is of importance also in the western understanding of the doctrine of
the Trinity.

That we may penetrate more easily into the knowledge of this most
difficult question we must first understand the Father and the Son
according to the teaching of the divine scriptures, in order that, when
we have learned to know them and have become familiar with them,
our words may become clearer. As we explained in the preceding
book, the eternity of God transcends places, times, appearances, and
whatever can be conceived by the human mind. He is outside of all
things and within all things; he comprises all things and is com-
prised by none; he does not change either by increase or decrease,
but is invisible, incomprehensible, complete, perfect, and eternal; he
does not know anything from elsewhere, but he himself is sufficient
unto himself to remain what he is.

This unbegotten one, therefore, brought forth the Son from himself before all time, not from any pre-existing matter, because all

things are through the Son; nor from nothing, because the Son is from him; nor as an ordinary birth, because there is nothing change-able or empty in God; nor as a part that is divided, cut off, or extended, because God is incapable of suffering and is incorporeal and these things are characteristic of suffering and the flesh, and according to the apostle: 'In Christ dwells all the fullness of the God-head bodily' (Col 2:9).

But in an inconceivable and ineffable manner, before all time and ages, he gave birth to the only-begotten God from that which in him was unbegotten, and through his charity and power he bestowed upon his birth everything that God is, and thus from the unbegotten, perfect, and eternal Father there is the only-begotten, perfect, and eternal Son. But that which belongs to him because of the body that he assumed results from the eagerness of his good will for our salva-tion. For, since he as one born from God is invisible, incorporeal, and inconceivable, he has taken upon himself as much matter and abase-ment as we possessed the power to understand, perceive, and com-prehend, adapting himself to our weakness rather than abandoning those things which belonged to his own nature.

He is, therefore, the perfect Son of the perfect Father, the only-begotten offspring of the unbegotten God, who has received every-thing from him who possesses everything. He is God from God, Spirit from Spirit, Light from Light, and he proclaims with assur-ance: 'I in the Father and the Father in me.' As the Father is Spirit, so the Son also is Spirit; as the Father is God, so the Son also is God; as the Father is Light so the Son also is Light. From those things, there-fore, which are in the Father are also those things which are in the Son, that is, from the whole Father the whole Son is born; he is not from anywhere else, because nothing was before the Son; he is not from nothingness, because the Son is from God; he is not a God in part only, because the fullness of the Godhead is in the Son, not in some things because he is in all things, but as he willed who could, as he knows who begot him.

St Hilary, *The Trinity*, III, cc 2-4

17 January
Saint Anthony, *abbot*
MEMORIAL

Anthony, 'Father of christian monks', died in the year 356. He was born of a christian Coptic family in Upper Egypt early in the latter half of the third century. Both his parents died while he was still in his teens, and Anthony was prompted when listening to the gospel at Mass to become an ascetic.

As he grew in age, sanctity and fame Anthony sought greater and greater solitude. This, however, did not stop him from becoming a great father of monks who was deeply concerned for the spiritual and temporal well-being of others. His 'Life', attributed to St Athanasius, is really a theological treatise on the power of the risen and divine Christ, and on prayer. In it the simple and very human subject, Anthony himself, is transformed beyond recognition. He was, however, a very great and holy monk, and that fact, combined with the theological presentation of the 'Life', gave great impetus to the development and spread of the monastic ideal in the fourth and fifth centuries.

In the wholeheartedness of his response to God Anthony remains as an example and stimulus to us today.

The last words and death of Anthony

'Let Christ be as the breath you breathe; in him put your trust. Live as dying daily, heeding yourselves and remembering the counsels you have heard from me. And let there be no communion between you and the schismatics, nor the heretical Arians. For you know how I also have avoided them for their false and anti-christian heresy. So do you also be earnest always to be in union first with the Lord and then with the saints; that after death they also may receive you into everlasting tabernacles as known friends. Ponder these things, and mean them. And if you have any care for me, and remember me as your father, do not allow anyone to take my body to Egypt, lest they should deposit it in houses; for that is the reason why I entered the mountains and came here. And you know how I have always reproached those who do this, and bade them stop the practice. Therefore care for my body yourselves, and bury it in the earth; and let my words be so observed by you, that no one shall know the place but yourselves only. For in the resurrection of the dead I shall receive it back from the Saviour, incorruptible. Distribute my garments; the one sheepskin give to Athanasius the bishop, and the cloak I used to lie on, which he gave me new, but it has worn out with me; and the other sheepskin give to Serapion the bishop; and do you have the hair-cloth garment. And now God save you, children, for Anthony departs and is with you no more.'

Having said this and been embraced by them, he drew up his feet; then gazing as it seemed on friends who came for him, and filled by them with joy — for his countenance glowed as he lay — he died and was taken to his fathers. Then they, as he had given them orders, cared for his body and wrapped it up and buried it there in the earth; and no man yet knows where it is laid save only those two. And they who received the sheepskins of the blessed Anthony and the cloak that he wore out, each guard them as some great treasure. For to look on them is like looking on Anthony; and to wear them is like joyfully taking on us his teachings.

St Athanasius, *The Life of St Antony the Hermit*, c 20

20 January
Saint Fabian, *pope and martyr*
OPTIONAL MEMORIAL

St Fabian was martyred in the year 250, one of the first victims of the persecution of Decius. He had been pope for fourteen years. St Cyprian, a contemporary, wrote of him that the glory of his death corresponded to the purity and goodness of his life. We do not know much else about him, but traditionally he was attributed with several administrative decisions in the Church of Rome itself. His epitaph in the cemetery of Calixtus is still preserved.

Eusebius in his *Ecclesiastical History* (VI, 29), relates that no one had thought of him at the election but a dove flew down and settled on him and this was taken as a sign from the Holy Spirit. . . . The dove motif in part inspired my choice of the following reading from St Cyprian, though the thought and context are quite different.

If anyone will consider and weigh these things, there is no need for a long treatise and long arguments. An easy proof for faith exists in a short summary of the truth.

The Lord speaks to Peter:

'I say unto thee' — these are his words — 'that thou art Peter, and upon this rock I will build my Church, and the gates of hell shall not overcome it. I will give unto thee the keys of the kingdom of heaven, and what thou shalt bind upon earth, shall be bound also in heaven, and whatsoever thou shalt loose upon earth shall be loosed also in heaven.'

Upon one does he build his Church.

And, although after his resurrection he bestows upon all the apostles a like power, and says: 'Even as the Father hath sent me, so do I also send you. Receive the Holy Spirit — whose sins you shall forgive, they shall be forgiven, whose sins you shall retain they shall be retained,' still — that he might show forth unity — by his authority he has provided that the origin of this unity should begin from one.

Assuredly, the other apostles were also that which Peter was too, endowed with a like fellowship both of office and of power. Still the beginning goes forth from oneness, so that it may be shown that the Church of Christ is one.

This one Church was also pointed out by the Holy Spirit in the canticle of canticles, when he said in the person of the Lord:

'My dove, my spotless one is but one; she is the only one of her mother, elect of her that bore her.'

Does he who holds not this unity of the Church, think that he holds the faith? Does he who strives against and resists the Church, believe that he is in the Church, though the blessed apostle Paul teaches and exhibits this same mystery of unity, saying:

'One Body and one Spirit, one hope of your calling, one Lord, one faith, one baptism, one God'?

Now we ought to hold fast and defend this unity — especially we bishops, who preside in the Church, that we may show that the episcopate too is itself one and undivided. Let no one lead astray the brotherhood with falsehood — let no one corrupt the truth of the faith by faithless prevarication.

St Cyprian, *The Unity of the Catholic Church*, cc 4, 5

20 January, also
Saint Sebastian, *martyr*
OPTIONAL MEMORIAL

St Sebastian died for the faith in Rome, but, according to St Ambrose, he was a native of Milan. He gave his witness for Christ in the last persecution in the early years of the fourth century. He was buried on the Appian Way, close to where the basilica, *ad catacumbas*, was subsequently built. There are three fourth century accounts of his martyrdom and they illustrate very clearly for us how inaccurate oral tradition can be, for all three accounts differ on how the martyr died, though all agree on his name and the place of his death, Rome. Among the traditions of Sebastian's bearing witness is the statement that he actually sought out martyrdom. This is not something generally encouraged, but it has prompted the choice of the following excerpt from St Augustine.

The day is to come which the Lord mentions, 'When all those who are in their tombs will hear his voice, and come forth' (Jn 5:28, 29); but with a great difference! All come forth, but not all come forth to the same thing. All are to rise, but not all must be changed. 'For they who have done well,' he says, 'rise to the resurrection of life; they, on the other hand, who have done evil, to the resurrection of judgement.' When he says, 'All who are in their tombs', beyond doubt he sets forth the resurrection of bodies. When, however, you hear 'judgement', lest you delude yourself as to its being a temporary judgement, judgement here stands for eternal punishment. In this connection it is said: 'He who does not believe, is already judged' (Jn 3:18). This then is the difference which will separate the just from the unjust, believers from unbelievers, confessors from deniers. This will be the distinction separating the lovers of this perishable life from the lovers of eternal life. 'And the just will go into eternal life, sinners, however, into eternal fire' (Mt 25:46). There they will be tormented in the body, the body they spared. For, by fearing the sufferings of the body, they spared the body, and in sparing the body, they denied Christ; and, by denying Christ, they did indeed postpone eternal punishments for their body. If they postponed them, did they remove them?

Prudently, therefore, the martyrs of Christ did not despise their own bodies. That perverse and worldly philosophy belongs to those who do not believe in the resurrection of our bodies. Our God, however, made body and spirit: he is the maker and the maker anew of both; he it is who establishes both and reestablishes them. Therefore the martyrs did not despise or persecute the flesh as an enemy, 'For no one ever hates his own flesh' (Eph 5:29). Rather they took care of it, when they seemed indifferent to it: when, persisting faithfully in it, they bore passing torments, for that very flesh, in truth, they purchased eternal glory!

Who, however, will explain in words what the future glory of the flesh will be? None of us yet knows the experience of having it. Now we bear the flesh as burdensome because it is needy, infirm, mortal, perishable. 'For a perishable body weighs down the soul' (Wis 9:15). But don't be anxious about this in the resurrection — 'For this perishable nature must put on the imperishable, and this mortal nature must put on immortality' (1 Cor 15:53).

St Augustine, *Sermon 277*, nn 2, 3, 4

21 January
Saint Agnes, *virgin and martyr*
MEMORIAL

Agnes gave her life for her faith in Christ towards the end of the era of persecution by the Roman Empire. This would have been, most probably, in the early years of the fourth century. The nearest contemporary account we have is in a sermon by St Ambrose, but it is clear that by his time legend had already taken over and had begun to embroider the facts. This growth of legend, in a predominantly oral culture, was the result of her popular fame and not the cause of it — at least initially. At the root of her legend there must have been something rather special about her and the circumstances of her death.

Even in our own day there are few stories that do not grow with the telling, but in those times the love of rhetoric was an added peril to the dangers of hearsay. The preachers of the fourth and later centuries loved to develop and embroider *themes*, with the result that, from the point of view of twentieth century history, the original very real person was quite smothered. With our sense of the incarnational, we tend to find this approach frustrating.

The reading given below, though not in the mainstream of orthodox christian teaching, does serve to give us the inspirational background to the ideal of the martyrs.

Seeing, then, that Christ has had such pity on us, firstly, in that we who are alive do not sacrifice to dead gods or worship them, but through him have come to know the Father of truth — what is knowledge in reference to him, save refusing to deny him through whom we came to know the Father? He himself says, 'He who acknowledges me before men, I will acknowledge before my father' (Mt 10:32; Lk 12:8). This, then, is our reward if we acknowledge him through whom we are saved. But how do we acknowledge him? By doing what he says and not disobeying his commands; by honouring him not only with our lips, but with all our heart and mind (cf Mk 12:30). And he says in Isaiah as well, 'This people honours me with their lips but their heart is far from me' (Is 29:13; cf Mt 15:8; Mk 7:6).

Let us not merely call him Lord, for that will not save us. For he says, 'Not everyone who says to me, Lord, Lord, will be saved, but he who does what is right' (Mt 7:21). Thus, my brothers and sisters, let us acknowledge him by our actions, by loving one another, by refraining from adultery, backbiting, and jealousy, and by being self-controlled, compassionate, kind. We ought to have sympathy for one another and not to be avaricious. Let us acknowledge him by acting in this way and not by doing the opposite. We ought not to have greater fear of men than of God. That is why, if you act in this way, the Lord said, 'If you are gathered with me in my bosom and do not keep my commands, I will cast you out and will say to you: "Depart from me. I do not know whence you come, you workers of iniquity."'*

Therefore, my brothers and sisters, ceasing to tarry in this world, let us do the will of Him who called us, and let us not be afraid to leave this world. For the Lord said, 'You will be like lambs among wolves.'* But Peter replied by saying, 'What if the wolves tear the lambs to pieces?' Jesus said to Peter: 'After their death the lambs should not fear the wolves, nor should you fear those who kill you and can do nothing more to you. But fear him who, when you are dead, has power over soul and body to cast them into the flames of hell.' You must realize, my brothers and sisters, that our stay in this world of the flesh is slight and short, but Christ's promise is great and wonderful, and means rest in the coming kingdom and in eternal life.

* Source unknown, possibly the Gospel of the Egyptians.

What, then, must we do to get these things, except to lead a holy and
upright life and to regard these things of the world as alien to us and
not to desire them? For in wanting to obtain these things we fall from
the right way.

Clement (Pseudo), *The Second Letter of Clement*, cc 3, 4, 5

22 January
Saint Vincent, *deacon and martyr*
OPTIONAL MEMORIAL

Vincent was a deacon of the Church of Saragossa in Spain, who died as a martyr in the year 304. He bore his witness to Christ in Valencia. According to
legend he endured his frightful torments with patience, calm, love and even
joy. In the fourth and fifth centuries he was one of the most renowned and
celebrated of the western martyrs, and both St Augustine and Prudentius
mention him with honour. For us, again, legend has obscured the human
person.

Vincent was a deacon. In the first centuries of the Church's history this put
him in the public eye. The deacons were responsible for the local churches'
works of corporal mercy — most often the only form of organised relief there
then was — and to these activities the preaching of the word was regularly
joined (cf Acts 6:1-8). In any situation certain individuals shine out for their
zeal, and quite evidently Vincent did so in his time. So it was that he became
known to the hostile Roman authorities, was arrested and condemned.

Who gave this endurance to his soldier, save the one who first shed
his blood for him? To him it is said in the psalm (70:5) 'For you, O
Lord, are my endurance; my hope, O Lord, from my youth'. A great
struggle procures great glory; not a human or temporary glory, but
one that is divine and everlasting.

It is faith which contends, and when faith contends no one overcomes the flesh. For although he is torn to pieces, although cut to
shreds; when does he perish who is redeemed by the blood of Christ?
A man of power cannot bear to lose what he bought with the best of
his wealth, and is Christ to lose what he bought with his blood? —
Indeed the whole of this is of consequence not for the glory of men,
but for the glory of God. It is truly from him that endurance comes,
the true endurance, which is holy, religious and upright. Christian

endurance is a gift of God. For there are many robbers who bear torture with great endurance, not yielding and overcoming their torturer; afterwards they are punished by eternal fire. It is his *cause* which marks off the martyr from the endurance, rather, the toughness, of the evil-doer. The torment is like, the cause unlike!

In the saying of the martyrs — Vincent would have used the very words in his prayers — we have sung (Ps 42:1): 'Judge me, O God, and mark off my cause from an unholy nation.' His cause is marked off because he struggled for truth, for justice, for God, for Christ, for the faith, for the unity of the Church, for undivided love.

Who gave him this endurance? Who? The psalms will tell us; for there we read, there we sing (Ps 61:2): 'Will not my soul be subject to God? For from him is my endurance'. Whoever thinks St Vincent was able to endure these things by his own inner strength errs greatly. For whosoever were to presume he could do this by his own inner strength, even though he seems to overcome by endurance, is in fact overcome by pride. To overcome well means to overcome every device of the evil one. . . . When therefore does the holy soul overcome, except when he says (Ps 34:2): 'In the Lord my soul shall make its boast. The meek shall hear and be glad.' The meek in fact know what I am saying: truly the word lives in them, in them the image lives. For one who is not meek, does not know how that tastes of which is said: 'In the Lord my soul shall make its boast.' For everyone who is not meek — the proud, the violent, the puffed-up, wishes to boast in himself, not in the Lord. He who says: 'In the Lord, my soul shall make its boast', does not say: 'The people shall hear and be glad; men shall hear and be glad'; but 'The meek shall hear and be glad'. They, for whom it has meaning, shall hear. Christ for his part was meek: 'He was led like a sheep to the slaughter' (Is 53:7).

St Augustine, *Sermon 274*

24 January
Saint Francis de Sales, *bishop and doctor of the Church*
MEMORIAL

St Francis died on 28 December, 1622. Today is the anniversary of his burial at Annecy in 1623.

From a young age Francis had wished to give himself to the service of the Church, but, out of obedience to his father's wishes, he first studied at Paris and Padua graduating as a doctor of law. In 1593 he was ordained priest and was appointed provost of the chapter at Geneva. He then devoted himself to bringing the region of the Chablais back to the Catholic Church, a task in which he succeeded. In 1599 he was named coadjutor to the bishop of Geneva and he succeeded to the see in 1602. As bishop he reorganised the diocese and established a diocesan seminary at Annecy. With Jane Frances de Chantal he founded the nuns of the Visitation.

In his life and teaching St Francis gave expression to an almost unique blend of gentleness and firmness. He possessed in the highest degree that most fundamental of virtues — discretion.

I have chosen the following excerpt from his *Letters* not simply because it shows his fostering of holiness in the lay state — to profit from it we must make allowance for a very different cultural milieu — but also because it shows his awareness of the danger of becoming 'holier than thou'!

Having outlined various spiritual practices, the sacramental life, prayer and reading, he continues:

These are the chief means to unite yourself closely to God. Those to unite yourself properly with your neighbour, are in great number but I will only mention some of them.

We must regard our neighbour in God, who wills that we should love and cherish him. It is the counsel of St Paul, who orders servants to serve God in their masters and their masters in God. We must exercise ourselves in this love of our neighbour, expressing it externally: and though it may seem at first against our will, we must not give up on that account: this repugnance of the inferior part will be at last conquered by habit and good inclination, which will be produced by repetition of the acts. We must refer our prayers and meditations to this end: for after having begged the love of God, we must always beg that of our neighbour, and specially of those to whom our will is not drawn.

I advise you to take care sometimes to visit the hospitals, comfort the sick, pity their infirmities, soften your heart about them, and pray for them, at the same time giving them some help.

But in all this take particular care that your husband, your servants, and your parents do not suffer by your too long stayings in church, by your too great retirement, and giving up care of your household. And do not become, as often happens, manager of others' affairs, or too contemptuous of conversations in which the rules of devotion are not quite exactly observed. In all this, charity must rule and enlighten us to make us condescend to the wishes of our neighbour, in what is not against the commandments of God.

You must not only be devout, and love devotion, but you must make it amiable, useful, and agreeable to every one. The sick will love your devotion if they are charitably consoled by it; your family will love it if they find you more careful of their good, more gentle in little accidents that happen, more kind in correcting, and so on: your husband, if he sees that as your devotion increases you are more devoted in his regard, and sweet in your love to him; your parents and friends if they perceive in you more generosity, tolerance, and condescension towards their wills, when not against the will of God. In short, you must, as far as possible, make your devotion attractive.

Francis de Sales, Letters to Persons in the World, pp 62-3

25 January
The Conversion of Saint Paul, *Apostle*
FEAST

We do not know the origins of the association of the conversion of St Paul with this day, but it appears on it in the Martyrology of Jerome. The conversion itself, however, was one of the turning points in the history of the early Church. There are two accounts of it in the Acts of the Apostles, and we are offered a choice of them as the first reading at today's Mass. It was cause for celebration that a persecutor was turned by the grace of Christ into the teacher of the nations. As in any celebration of the saints the primary emphasis is upon God's saving power as manifested in Christ. Paul himself never failed to glorify God for his conversion.

Today we echo his praise, and from the change brought about in Paul, draw hope that we too may be saved. This is the lesson outlined for us in the reading chosen from the sermons of another great convert, St Augustine.

The benefit of this happening, as the apostle Paul himself sets out in his letters, is this — indeed, to this end, he says, pardon was given to him for all his sins, and for that fury and frenzy by which he was dragging Christians to death, he who was a minister of the fury of the Jews, whether in the stoning of the holy martyr Stephen, or in the delivering up and leading of others to punishment — that no one should despair about himself, involved as he may be in great sins and ensnared in really evil deeds, as if he were not to receive pardon though converted to him, who, hanging on the cross prayed for his persecutors, saying, 'Father, forgive them, for they know not what they do' (Lk 23:34).

Out of a persecutor he was made a preacher and teacher of the peoples. 'For I was first,' he says, 'a blasphemer, a persecutor, a mocker: but I received mercy for this reason, that in me, as the first, Jesus Christ might display every forbearance as an example for those who were to believe in him for eternal life' (cf 1 Tim 1:13, 16). For by the grace of God we are made whole from our sins, in which we lay ill. The medicine which heals the soul is his, *it is his;* for the soul can wound itself — it cannot heal.

For persons with regard to their own body, have it indeed under their control to become ill, but do not have it under their control likewise to recover. If, truly, they go beyond due measure and live intemperately, if they do those things which are incompatible with good health and break down the soundness of the body, one day, it goes without saying, they fall ill; they do not recover after they have fallen. Now, in order to fall ill they give themselves to excess, but to recover they have the physician round for their healing. For, as we have said, they cannot have it under their control to recover good health, as they had it under their control to lose it. So also with the soul. That man or woman should fall by sinning unto death, should become mortal from being immortal, should become subject to the seducer, the devil, was subject to their own free will. . . .

Christ, the physician, comes to the afflicted and troubled. He says, 'The healthy have no need of the physician, but those who are sick. I have not come to call the just, but sinners' (Mt 9:12, 13). He calls sinners to peace*, he calls the ailing to health.

* (i.e. salvation).   St Augustine, *Sermon 278*, nn 1, 2, 5

26 January
Saints Timothy and Titus, *bishops*
MEMORIAL

The *memorial* of these two disciples of St Paul has been allocated to this day because of their closeness to him in life, first as followers, then as associates and fellow-workers. Apart from the various references in the New Testament, we know virtually nothing about them — a situation which holds also for most of the Apostles and the other early preachers of the christian faith. What mattered was Christ, and him risen from the dead!

From the New Testament we learn that both Timothy and Titus were human and limited, yet they were chosen to help bring Christ's message to their fellows, for in their infirmity, as in St Paul's, the power of Christ's grace shone out.

I offer a reading from St John Chrysostom which comments on phrases from St Paul's Letters to Timothy and Titus. (The fundamental text is 2 Tim 2:24-26.)

'And the Lord's servant must not be quarrelsome'. He ought not to wrangle even in enquiries, for the Lord's servant must keep far from strife, since God is the God of peace, and what should the servant of the God of peace have to do with strife? 'but kindly to everyone'. How is it then he says, 'reprove with all authority' (Tit 2:15), and again, 'let no one despise your youth' (1 Tim 4:12), and again, 'rebuke them sharply' (Tit 1:13)? Because this is consistent with gentleness. For a strong rebuke, if it be given with gentleness, is most likely to wound deeply: for it is possible to touch more effectually by gentleness, than to overawe by boldness.

'An apt teacher'; that is, of those willing to be taught. For 'one who is factious', he says, 'after admonishing him once or twice, have nothing more to do with him' (Tit 3:10). 'Forbearing'. He has well added this, for it is a quality which a teacher above all things ought to possess. All things are vain without it. And if fishermen do not despair, though often they cast their nets for a whole day without catching anything, much more should not we. For see what is the result. From constant teaching it often happens that the plough of the word, descending to the depth of the soul, roots out the evil passion that troubled it. For he that hears often will at length be affected. Someone cannot go on hearing continually without some effect being produced. Sometimes therefore, when he was on the point of being persuaded, he is lost by our becoming weary. . . . And having said, 'forbearing', he is not satisfied but goes on to say, 'correcting one's opponents with gentleness'. For he that teaches must be especially careful to do it with gentleness. For a soul that wishes to learn cannot gain any useful instruction from harshness and contention. For when it would set itself to the matter it will learn nothing, becoming bewildered on this account. Someone who would gain any useful knowledge ought above all things be well disposed towards his teacher, and if this be not first attained nothing that is called for or useful can be accomplished. And no one can be well disposed towards someone who is violent and over-bearing. How is it then that Paul says, 'As for those who are factious, after admonishing them once or twice, have nothing more to do with them'? He speaks here of those who are incorrigible, those whom he knows to be diseased beyond the possibility of cure.

'God may perhaps grant that they will repent and come to the truth, and they may escape from the snare of the devil'. What he says amounts to this. Perhaps there will be a reformation. Perhaps! for it is uncertain. So that we ought to withdraw only from those of whom we can show plainly, and concerning whom we are fully persuaded, that whatever be done, they will not be reformed. 'With gentleness', he says. In this disposition, you see, we ought to address ourselves to those who are willing to learn, and never cease from conversing with them until we have made our point.

'After being captured by him, to do his will.' It is truly said, 'after being captured', for meanwhile they swim in error. Observe here, how he teaches us to be humble-minded. He has not said, 'if perhaps you should be able', but, 'God may perhaps grant that they will repent'; if anything be done, therefore, all is of the Lord. You plant, you water, but he sows and makes it produce fruit. Let us not then get it into our heads that we ourselves succeeded in the persuading, even if we should persuade anyone! 'after being captured by him', he says, 'to do his will'. This no man will relate to doctrine, *but to life*. For his will is that we live rightly.

Sermon VI on 2 Timothy

27 January
Saint Angela Merici, *virgin*
OPTIONAL MEMORIAL

Angela Merici was born near Brescia in Italy about the beginning of the last quarter of the fifteenth century. That century witnessed a great flowering of the arts and letters in Italy, but the religious picture was far from attractive. Angela was prepared to go against the tide. As a young woman she joined the third Order of St Francis and gave herself to various pious works as well as to prayer. She became convinced that the education of girls was one of the great needs of the time, and opened a school in her own house. In 1535, for the furthering of her various works, she founded the Company of St Ursula. Those who gave themselves to this Company lived lives of consecrated virginity, but in their own homes, coming together for prayer and the works of the Company. After St Angela's death in 1540 her ideals spread and in some centres life in common began. Thus step by step the sisterhood known as the Ursulines came into being. In Paris the followers of St Angela were enclosed but continued to run schools. The principles she put before her followers on education are as valid today as they were in the sixteenth century: love, concern and respect for the individual, coupled with a firm gentleness, all flowing from and inspired by deep christian faith and love. St Angela was canonized by Pope Pius VII in 1807.

In one way Angela was a true child of the Italian 'Quattro Cento': her feeling for group discussion as a way to determining the working of the Spirit. This, perhaps, finds an echo in our day.

For all their influence, her writings were slight. The reading from her *Legacy* shows both her conviction of the guidance of the Holy Spirit, and the possibility of changing the rules she lays down.

Be on guard, therefore, and take special care that there is unity and harmony of purpose, just as we read of the apostles and other christians of the early Church: 'They were all of one mind'. You must try to be like this with all your daughters, because the more united you are, the more Jesus Christ will be there among you as a Father and a good Shepherd. There will be no other sign that one enjoys the Lord's favour than the love and unity existing among all, for he himself says: 'By this love you have for one another, everyone will know that you are my disciples'. See how love and harmony are a sure sign that one is on the right road and pleasing to God. Therefore, my dear sisters and mothers, be vigilant over this, because it is especially in this matter that the devil will set traps for you under the guise of good. So, as soon as you suspect even the slightest shadow of this plague, remedy it at once, according as God will enlighten you. On no account allow seeds of this kind to sprout in the Company, because that would also be a source of bad example in the town and further afield. Because where there is dissension of wills, discord is always to be found; and where there is discord there is undoubtedly ruin. Just as our Saviour says: 'Every government that is a prey to discord will soon be in ruins'.

Lastly, take great care that the good directives given you, and especially those of the Rule, are observed in earnest. If, with change of times and circumstances, it becomes necessary to make fresh rules or to alter anything, then do it with prudence, after taking good advice. Let your first refuge always be to have recourse to Jesus Christ, to pray fervently together with all your daughters. In this way Jesus Christ will undoubtedly be in your midst, and like a true and good Master, he will enlighten and instruct you as to what you should do. Hold it for certain that this Rule has been planted directly by his holy hand and that he will never abandon this Company till the end of time. If it was he who planted it in the first place, who is there that can uproot it? Believe this: do not doubt but have firm faith that this will be so. I know what I am talking about. Blessed are they who sincerely take up this work.

If you carry out these and other like things faithfully, as the Holy Spirit will direct you according to times and circumstances, then rejoice and be of good heart. Look at what a great reward awaits you; where the children are, there also the mothers will be. Rest assured then and do not doubt; we hope to see you united with us one day in heaven, as indeed does he who loves us all. And who can withstand him? His light, and the joyous splendour of his truth will encompass you at the moment of your death, and deliver you from the hands of your enemy. Persevere, then, faithfully and joyfully with the work you have begun. Take care, I say again, take care that you do not grow lukewarm, because every promise I have made you will be fulfilled in full measure. Now I must take my leave, while you must wait and continue with your work. But first I embrace you and I give you all the kiss of peace, asking God to bless you.

Angela Merici, *Legacy*

28 January

Saint Thomas Aquinas, *priest and Doctor of the Church*
MEMORIAL

Thomas was a native of south central Italy and was educated at Monte Cassino. When aged about nineteen he joined what was then the rather new Order of Friars Preachers and studied in Italy and France. Later he became a teacher himself. Thomas' clear, penetrating and tranquil mind and his deeply contemplative spirit of prayer are abundantly clear from his writings. Thomas died in 1274 and was canonized in 1323. He was declared a Doctor of the Church in 1567 and was proclaimed patron saint of universities and schools in 1880. His memorial day was formerly on 7 March, the day of his death; today is the anniversary of the transfer of his remains to Toulouse in 1369.

Though there have been periods since his death when the teaching of St Thomas has been accorded excessive reverence, today's real neglect is probably equally unbalanced. St Thomas had not only a clear mind and enlightened understanding, but also a wide and sure knowledge of scripture and tradition.

The following extracts from the *Summa Theologica* are offered as a continuous reading.

Bear in mind that human and divine law differ in their immediate aims. Human law, the purpose of which is the tranquillity of the state, operates by policing external acts which could break the public peace. The purpose of divine law, on the other hand, is to lead us through to eternal happiness, the obstacles to which are sins, internal as well as external. The effective putting down of crime and the enforcement of sanctions suffices for human law, but not for divine law, which would adapt the whole human being to everlasting joy.

Only the grace of the Spirit can do this, the grace by which 'love is shed abroad in our hearts' (Rom 5:5). 'The grace of God which is eternal life' (Rom 6:23). The giving is reserved to our Lord; it was beyond the power of the old law: 'the law was given by Moses, but grace and truth by Jesus Christ' (Jn 1:17). Hence the old law was good, but imperfect: 'for the law made nothing perfect, but the bringing in of a better hope' (Heb 7:19).

The predominant note, indeed the general tenor, of the gospel law is the grace of the Holy Spirit given through faith in Christ: 'where is then thy boasting? It is excluded. By what law? Of works? No, but by the law of faith' (Rom 3:27). The grace of faith is here called a law. More expressly St Paul says, 'the law of the spirit of life, in Christ Jesus, has delivered me from the law of sin and death' (Rom 8:2). Augustine remarks that while the law of works was graven on stone tablets the law of faith is written in the hearts of the faithful, and then he asks: 'What else are the laws of God written in our hearts but the very presence of the Holy Spirit?'

Primarily, then, the Gospel is the grace of the Spirit shed in our hearts which makes us justified. Nevertheless there are also accompanying ordinances which prepare for the grace and activity of the Spirit. They concern faith and morals, and Christians have to be instructed in them. But they are secondary, for these documents of doctrine and order directing human affections do not themselves make us righteous: 'the letter kills but the spirit gives life' (2 Cor 3:6). Augustine applies this conclusion to anything written down, to any code external to our minds and hearts, even to the commandments contained in the Gospel: yes, even the Gospel words would kill but for the presence of inward healing grace.

St Thomas Aquinas, *Summa Theologica*, Ia-IIae, q 98:1; 106:1, 2

31 January
Saint John Bosco, *priest and confessor*
MEMORIAL

John Bosco was a native of Piedmont, where he was born in 1815. He studied for the priesthood and was ordained in Turin. Don Bosco, [Don is the Italian title for a priest in the secular clergy and for some religious], devoted himself from the first to work among boys. To carry on this work he founded a Society which he called the Salesians after St Francis de Sales. The first steps in this foundation were taken in 1854. Don Bosco believed in equipping boys positively for life in the world, and trade schools have been a large part of the Salesian apostolate. It is quite clear that he had a charisma for dealing with boys, whom he handled with gentleness and firmness, but he taught a universal lesson by his life and deeds: if we desire to influence anyone *we* must reach out to them.

With the aid of St Mary Mazzarello he also founded the Daughters of our Lady Help of Christians, to do similar work among girls.

St John was canonized in 1934.

I have chosen the following reading from Henri Gheon, *The Secret of St John Bosco*, because it indicates the relationship of St John's ideal to that of St Francis de Sales as set out on 24th January above.

The primary lesson he learned from his patron saint was, 'First give yourself, then give God.' Give yourself whole and entire with no reservations whatever — all your time and strength and experience and knowledge, all your heart, all your joy. And the joy to be communicated above all was the joy of a pure conscience, an active body, a life well filled, a heart open to every appeal, a soul elevated to God. Show the happiness of the Christian, make people feel its reality without too much emphasis upon the Christian's sufferings; make them admire the Christian ideal, want it, accept it. Those were the three steps. Do not preach fear until you have preached love. Hence the necessity of limitless patience and sympathy and simplicity. Do not deal with souls as from on high; take them where they are — on the very level of the earth if it must be so; listen to them, win their confidence, tame them as you would tame a wild bird. Draw the sting of the evil in them by cultivating and bringing to life whatever tiny spark of good is still hidden within them. Teach them to spread and strengthen their spiritual wings; teach them to fly in that new air; without hurting them, without their even feeling it, break the strands of the net that trammels their flight. Once they have known the upward flight, how could they ever wish to sink back again to earth, when every impulse bears them towards God?

The idea of the Salesians was to humanise the approach to the eternal truth by kindly will and kindly action. 'You can bring salvation to anyone,' St Francis de Sales insists, 'provided you make him like salvation.'

'You can't begin too soon,' adds Don Bosco, 'the task of making him like it.'

That is why the Salesian apostolate is aimed first at the young, at those, above all, who are most unloved, poor, unreceptive.

Henri Gheon, The Secret of St John Bosco pp 146-7

2 February
The Presentation of the Lord
FEAST

This Feast is also presented in the *Glenstal Bible Missal*. The name given to today's feast in the East was 'The Meeting' or 'Coming to meet'. In Jerusalem it was celebrated as the commemoration of the coming of the Lord into his temple and there being met by the 'ideal' representatives of the Old Covenant — Simeon and Anna. The custom of processing with lights is perhaps derived from the Roman practice of greeting the emperor or his representative with a procession in which lights were carried and flowers thrown; Christ is our true ruler come to his people — the light of the nations.

Coming forty days after the Nativity, the Presentation closes the Christmas cycle.

The reading is from John Henry Newman's *Parochial and Plain Sermons* II, 10, given on this feast. Part of the same sermon is quoted in the *Bible Missal* for Sunday in the Octave of Christmas, Year B.

Our Saviour was born without sin. His mother, the blessed virgin Mary, need have made no offering, as requiring no purification. On the contrary, it was that very birth of the Son of God which sanctified the whole race of woman, and turned her curse into a blessing. Nevertheless, as Christ himself was minded to 'fulfil all righteousness,' to obey all ordinances of the covenant under which he was born, so in like manner his mother Mary submitted to the Law, in order to do it reverence.

This, then, is the event in our saviour's infancy which we celebrate today; his presentation in the temple when his virgin mother was ceremonially purified. It was made memorable at the time by the hymns and praises of Simeon and Anna, to whom he was then revealed. And there were others, besides these, who had been 'looking for redemption in Jerusalem,' who were also vouchsafed a sight of the infant saviour. But the chief importance of this event consists in its being a fulfilment of prophecy. Malachi had announced the Lord's visitation of his temple in these words, 'The Lord whom ye seek shall suddenly come to his temple;' words which, though variously fulfilled during his ministry, had their first accomplishment in the humble ceremony commemorated on this day. And, when we consider the grandeur of the prediction, and how unostentatious this accomplishment was, we are led to muse upon God's ways, and to draw useful lessons for ourselves. . . .

Such has ever been the manner of his visitations, in the destruction of his enemies as well as in the deliverance of his own people — silent, sudden, unforeseen, as regards the world, though predicted in the face of all men, and in their measure comprehended and waited for by his true Church. . . .

Whether we take the first or the final judgment upon Jerusalem, both visitations were foretold as sudden. Of the former, Isaiah had declared it should come '*suddenly*, at an instant;' of the latter, Malachi, 'The Lord whom ye seek shall *suddenly* come to his temple.'

J.H. Newman, Parochial and Plain Sermons, 10, pp 108-11

3 February
Saint Blaise, *bishop and martyr*
OPTIONAL MEMORIAL

Blaise was bishop of Sebastea in Armenia, and died for his faith in Christ about the year 315 or 316. One of the very popular early martyrs he has become lost in legend. Among the good deeds recorded in his *Legend* was the healing of a small boy choking on a fishbone. This, it would seem, has led to his becoming the patron of throats. Many places claimed to possess his relics, but relics believed to be his were brought by the Irish monk, St Fintan, from Rome to the monastery of Rheinau in the ninth century. These relics were subsequently brought to the monastery dedicated to St Blaise in the Black Forest.

For the reading I have chosen a passage from the *Catechetical Lectures* of St Cyril of Jerusalem on the Holy Spirit as the strength of the martyrs.

And he is called the Comforter, because he comforts and encourages us, and 'helps our infirmities; for we know not what we should pray for as we ought; but the Spirit himself makes intercession for us, with groanings which cannot be uttered', that is, makes intercession to God. Oftentimes a man for Christ's sake has been outraged and dishonoured unjustly; martyrdom is at hand; tortures on every side, and fire, and sword, and savage beasts, and the pit. But the Holy Spirit softly whispers to him, 'Wait thou on the Lord; what is now befalling you is a small matter, the reward will be great. Suffer a little while, and you shall be with angels for ever. The sufferings of this present time are not worthy to be compared with the glory which shall be revealed in us.' He portrays to the man the kingdom of heaven; he gives him a glimpse of the paradise of delight; and the martyrs, whose bodily countenances are of necessity turned to their judges, but who in spirit are already in paradise, despise those hardships which are seen.

And would you be sure that it is by the power of the Holy Spirit that the martyrs bear their witness? The Saviour says to his disciples, 'And when they bring you unto the synagogues, and the magistrates, and authorities, be not anxious how you shall answer, or what you shall say; for the Holy Spirit shall teach you in that very hour, what you ought to say'. For it is impossible to testify as a martyr for Christ's sake, except a man testify by the Holy Spirit; for if 'no man can say that Jesus Christ is the Lord, but by the Holy Spirit', how shall any man give his own life for Jesus' sake, but by the Holy Spirit?

Great indeed, and all-powerful in gifts, and wonderful, is the Holy Spirit. Consider, how many of you are now sitting here, how many souls of us are present. He is working suitably for each, and being present in our midst, beholds the temper of each, beholds also his reasoning and his conscience, and what we say, and think, and believe. Great indeed is what I have now said, and yet is it small. For consider, I pray, with your mind enlightened by him, how many Christians there are in all this diocese, and how many in the whole province of Palestine, and carry forward your mind from this province, to the whole Roman Empire; and after this, consider the whole world; races of Persians, and nations of Indians, Goths and Sarmatians, Gauls and Spaniards, and Moors, Libyans and Ethiopians, and the rest for whom we have no names; for of many of the nations not even the names have reached us. Consider, I pray, in each nation bishops, presbyters, deacons, solitaries, virgins, and laity besides; and then behold their great protector, and the dispenser of their gifts — how throughout the world he gives to one chastity, to another perpetual virginity, to another almsgiving, to another voluntary poverty, to another power of repelling hostile spirits. And as the light, with one touch of its radiance sheds brightness on all things, so also the Holy Spirit enlightens those who have eyes; for if any from blindness is not granted his grace, let him not blame the Spirit, but his own unbelief.

St Cyril of Jerusalem, *Catechetical Lectures*, XVI, 20-22

3 February, also
Saint Ansgar, *bishop and confessor*
OPTIONAL MEMORIAL

Ansgar was born in present-day France and became a monk in the abbey of Corbie. He later transferred to New Corbie, or Corvey, as it is called, from where he was summoned by King Harold of Denmark to preach to the Danes. He was appointed archbishop of Hamburg, and, when that town was destroyed by the Northmen in 845, he took over the united dioceses of Hamburg and Bremen. Though most of his work perished even in his own lifetime, St Ansgar is regarded as the apostle of Scandinavia.

Ansgar was sincerely concerned to preach the good news of Christ, but, as one modern commentator has remarked, his disposition of soul was too contemplative, he was too unconcerned to 'fight his corner', too little of an organizer to achieve results in this world. The prayer I have chosen, from St Anselm, another saintly monk and bishop, expresses something of Ansgar's true aspirations.

Almighty God, merciful Father, and my good Lord,
have mercy on me, a sinner.
Grant me forgiveness of my sins.
Make me guard against and overcome
all snares, temptations, and harmful pleasures.

May I shun utterly in word and in deed,
whatever you forbid,
and do and keep whatever you command.
Let me believe and hope, love and live,
according to your purpose and your will.

Give me heart-piercing goodness and humility;
discerning abstinence and mortification of the flesh.
Help me to love you and pray to you,
praise you and meditate upon you.
May I act and think in all things according to your will,

purely, soberly, devoutly,
and with a true and effective mind.
Let me know your commandments, and love them,
carry them out readily, and bring them into effect.
Always, Lord, let me go on with humility to better things
and never grow slack.

Lord, do not give me over
either to my human ignorance and weakness
or to my own deserts,
or to anything, other than your loving dealing with me.
Do you yourself in kindness dispose of me,
my thoughts and actions, according to your good pleasure,
so that your will may always be done
by me and in me and concerning me.

Deliver me from all evil
and lead me to eternal life
through the Lord.

St Anselm, 'Prayer to God'

5 February

Saint Agatha, *virgin and martyr*

MEMORIAL

Agatha — her name means 'Good' — suffered for her faith in Christ at Catania
in Sicily. She is mentioned in all the martyrologies of East and West and her
very fame led to such a flowering of legend that we cannot now even date her
martyrdom with certainty.

   She is mentioned in Eucharistice Prayer I — the traditional Roman Canon —
in the Missal.

   Agatha died because she loved God supremely and solely, and the reading,
taken from St Gregory of Nyssa, treats of such love, although in a somewhat
different context.

Whenever the soul, then, having divested itself of the many diverse
emotions incident to its nature, gets its divine form and, mounting
above desire, enters within that towards which it was once incited by

60

that desire, it offers no harbour within itself either for hope or for memory. It holds the object of the one; the other is extruded from the consciousness by the occupation in enjoying all that is good: and thus the soul copies the life that is above, and is conformed to the peculiar features of the divine nature; none of its habits are left to it except that of love, which clings by natural affinity to the Beautiful. For this is what love is; the inherent affection towards a chosen object. When, then, the soul, having become simple and single in form and so perfectly godlike, finds that perfectly simple and immaterial good which is really worth enthusiasm and love, it attaches itself to it and blends with it by means of the movement and activity of love, fashioning itself according to that which it is continually finding and grasping. Becoming by this assimilation to the Good all that the nature of that in which it participates is, the soul will consequently, owing to there being no lack of any good in that thing itself in which it participates, be itself also in no lack of anything, and so will expel from within the activity and the habit of desire; for this arises only when the thing missed is not found. For this teaching we have the authority of God's own apostle, who announces a subduing and a ceasing of all other activities, even for the good, which are within us, and finds no limit for love alone. Prophecies, he says, shall fail; forms of knowledge shall cease; but 'charity never fails'; which is equivalent to its being always as it is: and though he says that faith and hope have endured so far by the side of love, yet again he prolongs its date beyond theirs, and with good reason too: for hope is in operation only so long as the enjoyment of the things hoped for is not to be had; and faith in the same way is a support in the uncertainty about the things hoped for; for so he defines it — 'the substance of things hoped for'; but when the thing hoped for actually comes, then all other faculties are reduced to quiescence, and love alone remains active, finding nothing to succeed itself. Love, therefore, is the foremost of all excellent achievements and the first of the commandments of the law. If ever, then, the soul should reach this goal, it will be in no need of anything else; it will embrace that plenitude of things which are, whereby alone it seems in any way to preserve within itself the stamp of God's actual blessedness.

St Gregory of Nyssa, *Of the Soul and the Resurrection*

6 February
Saints Paul Miki and companions, *martyrs*
MEMORIAL

St Paul Miki and his twenty-five companions suffered martyrdom at Nagasaki in Japan, in the year 1597. Six of the martyrs were Franciscans, seventeen
were Franciscan Tertiaries, and three, one of whom was Paul Miki, were
Jesuits. They were suspended on crosses in the Japanese manner and then
killed simultaneously by spear thrusts through the heart. The persecution
under which they suffered was primarily nationalist in origin and spirit.
Renewed persecution broke out in 1613 and very many more then suffered
for the faith. From then on, until 1859, no foreigner could enter Japan. The
martyrs were canonized in 1862. In 1865 it was discovered that there were
thousands of Catholics in Japan. The faith had been handed down for over two
hundred years without any priests and with only the sacrament of baptism —
a record perhaps unique in the annals of the Church. The atom bombing of
Nagasaki in 1945 must cause us in the West to pause in shame.

  As a reading I have chosen excerpts from Robert Bogan's version of Pope
Paul VI's encyclical letter, *This is the Gospel.*

Witness
must always be justified,
and made explicit
by the living word.
There is no true evangelization
if the name of Jesus,
the Son of God;
his teaching, his life,
his promises;
his kingdom, or his mystery,
are not proclaimed.
From its beginning,
the Church has been seized
by the desire to evangelize.
This proclamation, or *kerygma,*
preaching, or catechesis,
have often become synonymous
with evangelization.

In fact
proclamation reaches

full development
only when listened to;
accepted and assimilated;
when it arouses
genuine adherence
to the truths
the Lord revealed;
adherence, still more,
to a programme of life
henceforth transformed.
It means adherence
to the kingdom;
to the 'new world';
the new state of things;
the new manner of being;
of living;
of living in that community
which the Gospel
inaugurates.

Such an adherence
cannot remain abstract
or disincarnated;
it manifests itself visibly
by entry
into the community of believers.
Those whose lives
have been transformed
enter a community
which is in itself
a sign of transformation;
a sign of newness of life.
This is the Church,
the visible sacrament
of salvation.
One who accepts the Church
as the Word which saves,

adheres to the Church,
and accepts the sacraments,
which manifest and support
this adherence
through the grace they confer.

He who has been evangelized
evangelizes others.
It is unthinkable
that anyone
should accept the Word,
and give himself
to the Kingdom,
without becoming
a witness to it.
Evangelization
is a complex process;
it involves the renewal of humanity;
witness;
explicit proclamation;
inner adherence;
entry into community;
acceptance of signs;
apostolic initiative.
Each element must be seen
in the context of the others.

Paul VI, *This is the Gospel*, nn 22-24

8 February
Saint Jerome Emilian, *priest and confessor*
OPTIONAL MEMORIAL

Jerome was born in Venice in the fifteenth century and, as an adult, followed a
military career. As a young man he gave little thought to God and had little
care for God's law. He underwent a conversion, however, gave away all his
possessions to the poor, became a priest, and devoted himself to the instruction of orphans and the care of the poor. To further these works, in the year

1532, he founded the Clerks Regular of Somascha — generally known today as the Somaschi. St Jerome died as the result of catching fever from those whom he was nursing at Somascha in 1537.

The reading given, taken from St Cyprian's treatise on *Almsgiving*, was chosen because of the same literal interpretation of the Gospel which inspired both saints, although they were separated by nearly thirteen centuries.

But you are fearful and hesitate lest, if you were to undertake much doing of mercy, your assets having been exhausted by liberal action, you might perhaps be reduced to want. Rest unshaken in this matter, rest secure — that cannot come to an end which is the source of what is spent for Christ's sake. In no way do I promise this to you on my own authority, but I predict it confidently by the faith of the holy scriptures, and the authority of God's own promise. The Holy Spirit speaks by Solomon and says: 'He who gives to the poor will never want; he, however, who turns his gaze away will be in great want'; showing that the merciful and the doers of mercy can never want, but that the niggardly and unfruitful afterwards arrive at need. Again the blessed apostle Paul, full of the grace of divine inspiration, says, 'He who supplies seed to the sower and bread for the eating will supply and multiply your sowing and increase the harvest of your right-eousness, so that in everything you will be enriched.' And again, 'The administration of this service will not only make up those things which are lacking to the saints, but will abound by many thanks-givings in the Lord': for while thanksgiving is directed by the prayer of the poor to God for our alms and works of mercy, the riches of the doer are heaped up by the recompense of God. And the Lord in the Gospel considering already then the hearts of such kind of men brings an action against the faithless and unbelieving, and says, denouncing with a prophetic voice: 'Do not think, saying, what shall we eat? or what shall we drink? or what shall we wear? For the nations seek these things. For your Father knows that you need them all. Seek first the kingdom and justice of God, and all these will be set before you.' He says all things will be set before and given to those who seek the kingdom and justice of God: for the Lord tells us that when the day of judgement shall have come, those who have been active in his Church will be admitted to receive his kingdom.

St Cyprian of Carthage, *Of Mercy and Almsgiving*, c 9

10 February
Saint Scholastica, *virgin*
MEMORIAL

Scholastica was a sister of St Benedict. All we know of her is contained in two chapters of the second book of *The Dialogues* attributed to St Gregory the Great. We learn from them that she was a consecrated virgin, who died before her brother. Benedict had his disciples bring her body to be buried in the tomb prepared for himself. Although the *Dialogues* would by some be dated to more than one hundred years after the events recounted, and the destruction of the monastery of Monte Cassino by the Lombards was a thing of the past, we can perhaps trust these details. The story of Scholastica's overcoming of her brother's legal scruples is told so vividly and the comment so neat — she who loved more was the stronger *(plus valuit quae amplius amavit)* — that if it is not authentic, it ought to be.

The reading is taken from a letter which is variously attributed in the manuscripts to Augustine, Jerome or Sulpitius Severus, but which contemporary scholars believe should be ascribed to Pelagius. Pelagius was, for quite a time, a highly respected spiritual guide in Rome.

How great blessedness, among heavenly gifts, belongs to holy virginity. Besides the testimonies of the scriptures, we learn also from the practice of the Church, by which we are taught that a peculiar merit belongs to those who have devoted themselves to it by special consecration. For while the whole multitude of those that believe receive equal gifts of grace, and all rejoice in the same blessings of the sacraments, those who are virgins possess something above the rest, since, out of the holy and unstained company of the Church, they are chosen by the Holy Spirit, and are presented by the bishop at the altar of God, as if being more holy and pure sacrifices, on account of the merits of their voluntary dedication. This is truly a sacrifice worthy of God, inasmuch as it is the offering of so precious a being, and none will please him more than the sacrifice of his own image. For I think that the apostle especially referred to a sacrifice of this kind, when he said, 'Now, I beseech you, brethren, by the mercy of God, that you present your bodies a living sacrifice, holy and acceptable to God.' Virginity, therefore, possesses both that which others have, and that which others have not; while it obtains both common and special grace, and rejoices (so to speak) in its own peculiar privilege of consecration. For ecclesiastical authority permits us to style virgins also the brides of Christ; while, after the manner of brides, it veils those whom it consecrates to the Lord, openly exhibiting those as very especially about to possess spiritual marriage who have fled away from carnal fellowship. And those are worthily united, after a spiritual manner, to God, in accordance with the analogy of marriage, who, from love for him, have set at naught human alliances. In their case, that saying of the apostle finds its fullest possible fulfilment, 'He who is joined to the Lord, is one spirit.'

For it is a great and a divine thing, almost beyond a corporeal nature, to lay aside luxury and to extinguish, by strength of mind, the flame of concupiscence kindled by the torch of youth; to put down by spiritual effort the force of natural delight; to live in opposition to the practice of the human race; to despise the comforts of wedlock; to disdain the sweet enjoyments derived from children; and to regard as nothing, in the hope of future blessedness, everything that is reckoned among the advantages of this present life. This is, as I have said, a great and admirable virtue, and is not undeservedly destined to a vast reward, in proportion to the greatness of its labour.

Sulpitius Severus, *Letter* II:1, 2 (possibly by Pelagius)

11 February
Our Lady of Lourdes
OPTIONAL MEMORIAL

The Blessed Virgin Mary has been venerated under this title, first in popular devotion and then in the Church's liturgy, since the apparitions of 1858 to St Bernadette Soubirous in the cave of Massabielle. It is Mary in the mystery of her Immaculate Conception who is honoured in today's Memorial and not the apparitions.

The reading is a free rendering of a homily pronounced by Pope John Paul II during a Mass he celebrated in French on 10 February, 1979, and which he devoted to Our Lady of Lourdes.

'The Almighty has done great things for me, holy is his name. He has mercy on those who fear him in every generation. . . . He has cast down the mighty from their thrones, and has lifted up the lowly. He has filled the hungry with good things and has sent the rich away empty.' Words we hear, words we repeat so often! Let us try, just for once — and when better than now — to linger on the marvellous and unaffected heart of Mary: God speaks in and through it. He speaks at a level beyond the usual level of men, and perhaps beyond the level of Myriam's own daily use — the young girl of Nazareth, related to Elizabeth and Zachary, recently become engaged to Joseph. In reality, isn't Mary acting as the spouse of the Holy Spirit?

It is indeed the Spirit who makes her heart so transparent (the simple and humble heart of a child of Nazareth), thanks to the promise made 'to Abraham and his children for ever'.

God is also mysteriously present to the whole history of human-kind — to successive ages, to different peoples — always able in his own marvellous way to rouse up, when and where he will, here simplicity, there hope, now a call to holiness, then a purifying, or, in another, conversion. In this way he is present in the history of the lowly . . . and of the mighty: yes, in the history of the hungry, of the oppressed, of the forgotten, who know themselves to be loved by him and find again with him courage, dignity, hope; in the history too, of the rich, of the oppressors, of those who want for nothing, who do not escape from the judgement of God, and are also invited to be human, to be just — sharing in order to enter his kingdom. God is present in the history of those who direct and those who are victims of our spreading consumer society: he wants to save humankind from the slavery to things and always to bring it back to the love of persons — of God, and of his brothers and sisters — with the spirit of purity, of poverty, of simplicity.

Pope John Paul II, Homily in Honour of Our Lady of Lourdes,
10 February, 1979

14 February
Saints Cyril, *monk,* and **Methodius,** *bishop*
MEMORIAL

(Mass, in Europe, as of a Feast)

Cyril and Methodius were brothers, natives of Thessalonika. Cyril was the younger of the two but entered the service of the Church first. Both were highly accomplished, and when Rotislav, Prince of Moravia sent to Constantinople for missionaries who could speak Slav, the two were recommended by Photius. They set out in the year 863. Cyril had devised an alphabet for Slav and the brothers preached and celebrated the liturgy in the vernacular. Moravia was situated between Byzantium and the aggressive Germanic peoples, and the German clergy made many difficulties for the two brothers. They decided to go to Rome and were favourably received by Pope Adrian II. Cyril died in Rome and was buried in San Clemente. Methodius was consecrated bishop and returned to Moravia, working in Pannonia. His troubles were not over. He was imprisoned, released, then denounced to Rome. Pope John VIII vindicated him but withdrew permission to use Slavonic as the regular liturgical language. He died in 884. Much of St Methodius' work was undone by a German successor, and seeds of lasting bitterness sown among the Slavs.

Today is the day of St Cyril's death in 869.

Pope John Paul II, on 31 December 1980, declared them heavenly patrons of Europe. The reading is taken from the Jerusalem Catechesis sometimes given as part of the Mystagogical Catechesis of St Cyril.

Let no one come here who could say with his mouth, 'We lift up our hearts unto the Lord', but in his thoughts have his mind concerned with the cares of this life. At all times, rather, God should be in our memory; but if this is impossible by reason of human infirmity, in that hour above all this should be our earnest endeavour.

Then the priest says, 'Let us give thanks to the Lord.' For truly we are bound to give thanks, that he called us, unworthy as we were, to so great grace; that he reconciled us when we were his foes; that he gave us the Spirit of adoption. Then you all say, 'It is fitting and right': for in giving thanks we do a fitting thing and a right; but he did not right, but more than right, in doing us good, and counting us fit for such great benefits.

After this, we make mention of heaven, and earth, and sea; of sun and moon, of stars and all the creation, rational and irrational, visible and invisible; of angels, archangels, virtues, dominions, principalities, powers, thrones; of the cherubim with many faces: in effect repeating that call of David's, 'Magnify the Lord with me'. We make mention also of the seraphim, whom Isaiah in the Holy Spirit saw standing around the throne of God, and with two of their wings veiling their face, and with two their feet, while with two they flew, crying 'holy, holy, holy, is the Lord of Sabaoth'. For the reason of our reciting this confession of God, delivered down to us from the sera-phim, is this, that we may in this way be partakers with the hosts of the world above in their hymn of praise.

Then having sanctified ourselves by these spiritual hymns, we beseech the merciful God to send forth his Holy Spirit upon the gifts lying before him; that he may make the bread the body of Christ, and the wine the blood of Christ; for whatsoever the Holy Spirit has touched, is surely sanctified and changed.

Then, after the spiritual sacrifice and bloodless service is com-pleted, over that sacrifice of propitiation we entreat God for the com-mon peace of the churches, for the welfare of the world, for kings, for soldiers and allies, for the sick, for the afflicted, and, in a word, for all who stand in need of any help we all pray and offer this sacrifice.

Then we commemorate also those who have fallen asleep before us, first patriarchs, prophets, apostles, martyrs, that at their prayers and intercessions God would receive our petition. Then on behalf also of the holy fathers and bishops who have fallen asleep before us, and in a word of all who in past years have fallen asleep among us, believing that it will be a very great benefit to the souls, for whom the supplication is made, while that holy and most awful sacrifice is set forth.

Cyril of Jerusalem, *Mystagogical Lecture* XXIII, 4-9

17 February
The Seven Founders of the Order of Servites
OPTIONAL MEMORIAL

The Seven Founders were young Florentines who joined the Confraternity of our Lady in Florence between the years 1225 and 1227. Discovering they shared a similar zeal and the desire for a life of renunciation they formed a community dedicated to the service of Mary and settled on the slopes of Monte Senario. After some years of withdrawn life they believed themselves called to become friars, and did so, adopting the Rule of St Augustine. They were called the Servants of Mary: we call them Servites. The Seven Founders were canonized in the nineteenth century. Today was chosen for their Memo-rial because it is the traditional day of death of one of the number, St Alexius Falconieri.

One form of devotion to Mary has become very much part of Servite tradition, although it is not certain how or where it began. This is devotion to her Seven Sorrows. The following reading is taken from a Servite author of this century, on 'Resignation'.

Jesus said one day to his disciples: 'If any man will come after me, let him deny himself, and take up his cross, and follow me' (Mt 16:24). This means that if we want to be true Christians, we must suffer in this world. Mary took up her cross and followed Christ. Her cross was a heavy one indeed. It was heavier than any cross we have to bear.

God knows how much each one of us can bear, and never puts upon our shoulders a burden that we could not carry. But whether our cross be light or heavy, we all have to carry it and follow the footsteps of Christ. He leads us along the way of the cross, up towards the mount of Calvary. He himself carried his cross to the very end, and died on the summit. None of us is asked to go as far as he did. There is a place for each one of us on Mount Calvary, for some high up, for others lower down; but each one has to be at the appointed place with his cross when Christ comes to judge the world.

Our Lady was the only one who was called to the summit of Calvary. 'She stood by the cross' (Jn 19:25); by the cross, quite close to it, in order to encourage us in our efforts to follow her. We are condemned to carry our cross because we have sinned: 'we indeed justly, for we receive the due reward of our deeds' (Lk 23:41); but Mary would not have been obliged, if she had not wanted and freely accepted, to do so.

She carried her cross and stood by her Son on Calvary in order to encourage and comfort us. Only those who have suffered themselves know how to help others in their sufferings. Mary knew the value of the example she was setting.

The example she gave us in the practice of other virtues is different from that which she gave us in her sufferings. In the practice of her other virtues, we feel the great distance between the example and the efforts we make to imitate it, because her Immaculate Conception freed her from the opposition of fallen nature.

This privilege, however, made her all the more perfect and consequently more sensitive to pain. Thus in the practice of patience her very perfection seems to bring her nearer to us. It is a virtue which we all have to practise since we all have to suffer, and the perfection of Mary makes her our perfect example in our sorrows. Not that we shall ever be able to suffer as much as she did, but we can bear with great resignation our share of suffering.

Hilary M. Morris, OSM, *Our Lady of Sorrows*, pp 38-9

21 February
Saint Peter Damian, *bishop and doctor*
OPTIONAL MEMORIAL

Peter was a native of Ravenna, the youngest of a large family, whose parents died when he was quite young. Initially he was brought up by a married brother but then was cared for by another older brother, archpriest of Ravenna, whose name, Damian, Peter subsequently took as a mark of appreciation, and added to his own.

When grown up Peter Damian became a hermit monk in the current of Camaldoli, and in 1043 was chosen as superior of his community. From his own house he founded five other communities of hermits, and three of his disciples are canonized saints. In the year 1057 he was appointed cardinal bishop of Ostia, and as bishop was very successful. He ultimately prevailed on Pope Alexander II to allow him to resign his see and became once more a simple monk, though he was twice summoned from his hermitage to act as Papal Legate.

His own monastic ideal was akin to that of the Syrian desert but he came to appreciate the more moderate observance of Cluny for cenobites. In the realm of Church politics he was wise enough to see that the Gregorian position was extreme and unworkable. St Peter Damian died in 1072.

The reading I have taken from his work entitled, *The Book of 'The Lord be with you'*. The liturgical practice with which it is immediately concerned has been modified in contemporary practice, but Peter Damian's understanding of and sense for the mystical body of Christ remain as true as they were over nine hundred years ago.

Consider carefully, therefore, all these things and those others which are too numerous to mention, and be punctilious in your observance of the laws of ecclesiastical custom whether you are alone or with others. For if the doctors of the Church had deemed it necessary, they would have given us one version of the offices of the Church for the use of solitaries and another for the use of communities; but by being content to compose one only, without any variation, they taught us to hold to this one order with inviolable respect. For they perceived that whatever is reverently offered up in God's service by any member of the Church is sustained by the faith and devotion of the whole body, since the Spirit of the Church, which gives life to the whole body which is preserved by Christ its head, is one. The whole Church is composed of the joining together of its different members; but it is certainly a single body, established on the firm foundation of a single faith and filled with the power of one life-giving Spirit. This is why the apostle says: 'There is one body and one Spirit, even as you are called in one hope of your calling.' And so it is good that whatever action in the holy offices is performed by any one section of the faithful should be regarded as the common act of the whole Church, joined in the unity of faith and the love of charity.

Now this is why, when in offering the mass we say: 'Be mindful, O Lord, of thy servants and handmaids', we add a little later 'For whom we offer, or who offer to thee, this sacrifice of praise'. These words make it quite plain that the sacrifice of praise is offered by all the faithful, women as well as men, even though it appears to be offered by the priest alone; for that which he performs with his hands in offering sacrifices to God is rendered pleasing by the earnest piety in the souls of the multitude of the faithful. This is made clear by another passage: 'We beseech thee therefore, O Lord, graciously to accept this oblation of our service and that of thy whole family.' These words make it even clearer that the sacrifice which is placed upon the holy altar by the priest is offered up by the whole of God's family. This unity of the Church was clearly proclaimed by the apostle when he said: 'For we being many are one bread and one body'. For so great is the unity of the Church in Christ that throughout the whole world there is but one bread which is the body of Christ and one chalice which is the chalice of his blood. Just as the divinity of the Word of God is one and fills the whole world, so although that body is consecrated in many places and on many days, yet there are not many bodies but the one body of Christ. And just as this bread and wine are truly changed into the body of Christ, so all those who worthily partake of it in the Church are made into the one body of Christ, as he himself bore witness when he said: 'He that eats my flesh and drinks my blood dwells in me and I in him.'

If, therefore, we are all one body in Christ and we who dwell in him cannot be separated from one another in spirit even though we are separated in the flesh, I can see no harm in our observing, when we are alone, the common custom of the Church, since by the mystery of our undivided unity we are never apart from her. When I in my solitude utter the common words of the Church I show that I am one with her and that by the indwelling of the Spirit I truly dwell in her: and if I am truly a member of her it is not unfitting that I fulfil my universal duty.

St Peter Damian, *The Book of 'The Lord be with you'*, pp 60-2

22 February
The Chair of Saint Peter
FEAST

It is not quite clear how this feast originated, or where. The texts indicate that what we are celebrating is the office of St Peter as bishop of Rome. The phrase 'at Antioch' which for a time appeared in the title of the feast was added in Gaul.

We dwell in gratitude on Peter's being bishop of Rome in the sense St Leo sets forth in the reading given below, taken from the sermon preached on the fourth anniversary of his own ordination as bishop in succession to St Peter. The first part of this same sermon is assigned in the *Divine Office* for this day.

The Lord, on the approach of his passion, a passion which was to shake the steadiness of the apostles, says, 'Simon, Simon, behold satan demanded to have you, that he might sift you like wheat, but I have prayed for you, that your faith may not fail; and when you have turned again, strengthen your brethren, so that you do not enter temptation.' Common to all the apostles was the danger of the temptation to fear. All likewise needed the help of the divine protection, for the devil wanted to disturb them all. And yet, a special care of Peter is taken on by the Lord, and prayer is made for the faith of Peter in particular, as if the future state of the others would be the surer, were the spirit of their leader not overcome! The resolve of all is strengthened in Peter, and the help of divine grace is so ordered, that the constancy, which through Christ, is bestowed on Peter, through Peter is conferred on the other apostles.

Since then, dearest ones, we see such protection divinely set over us, we, rightly and with good reason, rejoice in the favours and dignity of our leader, thanking our everlasting redeemer king, the Lord Jesus Christ, that he gave power of such kind to him whom he made head of the whole Church. This power is such that if anything is done rightly by us, if anything is rightly decided, even in our own times, it is to be attributed to his doing, his direction, to whom it was said: 'And when you have turned again, strengthen your brethren'; and, to whom the Lord, after his resurrection, in response to his three times professing eternal love, declared three times with mystic inner meaning: 'Feed my sheep'. Beyond all doubt, he now indeed does that, and, devoted shepherd, fulfils the Lord's command, strengthening us by his exhortations, and, lest we be overcome by any temptation, not ceasing to pray for us. If, moreover, as is to be believed, he extends this dutiful care of his to all God's people, how much the more will he deign to devote his help to us his disciples, among whom he rests on the sacred bed of a blessed sleep in that same flesh by which he presided!

Leo the Great, *Sermon 4* 'On the anniversary of his ordination'

23 February
Saint Polycarp, *bishop and martyr*
MEMORIAL

There are few of the Fathers of the early Church about whom we are so well informed as we are about Polycarp. He was a disciple of St John and became bishop of Smyrna. He was martyred in the middle of the second century, probably in the year 155, venerable for his years as for his faith. He had known St Ignatius of Antioch, and St Irenaeus of Lyons was one of his own disciples. We possess the circular letter written by the church at Smyrna describing his martyrdom, which took place on this day. The reading given below is taken from that letter and follows almost immediately on the extract from it used in the *Divine Office*. It is of importance as an early witness to the reverence and commemoration accorded the martyrs and to the place of such a commemoration in christian worship.

The Evil One put it into the head of Nicetas (the father of Herod, and brother of Alce) to make an application to the Governor not to release the body; 'in case', he said, 'they should forsake the Crucified and take to worshipping this fellow instead'. This was said under strong pressure from the Jews, who had been observing us as we were about to draw it out of the fire. Little do they know that it could never be possible for us to abandon the Christ who died for the salvation of every soul that is to be saved in all the world — the Sinless One dying for sinners — or to worship any other. It is to him, as the Son of God, that we give our adoration; while to the martyrs, as disciples and imitators of the Lord, we give the love they have earned by their matchless devotion to their king and teacher. Pray God we too may come to share their company and their discipleship.

However, when the centurion saw that the Jews were spoiling for a quarrel, he had the body fetched out publicly, as is their usage, and burnt. So, after all, we did gather up his bones — more precious to us than jewels, and finer than pure gold — and we laid them to rest in a spot suitable for the purpose. There we shall assemble, as occasion allows, with glad rejoicings; and with the Lord's permission we shall celebrate the birthday of his martyrdom. It will serve both as a commemoration of all who have triumphed before, and as a training and a preparation for any whose crown may be still to come.

Such then is the record of Polycarp the blessed. Including those from Philadelphia, he was the twelfth to meet a martyr's death in Smyrna; though he is the only one to be singled out for universal remembrance and to be talked of everywhere, even in heathen circles. Not only was he a famous Doctor, he was a martyr without a peer; and one whose martyrdom all aspire to imitate, so fully does it accord with the gospel of Christ. His steadfastness proved more than a match for the Governor's injustice, and won him his immortal crown. Now, in the fullness of joy among the apostles and all the hosts of heaven, he gives glory to the almighty God and Father, and utters the praises of our Lord Jesus Christ — who is the saviour of our souls, the master of our bodies, and the shepherd of the Catholic Church the wide world over. . . .

And now to him whose plenteous grace is able to bring us all into his heavenly kingdom, through his only-begotten Son Jesus Christ, be all glory, honour, might and majesty, for ever and ever. Our greetings to all the people of God. Our companions here send their greetings.

Letter from the Church at Smyrna on the death of Polycarp, nn 17-20

4 March
Saint Casimir, *confessor*
OPTIONAL MEMORIAL

Casimir was son of Casimir IV, king of Poland, and was born in 1458. He was directly involved in the affairs of government, was capable and intelligent, but truly just, gentle and pious. He was renowned for his love of the poor. Such goodness could not have been sustained without a life of real and deep prayer; fed, in Casimir's case, by a deep devotion to the Blessed Sacrament and to our Lady.

He died of consumption in 1484, when aged twenty-six, and was buried at Vilna in Lithuania. St Casimir was canonized in 1521 and is venerated as the patron saint of Lithuania and one of the patrons of Poland.

The reading is translated and adapted from a homily, preached by Pope John Paul II, which relates the readings offered in the Lectionary for St Casimir, to his life.

In Casimir the vocation to holiness given to the whole people of God as their lot is confirmed, and continues to shine upon his compatriots from generation to generation.

His earthly life was short, a mere twenty-six years, yet, for all its shortness, to him the words of scripture may be applied — he was 'perfected in a short time' (Wis 4:13).

The proper standard by which to judge human life is the degree of moral maturity attained, and, more especially, the quality of the love of God and neighbour with which it manages to fill each day of its existence.

Of Casimir we can say with the psalmist that he is one 'who walks blamelessly, and does what is right, and speaks truth from his heart' (Ps 14:2), showing by this the great uprightness of his life. In this spirit of uprightness he did not hesitate to influence his father the king, as the chronicles tell us, when justice with regard to his subjects demanded it.

Above all, Casimir was that disciple who faithfully followed Jesus Christ. He would have been able to quote the apostle's words as his own: 'For his sake I have suffered the loss of all things, and count them as refuse, in order that I may gain Christ and be found in him' (Phil 3:8-9). This great love burned up his soul like some inner flame.

He was like the gospel 'athlete' who strained 'ahead for what is still to come, racing for the finish' (Phil 4:13-14). Casimir lived on in the memory of posterity, in fact, as an ascetic full of zeal, for himself content with little, of himself demanding much.

The way of holiness by which this young man drew nearer to God in Jesus Christ, had love as its principal inspiration. It was upon love that he fed his thoughts, his feelings, it was from love he acted. This abiding in love was something he learned each day from the divine Master who said: 'As the Father has loved me, so have I loved you; abide in my love. If you keep my commandments you will abide in my love, just as I have kept my Father's commandments and abide in his love' (Jn 15:9-11).

Well then, Casimir abided in the love of Christ, Son of God, becoming an always more perfect 'friend' of his Master. He likewise grew continually more and more determined in this choice, and more and more into that solid structure concerning which the Master himself spoke to the apostles: 'I chose you and appointed you that you should go and bear fruit, and that your fruit should abide; so that whatever you ask the Father in my name, he may give it to you (Jn 15:16).

Pope John Paul II, Homily on the Fifth Centenary of the Death of St Casimir,
4 March, 1984

7 March
Saints Perpetua and Felicity, *martyrs*
MEMORIAL

Vivia Perpetua was a young married woman of the patrician or upper class. Felicity was a slave-girl. They were martyred with others for their faith in Christ in Carthage in the year 203.

We possess a contemporary account of their last days, written in part by Perpetua herself. Perpetua had a young son whom she was nursing when brought to trial. The choice she had to make is set out in the extract from their *Acts* given below. The tender love which was manifested between the two christian women of such different social conditions explains their memories being coupled together in the prayer and worship of the Church. In their steadfast love for Christ and for each other they bore triumphant witness to the power of the Spirit of their Risen Lord. This love was shown to all by their conduct in their last moments (cf the section of their *Acts* given in The Divine Office). The excerpt given below is from an earlier part of those Acts, written by Perpetua herself, and apparently written in Greek. It is this Greek text which I have followed.

After a few days it was understood we were going to be called. And, moreover, it came about that my father, depressed in spirit by long absence from home, made his way up to me, having taken it into his head to overcome me, saying: 'Daughter, have pity on my grey hairs, have pity on your father, if I am worthy to be called your father at all, bear in mind that with these hands I raised you to the very perfection of the prime of life, and I preferred you to your brothers and sisters. Look at your brothers and sisters, look at your mother and at your mother's sister, see your son who after you will not be able to live. Put aside these purposes and do not crush us all; for not one of us will speak with freedom if anything happens to you.'

He said this as a father, with the concern that parents have, and, kissing my hands and casting himself at my feet, and weeping, called me not his daughter but his lady.

I, on the other hand, grieved over my father's state, for alone of all my family he was not to exult in my suffering; I also consoled him saying: 'This will come about in the dock, if the Lord wills it, for know that we are not in our own power, but in that of God.' And he parted from me in great distress.

And on the appointed day, at lunchtime, we were whisked away for our hearing, and even as we came into the forum, the news went straightway through the neighbouring quarters and a great throng gathered together. And as we went up into the dock, the others, being questioned, confessed their faith. And it came to me to be interrogated. And my father appeared with my child there, and drawing me down to himself, said: 'Offer sacrifice, have pity on the babe'. And Hilarian, the Procurator, who then held the deceased Proconsul Minucius Oppianus's power of the sword, said to me: 'Spare your father's grey hairs, spare the helplessness of your child. Offer sacrifice for the well-being of the emperors.' And I replied: 'I do not sacrifice.' And Hilarian said: 'Are you a Christian?' And I said: 'I am a Christian.' And as my father sought earnestly to draw me away, Hilarian ordered that he be put down, and besides that one of the guard hit him with the butt of his spear, and I was deeply grieved, having pity on his old age. . . . At that time the Procurator condemned us all to the beasts, and rejoicing we went down into prison.

After that as I was accustomed to give suck to the child and it to remain with me in the prison, I sent the deacon Pomponius to my father, to ask for the babe. But my father did not give him over. Further, as God arranged, neither did the child from then on suck the breast, nor did I suffer any discomfort, perhaps in order that I might not be worn out by suffering at the thought of my child, and by the sense of pain in my breasts. . . .

The Acts of the Martyrdom of Perpetua and Felicitas, nn 5 & 6

8 March
Saint John of God, *religious*
OPTIONAL MEMORIAL

John was born in Portugal in 1495. As a young boy he wandered from home and so it happened that he was reared to manhood by a kindly and deeply christian couple far from his native place. He developed a fine physique as well as progressing in and deepening his life of prayer. This life was ended, when in the latter half of his twenties, to avoid a difficult emotional situation he enlisted as a soldier. The comments of his fellows soon occasioned his abandoning of prayer, and, it would seem, of much else that is christian besides.

An accident of war brought before him his real situation, and John returned to the sacraments. The change did not please his fellows, and they so arranged things that after a summary court martial he was discharged, having narrowly escaped a hanging. He returned briefly to where he had been brought up, but then set out again as a soldier in Charles V's army against the Turks. The war did not last long, and when John returned to Spain it was to his life as a shepherd. His prayer life was growing deeper all the time and with it his desire to expiate his past sins.

By God's providence and after many wanderings John was led to the care of the poor and despised. This was to be in Granada, and the catalyst was Blessed John of Avila. John did not come overnight to a realization of his call but through many sufferings, many of them brought on him by his wish to lower himself.

For the remainder of his life John was to devote himself to the care of the sick poor, caring for the whole person in whom he saw Christ himself. St John was particularly remarkable in his times for this sense of the person, as he was too, for his awareness of the importance of the practice of hygiene. He died in 1550, having spent all his forces. The companions he had gathered to aid in his work were to form the Order of Hospitallers of Saint John of God.

The reading offered, from his Letters, explains something of St John's religious psychology. It must not be forgotten, in reading it, that for John the love and service of Jesus was to a great measure to be expressed in the love and service of him in our neighbour.

My good duchess, if we consider carefully this present life we shall see that it is nothing else than a continual warfare as long as we remain in this valley of tears. We are constantly being persecuted by three mortal enemies, the devil, the world and the flesh. The world attracts us by its vices and its riches. It promises us a long life, saying: 'you are young, have a good time, enjoy yourself, it will be time enough to think of repentance when you are old.'

The devil is always setting traps in order to make us fall and to harm us. He tries to prevent us from doing good and being charitable. He inspires us with an exaggerated love of the goods of this world, so that we become forgetful of God and the care which we should have to preserve our soul pure and pleasing in his sight. When we have finished one affair he persuades us to engage in another and always to put off the amendment of our life to a later date. Thus we never manage to escape from the toils of the demon until the hour of our death comes, and then we shall see how false all that the world and the devil promised us was. But the Lord will judge us as he finds us at the hour of our death and, for that reason, it is well to mend our ways in time and not to be like those who are always putting it off till tomorrow.

Our other enemy, which is the worst, because it is one that we carry about with us, seeks by flattering attentions to lead us into perdition. This is the flesh, our body, which desires only to eat well, drink well, sleep well, be well dressed, do little work and satisfy all the desires of our carnal nature and of our vanity.

In order to overcome these three enemies, we have need of the grace and of the assistance of Jesus Christ. We must despise self and trust only in our Lord, confessing our sins humbly at the feet of our confessor, performing the penance imposed on us and resolving never more to sin. If we have the misfortune to sin, we must confess it truthfully. In this way can we hope to overcome the three enemies of which I have spoken. We must not trust in ourselves, otherwise we shall fall into sin a thousand times a day. We must put our trust in Jesus Christ and refrain from sinning for his sake. We must not grumble nor do evil, nor judge our neighbour nor do to him other than what we would have others do to us. Let us desire that all should be saved; and let us love Jesus Christ and serve him for his own sake and not through fear of hell.

From a letter of St John of God

9 March
Saint Frances of Rome, *religious*
OPTIONAL MEMORIAL

Frances was born in Rome in 1384 and from childhood had close links with the Olivetan Benedictines of Santa Maria Nuova. When of age she married Lorenzo Ponziano, a wealthy fellow citizen. Her married life was happy, the family circle devout, features we do not often associate with 15th century Rome.

She and Lorenzo had three children, two of whom died before the age of ten. Her son Battista alone was to survive her. These and other losses served to deepen her life of prayer; she came to live an intense mystical life, favoured with many visions and ecstacies.

This prayer life did not cut her off from the realities of suffering in the world around her, but rather sustained her in caring for the less fortunate. She distributed food to the poor, visited the sick and needy in their homes to care for them, among other things bringing them firewood to heat their rooms.

Not surprisingly the poor of Rome revered her as a saint. She associated other pious women who were accustomed to pray in Santa Maria with her in these activities. This association developed into a community of Oblates under the Rule of Benedict, dedicated to Our Lady, established at Tor de' Specchi. Oblates do not take vows but merely undertake to observe the rules of their association, and so the comunity founded by Frances was not enclosed. The community was not large and was made up of widows and young girls who not only lived a life of prayer but also cared for the needs of others, even visiting and ministering to them in their homes. This it would appear was something new in the Church, and was a stepping stone to future developments. When Frances' husband died she joined the community she had founded. She herself died in 1440 and was canonized in 1608.

The ideal of the Oblates of St Frances served as the initial inspiration for St Francis de Sales when he founded with St Jane Frances the community which was to develop into the rather different Order of the Visitation.

The reading, from Cardinal Hume, serves as a comment on the life and spirit of St Frances.

I would like to touch upon two important processes in the spiritual life.

The first is the need to become less and less egocentric and more and more God-centred. The more we learn of our own lives in a monastery and see of others' lives, the more we appreciate the importance of becoming increasingly selfless. The instinct in each of us is to want the incense to be offered to 'self': it is not instinctive to kneel down and offer it to God. The latter act would have been instinctive to unfallen human nature; but ours is a fallen nature and our instinct is to draw things to self — a terrifying thought, a frightening discovery. And even when we think we are becoming increasingly spiritual, we discover how much self there is in all this. And becoming God-centred entails suffering: there is no other way. It is going to be painful. That is why I believe in the arrangements we have here for the development of the spiritual life, because in the conflicts of day-to-day living we are presented with many opportunities of dying to self and rising with Christ. This dying and rising is fundamental to the spiritual life. It is a truth we ignore at our peril.

Secondly, I would remind you that there is no progress in charity without purification of faith. This is exemplified in our Blessed Lady. She was often baffled. She did not understand. She 'kept these things in her heart' (Lk 2:51). Read those texts closely and you will see what I mean. Faith must be purified. Those many props which seem important must, in a truly spiritual life, be removed so that there is no prop left, only God. This is very hard. But we know it is so from our reading, in the spiritual writers, of the aridities in prayer; the difficulties in understanding the things of God. After all, we have given our lives to God and yet, so often, he seems elusive. We long for light and are left in darkness. We long for consolation and find only pain. And faith is sorely tried, because faith ultimately is dependence on and acceptance of God alone.

George Basil Hume, OSB, *Searching for God,* p 140

17 March
Saint Patrick, *bishop*
OPTIONAL MEMORIAL

Patrick is Patron of Ireland, where this day is celebrated as a solemnity. He holds an almost unique place among the patron saints of western Europe, having become part of Irish tradition. This is the result of the growth of tradition over the centuries, but his writings show this Briton worthy of a place among the great national apostles. In Latin we have his *Confession,* an account and justification of his life and vocation, and his *Letter* to the soldiers of Coroticus. There is also, in Old Irish, his *Lorica* or *Breastplate,* set down in the ninth century, but certainly from the time of Patrick. It must be reckoned one of the truly great christian hymns. We have, too, an early witness to him in the hymn *Audite omnes.* The text of the latter is given in the *Glenstal Bible Missal.*

Christ was everything to Patrick, and his call to preach to the Irish came from God. These were his deep convictions. Just as deep was the conviction of his own unworthiness before God, and the consciousness of his limitations.

The reading is taken from the *Confession,* but from an earlier part of it than the reading given in *The Divine Office* under this day.

And it was there (among foreigners), that the Lord 'opened the understanding of my unbelieving heart', so that I should recall my sins even though it was late and 'I should turn with all my heart to the Lord my God', and 'he took notice of my humble state' and pitied my youth and my ignorance and protected me before I knew him and before I had sense or could distinguish between good and bad and strengthened me and comforted me as a father comforts his son.

So that is why I cannot keep silent, 'and it is not expedient', about the great acts of goodness and the great grace which the Lord generously gave me 'in the land of my captivity', because this is my repayment, after I have been chastened and have recognized him 'to praise and confess his wonderful works' among 'every nation that is under the sky'.

Because: there is no other God nor was there ever in the past nor will there be in the future except God the Father ingenerate, without beginning, from whom all beginning flows, who controls all things, as our formula runs: and his Son Jesus Christ whom we profess to have always existed with the Father, begotten spiritually before the origin of the world in an inexpressible way by the Father before all beginning, and through him were made things both visible and invisible; he was made man; when death had been overcome he was received into heaven by the Father, and 'he gave to him all power above every name of things heavenly and earthly and subterranean and that every tongue should confess to him that Jesus Christ is Lord and God'; and we believe in him and await his Advent which will happen soon, as 'judge of the living and the dead, and he will deal with everybody according to their deeds' and he poured out upon us richly the Holy Spirit the gift and pledge of immortality, who makes those who believe and obey to be sons of God and coheirs with Christ and we confess and adore him, one God in the Trinity of sacred name.

For he himself said through the prophet, 'Call upon me in the day of your trouble and I will deliver you and you will glorify me', and elsewhere it says 'Now it is honourable to display and confess the works of God.'

However though I am unsatisfactory in many points I want my brothers and relations to know what I am like, so that they can perceive the desire of my soul.

St Patrick, *The Confessions*, nn 2-6

18 March

Saint Cyril of Jerusalem, *bishop and doctor of the Church*
OPTIONAL MEMORIAL

Cyril was born about 315 and succeeded St Maximus as bishop of Jerusalem in 348. This was the time of the Arian controversy, for there were those who refused to accept the decrees of the Council of Nicaea. Cyril was exiled several times from his see as a result of the various changes in imperial policy but died in Jerusalem in 386. His own nature was gentle and conciliatory, but his faith very firm. His eighteen *Catechetical Instructions* are justly famous, and have already been cited. The reading is taken from the eighteenth of these Instructions.

In this holy catholic Church receiving instruction and behaving ourselves virtuously, we shall attain the kingdom of heaven, and inherit eternal life; for which also we endure all toils, that we may be made partakers thereof from the Lord. For ours is no trifling aim, but our endeavour is for eternal life. Wherefore in our profession of faith, after the words, 'and in the resurrection of the flesh', that is, of the dead, we are taught to believe also 'in the life eternal', for which as Christians we are striving.

The real and true life then is the Father, who through the Son in the Holy Spirit pours forth as from a fountain his heavenly gifts to all; and through his love for man, the blessings of the life eternal are promised without fail to us men also. We must not disbelieve the possibility of this, but having an eye not to our own weakness but to his power, we must believe; 'for with God all things are possible' (Lk 1:37). And that this is possible, and that we may look for eternal life, Daniel declares, 'And of the many righteous shall they shine as the stars for ever and ever' (Dan 12:3). And Paul says, 'And so shall we be ever with the Lord' (1 Thess 4:17): for the being for ever with the Lord implies eternal life. But most plainly of all the Saviour himself says in the Gospel, 'And these shall go away into eternal punishment, but the righteous into life eternal' (Mk 25:46).

And many are the proofs concerning eternal life. And when we desire to gain this eternal life, the sacred scriptures suggest to us the ways of gaining it; of which, because of the length of our discourse, the texts we now set before you shall be but few, the rest being left to the search of the diligent. They declare at one time that it is by faith, for it is written, 'He that believes in the Son has eternal life' (Jn 3:36), and what follows; and again he says himself, 'truly, truly', I say to you, he that hears my word, and believes him that sent me, has eternal life' (Jn 5:24), and the rest. At another time, it is by the preaching of the Gospel; for he says, that 'He that reaps receives wages, and gathers fruit unto life eternal' (Jn 4:36). At another time, by martyrdom and confession in Christ's name; for he says, 'And he that hates his life in this world, shall keep it unto life eternal' (Jn 12:25). And again, by preferring Christ to riches or kindred, 'And every one that has forsaken brethren, or sisters', and the rest, 'shall inherit eternal life' (Mt 19:29). Moreover it is by keeping the commandments, 'You shall not commit adultery, You shall not kill' (Mt 19:16-18), and the rest which follow; as he answered to him that came to him, and said, 'Good Master, what shall I do that I may have eternal life'? (Mk 10:17). But further, it is by departing from evil works, and henceforth serving God; for Paul says, 'But now being made free from sin, and become servants to God, you have your fruit which is sanctification, and the end eternal life' (Rm 6:22).

And the ways of finding eternal life are many, though I have passed over them by reason of their number. For the Lord in his loving-kindness has opened, not one or two only, but many doors, by which to enter into eternal life, that, as far as lay in him, all might enjoy it without hindrance.

Thus much have we for the present spoken within compass concerning eternal life, which is the last doctrine of those professed in the Faith, and its termination; which life may we all, both teachers and hearers, by God's grace enjoy!

St Cyril of Jerusalem, Instruction XVIII, nn 28-31

19 March

Saint Joseph, *husband of the Blessed Virgin Mary*
SOLEMNITY

Of Joseph we know very little — and yet a great deal. The gospel accounts tell us that he was a village carpenter and a descendant of David. He was the husband of the Blessed Virgin Mary and so foster father of Jesus. He was a just man, a man of faith and obedient to God's word. What could any of us wish more than that God's inspired word would call us 'just'?

Joseph had to find his way through several difficult situations, and the reading offered, from Fr Faber on 'discretion', surely highlights a quality of his spirit rarely dwelt on.

St Joseph is the most perfect model of this virtue. . . . It may briefly be defined as persevering love . . .

I must say a few words of the share discretion claims in the method of our actions. Generally speaking, discretion may be resolved into obedience, the not worshipping our own lights nor following our own wills. A very eminent spiritual writer simply speaks of the two virtues as if they were one, or of discretion as if it were but a function of obedience. Speaking, however, in detail, discretion of manner consists in five things which I will state as briefly as possible, in order that they may be the more readily impressed upon the memory.

Discretion acts slowly and after prayer, doubts impulses, and takes counsel.

Discretion does little, one thing at a time, calculates its own strength, perseveres in its little, is on the look out to add, and prognosticates nothing.

Discretion does its work very carefully, attends to the circumstances of its actions, and never pulls them to pieces again when it has once made them up.

Discretion gently forces itself to its work, and insists on an interior spirit, pure motives, and the practice of God's presence.

Discretion does all its work for God supremely, as a man's chief work, and indeed only great work, appreciates its importance, estimates its difficulty, and is not merely hopeful, but sure of its results.

What is not discretion then, but the most temerarious indiscretion, is to be afraid of God and of holiness, to wish to stand well with the world, to be in a visible mean, that is a mean everyone can see and praise, between extremes, to fear committing ourselves with God, to be frightened of enthusiasm when we know that we are really not at all drawn to it, as a rule rather to give God a little less than his due than a little more, for safety's sake.

Now look at the beautiful contradiction of all this in St Joseph's life, so tried and chequered with gravest doubts, and dreams, and changes, as if he were set to be the sport of all the unlikelihoods of grace and of all the perplexing unearthly ways of God: and how quiet, how docile, how all for God, how interior, how never looking before light and grace came, how childlike and prompt the moment they did come!

Fr Faber, Growth in Holiness, pp 359, 362-3

23 March
Saint Turibius of Mongorvejo, or, of Lima, *bishop*
OPTIONAL MEMORIAL

Turibius was born in Spain about the year 1538 and became a professor of law. Philip II noticed his ability and uprightness and appointed him a judge of the Inquisition of Granada, an unusual appointment for a layman. A stranger appointment was to come, for in 1580 Philip nominated him to be archbishop of Lima in Peru. In vain did Turibius plead the irregularity of his appointment. He received all the orders and was ordained bishop.

In Lima he found an appalling situation. The Spanish conquerors were exploiting the country and the native population with the practice of every kind of tyranny and injustice. Not only were the native Indians neglected spiritually, their treatment was such that conversion would be almost impossible. Turibius set about combatting these abuses in themselves and also providing for the spiritual and physical needs of the people. He travelled the whole of his huge diocese, learned the language of the Indians, and established the first seminary in Latin America. He died in 1606 on this day, and was canonized in the eighteenth century.

The reading is from St Ambrose, another layman made bishop! The attitudes of the rich had not changed much over the centuries — not that all the rich were as bad as those Ambrose had in mind!

What cause have you rich for pride, what right to shrink from a poor man's touch? Were you not conceived in the womb and born as the poor was born? Why do you flaunt your noble stock? Among you and your like the ancestry of a dog is traced like a wealthy man's, and a horse's fine breed is boasted of like a consul's. This horse has such and such a sire, such and such a dam, another can vaunt his ancestry two or three generations back. But all this is no help in the race; speed not breed wins the prize, and one with a famous name to risk is all the more disgraced if he loses.

You then, my rich man, take care that the virtues of your fathers are not put to the blush in you; otherwise they too may have to bear the reproach: 'Why did you choose *him*, why make *him* your heir? It is no credit to an heir to have gilded ceilings or slabs of porphyry. The praise for this must not go to men but to mine and quarry where men are punished. It is the poor who dig for gold, though to them the gold is denied, and they toil in the search for what they cannot keep. But I find it strange that you rich should brag of gold, since it is rather an occasion of stumbling than ground for praise: 'Gold also is a stumbling block, and woe to them that seek after it'. Again, there is a blessing for the rich man 'who has been found without blemish and who has not gone after gold or put his trust in treasure of money'. But it seems he is hard to find, for the writer wishes to be shown such a man: 'Who is he, that we may praise him?' His actions are to be praised as rare rather than accepted as customary. Thus a man who remains commendable amid riches is a man truly perfect and one to be glorified — 'he who might have transgressed and did not transgress, and might have done evil and did it not' (Sir 31:7-10).

Gold then, a thing which so often leads astray, is less esteemed for its own virtues than for the human misery it represents. The great halls which are your pride ought rather to be your shame, since while they are big enough for multitudes they shut out the poor man's voice — true, the voice if heard would fall on deaf ears. . . . You give coverings to walls and bring men to nakedness. The naked cries out before your house unheeded; your fellow-man is there, naked and crying, while you are perplexed by the choice of marble to clothe your floor. A poor man begs for money in vain; your fellow-man is there, begging bread, and your horse champs gold between his teeth (Virg., Aen. VII, 279). Other men have no corn; your fancy is held by precious ornaments. What a judgment you draw upon yourself! The people are starving, and you shut your barns; the people are groaning, and you toy with the jewel upon your finger. Unhappy man, with the power but not the will to rescue so many souls from death, when the price of a jewelled ring might save the lives of a whole populace! . . .

St Ambrose, *Naboth*

25 March
The Annunciation of the Lord
SOLEMNITY

The sense of what we are celebrating today is set out by Pope Paul VI in the extract from *Marialis Cultus* given below, and an enriched treatment of the texts of the celebration is given in the Glenstal Bible Missal.

On this day in the oldest martyrologies the first entry was the death of the Lord. Then there followed an entry commemorating his conception. The belief that Christ died on the anniversary of his conception is explicit in St Augustine and so it became part of western tradition.

The first liturgical celebration of the Annunciation would seem to have been in the East in the sixth century. It was probably introduced into Rome by Pope Sergius towards the end of the seventh century. The feast is celebrated by the Greek Church today even if it happens to be Good Friday.

In the Irish Martyrology of Tallaght, to the death and conception of the Lord is added the making of the world.

1 A reading from Pope Paul VI's Marialis Cultus

For the solemnity of the Incarnation of the Word, in the Roman Calendar the ancient title — the Annunciation of the Lord — has been deliberately restored, but the feast was and is a joint one of Christ and the Blessed Virgin: of the Word, who becomes 'Son of Mary' (Mk 6:3), and of the Virgin, who becomes Mother of God.

With regard to Christ, the East and the West, in the inexhaustible riches of their liturgies, celebrate this Solemnity as the commemoration of the salvific 'fiat' of the Incarnate Word, who, entering the world said: 'God, here I am! I am coming to obey your will' (cf Heb 10:7; Ps 39:8-9). They commemorate it as the beginning of the redemption and of the indissoluble and wedded union of the divine nature with human nature in the one person of the Word.

With regard to Mary, these liturgies celebrate it as a feast of the new Eve, the obedient and faithful virgin, who with her generous 'fiat' (cf Lk 1:38) became through the working of the Spirit the Mother of God, but also the true mother of the living, and, by receiving into her womb the one mediator (cf 1 Tim 2:5), became the true ark of the covenant and true temple of God. These liturgies celebrate it as a culminating moment in the salvific dialogue between God and man, and as a commemoration of the Blessed Virgin's free consent and cooperation in the plan of redemption.

Pope Paul VI, Marialis Cultus

2 A reading from Guerric of Igny, Sermon 2 on the Annunciation

Today the Word is made flesh and has begun to dwell among us, according, that is, to the rule of sound faith which the definition of Church doctrines has passed down to us. . . .

Today Wisdom has begun to build for himself a house of our body, in the womb of the Virgin; and for the building up of the unity of the Church, he cut out from the mountain without any hands (Dn 2:34), the corner stone, when, without human labour he obtained flesh for himself, the flesh of our redemption, from a virginal body. From this day, therefore, 'the Lord of hosts is with us, the God of Jacob is our protector', because today 'the Lord is our lifting up, that glory may dwell on our earth'.

Truly today, 'Lord, you have blessed your earth' — that blessed One among women — today you have given the favour of the Holy Spirit, that our earth might bring forth the blessed fruit of its womb, and with the heavens dropping down dew from above, the virginal womb produced the Saviour.

The earth cursed by the work of the prevaricator, which, even laboured on, produced thorns and thistles for the heirs of the curse, is now, by the work of the Redeemer, a blessed earth, bringing forth the remission of sins and the fruit of life for everyone, and dissolving for the offspring of Adam the stain of the original curse. Further, that earth is blessed, which altogether untouched — neither dug nor sown — produces the Saviour by the dew of heaven alone, and offers to mortal beings the bread of angels as the sustenance of eternal life. This earth then, which was uncultivated, seemed to be abandoned, but was filled full with the most excellent fruit; it seemed to be a desert of loneliness, but was a paradise of blessedness. Clearly a garden of delights, this God's solitude, the fields of which produced the sweet-smelling shoot, clearly a desert filled full, from which the Father sent forth the Lamb 'the ruler of the earth'.

Guerric of Igny, Sermon 2 on the Annunciation, n 1

2 April
Saint Francis of Paola, *hermit*
OPTIONAL MEMORIAL

Francis was born at Paola in Calabria in 1416. From his youth he gave himself
to the ideal of St Francis of Assisi as regards poverty and simplicity of life,
although he interpreted these counsels in the light of his own vocation which
was markedly eremitical and contemplative. His fervour and sanctity
attracted followers and these he ultimately formed into the Minims — the least
of the Friars.

King Louis XI of France invited him to his country where St Francis lived for
the last few decades of his life, dying at an advanced age at Plessis-les-Tours
in 1507. He was canonized by Pope Leo X in 1519. As a saint he came to be
much revered in his own part of Italy and to be regarded as a secondary patron
of Naples.

St Francis typifies that constant renewal in the Church of the spirit of the
early Fathers of the Desert, the urge to give up literally all things in order to
cleave to and have Christ.

The reading given is taken from Boniface Maes, a writer in the Franciscan
school and not far distant in time from St Francis of Paola.

The soul which, by the preceding exercises of the active life and of the
contemplative life, has come to the perfect renouncement of all
created things, to an entire abandonment of self to the good pleasure
of God for time and for eternity, and finally to a love of God purified
from all regard to any reward or consolation, so that the heart, having
become perfectly free and ready for good, is henceforth drawn to the
good by an almost natural tendency, this soul will exercise itself in
the following manner:

It will apply itself to understanding and to believing with a lively
faith that it is in God and that God is in it, as the light is in the air and
the air in the light, according to the words of the apostle: 'We live, we
move, and we exist in him' (Acts 17:28). And let it not represent to
itself any modality for this divine presence: for God is present in us in
an ineffable manner which surpasses our spirit and our imagination.
Then let it address God thus present to tell him its loving adoration,
and let it renew to him its gift of the abnegation of self, and of all the
rest, and the offering of a most pure love.

Having done that whole-heartedly, the soul should rest content
with a pure and simple act of faith in the presence of God in it, re-

straining itself as much as possible from all flights of the imagination
and from all discursive thought. Let it simply turn the heart to God,
and glide towards him by the sole force of love, or rather let it repose
in him, leaving the heart to move smoothly and without effort under
the action of his grace, and ignoring everything else save this serene
sweetness, this isolation of the spirit of God, this loving outpouring
of the heart, all distraction being shut out. And then it will experience
deep within itself a sort of void and forgetfulness of all things; and
the heart will little by little accelerate, gently and without check, and
the breathing quicken with spiritual fervour: for this loving emotion
of the heart is, according to St Bonaventure, 'the fire of wisdom.'

As for what God then works in the soul thus prepared, that, no one
can understand, neither he who writes, nor he who reads, nor he
who experiences it, for it is incomprehensible.

Boniface Maes, *Mystical Theology*

4 April
Saint Isidore, *bishop and doctor of the Church*
OPTIONAL MEMORIAL

Isidore was born in Seville, in Spain, about 560. He was made bishop of his
native city in 601 and was an extremely active churchman playing a major role
in several Spanish synods, particularly in the Fourth Council of Toledo, which
was held in 633. A decree of that council for which Isidore was responsible laid down that cathedral schools were to be established where the arts,
medicine, law, Hebrew and Greek were to be taught. This decree became,
later on, the general law of much of the western Church, and the schools so
established were to develop into or inspire the first medieval universities.
Isidore is justly regarded as one of the founders of the Latin Middle Ages on
this account.

His writings also entitle him to be so considered. He tried to write what was
really an encyclopaedia of classical learning and so became one of the most
quoted of the Fathers. His etymology was scarcely scientific, but his work was
full of valuable and, on the whole, otherwise accurate information. His
writings were known in Ireland and England by at least 700. Isidore himself
had died in 636.

St Isidore was declared a doctor of the Church in 1722.

The reading offered reflects well his style. Entitled a sermon it should be
much better seen as sermon notes — thoughts set out in short pithy para-

graphs. The spiritual attitude would perhaps be too passive for modern minds, but the insight that for real justice we must wait until the next life remains as true today as ever.

St Isidore is not much read today, but his passivity before the rich did not reflect his general response to life. In fact, in a world which he recognized as collapsing he did what he could to save what was worthwhile of the past and to ensure it would be passed on to future generations. In this positive response to his life and times he should be an example to us.

The oppressors of the poor are to know that they win a heavier sentence when they prevail against those they seek to harm. The more strongly they prove their power on the lives of the wretched here, the more terrible is the future punishment to which they must be condemned.

Let the judges and rulers of the nations hearken; for the temporal miseries which they bring upon the people, they shall be burned with everlasting fire. So the Lord declares through the prophet Isaiah: I was angry, he says, with my people, and I delivered them into your hand. And you showed them no mercy, but made their yoke exceeding heavy. Go down into the dust; sit there; be silent, and enter into darkness. Evil shall come on you, and you shall not know from where; and calamity shall break upon you which you shall not be able to overcome; misery which you know not shall come suddenly upon you.

We ought rather to sorrow for men who do evil than for men who suffer it. The wrongdoing of the first leads them further into evil; the others' suffering corrects them from evil. Through the evil wills of some, God works much good in others.

The will of evil men cannot be fulfilled unless God permits it. When by God's permission men work the evil which they desire, God himself, permitting the evil, is said to do it. Hence it is that the prophet writes: 'Shall there be an evil which the Lord has not done?' The wicked seek a thing in the evilness of their will, but God gives them leave to accomplish it in the goodness of his, because he works much good from our evil.

Some men, resisting the will of God, unwittingly do his purpose. Understand then that so truly are all things subject to God that even those who oppose his ordinance nevertheless fulfil his will.

Why in this life are the good judged by the evil? Either that in the next life the evil may be judged by the good, or that the good may have temporal affliction here and eternal recompense there.

Evil men are necessary that through them the good may be scourged when they do amiss. Hence it is that the Lord declares the Assyrian to be the rod of his anger. When this is so, it proceeds from the indignation of God, who through such men wreaks his anger on those whom he would amend by chastisement. God works in this with a will of perfect justice, but his instruments often with the intent of cruelty, as the prophet says of this same Assyrian: 'Nevertheless he himself means not so, but his heart is set on destruction.'

Some simple folk, not understanding the dispensation of God, are scandalised by the success of evil men, and say with the prophet: 'Why does the way of the wicked prosper? Why is it well with all those who walk crookedly and deal ill?' Those who speak thus should not wonder to see the frail temporal happiness of the wicked. Rather let them consider their end at last, and the everlasting torments prepared for them; as the prophet says: 'They spend their days in wealth, and in a moment they go down into hell.'

St Isidore, *The Oppressors of the Poor*, nn 1-7, 13

5 April
Saint Vincent Ferrer, *priest*
OPTIONAL MEMORIAL

Vincent was born in Valencia, in Spain, in 1350. He joined the Dominicans in Spain, but, as a friar, studied and taught quite internationally. He developed into an amazingly successful popular preacher, enjoying something of the success of a 'pop-idol' in our times, a success which was all the more remarkable in that he did not mince matters, nor in any way temper the stern demands of a rigorous interpretation of the christian message. He persuaded many thousands of people to lead better lives. He was also of great importance as one of the chief architects of re-union after the Western Schism. Vincent died in 1419, and was canonized in 1455.

Reading his sermons today can only make one wonder at his popularity and success. We lack the experience of the voice, the presence of a personality, the ardent fervour which sustained both. The message must be for us that what one says does matter, but much more important is what one is.

The extract given here is from a sermon preached in Easter Week and its theme makes it topical.

Peter said: 'I am going fishing, otherwise I shall die of hunger'. The others answered: 'We shall come with you'. And they went to the sea of Galilee, also called Tiberias from the city on its banks. The whole night they laboured in fishing and caught nothing. Therefore, when morning dawned, they were both sad and hungry; then Christ appeared to them.

We have here two mysteries. Peter said: 'I am going fishing'. St Gregory asks whether it is lawful to return to secular business, which has been left in order to follow Christ? For, he says, that Christ said: 'No man setting his hand to the plough and looking back is fit for the kingdom of heaven'. The plough signifies penance; for, as the plough breaks up the earth in order to sow seed, so penance breaks the earth of the body, that it may bring forth spiritual fruit. Not to look back may be understood in either of two ways; that is, it may signify a return to business involving sin, or to one which does not involve sin. For example: a religious on entering a monastic order, of necessity puts his hand to the plough; but if he looks back by taking off the religious habit he is not fit for the kingdom of God. The same is true in regard to yourselves who, during Lent, have put your hand to the plough by penance, confession, and promise of amendment. But if you look back and say: 'Really, this is too much. Let us return to our dice, bad language and evil pleasure', you are not fit for the kingdom of God. The same is true of those whose business is sinful, or an occasion of sin to them or others. But with regard to business which does not involve sin, or occasions of sin, then it is lawful to return to it; as in the case of the business of fishing.

This leads us to a study of the hidden meaning of their occupation. Fishers are preachers, fishing for souls in the net of their sermons, in order to convert them from an evil life. Of this fishing Christ said: 'Follow me, and I will make you fishers of men'. It is necessary that these preachers should fish by day; that is, in leading a good life, and not by the night of an evil life. For in the latter case no one will accept their teaching. Of what use is it to preach against vice if the preacher himself is vicious? He will labour in vain, fishing all night; that is, while his own life is evil. Such people may truly say, as we read in St Luke's Gospel: 'Master, we have laboured all night and have caught nothing'. It is also necessary for preachers, fishing for souls, to cast the net on the right side; that is, by a good intention, in order to convert souls; and not on the left side of an evil intention, for vain glory, or in order to obtain money. Good fishers will obtain a multitude of great fishes; that is, a hundred and fifty-three, in the conversion of many people. A hundred signifies Christians; for, as ten times ten makes a hundred, so Christians should observe the ten Commandments. Fifty signifies the Jews, for, as five times ten makes fifty, so there are five books of the Law in the Old Testament. Three signifies the Saracens, for they believe three things; that Christ, born of a Virgin, is a holy Man and reigns in glory. So we read in St Luke: 'Launch out into the deep'.

St Vincent Ferrer, A Sermon preached on the Wednesday of Easter Week

7 April
Saint John Baptist de la Salle, *priest*
MEMORIAL

John Baptist de la Salle was born into an upper class French family in 1651 and was possessed of considerable personal means. He entered the service of the Church and, following what tended to be the pattern of the day for one of his social rank, became a canon of Rheims cathedral at the age of sixteen. He studied for the priesthood and was ordained. Then, by a series of providential encounters, he got involved in the education of the children of the poor at Rheims. He came ultimately to devote all his energies to education, but in the interim had resigned his canonry and sold all his possessions to relieve the victims of famine.

His first attempts at running schools ran into staffing difficulties and so he came to found the Brothers of the Christian Schools, mostly for the care of the poor. Among his works, though, were the first industrial schools. Through James II he became involved in the schooling of the upper classes, and this gained his work influence, but the chief thrust remained the education of the poor.

John Baptist de la Salle made several important innovations in educational practice, among which, perhaps, the use of the vernacular as the language of instruction (rather than Latin) was the most significant. His original ideas are set out in his Manual for Christian Schools. He died in 1719.

Canonized in 1900, St John Baptist de la Salle was declared patron saint of school-teachers in 1950. What he initiated and achieved under grace is certainly cause for us to celebrate his memorial.

The reading, taken from an address of Pope John XXIII, has been chosen for its observations on the vocation of the christian teacher, and particularly of the members of teaching Religious Congregations. Pope John's stress on the link between life and teaching is something we must defend today.

Dear Sons of Saint John Baptist de la Salle,
The vocation of a teaching Brother has always appeared to us as due a particular respect.

You hold a chosen place in the great body of Catholicism, a place to which you have brought your original and rich vocation of teaching Brothers. It cannot be too much underlined: the christian formation of youth is of prime importance. Nothing can replace that slow imbuing with christian values which is the fruit of teaching given by those who have consecrated their lives to such values. The blossoming of Catholic schools throughout the whole world is one of the greatest glories of the Church. You, dear Brothers of the Christian Schools, have an important share in this marvellous development. Everyone knows the inspiration your holy founder was in this field, and how much all owe to him, who since his time have drawn on his fruitful example. The story of all this is deeply engraved upon the heart of the Church, to the honour of St John Baptist de la Salle and of yourselves. Be faithful then, dear sons, to this finest of vocations, and continue to work with fervour in the Lord's field — your work marked with that special love for the least and poorest, which has, from its foundation, always marked your Institute.

To be sure, in these times, you have also to reckon with difficulties. It is heart-breaking to see the obstacles your apostolate encounters in so many lands. Have courage, dear sons, and unshaken confidence in the grace of Jesus Christ. May the trials which divine Providence mysteriously permits, serve to renew our energy and make us entrust ourselves gladly to God's disposition, to take up in another place the work interrupted in this one!

We must recall the Master's instruction to his disciples, given also for our enlightenment and warning: 'when they persecute you in one town, flee to the next . . .' (Mt 10:23). The Holy Spirit is always urging us forward to bear witness to the unfading youthfulness of the Church and to be living witnesses of its apostolic dynamism.

The work is pressing, and it demands many labourers. All over the world there are developing young minds in search of the truth, in this old Europe and further afield, among nations only now beginning to care for themselves and to take charge of their own futures and government. It is an admirable work, worthy to arouse the enthusiasm of young Catholics, this work of devoting oneself to the human and supernatural formation of those who will be the responsible adults of tomorrow. May you, dear sons, increase without ceasing your gallant ranks. May you continue to form in your schools future priests, religious who will continue your work, and laymen who will be in the world a strong leaven of Catholicism. This, dear sons of St John Baptist de la Salle, is the greatness of your vocation, this is the rich fruit of your renunciation: consecration to God in the religious life, consecration to men in teaching and education.

Pope John XXIII, Address to the Superiors of Christian Brothers Schools,
14 June, 1961

11 April
Saint Stanislaus, *bishop and martyr*
MEMORIAL

Stanislaus was born in Poland about the year 1030, and, having studied in Paris and Liege, was ordained priest. In 1071 he succeeded Lambert as bishop of Cracow. He was a zealous pastor and did much to raise the standards of his clergy as well as caring for the needs of the poor. Then, he differed with the King, Boleslav, over a series of interests, and was killed during the celebration of Mass as a result. This was in 1079.

St Stanislaus was canonized in 1253. Nine hundred years after his death a successor of his in the see of Cracow was elected pope.

St Stanislaus is venerated as one of the patrons of Poland.

The reading is on Love and is taken from an address by F.H. Drinkwater. St Stanislaus lived out such love and consummated his union with Christ by the shedding of his blood for him.

Everybody sees how important love is. If we get it more or less right, our life can be called a success. If we get it all wrong, our life is certainly a failure, however successful it may have been to the outside view.

'Without a lover thou canst not live,' says the author of the *Imitation of Christ*.

Does this mean only the passionate or romantic kind of love? Does it mean that life is not worth living if you can't find someone to get engaged to, or to go out with, or a bosom friend with whom you can spend all your time and share all your secrets?

No; about any of these ways we can say: It is well enough, but it is only one way.

The author of the *Imitation* means exactly what he says: that to live a life worth living we must love and be loved. Our heart is given us to use. We must not be afraid of loving.

Above all, we need to love God and to know that he loves us. Without that, in the long run, all the other loves will turn to dust and ashes and bitterness. To let ourselves be loved by God and to love him in return — that is the first and greatest commandment even of our own nature.

And is there any need to go further than that? Is not this divine love enough in itself to fulfil our life?

No, for God himself is the first to tell us that loving him involves loving others, too. Our neighbour — which means everyone that needs us. Our family, those of our own blood, whom it seems we must either love or hate. The friends whom God has given us. Those whose happiness in some way depends on us. The poor and suffering and discouraged whom we meet by the way.

And that reminds us that there are many different love-relationships, and that they can all be spoiled. Even mother-love may be too possessive and selfish, as we often see, especially in these days of small families.

All our loves must be in God and for God; and to please God they must be real — a merely formal outward attitude is not enough. There is a truly appalling English expression, 'cold as charity' — which indicates one of the wrong turnings which religious people may take.

How to manage love: that is the all-important thing that our Lord came to teach us. Nobody has solved these problems except Jesus Christ. He teaches us by his own words, as much as words can teach anybody: He gives us enough Truth for practical purposes. But these are things that we can learn only by living, and he teaches us most through the secret ways of his grace.

F.H. Drinkwater, 'The Great Lover'

13 April
Saint Martin I, *pope and martyr*
OPTIONAL MEMORIAL

Martin was born at Todi in Umbria and joined the Roman clergy. There were many contacts between the Roman Church and the Eastern Empire in the seventh century, and Martin was appointed papal legate to the Emperor in Constantinople. He then was elected Pope himself in 649. He opposed the monothelite heresy and had it condemned at a Council in the Lateran in 649. This heresy held that Christ had only one will, the divine will, and not a human one as well. The monothelite heresy was favoured by the emperor of the time, Constans II, and, as a result of the differences which followed, Martin was arrested on various charges, exiled first to Constantinople itself, and, when there, condemned to death and stripped of his honours. His death sentence was commuted to exile to Kherson in the Crimea. In Kherson, in conditions of misery and hunger, he died. Meanwhile, rather cravenly, the Roman clergy had accepted his deposition and elected a new pope.

The true faith triumphed, however, and in the Eastern Liturgy Martin is hailed: 'Glorious definer of the Orthodox faith . . . thou didst adorn the divine see of Peter'. Martin's letters from exile show his remarkable spirit of charity and forgiveness.

Martin's memorial is celebrated then for his firm defence of the faith, even to death, and his charity and forgiveness.

The reading is taken from the Greek Life of Martin, composed some fifty or so years after his death, but based on contemporary materials.

Saint Martin's Death in Exile

After these things he was ordered to be exiled in Kherson, and, after the lapse of some days, that most holy and apostolic man was shipped over there in secret. Having been deported there then; after many days, being in need, he wrote a letter to a certain dear friend of his in Byzantium asking for some supplies because of his severe and painful bodily ills and the manifold deprivations of that region in which nothing at all was to be found. To be specific, grain in particular was not at all to be found. On this account he wrote, with most earnest assurance, that when a boat had sailed there with a little grain in exchange for salt, he had been scarcely able to buy one measure of grain at four measures to the monetary unit, and that with much exhortation and entreaty.

Further, holy soul, he set down the many trials which he endured over there, not only from his bodily difficulties, but also from the local inhabitants and rulers, completely crushing him most evilly, as it seemed, so that he would die — a situation brought on clearly by the 'establishment' in Byzantium. In this way the blessed man endured the trials coming upon him on account of his upright confession of Christ our God, and his uncorrupted faith, and thanks to his condemnation of the heretics.

Now that apostolic man, the confessor and martyr of Christ our God, the most holy and thrice blessed Pope Martin of Rome had fulfilled his course. He had fulfilled it in accord with his own request of the Lord God — a request made of him with tears — having left the transport ship and walked on the ground there, in the same exile at Kherson. Having therefore fought the good fight, having finished the race and kept the faith, it is the very perfecting of him in that exile. On 13 April 656, he slept in death. He was buried in the tombs of the saints in the truly honourable church, called Blachernae, of the All-holy Lady, our undefiled and ever-Virgin Mother of God, Mary, not a furlong distant from the walls of that same town of the Khersonites.

He was a noble model for all who want to live piously and suffer for the real truth. . . . May Christ, our God, watch closely over his privileges, and preserve all of us, faithful hearers of his right actions, in integrity of faith and virtuous living, in peace and perfect love and all justice until the end.

from a Greek *Life of St Martin*

21 April

Saint Anselm, *bishop and doctor of the Church*
OPTIONAL MEMORIAL

Anselm was a native of Aosta, in Italy, who, as a young graduate, entered the monastery of Bec in Normany, where his fellow countryman, Lanfranc, had established a celebrated school. He succeeded Lanfranc as prior of his monastery, and, when aged forty-five, or so, was elected abbot. This was in 1078. Next he became abbot of Caen, and in 1093 was made archbishop of Canterbury. His zeal for the liberties of the Church caused him to be exiled under William Rufus and Henry I. He played a leading role at the Council of Bari. Anselm died in 1109 and, though never formally canonized, was declared a doctor of the Church in 1720.

Anselm was a very attractive person, and his writings on the mystical life are important, but he was marked by a peculiar intellectual intransigence. A feature of his spirituality and of his prayers is his obsession with sin and guilt. This led him to seek endless intercessors in his prayers; he was a true harbinger of medieval spirituality. The reading offered, taken from one of his prayers, reflects a more tranquil and biblical spirit.

In him we revere again a defender of the Church against temporal power, a man, and monk, remarkable for his ardent faith and love. And, though our spirituality may be more serene, we should also reflect on his hatred of sin and guilt.

Jesus, John's master, look on us.
Near to the waters my soul longs with thirst;
but there is nothing for it to drink
unless something flows from the fount.
Fount of mercy, flow from yourself through John
so that I may drink of you in him.
Good Lord, make answer on my behalf.
I go back to the fount itself, I can do no other.
Near to the fount of life no thirsting soul perishes.
Do not block the way of the thirsty to drink.
The one who is full of love hears your thought
and your thirsty one drinks your mercy through him.
Say to him, 'John, who seems to you to have been neighbour
to him that fell among thieves?'
And, blessed John, do you answer
in the words the human race applied to the Samaritan
and give thanks to him —

reply, 'He that had mercy upon him.'
Good Jesus, you have begun to help my prayer,
now into your hands I commend it,
so that your perfect goodness may perfect it.
Speak, I pray you, to your beloved John
to show him me, your servant,
and say to him, 'Go and do thou likewise.'

Hope and rejoice,
rejoice and love, O my soul!
He whom so doubtfully you asked to hear you
himself prepares for you an intercessor.
As a beggar I prayed through another
because I had no confidence before him myself;
and lo, he himself takes care of me,
and prays where I myself failed.
What goodness, piety, and love!
See, he shows how much he loves me —
he comes near to me so that I may love him!
So I press on and hope,
not in myself but in him,
for he listens to my desire who thus crowns my prayer.
'My heart and my flesh' rejoice in him and love him,
'and all that is within me' bless him. Amen.

St Anselm, Prayer in Honour of St John

23 April
Saint George, *martyr*
OPTIONAL MEMORIAL

St George died as a martyr at Lydda in Palestine in the first decade of the fourth century. He was, perhaps, a soldier in the Roman army. Of the many early martyrs George is one of those who received special veneration in all the mediterranean lands, and we find mentions of him in England and in Ireland around the early eighth century.

St George should be seen as a victim of conscience. All the martyrs were, of course, but as a soldier, George had to make a distinct act of preference — his loyalty to Christ as against loyalty to his profession of arms. This was the sense of devotion to him, a sense that is, and was, too frequently forgotten. The reading is from Pope John XXIII, *Pacem in Terris*, in which the Pontiff underlines the rights of the person and of conscience, rights which also constitute an obligation, for no one can renounce what God has given him.

The world's Creator has stamped our inmost being with an order revealed to us by our conscience; and our conscience insists on our preserving it. Men and women 'show the work of the law written in their hearts, their conscience being witness to them.' And how could it be otherwise? All created being reflects the infinite wisdom of God. It reflects it all the more clearly, the higher it stands in the scale of perfection.

But the mischief is often caused by erroneous opinions. Many people think that the laws which govern our relations with the State are the same as those which regulate the blind, elemental forces of the universe. But it is not so; the laws which govern men and women are quite different. The Father of the universe has inscribed them in our nature, and that is where we must look for them; there and nowhere else.

These laws clearly indicate how a human being must behave towards his fellows in society, and how the mutual relationships between the members of a State and its officials be conducted.

Any well-regulated and profitable association of men in society demands the acceptance of one fundamental principle: that each individual human being is truly a person. He or she is a nature, that is, endowed with intelligence and free will. As such he or she has rights and duties, which together flow as a direct consequence from that nature. These rights and duties are universal and inviolable, and therefore altogether inalienable.

When, furthermore, we consider our personal dignity from the standpoint of divine revelation, inevitably our estimate of it is incomparably increased. Men and women have been ransomed by the blood of Jesus Christ. Grace has made them sons and daughters and friends of God, and heirs to eternal glory.

Among men and women's rights is the right to be able to worship God in accordance with the right dictates of one's own conscience, and to profess one's religion both in private and in public. According to the clear teaching of Lactantius, 'this is the very condition of our birth, that we render to the God who made us that just homage which is his due; that we acknowledge him alone as God, and follow him. It is from this *ligature* of piety, which binds us and joins us to God, that religion derives its name.' Hence, too, Pope Leo XIII declared that 'true freedom, freedom worthy of the sons and daughters of God, is that freedom which most truly safeguards the dignity of the human person. It is stronger than any violence or injustice. Such is the freedom which has always been desired by the Church, and which she holds most dear. It is the sort of freedom which the apostles resolutely claimed for themselves. The apologists defended it in their writings; thousands of martyrs consecrated it with their blood.'

Pope John XXIII, Pacem in Terris, nn 5, 6, 7, 9, 10, 14

24 April
Saint Fidelis of Sigmaringen, *priest and martyr*
OPTIONAL MEMORIAL

St Fidelis was born in the town of Sigmaringen in South Germany in the year 1578. He first studied law and became an advocate, but then entered the Friars Minor Capuchins. He excelled as a friar and became a highly regarded preacher. Coming to the notice of the authorities of the newly constituted Congregation of Propaganda Fide in Rome, he was appointed to preach to the Calvinists of the Canton of the Grisons, Switzerland. His work was successful but also aroused intense hostility and he was killed by a group of fanatics at Seewis in 1622.

He was the first of those appointed by the Congregation for the Propagation of the Faith to die for that faith.

St Fidelis was remarkable not only for his fervour and loyalty with regard to the Catholic faith but also for his concern and love for the needy, suffering and deprived.

The reading is taken from *The Goad of Divine Love*, attributed to St Bonaventure, and certainly from his circle. The translation is based on an old English one, from approximately the same epoch as St Fidelis, who would certainly have been familiar with the text in one version or other.

Concerning your neighbours, take this lesson: 'Think every man in the world to be yourself.' If you do this well, and imprint it well on your heart, then there is no doubt you will love your neighbour's good as your own. You will be as careful to obtain by prayer, exhortation, help, and any way you are able, whatever you see in any way aids your neighbour's salvation, as you would be for yourself. And when you see him or her speak or do what is good, you will be as glad as if you spoke and did it yourself. If you know your neighbour to be in sin, or to have any spiritual failing, you will be made sad, and ready, as far as you are able to reclaim your neighbour from evil, and lead him or her back to goodness.

I, miserable wretch that I am, should never cease weeping, when I see the destruction of so many souls, and my God held as nothing. Let the souls of the just draw strength from the consideration of these two realities. Let them do all that they possibly can to free and deliver those souls from their sins, not accepting that God be treated with contempt, while grieving for the loss of so many souls.

How can one say that one loves God and seeks after God's love, who, seeing God's image stuck in the dunghill, does not take this to heart? Or, if they think that the Son of God died for the redemption of souls, how is it that they, also, do not desire to die in order to gain souls? But, above all, when one sees the blood of Christ trampled underfoot, how, I ask, can one possibly endure this injury to one's Lord?

Why do they not pour themselves forth wholly in prayer, continually calling upon their neighbour by preaching, or instructing their neighbour by reading, or by hearing confessions, so that they may preserve and save this same blood of their Lord from such contempt by the winning and converting of souls?

These things, my most dear ones — namely the contempt of God and the loss of souls — ought to inflame us to preach, to confess, to pray, and to build up by good example — but not vainglory, nor pride of heart, nor popular applause, nor any worldly profit whatsoever. Let us look for nothing from souls but Jesus Christ crucified — for they are bought with a great price!

St Bonaventure, *The Goad of Divine Love*, I, ix, 1, 5, 7

25 April
Saint Mark, *evangelist*
FEAST

John Mark was a native of Palestine and a kinsman of Barnabas. He first appears, in the New Testament, in the company of Paul and Barnabas. His conduct led to a difference between Paul and Barnabas, but later we find him at Paul's side in Rome. Traditionally, however, he has been more closely related to Peter. When the latter was miraculously delivered from prison in Jerusalem it was to the house of Mary, mother of John Mark, that he went, indicating that the family was of importance in the early Church there. The Gospel he wrote has been traditionally viewed as representing St Peter's approach to the preaching of the good news and would have been written in Rome. There are solid reasons for accepting that tradition. Mark is mentioned by St Peter in his first letter as 'my son', and this is read at today's Mass.

Again tradition would have it that Mark subsequently went to Alexandria and died there as a martyr in or about the year 74. His feast is celebrated today by the Copts and Byzantines, and was adopted by Rome in the eleventh century. Grace can make the weak strong, a lesson set out by Newman in the reading given here.

The encouragement which we derive from these circumstances in St Mark's history, is that the feeblest among us may through God's grace become strong. And the warning to be drawn from it is, to distrust ourselves; and again, not to despise weak brethren or to despair of them, but to bear their burdens and help them forward, if so be we may restore them. Now let us attentively consider the subject thus brought before us.

Some people are naturally impetuous and active; others love quiet and readily yield. The over-earnest must be sobered, and the indolent must be roused. The history of Moses supplies us with an instance of a proud and rash spirit, tamed down to an extreme gentleness of deportment. In the greatness of the change wrought in him when from a fierce, though honest, avenger of his brethren, he became the meekest of men on the earth, he evidences the power of faith, the influence of the Spirit on the heart.

St Mark's history affords a specimen of the other, and still rarer change, from timidity to boldness. Difficult as it is to subdue the more violent passions, yet I believe it to be still more difficult to overcome a tendency to sloth, cowardice, and despondency. These evil dispositions cling about a man, and weigh him down. They are minute chains, binding him on every side to the earth, so that he cannot even turn himself or make an effort to rise. It would seem as if right principles had yet to be planted in the indolent mind; whereas violent and obstinate tempers had already something of the nature of firmness and zeal in them, or rather what will become so with care, exercise, and God's blessing. Besides, the events of life have a powerful influence in sobering the ardent or self-confident temper. Disappointments, pain, anxiety, advancing years, bring with them some natural wisdom as a matter of course; and, though such tardy improvement bespeaks but a weak faith, yet we may believe that the Holy Ghost often blesses these means, however slowly and imperceptibly. On the other hand, these same circumstances do but increase the defects of the timid and irresolute, who are made more indolent, selfish, and faint-hearted by advancing years, and find a sort of sanction of their unworthy caution in their experience of the vicissitudes of life.

St Mark's change, therefore, may be considered even more astonishing in its nature than that of the Jewish Lawgiver. 'By faith,' he was 'out of weakness made strong', and becomes a memorial of the more glorious and marvellous gifts of the last and spiritual dispensation.

J.H. Newman, *Parochial and Plain Sermons II*, 16

28 April
Saint Peter Chanel, *priest and martyr*
OPTIONAL MEMORIAL

Peter was born in the town of Cuet in France in 1803. He entered the ranks of the secular clergy, but then believed himself called to join the Society of Mary or Marists. He was sent as a missionary to Oceania, to the group of islands called 'Friendly Islands', and there, on the island of Futuna he preached the Gospel. It was not very fruitful work but he persevered and made some converts. Eventually he was set upon by a group of resentful pagan islanders and clubbed to death. In his case the old saying proved true: 'the blood of martyrs is the seed of Christians', for after his death conversions proved more frequent.

St Peter was canonized in 1954, one hundred and thirteen years after his death. His faith and perseverance should inspire us, when so much seems to be lost. The reading is taken from Pope Paul VI, *Evangelii Nuntiandi*.

As the kernel and centre of his good news, Christ proclaims salvation, this great gift of God which is liberation from everything that oppresses human beings but which is above all liberation from sin and the evil one, in the joy of knowing God and being known by him, of seeing him, and of being given over to him. All of this is begun during the life of Christ and definitively accomplished by his death and resurrection. But it must be patiently carried on during the course of history, in order to be realized fully on the day of the final coming of Christ, whose date is known to no one except the Father.

This kingdom and this salvation, which are the key words of Jesus Christ's evangelization, are available to every human being as grace and mercy, and yet at the same time each individual must gain them by force — they belong to the violent, says the Lord, through toil and suffering, through a life lived according to the gospel, through abnegation and the cross, through the spirit of the beatitudes. But above all each individual gains them through a total interior renewal which the gospel calls 'metanoia'; it is a radical conversion, a profound change of mind and heart.

Christ accomplished this proclamation of the kingdom of God through the untiring preaching of a word which has no equal elsewhere: 'Here is a teaching that is new, and with authority behind it'; 'And he won the approval of all, and they were astonished by the gracious words that came from his lips'. 'There has never been anybody who has spoken like him'. His words reveal the secret of God, his plan and his promise, and thereby change the heart of man and his destiny.

The Church knows this. She has a vivid awareness of the fact that the Saviour's words, 'I must proclaim the good news of the kingdom of God', apply in all truth to herself. She willingly adds with St Paul: 'Not that I boast of preaching the gospel, since it is a duty that has been laid on me; I should be punished if I did not preach it!'

Evangelizing is in fact the grace and vocation proper to the Church, her deepest identity. She exists in order to evangelize, that is to say, in order to preach and teach, to be the channel of the gift of grace, to reconcile sinners with God, and to perpetuate Christ's sacrifice in the mass, which is the memorial of his death and glorious resurrection.

Anyone who re-reads in the New Testament the origins of the Church, follows her history step by step and watches her live and act, sees that she is linked to evangelization in her most intimate being:
— The Church is born of the evangelizing activity of Jesus and the Twelve. She is the normal, desired, most immediate and most visible fruit of this activity: 'Go, therefore, make disciples of all the nations.' Now, 'they accepted what he said and were baptized. That very day about three thousand were added to their number. 'Day by day the Lord added to their community those destined to be saved.'
— Having been sent and evangelized, the Church herself sends out evangelizers. She puts on their lips the saving Word, she explains to them the message of which she herself is the depositary, she gives them the mandate which she herself has received and she sends them out to preach. To preach not their own selves or their personal ideas, but a gospel of which neither she nor they are the absolute masters and owners, to dispose of it as they wish, but a gospel of which they are the ministers, in order to pass it on with complete fidelity.

Pope Paul VI, *Evangelii Nuntiandi*, nn 9, 10, 11, 14, 15

29 April
Saint Catherine of Siena, *virgin and doctor of the Church*
MEMORIAL

Catherine was born in Siena in Italy, in 1347, and joined the third Order of St Dominic. Among the many striking personalities of the Middle Ages, there were not a few women. Catherine was one such, but she would have been striking in any place or time. She was an ascetic and a mystic, a true contemplative and one for whom the supernatural penetrated every moment and action of her life, yet full too, of an active love of God and of her neighbour. As a member of the third Order she gradually attracted a body of men and women who aided her in the care of the sick and the poor. She worked for peace and reconciliation in her native place of Siena with success, and on the level of Church politics persuaded Pope Gregory XI to return from Avignon to Rome. When the great Western Schism subsequently developed she supported Pope Urban, and tried, unsuccessfully, to bring about re-union.

She dictated a number of works which are remarkable for their spiritual content and soundness of doctrine. The reading offered is taken from the 'epilogue' of her Dialogue as translated from the original Italian into Latin by Blessed Raymond of Capua, who acted as her confessor and confidant, in his account of her life.

St Catherine died in 1380 and was canonized in 1461.

She is revered as one who was always faithful to grace and so grew in infused wisdom and love.

My truth was and is this, that I created you to have eternal life; and this truth I revealed to you through the blood of the only begotten Word, my Son.

Finally I satisfied your desire and the promise I had made you, that I should tell you about the perfection of obedience and the imperfection of disobedience, and whence it arises, and what it is that prevents you from being obedient. I presented this to you as the key to everything else, and so it is. I also told you about the kinds of obedience that are appropriate to the perfect and the imperfect, religious and layfolk, speaking of each one separately in turn; describing the peace that comes from obedience, the war that comes from disobedience, and how the disobedient deceive themselves, adding in explanation how death came into the world through the disobedience of Adam.

Now I, the Eternal Father, the supreme eternal truth, end by saying that in the obedience of my only begotten Son and Word you have life. And as all inherit death from the first old man, so all who bear the key of obedience draw life from the new man Christ, sweet Jesus, whom I gave you as a bridge after the way to heaven had been disrupted. Pass through this sweet straight way, the way of clear straight truth with the help of the key of obedience, and then you will pass through the darkness of this world without offending me, and at last will open heaven with the key of my Word.

Now I ask you and my other servants for tears; for it is through tears and continual humble prayer that I will have mercy on the world. Run mortified along this way of truth, so that you may not be accused of dawdling, for more will be expected of you than ever now that I have shown myself to you in my truth.

Take care never to emerge from the cell of self-knowledge, but in that cell both spend and store the treasure I have given you. For this treasure is a doctrine of truth, founded on the solid living rock of Christ, sweet Jesus; and this doctrine is clothed in light, which banishes darkness. Clothe yourself in this, most beloved daughter — in truth.

St Catherine of Siena, 'Dialogue'

30 April

Saint Pius V, *pope*

OPTIONAL MEMORIAL

Pius was born in Piedmont in Italy in 1504 and entered the Dominicans as a youth. He became a professor of theology with time and then in 1556 was made bishop. In the following year he was appointed a cardinal and in 1566 was elected as Pope taking the name Pius V. Pius was an austere and stern reformer, imposing the decrees of the Council of Trent, which had ended in 1563, with a firm hand. As implementation of those decrees he thoroughly reformed the Roman Missal and Breviary — much of his work being undone by the popes of later centuries. With regard to Church polity his actions against Protestantism in Spain and France were successful, but disastrous for the Catholics of England and Ireland. On another level he was responsible for stemming the Turkish advance into Europe, as he had fitted out the fleet which defeated the Turks at the battle of Lepanto. Pius V also encouraged the saying of the rosary. In all his actions, in his austerity and in his holiness he was a very typical son of St Dominic. He died in 1572 and was canonized in 1712.

We revere him as one who took seriously the work of Church renewal after Trent and a man who had the courage of his convictions.

The reading, from St Augustine, is chosen because of its reference to the Gospel given for the memorial, its paschal relevance, the note of authority, and the seriousness of christian renewal.

Your charity will have observed in today's reading that it was said to Peter by his Lord, 'do you love me?' This by way of interrogation. And Peter's making answer to him, 'Lord, you know I love you'. This exchange was repeated a second and a third time: and to each profession of Peter the Lord said: 'Feed my lambs'. Christ was entrusting to Peter his lambs to be fed, while he was feeding Peter. For what was Peter able to offer the Lord, especially as he already had a glorified body and was about to ascend to heaven? Christ was saying as it were to him, '"do you love me?", show that you love me in this: "feed my sheep"'.

Brothers, hear then with submission that you are the sheep of Christ, while we, with apprehension, hear: 'Feed my sheep'. If with apprehension we feed and are anxious for the sheep, how ought those same sheep be anxious for themselves? Let the care then be ours, submission yours: ours the shepherd's watchfulness, yours the lowliness of the flock. Although we, yes we, appear to speak to you from the place of authority, by virtue of our apprehension we are subject to you: for we know how perilous is the account to be rendered for this so lofty seeming seat.

Wherefore, dearly beloved, newborn as Catholics, members of Christ, think what kind of head you have. Sons of God, think what kind of Father you have found. Christians, think of the heritage promised to you. Not such a heritage as on earth — it cannot be possessed by the sons unless the parents are dead. For on earth no one possesses the inheritance of a father unless he has died. We shall possess what our Father still alive will give: because our Father cannot die. I add more, I say more, and I speak the truth: the Father himself will be our inheritance.

Live fittingly, especially you, Christ's new cleansed, the recently baptized, just now reborn, as I encouraged you before, and now say again, and proclaim my solicitude; because the gospel reading we have just heard has made me greatly apprehensive! Watch over yourselves, do not imitate evil Christians. And do not say: I shall do this, because many faithful do it. This is not preparing a defence for the soul, but seeking companions on the road to hell. Grow in this, the Lord's piece of ground, here you will find good companions, who will be suitable for you, if you in turn are good.

St Augustine, *Sermon 146*, nn 1, 2

1 May
Saint Joseph the worker
MEMORIAL

This modern memorial of St Joseph, the foster father of our Lord Jesus was established by Pope Pius XII in 1955. His intention was to consecrate the observance of the May Labour Day, and, at the same time, to propose the example of a workman who though only a village craftsman, served God in a most exceptional way.

The reading is taken from the encyclical letter *Laborem Exercens* of Pope John Paul II, and the passages chosen underline the value of work for the individual; through it he becomes 'more a human being', and the link between this, the family and education.

Work is a good thing for man. It is not only good in the sense that it is useful or something to enjoy; it is also good as being something worthy, that is to say, something that corresponds to human dignity, that expresses this dignity and increases it. If one wishes to define more clearly the ethical meaning of work, it is this truth that one must particularly keep in mind. Work is a good thing for man — a good thing for his humanity — because through work the individual not only transforms nature, adapting it to his own needs, but he also achieves fulfilment as a human being and indeed, in a sense, becomes 'more a human being'.

Without this consideration it is impossible to understand the meaning of the virtue of industriousness, and more particularly it is impossible to understand why industriousness should be a virtue: for virtue, as a moral habit, is something whereby the human being becomes good as a human being.

Having thus confirmed the personal dimension of human work, we must go on to the second sphere of values which is necessarily linked to work. Work constitutes a foundation for the formation of family life, which is a natural right and something that man is called to. These two spheres of values — one linked to work and the other consequent on the family nature of human life — must be properly united and must properly permeate each other. In a way, work is a condition for making it possible to found a family, since the family requires the means of subsistence which man normally gains through work.

Work and industriousness also influence the whole process of education in the family, for the very reason that everyone 'becomes a human being' through, among other things, work, and becoming a human being is precisely the main purpose of the whole process of education. Obviously, two aspects of work in a sense come into play here: the one making family life and its upkeep possible, and the other making possible the achievement of the purposes of the family, especially education. Nevertheless, these two aspects of work are linked to one another and are mutually complementary in various points.

Pope John Paul II, *Laborem Exercens*, cc 9 & 10

2 May

Saint Athanasius, *bishop and doctor of the Church*
MEMORIAL

Athanasius was a native of Alexandria and born in the year 295. As a young man he entered the service of the Church in his native city and quickly came to prominence. Ordained deacon, he was made theological adviser to bishop Alexander and accompanied him to the Council of Nicaea in 325. The Council had been summoned to deal with the difficulties raised by the teaching of the priest Arius, who was also a native of Alexandria, and who denied the divinity of Christ. The Council solemnly affirmed the faith of the Church in the divinity of Christ and condemned the teaching of Arius. The heresy, unfortunately, was to trouble men for many years to come.

Athanasius was chosen to succeed Alexander as bishop in 328, and, as one of the champions of Nicaean orthodoxy was exiled five times from his see, spending seventeen years of the forty-five he was bishop in exile.

He had friendly and close contacts with the early monks of Egypt, especially with St Antony and St Pachomius. This was of significance for the Latin West, for during Athanasius' first exile in Rome and Trier he spread the fame of these early monks and so inspired their imitation.

He died in Alexandria in 373.

The reading is taken from his treatise on The Incarnation.

It is the function of soul to behold even what is outside its own body, by acts of thought, without, however, working outside its own body, or moving by its presence things remote from the body. Never, that is, does a man, by thinking of things at a distance, by that fact either move or displace them: nor if a man were to sit in his own house and reason about the heavenly bodies, would he by that fact either move the sun or make the heavens resolve. But he sees that they move and have their being, without being actually able to influence them.

Now, the Word of God in his man's nature was not like that; for he was not bound to his body, but rather was himself wielding it, so that he was not only in it, but was actually in everything, and while external to the universe, abode in his Father only. And this was the wonderful thing, that he was at once walking as man, and as the Word was quickening all things, and as the Son was dwelling with his Father. So that not even when the Virgin bore him did he suffer any change, nor was his glory dulled by being in the body, but on the contrary he sanctified the body also. For not even by being in the universe does he share in its nature, but all things, on the contrary, are quickened and sustained by him. For if the sun too, which was made by him, and which we see, as it revolves in the heaven, is not defiled by touching the bodies upon earth, nor is it put out by darkness, but on the contrary itself illuminates and cleanses them also, much less was the all-holy Word of God, maker and lord also of the sun, defiled by being made known in the body; on the contrary, being incorruptible, he quickened and cleansed the body also, which was in itself mortal: 'who did', for so it says, 'no sin, neither was guile found in his mouth' (1 Peter 2:22).

Accordingly, when inspired writers on this matter speak of him as eating and being born; understand that the body, as body, was born, and sustained with food corresponding to its nature, while God, the Word himself, who was united with the body, while ordering all things, also by the works he did in the body showed himself to be not man, but God the Word. But these things are said of him, because the actual body which ate, was born, and suffered, belonged to none other but to the Lord: and because, having become man, it was proper for these things to be predicated of him as man, to show him to have a body in truth, and not in seeming.

But just as from these things he was known to be bodily present, so from the works he did in the body he made himself known to be Son of God. Whence also he cried to the unbelieving Jews: 'If I do not the works of my Father, believe me not. But if I do them though you

believe not me, believe my works; that you may know and understand that the Father is in me, and I in the Father' (John 10:37 f). For
just as, though invisible, he is known through the works of creation;
so having become man, and being in the body unseen, it may be
known from his works that he who can do these is no man, but the
Power and Word of God.

St Athanasius, *On the Incarnation*, cc 17, 18

3 May
Saints Philip and James, *apostles*
FEAST

Philip is mentioned several times in the gospels, particularly in that of St John.
He was a native of the town of Bethsaida, a fellow townsman of Andrew and
Peter, and had been first a follower of John the Baptist. According to an old
tradition he preached the gospel in Phrygia and died at Hierapolis. James the
Less, so-called to distinguish him from the brother of St John, was the son of
Alphaeus, and has been traditionally identified with the 'brother of the Lord',
and author of the epistle which bears his name. He was also considered to
have been the first bishop of Jerusalem. Whether or not that is the case, he was
certainly one of the leading figures in the Church in Jerusalem and died there
as a martyr in the year 62.

The reading is taken from St Augustine, and is an extract from a sermon he
preached on Ascension Day. Today's feast usually falls in Eastertide and the
passage used comments on today's gospel reading, hence its choice.

With that same mind the disciples wished the Lord to be always with
them in the flesh, as Peter feared for his suffering. For they saw the
man with them as master, comforter, consoler and protector, in just
the way they saw themselves. If they were not to see something of
the kind, they believed him absent; while, by his sovereign power, he
is present everywhere! He was indeed caring for them as a hen for
her chicks, just as he had told them.

However it was necessary that they should be somewhat raised,
and already begin to think of him in a spiritual manner, as the Word
of the Father, God with God, through whom all things were made:
and the flesh which they saw did not allow them to do so. It was
good, therefore, for them to be confirmed in the faith by his being

with them for forty days; but it was better for them that he withdrew himself from their eyes, and that he, who had lived on earth as a brother, should assist from heaven as Lord; and that they should learn to think of him as God.

This indeed John the Evangelist cried out: if anyone should heed, if anyone should understand — for the Lord says: 'Let not your hearts be troubled. If you love me, he says, you would rejoice, because I go to the Father; for the Father is greater than I.' And in another place he says: 'I and the Father are one.' He claimed such equality for himself not by robbery but by nature, since he said the following to one of the disciples saying to him: 'Lord, show us the Father and we shall be satisfied', and he, 'Philip, I have been with you all this time, and you do not know the Father? He, who sees me, sees the Father.' What is this — 'He who sees me'? — If after the manner of the eyes of the flesh, they who crucified him saw! What then is 'Who sees me', save, who has understood, who sees with the eye of the heart? For in the same way as there are inner ears, which the Lord sought when he said: 'Let him hear who has ears to hear', when no deaf person was standing before him; so also there is an inner gaze of the heart, by which if one has seen the Lord, he has seen the Father: for he is equal to the Father.

St Augustine, *Sermon 4 on the Ascension of the Lord,* 2

12 May
Saints Nereus and Achilleus, *martyrs*
OPTIONAL MEMORIAL

These were two soldiers in the Roman army who were converted to christianity and subsequently refused to serve. They were put to death, probably in the year 304, under the Emperor Diocletian. They were buried in the cemetery of Domitilla on the Ardeatine Way, and are mentioned in the martyrology of St Jerome.

The reading is taken from St Augustine and is extracted from a sermon preached by him in honour of some North African martyrs.

A sermon is due about the suffering glory of the holy martyrs. For the very reason they suffered most gloriously, bearing with the raging mobs, they set patience before us.

The constancy of the martyrs is to be praised, but what eloquence suffices to praise it? From whence then such a gift of patience? From whence, except from whence every best gift? From whence the best gift, except from whence the perfect gift? For so it is written in the book: 'For patience has a perfect work'. 'Every good endowment,' he says, 'and every perfect gift is coming down from the Father of lights, with whom there is no variation nor shadow due to change' (James 1:17). Patience comes down from the unchanging Fount on our changeable human minds, and makes them unchanging. From whence comes it to man to please God, save from God? From whence to man a good life, save from the Fount of life? From whence enlightenment to man, save from Light eternal? 'For with you,' he says, 'is the fount of life' (Ps 35:9). 'With you', he says: I could have said, 'from me'; but if I were to say, 'from me', I depart from you. 'With you' then, 'is the fount of life. In your light', not in ours; 'In your light we shall see light.' Wherefore, 'Approach him and you will be enlightened.' He is the fount of life; approach, drink, live: he is the light, approach, seize, and see. If he does not stream into you, withered will you be. It was from this source, then, that our martyrs drank.

Christ wished to suffer for us. The apostle Peter says: 'He suffered for you, leaving you an example, that you might follow his footsteps.' He taught you to suffer, and he taught by suffering. The teaching was slight, unless the example were added to it. And how, brothers, did he teach? He hung upon the cross, the Jews raged: he hung on the harsh nails, but did not lose his gentleness. They raged against, they roared around, they insulted him hanging there; as madmen they raged from every side against the one supreme doctor set in their midst. He was hanging there and healing. 'Father,' he said, 'forgive them, for they know not what they do' (Lk 23:34). He made petition and still he hung: he did not come down, because he was making a remedy for the mad from his blood. Then because of the words of the petitioning Lord, the mercy of the same Lord giving ear, because he petitioned the Father, and heard with the Father; because those words could not be poured out in vain, after his resurrection he healed those most insane ones he bore with while hanging.

He ascended into heaven, he sent the Holy Spirit; nor did he show himself to them after his resurrection, but to his faithful disciples alone, lest he should seem to have wanted to taunt those who killed him. For it was of more importance to teach his friends lowliness, than to charge his enemies with the truth. He has risen: he has done more than they demanded, when not believing, but taunting, they said: 'If he is the son of God, let him come down from the cross.' And because he would not come down from the cross, he rose from the grave. He ascended into heaven, he sent from there the Holy Spirit: the Spirit filled the disciples, corrected the fearful, formed the brave!

St Augustine, *Sermon 284* nn 1, 2, 6

12 May, also
Saint Pancras, *martyr*
OPTIONAL MEMORIAL

He was a Roman, perhaps only a boy of fourteen, who it would seem, likewise suffered under the emperor Diocletian. He was buried on the Aurelian Way and a basilica over his tomb was built by Pope Symmachus. In the Middle Ages the monastery attached to the basilica was one of the most important in Rome, and today is the site of the Teresianum of the Discalced Carmelites.

The reading is extracted from Lactantius' Epitome of the Divine Institutes. Lactantius, called the last of the Apologists, was a convert from paganism and had been deprived of his position as professor of rhetoric for his christian faith under Diocletian.

Faith, too, is a large part of justice, and we, who bear the name of Christian, must cling to it especially in matters religious, because God is prior to and mightier than, man. Though it is glorious to lay down life for friends, parents, children (that is, for man), and he that does this wins lasting remembrance and praise; how much more glorious for the sake of God, who can dower us with life eternal in place of death in time! When forced of necessity to turn aside from Him and have recourse to heathen rites, no fear, no terror, can hinder us from guarding the faith delivered to us.

Let God be ever in our eyes, in our hearts, by whose inward help we may master bodily pain, and agonies inflicted on our persons. Let us think of nothing except the prize of immortality. Even if our limbs are to be hacked asunder or burnt, we shall endure whatever is devised by the insanity of tyrannic cruelty. Lastly, let us strive to bear death itself, not grudgingly nor with faint hearts, but freely, unterrified, as knowing what glory shall be ours to enjoy in the presence of God, triumphant over this world and attaining his promises. What good things, what blessedness, shall be ours in exchange for our brief afflictions and the losses of our present life! Even if we be denied this splendid chance, yet will faith have its reward in the day of peace.

Even though we have not fallen into sin, we are bound to make confession to God, and pray to him continually to forgive us our trespasses, and to yield him thanks even in misfortunes. Let us ever show ourselves obedient to the Lord. For humility is dear and acceptable to God. He accepts the sinner that confesses rather than the just man in his pride; how much more, then, will he accept the just man who confesses his faults, and, in proportion to his humility, will exalt him in his heavenly kingdom! These are the characteristics that the genuine worshipper should exhibit; these are the offerings, this the sacrifice, with which God is well pleased; this is real worship when a man brings to God's altar the pledges of his heart and soul. In such a worshipper the Most High delights; He welcomes him as a son, and grants him the due reward of immortal life.

Lactantius, Epitome of the Divine Institutions, cc 66-67

14 May
Saint Matthias, *apostle*
FEAST

The account of Matthias' choice as an apostle is given in Acts 1:15-26, which is today's first reading, and the idea of this date for his feast is to locate it in Eastertide and near the Ascension, in memory of that choice. In the Coptic rite his day is on the 4 March and in the Byzantine the 9 August.

Traditionally he was martyred in Colchis and his relics brought to Rome by the empress Helena. Subsequently they were divided and part of them

123

is venerated in the monastery of St Justina in Padua and another part in
St Matthias' in Trier.

The reading, taken from the Sermons of St Vincent Ferrer, treats of the
excellence of the Resurrection, the resurrection to which Matthias was chosen
to witness.

The meaning of the word 'Gospel', Good News, suggests the glorious resurrection of Jesus Christ, which the Angel announced to the
three Marys as they were hastening with the greatest devotion to
Christ's sepulchre. He told them: 'He is risen,' as though to say: now
his body has departed from the tomb and his soul is no longer in
Limbo. His humanity is not here, for he has risen as he said. Do not
seek him here.

To understand these words aright, you must know that the resurrection of Christ possesses two excellencies, which surpass every
other resurrection. First, it is full of power; second, it is glorious.
Many have risen from death to life in both the Old and the New Testament; but they did not rise by their own power. Christ, however,
rose from the dead by his own power and not by that of another,
since he is true God. For his body by its union with the Godhead had,
in the tomb, the infinite power of rising from the dead; this is also
true of his soul in Limbo. This is possible to no other dead person,
since neither the body nor the soul has the power of restoring life. As
David says: 'The spirit going — that is, in death — and not returning'
— by its own power to life. We read of Elias and Eliseus, in the Old
Testament, that they raised the dead to life. We read likewise in the
New Testament that the Apostles did the same. But how? By prayer
and supplication, not by their own power, nor by that of the dead
person, but solely by the power of God and as God's ministers.
Christ's resurrection today was effected by his own power, therefore
he said: 'I lay down my life that I may take it up again. No man takes it
from me — that is, by violence — but I lay it down — by death — and I
have the power to take it up' — by resurrection (John 10:17, 18).

The second excellence is that this resurrection was glorious; for
Christ rose to a glorious life, immortal and impassible. Others have
been raised again to a mortal life and the miseries of this world, to die
once more. But Christ, by a singular privilege, rose from the dead to

glory. 'Christ, rising again from the dead, dies now no more. Death shall no more have dominion over him' (Rom 6:9).

Concerning this mystery, I have noted three points in which the whole practical application to us of Christ's blessed resurrection consists:

The resurrection of Christ was lovingly celebrated.

It was proved most graciously.

Its truth was spread abroad with might.

St Vincent Ferrer, A Sermon Preached on Easter Sunday

18 May

Saint John I, *pope and martyr*
OPTIONAL MEMORIAL

John was a native of Tuscany who joined the clergy of Rome and in 523 was elected pope. Theodoric, king of the Goths, and an Arian, sent Pope John to Byzantium to persuade the emperor, Justin I, to stop persecuting the Arians within the empire. At Constantinople the pope was received with honour but neither he, nor the emperor were disposed to go along with Theodoric's wishes. Pope John's manifest friendship with the emperor aroused the suspicions of Theodoric on his return to Rome and he was imprisoned by the king in Ravenna, where he died in 526.

The reading is taken from Origen, written long before the Arian conflict but already refuting it and other christological heresies.

Now if it were only the man whose opinions about God the Father are at variance with the requirements of the rule of religion who must be accounted a heretic, the foregoing account would clearly be sufficient. But our conviction must be identically the same with regard to him who has any erroneous views about our Lord Jesus Christ, whether he follow those who say he was born of Joseph and Mary, as do the Ebionites and the Valentinians; or whether he follow those who deny that he is the firstborn, the God of all creation, the Word, the Wisdom which is the beginning of the ways of God, established before anything else was made, brought forth before all the hills (Prov 8:22-26). Such say that he was only a man.

Or a heretic may follow those who allow indeed that he was God, but not that he took upon him human nature, a soul, that is, and a body of earth. These, on the pretext of giving greater glory to Jesus the Lord, declare that all his actions were in appearance rather than in reality. They do not acknowledge that he was born of a virgin, but say that he appeared in Judaea as a man of thirty years.

Others believe indeed that he was born of a virgin, but maintain that the virgin rather imagined that she had given him birth, though she had not in reality done so. The mystery of the attributed birth was, as they declare, hidden even from the virgin. Such people must be kept right away from the church. Sufferers from the malady of abstraction they set up doctrines by which they entice many disciples to their sect.

Those too who say the Lord Jesus was a man foreknown and fore-determined, who before his coming in the flesh had no personal and independent existence, but when born as a man had only the God-head of the Father within him — they also may not without risk be associated with the church's membership. To the same class belong those who, with more superstition than religion, not wishing to appear to say there are two Gods, nor yet to deny the divinity of the Saviour, maintain that the Father and the Son have one and the same personal being.

Origen, Commentary on Titus

20 May
Saint Bernardine of Siena, *priest*
OPTIONAL MEMORIAL

Bernardine was born in 1380 near Siena and entered the Friars Minor. Ordained priest, he developed into a popular preacher, going up and down Italy, preaching in italian with a great deal of liveliness and wit. With his contemporary, St John of Capistrano, he spread devotion to the Holy Name of Jesus and encouraged the use of the monogram IHS in houses. His practice of preaching with a card showing this monogram surrounded by rays led to his being denounced as an idolatrous heretic. Tried by ecclesiastical court he vindicated his orthodoxy. Another devotion which he was largely responsible for popularizing was to the foster father of our Lord, St Joseph.

St Bernardine died in 1444 and was canonized by Pope Nicholas V in 1450, just six years later.

The reading is taken from the very interesting testimony of Leonardo Benvoglienti, a leading citizen of Siena and a layman. It was written two years after Bernardine's death.

O happy Bernardine, you are to be offered the highest of praises. O truly are you, our age, to be called happy, which had the most excellent Bernardine, a holy man, sent as it were from heaven by divine mercy.

Why are you to be called happy, Bernardine? In what does your happiness consist? Certainly you are to be called glorious and happy. For the most High God, from whom all good things come down, gave you that happiness which he gives to few indeed. What happiness did he give you? In this world overflowing grace, in heaven eternal glory. What grace did you have in this world? — and whence do you prove glory in heaven? Let us first speak of the grace and then let us point out the glory. Truly on Bernardine were conferred from heaven the most excellent and uncountable gifts, which so showed forth in his life from youth to old age, that he was judged a marvel and divine by all. For if simplicity, truth, integrity of life, uprightness and perseverance are sought in the best proven and indeed divine man, whom have we known more simple than Bernardine, and more uprightly progressing with perseverance in the way of truth? If we seek austerity, it will be found of a most amazing kind and exceeding human strength in this man, coupled with the most exact religious sense. If we seek love from a man, in whom shall we find a greater and more fervent love for God and for neighbour, on whose behalf he laboured for such a time with an ardent spirit, always active in word and deed? If we praise in a good and happy man the rejection of worldly goods and honours, whom shall we more praise than this man, who, born of noble parents in this splendid city, following the gospel counsel, having distributed all he possessed to the poor of Christ and cast aside all kinds of worldly honours, defenceless, would only follow the defenceless Christ? What shall I say of his prudence and carefulness? Was he not held by the popular esteem of all Italy to be the most prudent and wise of men? All indeed wondered at his control, pleasantness and constancy in the face of hostility. If we test holiness by piety and lowliness, rightly we praise this man above others in all these matters. But what shall we say of his marvellous teaching directed to the progress of peoples and souls? — For a long time, for a very long time indeed, no one such as he has been found who could melt the hardest and most stubborn hearts, and bend them as he wished, and turn them to the love and honour of the Lord.

Testimony of Leonardo Benvoglienti

25 May
Saint Bede the Venerable, *priest and doctor of the Church*
OPTIONAL MEMORIAL

Bede was born about the year 673 on lands which shortly afterwards were deeded to the monastery of Wearmouth. He was given by his parents to the monastery as a child oblate when aged barely seven. He died as a monk in 735, having spent the greater part of his life in the twin monastery of Jarrow. He would seem to have done all his studies in one or other of the twin monasteries, and surely was a credit to them, as he was one of the finest products of the springtime of Anglo-Saxon monasticism. As a biblical commentator and historian his combination of acumen, honesty, hard work and native good sense made him outstanding in his age. Much of his work still has its value. When we reflect on the times in which he lived we can only wonder at his serenity and balance of mind and thought.

He was first buried at Jarrow, but his remains were eventually laid to rest in the Galilee chapel of Durham cathedral.

The reading, from his Commentary on St Luke, shows something of his mind.

'And after three days they found him in the temple, sitting among the teachers, listening to them and asking them questions' (Lk 2:46). He sits among the teachers as the fount of wisdom, but, as the model of lowliness, he first seeks to listen to the teachers and ask them questions before instructing the unlearned. God is not ashamed to listen to men, because such is fitting to his age as a human being — that small boys be not ashamed to learn from their elders! And lest any not well developed should dare to teach, he as a boy wished to be taught by asking questions, who, by his divinity's power, gave to his very teachers the word of knowledge.

'And all who heard him were amazed at his understanding and his answers. And when they saw him they were astonished' (Lk 2:47-48). Note the distinction of words, and being careful of the mysteries of your salvation and of the faith, consider their meaning.

Those who heard him were amazed, and when they saw him they were astonished. And they were the more amazed at the intelligence of his answers, the more they saw and thought little of his few years. His tongue showed forth divine wisdom, his age set out human weakness. Truly these matters amazed the teachers of the Jews as something new, and between the lofty things they heard and the weak ones they saw, they were disturbed in astonished doubt. We, however, know him to be the one about whom the prophet in days gone by joyfully exulted: 'To us a child is born, to us a son is given, and his name will be called wonderful, counsellor, mighty God' (Is 9:6). Let us, then, in no way be astonished, that he, who was thus made man as a child as nevertheless always to remain what he was, God and mighty, should now have given tokens of his divinity, now of his humanity, to those he wished to instruct. Rather, let us offer thanks to him with fitting faith, hope and love, because he who was great and exceedingly to be praised had come and we did not know him. A child is born to us, that by growing and developing among children, he might little by little bear them along to grasp the secrets of his power and greatness.

'And his mother said to him: "Son, why have you treated us so? Behold, your father and I have been looking for you anxiously." And he said to them, "How is it that you sought me? Did you not know that I must be in my Father's house?" And they did not understand the saying which he spoke to them. And he went down with them and came to Nazareth, and was obedient to them' (Lk 2:48-51). How great an example of dutifulness and also of lowliness in our Lord! His parents do not understand the saying about his divinity which he speaks to them; nevertheless he, not ungrateful for their human concern in his regard, goes down where they command, and is obedient to them. For how a virtuous master if he were not to fulfil the observance of dutifulness? What else did he do among us than what he wishes us to do? He submitted to the man, he submitted to the hand-maid. For she herself says: 'Behold the handmaid of the Lord' (Lk 1:38). He submitted to one apparently his father, he submitted to God, his true Father.

St Bede, *An Exposition of Luke's Gospel*, bk 1

25 May, also
Saint Gregory VII, *pope*
OPTIONAL MEMORIAL

Gregory VII, also known by his earlier name of Hildebrand, was a native of Tuscany and born about 1028. His family background was simple and he would seem to have been brought up by an uncle in the Cluniac priory on the Aventine in Rome. This background and upbringing coloured both his view of the world and the world's, as represented by its lords, view of him. He became a monk in one or other house of the Cluniac observance, having been for a while in the papal service. In the company of St Hugh of Cluny he again came into contact with the papal household and was released to serve the pope, Leo IX. He was appointed papal 'provisor' of the monastery of St Paul's outside the Walls and retained that position until elected pope in 1073.

As pope he was an ardent reformer, he sought to free the Church from lay control and, indeed, to establish the primacy, in real terms, of the spiritual power over the temporal. As a result of the bitter feud which followed with the emperor, he died in exile in Salerno in 1085.

It is interesting that Hugh of Cluny, his former abbot who long outlived him, while sympathetic to the same general principles, realised that St Gregory's position was an overstatement and unworkable. While a failure as an ecclesiastical politician, there can be no doubting St Gregory's holiness of life and spirit of prayer.

The reading is taken from a letter of his to one of his episcopal supporters, and sets out very clearly his view of how secular rulers should conduct themselves.

Therefore let those whom holy Church, of its own will and after proper counsel, not for transitory glory but for the salvation of many, calls to have rule or dominion, humbly obey. And let them always beware in that point as to which St Gregory in that same pastoral book bears witness: 'Indeed, when a man disdains to be like to men, he is made like to an apostate angel.'

Thus Saul, after having possessed the merit of humility, came to be swollen with pride when at the summit of power. Through humility, indeed, he was advanced; through pride, rejected — God being witness who said: 'When you were small in your own eyes, did I not make you head over the tribes of Israel?' (1 Sam 15:17). And a little further on: 'Moreover, strange to say, when he was small in his own eyes he was great in the eyes of God; but when he seemed great in his own eyes he was small in the eyes of God.' Let them also carefully retain what God says in the gospel: 'I seek not my own glory'; and, 'He who will be the first among you shall be the servant of all.' Let them always prefer the honour of God to their own; let them cherish and guard justice by observing the rights of every man; let them not walk in the counsel of the ungodly but, with an assenting heart, always consort with good men. Let them not seek to subject to themselves or to subjugate the holy Church as a handmaid; but above all let them strive, by recognizing the teachers and fathers, to render due honour to the eyes of the Church — the priests of God.

For if we are ordered to honour our fathers and mothers after the flesh — how much more our spiritual ones! And if he who has cursed his father or mother after the flesh is to be punished with death — what does he merit who curses his spiritual father or mother? Let them not, led astray by worldly love, strive to place one of their own sons over the flock for which Christ poured forth his blood, if they can find some one who is better and more useful than he: lest, loving their son more than God, they inflict the greatest damage on the Holy Church. For he who neglects to provide to the best of his ability for such a want — and, one might say, necessity — of Holy Mother Church is openly convicted of not loving God and his neighbour as a Christian should.

For if this virtue, love, has been neglected, no matter what good any one does he shall be without any fruit of salvation. And so by humbly doing these things, and by observing the love of God and of their neighbour as they ought, they may hope for the mercy of him who said: 'Learn of me, for I am meek and lowly of heart.' If they have humbly imitated him they shall pass from this servile and transitory kingdom to a true kingdom of liberty and eternity.

A Letter of Pope Gregory VII (excerpt)

25 May, also
Saint Mary Magdalene de' Pazzi, *virgin*
OPTIONAL MEMORIAL

She was born in Florence in 1566 and died there in 1607. From childhood she lived a life of remarkable piety and entered the Carmelites in her native city particularly because of their practice of frequent Communion. As a nun her life was one of prayer and self-denial, and she was favoured with mystical union, the power of miracles, knowledge of hearts and prophecy. Her whole life was offered for the spiritual renewal of the Church.

The Council of Trent had favoured the practice of frequent Communion but this was obscured by other reforms and remained practically a dead letter. The reading offered is taken from Pope Paul VI's encyclical 'Mysterium Fidei', where he recalled the advantage of frequent Communion and also where he invoked the intercession of those saints marked by a special devotion to the Holy Eucharist. St Mary Magdalene is surely one of these.

What here follows is something which, at your insistence, should be increasingly known and put to the proof by Christ's faithful: 'The man who wants to live has a place to live in, means to live on. He must approach, believe, be incorporated, if he is to be given life. He must not hold back from the close union of the members: it is not for him to be the corrupt member which deserves to be pruned; not for him to be the twisted member, the occasion of blushing. He is to be fair, fit, sound. He must hold fast to the body, live to God, on God. He should toil now on earth to reign hereafter in heaven' (St Augustine).

Every day, as is desirable, and in the greatest possible numbers, the faithful must take an active part in the sacrifice of the Mass, avail themselves of the pure, holy refreshment of holy communion and make a suitable thanksgiving in return for this great gift of Christ the Lord. Here are words they should keep in mind: 'Jesus Christ and the Church desire all Christ's faithful to approach the sacred banquet every day. The basis of this desire is that they should be united to God by the sacrament and draw strength from it to restrain lust, to wash away the slight faults of daily occurrence and to take precautions against the more serious sins to which human frailty is liable' (Pius X).

Christ the Lord took from the Blessed Virgin Mary the flesh which 'is contained, offered, taken' in this sacrament under the appearances of bread and wine. May she, and all the saints, especially those whose devotion for the divine eucharist was fired with exceptional ardour, intercede before the Father of mercies so that the faith and the eucharistic cult, which they have in common, may give rise to perfect unity of fellowship among all who go by the name of Christian, and that this unity may grow strong. The words of the holy martyr Ignatius to the Philadelphians come to mind. He was warning them against the evil of division and dissensions, the remedy for which is the eucharist: 'You must strive therefore to employ one thanksgiving. There is one flesh of our Lord Jesus Christ, one chalice for the gathering of his blood, one altar, one bishop. . . .'

Pope Paul VI, *Mysterium Fidei*, nn 65, 66, 75

26 May
Saint Philip Neri, *priest*
MEMORIAL

Philip was born in Florence in 1515 and died in Rome, where he spent most of his life, in 1595. He had come to Rome as a young man and was moved to do something about the appalling spiritual and moral degradation he found. As well as a true product of the Florentine renaissance, he was a deep and convinced Christian, and worked as a man to bring his contemporaries back to Christ. He exemplified the overcoming of evil by good, consistently refraining from denunciation. For many years his was active in the lay apostlate — he was only ordained priest in 1551, when aged forty-six.

As a priest he came to be called 'the apostle of Rome', for he really spread around him the light of Christ. Among other activities he founded the Oratory of Divine Love and fostered the serious development of religious music and song: to this day we still speak of 'oratorio'.

Very warm and joyful in his relations with others, in his prayer-life he sought for complete union with Christ, and was favoured with mystical experiences. He was, as well, endowed with the gifts of miracles and prophecy.

The reading given is taken from a letter he wrote to a niece who was a nun. The underlying thread of the whole letter is generous love, which opens and surrenders itself to God and to others.

The mole is a blind animal which abides always in the earth; it eats earth and burrows in earth, and is never satiated with earth. And such is the avaricious man or woman; women are by nature avaricious. And what a revolting thing is avarice! A man has received so much from God — he has given him, besides his being, and all created things from the angels downwards, his own Son. The sweet Christ, the incarnate Word, gave himself to us, without reserve, even to the hard and shameful death of the cross, and then gave himself to us in a sacrament, as at first he left heaven, humbling himself to become man for us; and on the cross he was stripped of his garments, and shed his precious blood, and his soul was separated from his body.

All things created are open-hearted and liberal, and show forth the goodness of their Creator; the sun pours abroad light, and fire gives out heat; every tree stretches forth its arms and reaches to us its fruit; the water and the air, and all nature, declare the bounty of the Creator. And we, who are yet his living images, we do not represent him, but with base degeneracy deny him in our works, however much we confess him with our mouths.

Now, if avarice is a monstrous thing in any one, what is it in a religious who has made a vow of poverty, abandoning everything for the love of God! We must, at whatever cost of pain, get rid of this foul pestilence of avarice; nor shall we feel the pain if we seriously reflect that as soon as we cast off this sordid garb, our soul is clothed with a regal and imperial garment. I mean not only that we must despise gold and silver and pleasure and all else that is so prized by a blind, deluded world, but that we are to give even the very life we love so much for the honour of God and the salvation of our neighbour, having our hearts ever ready to make this sacrifice, in the strength of divine grace.

Greatly love holy obedience, and put this before and above every other thing, and never take anything to your own use unless it has been signed and sealed to you with the blessing of your Superior. Together with obedience love prayer; but carefully remember that while you love and desire prayer and holy communion with the utmost affection of your heart, you must be always ready to leave either or both at the call of obedience. Regard holy obedience as a true prayer and a real communion; for you must not desire prayer and communion for the sake of the sweetness of devotion you find in them — that would be seeking yourself and not God — but that you may become humble and obedient, gentle and patient. When you find these within you, then you will gather the fruit of prayer and communion, and above all, you will live in peace with all.

Take great delight in the life of holy community; shun all singularity, take heed of purity of heart, for the Holy Spirit dwells in pure and simple souls, and he is the great Master of prayer, and makes us dwell in that abiding peace and gladness of heart which are as a foretaste of paradise; while anger, discord, and bitterness abiding in the soul are as a fume from hell.

God give you grace that you may so gather yourself up into his divine love, and enter so deeply through the wound of his side into the living fount of the God made man, that you may annihilate yourself and all self-love, and never more find a way to come out thence. And there, within that wound, remember me, and pray for me, a wretched, worthless sinner.

St Philip Neri, A Letter to his Niece

27 May
Saint Augustine of Canterbury, *bishop*
OPTIONAL MEMORIAL

Augustine was a monk of the monastery of St Andrew 'in clivo Scauri', St Gregory the Great's own monastery in Rome, and was prior of the house in the early years of the latter's pontificate. In 596 he was sent as the head of a group of monks to preach to the English. The decision was the pope's and it was his resolution which held the group to their task. Augustine was consecrated bishop in Gaul. The party arrived in south-east England in 597. They were accepted there by king Ethelbert. Their preaching of the faith was more-or-less confined to the kingdom of Kent, and at Canterbury Augustine established his archiepiscopal see, with suffragans at London and Rochester.

St Gregory would have preferred London as the primatial see, and would seem to have been rather disappointed with the group's lack of spirit and drive. No one can give what they have not got, however, and the giving of the best, under grace, is what marks one as a saint. This Augustine manifestly did.

He was not a Gregory the Great, nor, to mention their great Irish contemporary, a Columbanus, but what he could do he did well, his work endured and ultimately prevailed.

He died on 26 May in the year 604 or 605. In his life he had worked miracles.

The reading is taken from a letter of St Gregory the Great to him. The first part of the letter is used in the Divine Office for today, and extracts from it are used by St Bede the Venerable. The real miracle is mutual love.

Dearest brother, if then we recognize that Moses, whom we know to have been especially chosen by God, died for his sin (without entering the Promised Land) after all the signs he wrought, with what great fear ought we not tremble, who do not yet know if we are chosen?

What need is there for me to say anything then of the miracles of the condemned, since you, my brother, well know what the Truth says in the gospel: 'Many will come in that day saying to me: Lord, in your name we prophesied, and in your name we cast out demons, and in your name we performed many wonders. But I shall say to them that I know not who you are. Depart from me, all you workers of iniquity' (Mt 7:22; Lk 13:27). For by signs the gaining of souls is to be sought, and the glory of him, by whose power those same signs are performed. The Lord indeed gave us one sign in which we can both exceedingly rejoice and recognize in ourselves the glory of being chosen when he said: 'By this it shall be known that you are my disciples, if you have love for one another' (Jn 13:53). This is the sign the prophet was seeking when he said: 'Lord, perform for me a good sign, that those who hate me may see and be confounded' (Ps 85:17).

These things I say, because I desire to prostrate the mind of him who hears me in lowliness. But your very own lowliness may have its confidence. For I, a sinner, have the most certain hope, that by the grace of our all-powerful creator and redeemer, God and Lord, Jesus Christ, your sins are already forgiven, and therefore you have been chosen so that through you others should be forgiven. Nor will you grieve concerning any guilt in the future, who will have tried to cause joy in heaven over the conversion of many.

Indeed, our same Creator and Redeemer, speaking of the sinner's repentance, said: 'So I say to you, there will be greater joy in heaven over one sinner doing penance, than over ninety-nine just who have no need for repentance' (Lk 15:7). And if there be great joy in heaven over one doing penance, how much joy do we believe will be caused over such a multitude converted from their error, who coming to the faith condemn the evil they have done by repentance? Wherefore, in that joy of heaven and the angels, let us repeat again those same words of the angels with which we began: let us say then, let all say: 'Glory to God in the highest, and on earth peace to men of good will' (Lk 2:14).

St Gregory the Great, Letter to St Augustine

31 May
The Visitation of the Blessed Virgin Mary
FEAST

In the West this wholly scriptural celebration was first introduced among the Franciscans in 1263 and was assigned to 2 July. Pope Urban VI took it into the Roman Calendar in 1389 with a view to obtaining Mary's help in the ending of the great Western Schism.

In recent times it has been transferred to today's date in order to fall between the solemnities of the Annunciation and of St John the Baptist, thus emphasising its scriptural foundation and theological significance. The prayer of the contemporary Roman liturgy stresses the example of Mary in hastening to help Elizabeth in her need — may we also be so concerned for others, and obedient to the Spirit.

There are other aspects of the Visitation; as those set forth in the very beautiful prayer given for this day in the Alternative Service Book of the Church of Ireland.

Almighty God,
by your grace Elizabeth rejoiced with Mary,
and hailed her as the mother of the Lord:
Fill us with your grace
that we may acclaim her Son Jesus as our Saviour
and rejoice to be called his brethren.

The reading given is from the same homily of St Bede the Venerable as used in the Divine Office for today. It is interesting to compare its more natural presentation with that of Guerric of Igny given, above, for the Annunciation.

'And she said: Blessed are you among women, and blessed is the fruit of your womb.' Not only blessed among women, but with an eminent blessing among all blessed women. Nor is he the fruit of her womb blessed after the manner of the saints, but, as the apostle says: 'Of whom is Christ according to the flesh, who is over all things, God blessed for ever' (Rom 9:5). Of the origin of this fruit the psalmist speaks in mystic words, when he says: 'The Lord will give goodness, and our earth shall yield her fruit' (Ps 84:13). The Lord 'gave goodness' when he decreed to save the human race from guilt by his only-begotten Son; he 'gave goodness' when, by the grace of the Holy Spirit, he consecrated to himself a temple in the virgin's womb. And 'our earth gave its fruit' when the same virgin, whose body was of our earth, gave birth to a Son co-equal to his Father in his divinity, though consubstantial with his mother in the truth of his humanity.

Isaiah also, looking forward to the time of our redemption, says: 'In that day the bud of the Lord shall be in magnificence and glory, and the fruit of the earth shall be high' (Isaiah 4:2). The bud of the Lord was indeed in glory when the everlasting Son of God appeared in time in the flesh, and by the greatness of his heavenly virtues shone before the world. The fruit of the earth was high when, in the power of his resurrection, God raised to the highest heaven in immortal glory the flesh which he had taken from our nature in its mortality. Truly, then, is it said: 'Blessed are you among women, and blessed is the fruit of your womb.' Incomparably blessed is she who received the glory of that divine bud, yet preserved the crown of her integrity. Blessed among women, by whose virginal childbirth the curse of the first mother is turned aside from the sons of women. Blessed is the fruit of her womb, by whom we have received both the seed of incorruption and the fruit of the heavenly inheritance which we had lost in Adam.

The Homilies of the Venerable Bede, Bk 1, 4

Saturday following the Second Sunday after Pentecost
The Immaculate Heart of Mary
OPTIONAL MEMORIAL

This optional memorial follows normally on the solemnity of the Sacred
Heart, but is only celebrated when the Saturday in question is free.

As in every celebration of Mary what we celebrate is God's work in her, and
in today's memorial, his keeping of her heart for himself. Mary was conceived
without sin, but also preserved from sin all through her life. The reading is
taken from Cardinal Newman on the Immaculate Conception.

God, in his mercy, has communicated in various measures his great
attributes to his rational creatures, and first of all, as being most
necessary, holiness. Thus Adam, from the time of his creation, was
gifted, over and above his nature as man, with the grace of God, to
unite him to God and to make him holy. Grace is therefore called holy
grace; and, as being holy, it is the connecting principle between God
and man. Adam in paradise might have had knowledge, and skill,
and many virtues; but these gifts did not unite him to his Creator.
It was holiness that united him, for it is said by St Paul, 'Without
holiness no man shall see God'.

And so again, when man fell and lost this holy grace, he had
various gifts still adhering to him; he might be, in a certain measure,
true, merciful, loving, and just; but these virtues did not unite him to
God. What he needed was holiness; and therefore the first act of
God's goodness to us in the gospel is to take us out of our *un*holy state
by means of the sacrament of Baptism, and by the grace then given us
to re-open the communications, so long closed, between the soul and
heaven.

We see then the force of our Lady's title, when we call her '*Holy*
Mary'. When God would prepare a human mother for his Son, this
was why he began by giving her an immaculate conception. He
began, not by giving her the gift of love, or truthfulness, or gentleness, or devotion, though according to the occasion she had them all.
But he began his great work before she was born; before she could
think, speak, or act, by making her *holy*, and thereby, while on earth,
a citizen of heaven. '*Tota* pulchra es, Maria!' Nothing of the defor-
mity of sin was ever hers. Thus she differs from all saints. There have

been great missionaries, confessors, bishops, doctors, pastors. They have done great works and have taken with them numberless converts or penitents to heaven. They have suffered much, and have a superabundance of merits to show. But Mary in this way resembles her divine Son: that is, that, as he, being God, is separate by holiness from all creatures, so she is separate from all saints and angels, as being *'full of grace'*.

J.H. Newman, *Meditations and Devotions*, 'Sancta Maria', pp 26-27

1 June
Saint Justin, *martyr*
MEMORIAL

Justin was born towards the beginning of the second century in Nablus in Palestine. His family were pagans, of Roman origin, apparently, and had been settled in Palestine for two generations. From his youth he was possessed by a thirst for truth and he explored many philosophical systems before discovering and embracing Christianity. He was well styled by Tertullian as 'philosopher and martyr'.

It is clear from his own writings that he preserved the characteristic dress of a professional philosopher, and taught Christianity as a philosophy. In the classical world, however, philosophy normally implied more than a system of thought, rather a whole system of values and a way of life.

He finally settled in Rome, where he wrote his Apologies, addressed to the emperors.

He was martyred in Rome under the city prefect Junius Rusticus, Marcus Aurelius being emperor, about the year 165.

Today has been celebrated as his memorial by the Byzantines for at least a thousand years. Traditionally he is known as Justin Martyr, perhaps because of his manifold witnessing to Christ — in his life, his writings and his manner of dying.

The writing quoted below is from his Dialogue with Trypho, who was a Jew.

Jesus had gone to the river Jordan, where John was baptizing, and when he came out of the water, the Holy Spirit lighted on him like a dove, as the apostles of Christ wrote. Now, we know that he did not go to the river because he stood in need of baptism, or of the descent of the Spirit like a dove; even as he submitted to be born and to be crucified, not because he needed such things, but because of the human race, which from the time of Adam had fallen under the power of death and the guile of the serpent, and each one of which had committed personal transgression.

For God, wishing both angels and men, who were endowed with free-will, and at their own disposal, to do whatever he had strengthened each to do, made them so, that if they chose the things acceptable to himself, he would keep them free from death and from punishment; but that if they did evil, he would punish each as he sees fit. For it was not his entrance into Jerusalem sitting on an ass, which we have showed was prophesied, that empowered him to be Christ, but it furnished men with a proof that he is the Christ; just as it was necessary in the time of John that men have proof, that they might know who is Christ.

For when John remained by the Jordan, and preached the baptism of repentance, wearing only a leather girdle and a vesture made of camels' hair, eating nothing but locusts and wild honey, men supposed him to be Christ; but he cried to them, 'I am not the Christ, but the voice of one crying; for he that is stronger than I shall come, whose shoes I am not worthy to bear.' And when Jesus came to the Jordan, he was considered to be the son of Joseph the carpenter; and he appeared without comeliness, as the scriptures declared; and he was deemed a carpenter (for he was in the habit of working as a carpenter when among men, making ploughs and yokes; by which he taught the symbols of righteousness and an active life); but then the Holy Spirit, and for man's sake, as I formerly stated, lighted on him in the form of a dove, and there came at the same instant from the heavens a voice, which was uttered also by David when he spoke, prefiguring Christ, what the Father would say to him: 'You are my Son: this day have I begotten You.'

St Justin Martyr, *Dialogue with Trypho,* c 88

2 June
Saints Marcellinus and Peter, *martyrs*
OPTIONAL MEMORIAL

Marcellinus and Peter were members of the Roman clergy and suffered under Diocletian in the year 303. They were buried in the cemetery 'Inter duos Lauros' (Between the two laurels) on the Via Lavicana initially. There was considerable veneration for them in Rome in the centuries following their bearing witness, as their magnificent tomb and the church built on the site of their burial indicate, and their mention in the Roman canon testifies. Otherwise, however, we know little about them.

The reading is taken from St Augustine. The sermon used was preached by him on the memorial of the Milanese martyrs, Protasius and Gervase, on the 19 of this month.

The earth has been filled by the martyrs with, as it were, the seed of blood, and from that seed rose up the cornfield of the Church. Dead they sowed Christ more than when alive! They sow today, they preach today; their tongue is silent, their deeds cry out. They were held prisoner, bound, locked up, brought out, tortured, burned, stoned, struck, cast to the beasts. In all the ways they died they were mocked as worthless: but 'precious in the sight of the Lord is the death of his saints' (Ps 115:15). It was precious, then, only in the sight of the Lord, now in our sight too. For then, when it was a disgrace to be a Christian, the death of the saints was worthless in the sight of men: they were abhorred, held for an abomination. It was presented as a cursed thing: in this way you will die — you will be crucified — you will be burned. . . . What believer does not now desire such cursed things?

Look closely at the promises of God. What did he do to those very martyrs, do you think he gave them all for which they asked? Not at all Many of them desired to be released, and released with some miracle, as the three youths were released from the furnace. What was the utterance of king Nebuchadnezzar? 'Because, he said, they hoped in him, and set at naught the king's command.' What testimony does he offer, whose efforts were to kill? He wanted them to be burned, and afterwards came to belief through them. If they died in the fire, they would have been crowned in a hidden way, it would have been no use to him. They were preserved for a time, then, that an unbeliever might come to belief, that he who had condemned them might praise God (cf Dan 3). The God of the three youths was the same God as the God of Maccabees. He saved the first named from the fire, he caused the second named to die in the fire. Has he changed? Did he love one group more than the other? A greater crown was given to the Maccabees. One group certainly escaped the fire, but they were preserved for the perils of this world: the other finished with all perils in their fire! No trial remained for them anymore, only a crowning. It follows that the Maccabees received more (cf 2 Macc 7).

Stir up your faith, stretch the sight of your heart, not of your body: for within you you have the sight of your heart, which the Lord has made for you, who opened the eyes of your heart for you, when he gave you faith.

A few days ago a certain writing was read to you, in which, to a particular sick woman racked with severest pain, when she had said, I cannot bear it; to her the martyr himself, who had come to heal her, said: what if you were undergoing martyrdom? Many, then, undergo martyrdom in their sick-beds: truly many. There is a kind of persecution by satan, more hidden and more cunning than what then was. The believer lies in his bed, racked with pain, he prays and is not heard — in fact he is heard, but is proven, tried, scourged, that he may be received as a child of God.

Wherefore, when he or she is racked with pain, temptation comes by some utterance. Either some woman of little worth or a man, if he should be called such, approaches the sick-bed, and says to the sick one: Make such an amulet and you will be well: let such an incantation be used and you will be well. Such and such, so and so, such another, have been made well by doing this, just ask.* The sick person does not go along, does not submit, does not turn their heart that way; for all that, they struggle.*† They have no strength, yet they overcome the devil. They become a martyr in their bed, being crowned by him who hung for them upon the cross.

St Augustine, Sermon 286 nn 3, 6, 7

* Pagan superstitions and practices were still strong, as is evident.
*† The verb here used is the same as that used of the struggle of the martyrs in the arena and before their persecutors.

3 June
Saints Charles Lwanga and companions, *martyrs*
MEMORIAL

These are twenty-two named Ugandans of the Catholic faith who were put to death by king Mwanga, and who were canonized in 1964. They were all young men or boys, some of them initially only catechumens, who were in the king's service. Mwanga objected to their Christianity but also to their christian moral values which ran counter to his immoral sexual demands. Charles Lwanga baptized those who were catechumens before they suffered death. He and twelve companions were slain on this day in 1886; of the other nine some were slain in May of that year or through to January of 1887. Their various sufferings were most cruel.

Many other Christians were slain in the same period, many of whom were of the Anglican communion, for Anglican missionaries had preceded the White Fathers in Uganda by about three years.

The reading is from the address of Pope Paul VI on the occasion of the canonization of the martyrs, and just precedes the part of the address given on this day in the Divine Office.

Yes: they are Africans and also martyrs. 'These are they who have come out of the great tribulation. They have washed their robes and made them white in the blood of the Lamb. Therefore are they before the throne of God' (Apoc 7:14-15).

Every time we utter the word 'martyr' in the sense it has acquired in christian hagiography, we should bring to our mind's eye a drama evoking horror and wonder. Horror, because of the injustice which unlooses such a drama with the instruments of power and cruelty; horror, again, because of the blood which is shed and of the death so unfeelingly inflicted; wonder, then, because of the simple strength which submits without struggle or physical resistance to torment, happy and proud to witness to the unconquerable truth of a faith which has fused itself with life.

Life, however, dies, faith lives on. We see brute as opposed to moral force; the first knowing in its very success defeat; the second, triumph in failure! Martyrdom, then, is a drama: an appalling drama, be it said, but one rich in teaching. The unjust and evil violence which brings it about, tends almost to be forgotten, while in the memory of centuries the gentleness which makes the offering of self a sacrifice, a holocaust, remains with all its lustre and attractiveness; a supreme act of love and faithfulness with regard to Christ; an example and a witnessing, and enduring message to contemporary and future generations alike. Such is martyrdom: such has been the glory of the Church through the centuries.

Martyrdom is a happening of such quality that the Church lost no time in gathering together the accounts of 'the passions of the martyrs', and forming from them the choice book concerning its most illustrious children, the martyrology. Such beauty and greatness shine forth from martyrdom that legend and art have made it the theme of imaginative and fabulous development. But the actual history, which the martyrology to this day relates, rouses in us, and with good cause, an admiration which knows no limits, and rightly inspires praise of God for the great works he achieves in weak human beings. Then again it causes us to bestow on those heroes, who have written the pages of this matchless book with their blood, the honour due to them.

> Pope Paul VI, Address on the Occasion of the Canonization of the
> Twenty-two Ugandan Martyrs, 18 October, 1964

5 June
Saint Boniface, *bishop and martyr*
MEMORIAL

Boniface was an Anglo-Saxon, a native of Devonshire, born about the year 673, and originally known as Wynfrith. He was educated at Exeter and then became a monk at Nursling in Hampshire. In his mid-thirties he believed himself called to become a missionary in Germany and left England, going first to Rome to receive the papal mandate. At Rome the pope gave him the name Boniface — a Latin name to replace his, to the Romans, strange sounding Anglo-Saxon one.

He was first sent to help St Willibrord in Frisia and to gain experience, and, then, having been ordained bishop in Rome in 722, he went to Germany. Much of his work in Germany was concerned with organizing the embryonic Church which existed there, although he did undertake direct conversion as well. His regular pattern was to establish a monastery as a base and to develop the apostolate around that. Of the monasteries he founded the most cele-brated was to be Fulda, and there his relics are to be found to this day.

As part of his programme he introduced the Rule of Benedict into these monasteries and the observance at Fulda was modelled on that of Monte Cassino.

St Boniface and his companions were slain in Friesland in the year 754 by a heathen mob.

The reading is taken from his Letters. What he says has meaning for us all, but. to illustrate his Roman faith, the text of the oath he took on his ordination as bishop is given first. Note that the pope is referred to in the traditional, and more satisfactory, form of vicar of Peter.

I, Boniface, by the grace of God bishop, promise to you, blessed Peter, chief of the apostles, and to your vicar, the blessed pope Gregory, and to his successors, in the name of the indivisible Trinity, Father, Son and Holy Spirit, that I will uphold the faith and purity of holy catholic teaching and will persevere in the unity of the same faith in which beyond a doubt the whole salvation of a Christian lies. I will not agree to anything which is opposed to the unity of the universal Church, no matter who may try to persuade me, but in all things I will show, as I have said, complete loyalty to you and to the welfare of your Church on which, in the person of your vicar and his successors, the power to bind and loose has been conferred.

                          Boniface, 'Oath taken on his ordination as a bishop'

Lowly as I am, noble youth, I beg you not to disregard the words of Solomon the wise: 'In all thy works remember thy last end and thou shalt never sin' (Sir 7:40). Walk whilst you have the light lest the darkness of death come upon you (Jn 12:35). Temporal things pass swiftly away, but the eternal that never fade will soon be upon us. All the treasures of this world, such as gold, silver, precious stones of every hue, succulent and dainty food and costly garments, melt away like shadows, vanish like smoke, dissolve like foam on the sea. The psalmist uttered the truth when he said: 'Man's days are like grass: like the flower of the field he flourishes' (Ps 102:15). And again: 'My days are like a shadow that declines and I am withered like grass' (Ps 101:12).

Men who wallow in luxury are said in holy scripture to pass sleepless nights through anxiety, spinning their fragile webs that catch only dust or a breath of wind, for as the psalmist says: 'They gather together treasure and know not for whom they gather it' (Ps 38:7). And at the moment when death, the minion of baneful Pluto, barks at the door, foaming at the mouth and gnashing his teeth, they faint with fear; then, deprived of heavenly consolation, they lose in an instant both their precious souls and the deceitful gains for which they have slaved like misers night and day. Finally, they are snatched by the claws of fiends and borne off to the gloomy caverns of Erebus, there to suffer everlasting torments.

There is no doubting the truth of this. In all earnestness and affection I beg you to consider this matter very carefully. Give rein to your natural gifts and abilities; do not stifle your literary talents and your keen spiritual understanding with gross pleasures of the flesh. Keep in mind the words of the psalmist: 'His delight is in the words of the law of the Lord; in his law he meditates day and night' (Ps 1:2): and elsewhere: 'O how I love your law, it is my meditation all the day' (Ps 118:97). Call to mind also the words of Moses: 'This book of the law shall not depart out of your mouth, but you shall meditate therein day and night' (Jos 1:8). Put aside all harmful obstacles; strive with unflagging zest to pursue your study of the scriptures and thereby acquire that nobility of mind which is divine wisdom. It is more precious than gold, more beautiful than silver, more lustrous than onyx, clearer than crystal, more costly than topaz (Job 28:17, 19) and, according to the opinion of the Preacher, all things that may be desired are not to be compared with it (Prov 8:11).

Can there be a more fitting pursuit in youth or a more valuable possession in old age than a knowledge of sacred scripture? In the midst of storms it will preserve you from the dangers of shipwreck and guide you to the shore of an enchanting paradise and the everlasting bliss of the angels. Of it the same wise man has remarked: 'Wisdom overcomes evil: it stretches from end to end mightily and disposes all things sweetly. Her have I loved from my youth and have become enamoured of her form' (Wis 8:1).

Boniface, 'Letter to St Nithard'

6 June
Saint Norbert, *bishop*
OPTIONAL MEMORIAL

Norbert was born about the year 1080 close to Xanten in the duchy of Cleves, in the lower Rhineland. His family was aristocratic and he was linked by blood to the then German emperors. Destined by his family for an ecclesiastical career he was given a canonry in the cathedral of Xanten and was ordained subdeacon. His life-style was like that of any other worldly person.

He was converted suddenly in 1115 to more serious ways and spent some months in spiritual retreat in the abbey of Siegburg. After this he was ordained priest and set about persuading his fellow canons to embrace the regular life. He was not successful at Xanten and became an itinerant preacher in France, preaching renewal and penance. His ascetic and apostolic zeal led to the founding of a community at Prémontré of canons regular. The ideals and observance of Cîteaux greatly influenced the new community and the houses founded from it, the members of which became known as the 'White Canons', and developed into the Premonstratensian Order.

In 1126 Norbert himself was elected archbishop of Magdeburg and proved an energetic pastor, doing much to build up the religious life of the people and to complete the conversion of the Wends. He also set about improving relations between the imperial court and the Holy See.

St Norbert died in 1134.

The reading is taken from Clement of Alexandria's treatise, 'Who is the rich man that is being saved?' Norbert, in fact disposed of all his worldly goods, which was not quite what Clement advised. In the following passage, however, Clement set out his understanding of the real values of life. The ideal of Norbert would have been one with this.

Our Lord and Saviour was indeed glad to be asked a question corresponding exactly with his character: as being the Life he was questioned about life, as the Saviour about salvation, as the Teacher about the sum of the doctrines he was teaching, as the Truth about the true immortality, as the Word about his Father's word, as the Perfect One about the perfect rest, as the Incorruptible One about the sure incorruption.

He was questioned about the very things on account of which he came down to earth, in which he gives instruction, which he teaches, which he offers, that he may show the purpose of the gospel, namely, that it is the giving of eternal life. He foreknows as God both what questions he will be asked, and what answers will be given him; for who could know this better than the Prophet of prophets and Lord of every prophetical spirit? And being addressed as 'good', he takes his key-note from this very first word, and begins his teaching from this point, and directs the learner to God who is good, and before all, and alone dispenser of life eternal, which the Son has received from him and gives to us.

So then it is necessary to store up in the mind right from the very first the greatest of the lessons that concern true life, and the one that crowns all others, which is, to know God who is eternal, and giver of eternal gifts, and first, and highest, and one, and good. It is possible to possess God by way of knowledge and apprehension; for this is an immutable and fixed beginning and foundation of life, namely, knowledge of God who really is, and who gives the real, that is, eternal gifts, from whom all else receives existence and continuance. For ignorance of God is death, but full knowledge of him, and making him a friend, and love towards him, and becoming like him, is alone life.

It is to know this God, first of all, whom 'no one knows except the Son, and any one to whom the Son chooses to reveal him' (Mt 11:27), that he exhorts the man, who is to live what is truly life.

Clement of Alexandria, *Who is the Rich Man that is Being Saved*, nn 6, 7, 8

9 June
Saint Ephrem, *deacon and doctor of the Church*
OPTIONAL MEMORIAL

Ephrem, or Ephraim, was born of a christian family in Nisibis about the year 306, while Christianity was still a proscribed religion in the Roman empire. When he grew up he entered the service of the Church in Nisibis and was ordained deacon. His learning led him to being put in charge of the theological school which was founded there, but which was later moved to Edessa, when Nisibis fell to the Persians.

Ephrem died in Edessa about the year 378.

He wrote in Syriac, usually in metre and was a strenuous defender of the

Catholic faith, for then, as now, there were those who denied the fullness of that faith. His teaching on the sinlessness of the Virgin Mary foreshadowed the doctrine of the Immaculate Conception.

The reading is taken from a homily on Holy Martyrs given by him. It is an extract but the style and content is a presage of much subsequent Eastern christian thought and writing.

'With fear and trembling, work out your salvation' (Phil 2:12).

The wisdom of the pagan philosophers, and the eloquence of their orators, were confounded at the extraordinary sight of the death and triumphs of the early martyrs. The tyrants and judges were seized with astonishment when they witnessed the faith, courage, and even the gaiety of these holy champions of the faith. What will be our excuse at the tribunal of Jesus Christ if, after having been saved from persecution and torture, we have nevertheless neglected to love God, or even attempted to work out our salvation?

What a contrast! on one side the martyrs, ever attached to God in the midst of the severest trials; and on the other, the greater part of Christians who, in the bosom of a quiet peace, refuse to give to God a heart, which he certainly has a right to demand.

Once more, what could we do on that dreadful day, on which our eternity depends? Whilst the martyrs, full of a holy confidence, would show to Jesus the scars of their wounds, what should we have to show him? Can we offer him a lively faith, a sincere charity, a disinterested detachment from earthly things, successful victories over our passions, souls fond of silence and solitude, hearts pure and chaste, alms given to the poor, prayers, watchings, and tears? Happy the one who is the bearer of these good works, for he or she will appear with confidence before Jesus Christ and his angels.

Holy martyrs, who have merited by your triumphs to be intimately united to God in heaven, deign to intercede on our behalf. We are but miserable sinners; but if you will give us the help of your prayers, the grace of Jesus Christ will enlighten our souls, and our hearts will be inflamed with the fire of divine love.

St Ephrem, *Homily on Holy Martyrs*

11 June
Saint Barnabas, *apostle*
MEMORIAL

Barnabas was a Cypriot Jew, a Levite, Joseph by name originally, who was prominent in the early Church in Jerusalem and called Barnabas by the apostles, as Luke tells us in Acts 4:36. He is styled 'apostle' by extension. He was one of the outstanding converts among the Jews of the diaspora and was able to introduce the convert Saul into the Church in Jerusalem.

Later we find Barnabas entrusted with various missions and ultimately with the evangelizing of Cyprus along with St Paul. Traditionally he was martyred in Cyprus. We can hardly say more about him than does scripture, 'he was a good man, full of the Holy Spirit and of faith' (Acts 11:24).

The reading, from Newman's *Parochial and Plain Sermons*, develops another line however, and it is how even good people can be wrong. The whole of the sermon is devoted to the tolerance of religious error, the excerpt takes up just a point from Newman's thought but a point of universal validity.

'And the other Jews dissembled likewise with him; insomuch that Barnabas also was carried away with their dissimulation' (Gal 2:13). The other instance was his indulgent treatment of Mark, his sister's son, which occasioned the quarrel between him and St Paul. 'Barnabas determined to take with them', on their apostolic journey, 'John, whose surname was Mark. But Paul thought not good to take him with them who departed from them from Pamphylia, and went not with them to the work' (Acts 15:37, 38).

Now it is very plain what description of character, and what kind of lesson, is brought before us in the history of this holy apostle. Holy he was, full of the Holy Spirit and of faith; still the characteristics and the infirmities of man remained in him, and thus he is 'unto us for an example', consistently with the reverence we feel towards him as one of the foundations of the Christian Church.

He is an example and warning to us, not only as showing us what we ought to be, but as evidencing how the highest gifts and graces are corrupted in our sinful nature, if we are not diligent to walk step by step, according to the light of God's commandments. Be our mind as heavenly as it may be, most loving, most holy, most zealous, most energetic, most peaceful, yet if we look away from him for a moment, and look towards ourselves, at once these excellent tempers fall into some extreme or mistake. Charity becomes over-easiness, holiness is tainted with spiritual pride, zeal degenerates into fierceness, activity eats up the spirit of prayer, hope is heightened into presumption. We cannot guide ourselves. God's revealed word is our sovereign rule of conduct; and therefore, among other reasons, is faith so principal a grace, for it is the directing power which receives the commands of Christ, and applies them to the heart.

J.H. Newman, *Parochial and Plain Sermons II*, 23

13 June

Saint Anthony of Padua, *priest and doctor of the Church*
MEMORIAL

Anthony was born in Lisbon, Portugal, in 1195, into a knightly family. He opted, however, for the service of the Church and, at the age of fifteen joined the Canons Regular of St Augustine. Inspired by the martyrdom of five early Franciscans he had known, he joined the Friars Minor in 1221. As a friar he preached in Italy and France with marvellous effect. He was a strong opponent of heresy but made his greatest impact as a man of God.

He died in Padua in 1231, aged just thirty-six, and was canonized the following year, 1232.

His shrine in Padua is one of the greatest in Italy and a most popular centre of pilgrimage even in our day.

The reading is taken from a sermon on Jer 48:28 he preached to the Benedictines of St Martin at Limoges in 1226. The text he followed was the Vulgate Latin; his exegesis is quite arbitrary but both moving and beautiful.

'Leave the cities and dwell in the rock, inhabitants of Moab, and be like the dove that makes her nest in the mouth of the hole of the highest place.'

Jer 48:28

But to leave the world, to live remote from the tumult of cities, to keep oneself unspotted from their vices, is not sufficient for the religious soul. Hence the prophet adds: 'Dwell in the rock.' Now this rock is

Jesus Christ. Establish yourself in him: let him be the constant theme of your thoughts, the object of your affections. Jacob reposed upon a stone in the wilderness, and while he slept he saw the heavens opened and conversed with angels, receiving a blessing from the Lord. Thus will it be with those who place their entire trust in Jesus Christ.

'And be like the dove that makes her nest in the mouth of the hole of the highest place.' If Jesus Christ is the rock, the hole of the rock, in which the religious soul is to seek shelter and take up her abode, is the wound in the side of Jesus Christ. This is the safe harbour of refuge, to which the divine spouse calls the religious soul when he speaks to her in the words of the Canticle, 'Arise, my love, my beautiful one, and come, O my dove, that art in the clefts of the rock, in the deep hollow of the wall.' The divine spouse speaks of the numberless clefts of the rock, but he also speaks of the deep hollow. There were, indeed, in his body numberless wounds, and one deep wound in his side; this leads to his heart, and it is here that he calls the soul he has espoused. To her he extends his arms; to her he opens wide his sacred side and divine heart, that she may come and hide therein. By retiring into the clefts of the rock the dove is safe from the pursuit of birds of prey, and, at the same time, she prepares for herself a quiet refuge where she may calmly repose and coo in peace. So the religious soul finds in the heart of Jesus a secure refuge against the wiles and attacks of satan, and a delightful retreat.

However, we must not rest merely at the entrance to the hole in the rock, we must penetrate its depths. At the mouth of the deep hollow, at the mouth of the wound in his side, we shall indeed find the precious blood which has redeemed us. This blood pleads for us and demands mercy for us. But the religious soul must not stay at the entrance. When she has heard and understood the voice of the divine blood, she must hasten to the very source from which it springs, into the very innermost sanctuary of the heart of Jesus. There she will find light, peace and ineffable consolations. 'And be like the dove that makes her nest in the deep hollow of the rock.' The dove builds her nest with little pieces of straw she gathers up here and there. And how are we to build up an abode in the Heart of Jesus? This divine saviour, who so mercifully gives us the place wherein we are to make our abode, furnishes us at the same time with the materials with which to construct it.

O religious soul, dove beloved of Christ, behold these little pieces of straw which the world tramples under its feet. They are the virtues practised by your Saviour and spouse, of which he himself has set you an example: humility, meekness, poverty, penance, patience and mortification. The world despises them as useless pieces of straw; nevertheless, they will be for you the material from which to construct your dwelling place forever, in the profound hollow of the rock, in the heart of Jesus.

St Anthony of Padua, *Sermon to the Benedictines of the Abbey of St Martin,*
Limoges, 1226

19 June
Saint Romuald, *abbot*
OPTIONAL MEMORIAL

Romuald was born about the middle of the tenth century in Ravenna and became a Benedictine monk in the monastery of Classe which serves the beautiful church of S. Apollinare. He left there to live as a hermit, and might well be termed a roving recluse, for he travelled as far as Cuxa in the Pyrenees, before returning to Italy, where he continued his wanderings.

Everywhere he went he founded small communities of hermit monks and sought to spread the Cluniac reform among cenobites. He must really be seen as a reformer of the solitary life, for his aim was not to found a distinct Order but an institute where the solitary life, then much in vogue, could be lived under obedience. His most famous monastery was Camaldoli, and from it, his followers came to be called Camaldolese.

He died about 1027.

The reading is taken from another and later eremitical tradition, the Carthusian, but it would be universally accepted.

It is not in the light of words that we must seek light. The light of a word is still something created, ephemeral — part of our nothingness. If we become attached to that light, we are halting on the way; we shall never reach the goal. That is why God bestows on souls whom he loves the grace of refusing them this light. He leaves them in darkness, and it is that darkness that becomes light: 'And night shall be my light in my pleasures.'

The true light shines in the darkness, but one must get accustomed to finding it there. At first one is terrified: light is such a lovely and necessary thing. But, little by little, the day begins to dawn, and one sees that the light we miss is an inferior light, whilst that which is growing is much purer.

The light which is lacking at these times is our own light. We no longer perceive our state of grace, or rather we do not feel it. We no longer find within us that soothing assurance of belonging to God. What we do find in ourselves is division and darkness.

We must go beyond this stage. We must get out of ourselves, and despise the voice that doubts or argues or despairs. We must listen to that other voice which speaks to us from the depths of our soul, and says to us: 'God is Love: to be separated from him there must be an act of the faculty of loving — a love opposed to his love. I do not see that in myself; therefore. . . .'

That is the true light, the light that shines in the darkness. But because it does shine in the darkness, we have to pass through these hours of darkness, hours when one says: 'My God, I do not see that I have willed to offend you, but I am no longer conscious of my love for you. I no longer feel the attachment of my will to your goodness, or taste the union of my spirit with your truth. But I do know that to offend you one must will to do so, and since I do not wish that, then I believe that I have not done so'.

We must be content with this single light from within, and attach ourselves to it alone — the light of him who is the Voice or Word. That is why all other voices must be stilled. Even when they make themselves heard, they do not speak to us; they no longer tell us anything. God closes the ear that is conscious of them, in order that he may open the ear which listens to the voice from within.

The divine will — that is our true light, and it is the light of love. The soul desiring this will knows that it is in truth and holiness, even if everything else cries out to it that it is in error and evil.

Carthusian author, *They Speak by Silences*, pp 16-17

21 June

Saint Aloysius Gonzaga, *religious*

MEMORIAL

Aloysius, or Luigi, was born in the latter half of the sixteenth century, the eldest son of a very wealthy and aristocratic Italian family. He was brought up in a succession of courts. As a partial result of this upbringing he was separated for three critical years from his pious mother whom he deeply admired, loved and revered. Two of those years were spent in the court of Florence, which at that time was vicious in the extreme. It was the reaction to the atmosphere of that court of a devout, high spirited, but still young boy, which has led to the stories about Aloysius never looking at a woman's face, and even hesitating to be alone in his mother's company. It would seem to have been a passing phase.

Aloysius imposed on himself a discipline similar to that of the desert fathers — we may fault his discretion but not his zeal — and reached a high degree of prayer and holiness as a young man. He entered the Society of Jesus in 1585, much against his father's will, and renounced his rights in favour of his younger brother.

Aloysius died as a result of nursing the plague stricken, in Rome, in 1591.

He was canonized in 1726 and has since been proclaimed the patron saint of all christian youth.

For our reading an extract of a letter to his younger brother is given here. His brother's conduct left a lot to be desired and the references in the passage below are to undertakings given in response to Aloysius' efforts to bring him back to better ways. The formality of address used was typical of the age and of their social class. The Cardinal Borromeo mentioned is St Charles. Note the encouragement of daily Mass but with no mention of daily communion. On the latter point the recommendation of the Council of Trent had remained a dead letter.

As regards our blessed God, I will here remind you of what by word of mouth I recommended to you concerning his worship and service. And since the recommending of the virtue of religion, which we owe to God, seems peculiarly to belong to religious, I will descend to some particulars which you can put into practice according to the measure of grace which the Lord shall deign to communicate to you.

Amongst these, one is that you should commend yourself to the Lord every morning, making use of the 'Daily Exercise', or other such-like prayers, during which you might meditate on some of the points which you may find in the 'Daily Exercise' at the end of the little work I send you, which was compiled by the direction of Monsignor the Cardinal Borromeo, of happy memory; and as your lordship will there meet with suggestions which you can yourself read, I will not enlarge on this subject any further; only I would remind you besides to hear mass, according to the agreement between us.

Moreover, I would not have you lie down to rest at night before examining yourself as to whether you have offended God, so that if you should have any mortal sin on your conscience — from which may the Lord preserve you! — you may as soon as possible efface it by means of penance; bearing in mind that this is always needful whenever you have anything to repent of, and never waiting for a specific time, such as Easter or some other season; for no one can assure you of being then alive.

Next, as regards providing good things before men, I recommend to your observance the respect which you owe to your relatives and lords, upon which point I shall say nothing, as presuming how much you have this at heart; only, from my own personal obligation, and not from any idea that you need to be reminded thereof, I recommend to you the reverence you owe to the Signora Marchesa, your mother, as being your mother, and such a mother.

Moreover, as the head of your brethren, you know how fitting it is, both to have them united to you, and so to behave towards them as to endear this union to them. As for your vassals, I will simply observe that God has perhaps given them into your charge in a special and peculiar manner, only in order to signify to you the special and spiritual care which you ought to have for them, recognizing in the providence of God towards yourself a pattern of the manner in which you ought to provide for them.

St Aloysius Gonzaga, 'A Letter to his brother'

22 June
Saint Paulinus of Nola, *bishop*
OPTIONAL MEMORIAL

Paulinus was born at Bordeaux about the year 355 and came from a distinguished Gallo-Roman family. He was destined for high rank in the imperial
administration apparently, and married with such a career in view. Then in
389 he became a Christian and he and his wife opted for the ascetic life. While
living at Nola in the Campania he was ordained priest and then, about 409, he
was chosen as its bishop. He served as bishop until his death in 431. He is
referred to by his contemporaries among the Latin fathers. Many of his letters
and poems have been preserved.

The reading given here is taken from one of his letters in which he
comments on Luke 7:36ff.

So let us encourage each other and vie with one another in saying:
'Come, let us adore and weep before the Lord who made us.' By
weeping before him we shall engender our joys, by anointing the
soles of his feet we shall heal our wounds. For whatever we expend
on Christ we bestow rather on ourselves.

That woman cleansed herself by washing Christ, washed away
her sins by wiping his feet, and loved herself by loving him. So she
deserved to hear the words: 'Daughter, your faith has saved you',
whereas Simon, who was a son of the kingdom, did not. She won
greater justification from her service than he did from his feast.

For the Pharisee had not believed, but she did. In fact the Pharisee
said: 'This man, if he were a prophet, would surely know who this
woman is that is touching him.' So Simon was not justified by the
feast to which he had invited Christ as if he were a mere man.

Perhaps he thought that Christ, to the extent that Christ was for
our sakes poor, was indebted to him, because he considered it so
great that he, a rich man, invited a poor man to his table. But that
woman would not have hoped for the remission of her sins through
this great round of service, expense, and tears if she had not believed
in God in Christ; and so she found the head of her salvation at the
very tip of the Saviour's foot.

Poor Jew, where will you cast yourself? Our sinner anticipated you
by embarking on your tasks in your own house. You feasted to show

your arrogance; she fasted to play the servant. The water that you had refused to pour from your jugs she provided from her eyes. You did not wipe Christ's feet even with a towel, but she did so with her hair. You were unwilling to touch his feet even with your hands, but she did not cease to caress them with her kisses. Undoubtedly you ought to have provided this service to the guest you had received in your house, if you had preserved the law of hospitality even according to the example of your fathers; it is enough to cast up before your pride the example of father Abraham. So she was preferred to you, for by her faithful love she proved that she was more truly the child of your father.

St Paulinus of Nola, *Letter 23*, nn 39–40

22 June, also
Saint John Fisher, *bishop*
and Saint Thomas More, *martyrs*
OPTIONAL MEMORIAL

John Fisher was martyred in London on 22 June, 1535; Thomas More on 6 July in that same year. The two were very different, yet also remarkably alike for their learning, nobility of character, and firmness of conviction. They were canonized on 19 May, 1935.

John Fisher was born at Beverley in York in 1469, studied in the local grammar school and at Cambridge, where he was ordained priest. In 1501 he obtained his doctorate in divinity, and was elected Vice-Chancellor of the University. On University business he had already met Lady Margaret Beaufort, whose spiritual director he became and through her he was instrumental in the building of Christ's and St John's Colleges at Cambridge and the institution of the Lady Margaret Professorships of Divinity at both Oxford and Cambridge.

In 1504 her son, King Henry VII, had John appointed bishop of Rochester — because he judged him a man of God. As bishop he gave himself to the service of God in his people, visiting and instructing them and caring for them. His love of truth remained: this caused him to spend money on books and to set himself to the learning of Greek and Hebrew. Such a man could not bow to the whims of Henry VIII, and for his fidelity to the Holy See and God's law he was branded a traitor and slain.

Thomas More was just nine years younger than John Fisher, was a native of London and more a product of the renaissance than was John. He had mastered Greek as a lad at Oxford, but studied law at his father's behest. Incredibly gifted in mind and temper, he was blessed also in his family and his mentors. To resolve his hesitations about his vocation in life he spent four years in the guest-house of the London Carthusians while reading law, to pray and to reflect. He found his way: it was to be in the world. He came not to think so much about his merits and demerits but 'about his Lord and Love. That was the secret of his life, as of his laughter. He was at peace with himself because he was at peace with God. That was why he was so humble in success, so meek in high places, so gentle in contradiction, so firm in adversity, and so very gallant in death.' (R.L. Smith).

Thomas rose to be Lord Chancellor of England, the first commoner to do so, and died for the same cause and reason as John Fisher.

The readings offered are from their respective writings. For John Fisher the final third of a splendid prayer he wrote, it would seem towards the end of his life and perhaps in the Tower.

O Father, then, whither shall I turn in my necessity rather than to thee which have me call thee by this name, a name of much love and tenderness, of much delight and pleasure, a name which stirreth the heart with much hope and constancy and many other delectable affections. And if nothing were told me but only this name, it might suffice to make me steadfastly trust that thou, which hast commanded me to call thee by this name father, will help me and succour me at my need when I sue unto thee; but much rather because my saviour thy son Christ Jesus hath assured me that thou art a more kind and more loving father unto me than was mine own natural father. This assurance made by thy most entirely beloved son should specially move both thee and me. First it should move me to have an hope and a confidence that thou wilt deal with me according to the same promise. Second, it should also move thee to perform this promise effectually and so to show thyself a kind and loving father in this my petition. My petition, most dear father, is agreeable to that same promise made by thy most entirely beloved son my saviour Jesus. I ask no other thing but thy good Holy Spirit to be given unto me according to that same promise which he promised.

I know, most gracious Father, that thou art here present with me albeit I see thee not. But thou both seest me and hearest me and no secrecy of my heart is hid from thee. Thou hearest that I now ask thine Holy Spirit and thou knowest that I now pray therefor and that I am very desirous to have the same. Lo! dear Father, with all the enforcement of my heart I beseech thee to give thine Holy Spirit unto me. Wherefore unless thou wilt disappoint the promise of thy son Jesus thou canst not but give me this Holy Spirit; so by this means I shall be fully relieved of that my misery whereof I complained unto thy goodness at the beginning. Thy most Holy Spirit he shall make me to love thee with all my heart, with all my soul, with all my mind, with all my power, for he is the author of all good love, he is the very furnace of charity and he is the fountain of all gracious affections and godly desires. He is the spiritual fire that kindles in the heart of them where he enters all gracious love; he fills their souls in whom he is received with the abundance of charity; he makes their minds sweetly to burn in all godly desires and gives unto them strength and power courageously to follow all ghostly affections and specially towards thee. Wherefore, dear Father, when thou hast strictly commanded me thus to love thee with all my heart and thus would I right gladly do (but without thy help and without thy Holy Spirit I cannot perform the same), I beseech thee to shed upon my heart thy most Holy Spirit by whose gracious presence I may be warmed, heated and kindled with the spiritual fire of charity and with the sweetly burning love of all godly affections, that I may earnestly set my heart, soul and mind upon thee and assuredly trust that thou art my very loving Father and according to the same trust I may love thee with all my heart, with all my soul, with all my mind and all my power. Amen.

A Prayer of St John Fisher

The reading for St Thomas More is the very last letter he wrote, with charcoal, he was denied a pen, to his daughter Margaret. It has not the doctrinal content of the letter given under this day in the Divine Office but is wondrous in its love.

Our Lord bless you, good daughter, and your good husband and your little boy and all yours, and all my children and all my godchildren and all my friends. Recommend me when ye may to my good daughter Cecily, whom I beseech our Lord to comfort; and I send her my blessing and to all her children; and pray her to pray for me. I send her an handkercher: and God comfort my good son, her husband. My good daughter Dauncey [Elizabeth] hath the picture in parchment, that you delivered me from my Lady Coniers, the name is on the back. Show her that I heartily pray her, that you may send it in my name to her again, for a token from me to pray for me. I like specially well Dorothy Colley [Margaret's maid, who often bore him messages], I pray you be good unto her. I would wit whether this be she that you wrote me of. If not, I pray you be good to the other, as you may in her affliction, and to my good daughter Jane Aleyn [another of her maids], too. Give her, I pray you, some kind answer, for she sued hither to me this day to pray you be good to her.

I cumber you, good Margaret, much, but I would be sorry it should be any longer than tomorrow. For it is St Thomas's even, and the utas [Octave day] of St Peter: and therefore tomorrow long I to go to God: it were a day very meet and convenient to me.

I never liked your manner toward me better than when you kissed me last. For I love when daughterly love and dear charity hath no leisure to look to worldly courtesy.

Farewell, my dear child, and pray for me, and I shall for you and all your friends, that we may merrily meet in heaven. I thank you for your great cost. I send now to my good Clement [Margaret Gigs] her algorism stone, and I send her and my godson and all hers God's blessing and mine. I pray you at time convenient recommend me to my good son John More. I liked well his natural fashion [John and Margaret, separately, had broken through the guard to kiss their father, after his condemnation]. Our Lord bless him and his good wife, my loving daughter, to whom I pray him be good as he hath great cause: and that if the land of mine comes to his hand, he break not my will concerning his sister Dauncey. And our Lord bless Thomas and Austin [John's sons] and all that they shall have.

St Thomas More, A Letter to his daughter, Margaret

24 June
The Birth of Saint John the Baptist
SOLEMNITY

This Solemnity is also presented in the Glenstal Bible Missal. The Birth of St John the Baptist is one of the oldest of christian celebrations. It was seen as heralding the new age of redemption, and was very much a Christ-orientated feast.

John, the last and greatest of the prophets, was made holy in his mother's womb, filled with the Holy Spirit, and so born holy. While still in the womb he hailed Christ. The date chosen for the feast was inspired by the prior choice of the date for Christmas — a six month interval between the two births — and the symbolism of the summer solstice, after which the sun grows less and less, until the new birth at the winter solstice.

The reading is taken from a Sermon by Mgr Ronald Knox.

'Why is this granted to me', says St Elizabeth, 'that the mother of my Lord should come to me'; and the child in her womb, as if the spirit of the mother's salutation had passed into him, had only one thought all his life, to make way for another who was greater than himself. 'I am the voice of one crying in the wilderness' — that is his account of himself: don't listen to the voice, then; listen to what it says. 'He was a burning and shining light', our Lord says of him; don't look at the light, then, look at him on whom its rays are cast. Always we see St John is pointing, always away from himself. 'Behold the Lamb of God, who takes away the sins of the world' — there, don't look at me, look at him; don't ask who I am, ask who he is. There comes one after me, who is greater than I, the latchet of whose shoe I am not worthy to loose. Everyone is crowded round St John, everyone wanting to know who he is, and he will let them see nothing but the finger that points to a greater than himself, let them hear nothing but the voice of the fore-runner who preaches a gospel not his own.

And gradually, as our Lord more and more allowed this attention to be directed towards himself, he, instead of his fore-runner, became the centre of interest. 'The pupil is outstripping the master', people will have said; for I think it's fairly certain that our Lord, at the opening of his ministry, was regarded as the disciple of St John, the man who had baptized him. And one by one the little groups that listened to the Baptist on the rocky hills by Jordan melted away, and he knew that they had gone off to follow the new teacher, who, travelling from village to village, was more easy of access. Perhaps they even thought that in so transferring their allegiance from the stern prophet of the desert with his wild clothes and rough manner to the friend of publicans and sinners, they were taking an easier yoke upon themselves. Anyhow, the followers of John became fewer, the audiences of the Galilean prophet more numerous. And I want you to see that if St John had been a smaller man, if he had looked upon his winning popularity in the way in which you and I would look upon such a thing if it were to happen to ourselves, it would have been impossible for him not to feel a pang of jealousy at having been obeyed so well, at having been so successful in diverting attention from himself to his Master. 'He might have left me just a little work to do, just a few souls to deal with; he might have given me some part to play in his mission'; it's not difficult to imagine St John feeling like that. But that was not St John's way. 'He must increase, and I must decrease', so he assures the little band that still remain faithful to him, as if it were the most natural thing in the world. And again, 'The bridegroom's friend, who stands by and listens to him, rejoices too, rejoices at hearing the bridegroom's voice.' Our Lord has come to claim his promised Bride, the Church, and St John is content with the humble, the almost undignified role of what we call the 'best man'. And it's easy to see what St John is thinking of when he makes this comparison.

Ronald A. Knox, *University and Anglican Sermons, Additional Sermons 9*

27 June
Saint Cyril of Alexandria, *bishop and doctor of the Church*
OPTIONAL MEMORIAL

Cyril was born in the year 370. He became a monk and, in time, was ordained priest. In 412 he succeeded an uncle of his as patriarch of Alexandria, and has left many writings, sermons and homilies on scripture. He died in 444. He was a zealous champion of the faith and denounced the heresy of Nestorius, patriarch of Constantinople, to Pope Celestine I. Nestorius denied the title 'Mother of God' to Mary: this denial was as a result of his christology. Cyril guided the subsequent Council of Ephesus in 431, which affirmed the unity of person in Christ and proclaimed Mary to be truly the 'Mother of God'.

He was unfortunately a rather high-handed individual, and, unaware of their precise origins, actually used formulas in his definition which derived from heretical sources. In this way he sowed the seeds of many future difficulties, and the Council of Chalcedon just twenty years later, had to complete the definitions of Ephesus.

The reading is less concerned with polemics, and deals with confidence in prayer.

'Truly, truly, I say to you, if you ask anything of the Father, he will give it to you in my name. Hitherto you have asked nothing in my name: ask and you will receive, that your joy may be full' (John 16:23, 24).

In this way Christ urges his disciples to ask for spiritual gifts, and, at the same time, gives them confidence that they will not fail to obtain them, should they ask for them. He says further, 'Truly, truly', to confirm their belief that should they ask the Father for anything they would receive it from him, for he will act as their mediator, and relay their request, and, as one with the Father, grant it. This is what he means by 'in my name'; for it is only through the Son that we draw near to the Father, since, as it is written, it is through him we have access in the one Spirit to the Father (Eph 2:18). On this account he said: 'I am the door' (John 10:9), and 'I am the way; no one comes to the Father, but by me' (John 14:6). For, as the Son is God, he, one with the Father, gives good things to those he has made holy, and is found to be generous out of his abundant goodness to us.

Paul, a man close to God, has given us the clearest testimony in this regard, where he writes: 'Grace to you and peace from God our Father and the Lord Jesus Christ' (Rom 1:7). Christ intercedes with the Father for us as our mediator (1 Tim 2:5), our high priest (Heb 4:14), and our advocate (1 John 2:1). He is our assurance in the presence of the Father. Let us offer our prayers, then, in Christ's name. The Father will most readily agree to them when they are made in this way. He will grant his graces to those who ask for them, so that we may rejoice in receiving them.

It follows that filled with spiritual gifts, and made rich by the fullness of understanding because of his Spirit dwelling within us, we must strive vigorously against every unfitting as well as evil desire. We must do all things well, working with fervent zeal towards every virtue, being sustained by everything that leads to holiness. Leaving behind the sadness which arises from a bad conscience, we are especially to rejoice in the hope of the reward to come, and to enrich our minds with the joys of Christ.

St Cyril of Alexandria, *Commentary on John 16*

28 June
Saint Irenaeus, *bishop and martyr*
MEMORIAL

He was a native of Asia Minor, born at Smyrna about the year 130, and a disciple of St Polycarp the celebrated bishop of that see. Polycarp in his time had been a disciple of St John (see 23 February).

We do not know how, or why, but Irenaeus became a priest of Lyons in France, and succeeded to the martyred bishop there in the last quarter of the second century. He was deeply conscious of the preciousness of the tradition of faith and is in a sense the father of Catholic orthodoxy, as his writings against the Gnostic heretics are mines of information on the beliefs and teaching of the early Church.

He wrote in Greek, but only fragments of the original are preserved. His major work, *Against the Heresies,* exists in a very early Latin translation; the text quoted in the reading given here, exists only in an Armenian version. We can, however, be sure of the fidelity of the texts we have.

St Irenaeus is believed to have suffered martyrdom about the year 200/202.

It was to Jerusalem that the prophets were sent by God through the Holy Spirit. They instructed the people and turned them to the God of their fathers, the Almighty; and they became heralds of the revelation of our Lord Jesus Christ the Son of God, declaring that from the posterity of David his flesh should blossom forth; that after the flesh he might be the son of David, but according to the spirit, Son of God, pre-existing with the Father, begotten before all the creation of the world, and at the end of the times appearing to all the world as man, the Word of God gathering up in himself all things that are in heaven and that are on earth (Eph 1:10).

So then he united man with God, and established a community of union between God and man; since we could not in any other way participate in incorruption, save by his coming among us. For so long as incorruption was invisible and unrevealed, it helped us not at all: therefore it became visible, that in all respects we might participate in the reception of incorruption. And, because in the original formation of Adam all of us were tied and bound up with death through his disobedience, it was right that through the obedience of him who was made man for us we should be released from death: and because death reigned over the flesh, it was right that through the flesh it should lose its force and let man go free from its oppression. So 'the Word was made flesh' (Jn 1:14), that, through that very flesh which sin had ruled and dominated, it should lose its force and be no longer in us. And therefore our Lord took that same original formation as his entry into flesh, so that he might draw near and contend on behalf of the fathers, and conquer by Adam that which by Adam had stricken us down.

Whence then is the substance of the first-formed man? From the will and the wisdom of God, and from the virgin earth. 'For God had not sent rain', the scripture says, 'upon the earth', before man was made; 'and there was no man to till the earth' (Gen 2:5). From this then, whilst it was still virgin, God took dust of the earth and formed the man, the beginning of mankind. So then the Lord, summing up afresh this man, took the same dispensation of entry into flesh, being born from the Virgin by the will and the wisdom of God; that he also should show forth the likeness of Adam's entry into flesh, and there should be that which was written in the beginning, man after the image and likeness of God (Gen 1:26).

And just as through a disobedient virgin man was stricken down and fell into death, so through the Virgin who was obedient to the Word of God man was reanimated and received life.

St Irenaeus, *The Demonstration of the Apostolic Preaching* nn 30, 31, 32, 33

29 June
Saints Peter and Paul, *apostles*
SOLEMNITY

Referred to symbolically as the twin columns of the Church of God, Saints Peter and Paul have been celebrated together on this day since at least the fourth century. It is believed that Peter may have been martyred two years before St Paul, and it is generally accepted that Paul bore his witness in the year 67 of our era. Traditionally St Peter died by crucifixion, St Paul by beheading — as a Roman citizen he would have been exempt from the more ignominious form of death.

Long ago the pope celebrated two Masses on this day, one in St Peter's, the other in St Paul's. Subsequently the Mass of St Paul was transferred to 30 June, but that commemoration is now suppressed.

There is absolutely no reason to doubt the tradition that both apostles did die in Rome and were regarded as the founders of the Roman Church. The date may represent history, or, quite possibly, a theology; for this day, 29 June, was celebrated in pagan Rome as the day of the city's foundation by Romulus.

The reading is taken from the same sermon of St Augustine as is the reading given on this day in the Divine Office. (A reading from St Cyprian is given in the *Glenstal Bible Missal*.)

In Peter, firmness is especially commended to the Church: for he followed the Lord going to his passion, and a certain weakness is remarked: because when questioned by a handmaid, he denied his Lord. Strange! the lover suddenly turned denier! . . . He, who had been presumptuous about himself, discovers himself. For, as you know, he had said: 'Lord, I will never fall away. Even if I must die with you, I will not deny you' (Mt 26:33, 35); and the Lord replies to this presumptuous one: 'Will you lay down your life for me? Truly, truly, I say to you, the cock will not crow, till you have denied me three times' (Jn 13:38). What the doctor had foretold took place: the sick man was unable to do what he thought he could. But then what? — Immediately 'the Lord looked at him'. So it is written, so the Gospel says; the Lord looked at him, 'and he went out and wept bitterly' (Lk 22:61, 62). He went out, this means to confess. 'He wept bitterly', who had known what it is to love. In love sweetness followed, the bitterness of which in sorrow had gone before.

168

Paul comes out of Saul, the lamb out of the wolf; first enemy, then apostle; first persecutor, then preacher. Let him come, let him receive letters from the chief priests, so that wherever he might find Christians he should bring them, bound, for punishment. Let him, yes, let him receive, let him set out, journey, seek carnage, thirst for blood: 'He who dwells in the heavens, will mock him' (Ps 2:4). For he went, as is written, breathing carnage, and was drawing near Damascus. Then from heaven the Lord intervened: 'Saul, Saul, why do you persecute me?' I am here, I am there: here the head, there the body. Not for us to wonder, then, my brothers, we belong to the body of Christ. 'Saul, Saul, why do you persecute me? It hurts you to kick against the goad' (Acts 9:4; 26:15). You wound yourself; for my Church grows through persecutions.

Then frightened and trembling he said: 'Who are you, Lord?' And he, 'I am Jesus the Nazarene, whom you are persecuting.' Straightaway he is a changed man, awaits his orders: he lays aside his grudge, makes ready his obedience. He is told what he is to do. And before Paul is baptized, the Lord says to Ananias: Go to such a street, and to such a man, Saul by name, baptize him; because he is a chosen vessel of mine. A vessel ought to hold something, it ought not be empty! The vessel is to be filled: from whence save from grace?

Ananias, however, replied to our Lord Jesus Christ: 'Lord, I have heard that this man has done much ill to your saints. And now he bears letters from the chief priests, that wherever he should find men belonging to this way, he is to lead them off as prisoners.' And the Lord said to him, 'I shall show him what things he must suffer for my name.' Ananias was alarmed at the mention of Saul's name: even under the shepherd's care the feeble sheep was alarmed at the common talk about the wolf.

The Lord indeed showed him the things he had to suffer for his name. Afterwards he occupied him in his work. He occupied him in chains, in stripes, in prisons, in shipwrecks. He took care of suffering for him, he brought him to this day. One day of suffering for two apostles. But these two were one: although they suffered on different days, they were one. Peter went ahead, Paul followed. Let our way, then, be made straight in the Lord. It is narrow, thorny, hard: and for so many who go along it, it is made smooth! The Lord himself went along it, the unshaken apostles, afterwards the martyrs; boys, women, girls. But who in them? He who said, 'Without me you can do nothing' (John 15:5).

St Augustine, *Sermon 295*, nn 3, 6, 8

30 June
The First Martyrs of the Church of Rome
OPTIONAL MEMORIAL

This memorial celebrates those martyrs who suffered during the first persecution under the emperor Nero in the year 64. Rome had been in great part burnt and Nero sought to make the Christians the scapegoats. Most would have suffered in the Vatican Circus. The early Church Fathers recount the savagery with which the church in Rome was then assailed, and how firm it remained in the faith. The pagan historian Tacitus, who had absolutely no use for the Christians, nonetheless tells us that their sufferings moved the crowds to pity.

The pattern of fidelity and patience in suffering was to be followed by the Christians of Rome for nearly two hundred and fifty years.

St Clement's account of the persecution is given in the Divine Office under this date.

The reading offered here is taken from Lactantius' Epitome of the Divine Institutes. The passage is one where he sets out and rejects the pagan objections to the Christians in summary form, while outlining the cruelty of the persecutors.

If, however, someone, terrified neither by threats nor torments, prefers his faith to his life, against such a one cruelty puts forth all its strength, contrives torture unspeakable, unbearable; and just because it is known that death for God's sake is glorious, and that victory consists in rising superior to torment, and in laying down life itself for faith and religion — why, then, these men too strive to win a victory. Not by death do they afflict us, but devise new and unheard of cruelties, to compel human frailty to succumb to bodily anguish. Should this fail, they defer things; they apply to wounds every care, that reiterated torture may increase the pain in scars still raw, plying the rack against the innocent. They actually consider themselves pious, just, and religious (for with such rites their gods are well pleased), while they speak of the martyrs as impious and beyond remedy. What perversity is this, to call an innocent and tortured victim a desperate and impious creature, while the tormentor is called just and pious!

It is said that people are rightly and deservedly punished who revile the religious observances of the State, which have been handed down by their ancestors. What if those ancestors were fools in adopting vain rites (as we have already shown), are *we* to be hindered from pursuing a true and a better course? Why abandon our liberty and become slaves to alien errors, as though we were sold to them? Allow us to be wise and to search after truth. Yet, should they elect to defend ancestral religions, why are the Egyptians exempt, who worship cattle and creatures of every kind as deities? Why do actors on the comic stage ridicule the gods themselves? and why is he honoured who has mocked these gods with the greater wit? Why are philosophers listened to, when they affirm that there are no gods, or that, if they do exist, they have no care or regard for human affairs, or argue that there is no providential order in the world? Of all mankind those alone are judged irreligious who follow after God's truth! Since this truth is both justice and wisdom, these people brand it as a crime, counting it irreligion or folly; they obviously do not understand the nature of what is deceiving them, when they call evil good, and good evil.

Lactantius, *Epitome of the Divine Institutes*, cc 54, 55 (excerpts)

3 July
Saint Thomas, *apostle*
FEAST

Thomas was a Galilaean, one of the Twelve. His Syriac name means the Twin, the Greek form of which would be Didymus. He appears frequently in the Gospel narratives, particularly in the resurrection narratives of St John, and one such account is used in today's Mass. Otherwise we know nothing from early written sources about him. Traditionally he was believed to have preached the Gospel in India, where he is said to have been martyred. The

Christians of South India claim to be descended from his converts, and, while there are some difficulties with this, the claim cannot be discounted.

Today's feast derives from Edessa, where, on this day, since the sixth century, the feast of the translation of his relics has been kept.

The reading is from St Augustine and the sermon was originally given in Eastertide.

Call to mind the first stage of the world's making. 'Darkness was upon the deep; and the Spirit of God was borne upon the waters. And God said: 'Let there be light'; and there was light. . . . And God separated the light from the darkness, and he called the light Day and the darkness Night' (Gen 1:2-5). Call to mind the darkness of these newly baptized before they came for the remission of sins. Well, then, darkness was upon the deep before these same sins were remitted. But the Spirit of God was borne upon the waters: these went down into the water, the Spirit of God was borne upon the waters, the darkness of their sins was driven away. 'This is the day which the Lord has made.' For this day the apostle says: 'For you were once darkness, now however light in the Lord' (Eph 5:8). Did he say: you were darkness in the Lord? No, rather, darkness in you: light in the Lord. But the Lord called the light Day; because by his grace whatever is done is done. They were able by themselves to be darkness: they were not able to become light, except by the making of the Lord. 'For this is the day which the Lord has made'; the day did not make itself, no, the Lord made it!

Wasn't Thomas, one of the disciples, a man; one of the crowd, as it were? His fellow disciples said to him: 'We have seen the Lord'. And he said: Unless I shall have touched, unless I shall have placed my finger in his side, I shall not believe (cf John 20:25). The evangelists announce it to you, Thomas, and you do not believe. The world has believed them, and the disciple does not believe. Of them it is said: 'Their sound has gone through all the earth, and their words to the utmost bounds of the world' (Ps 18:5). Their words go out, they reach to the utmost bounds of the earth; the whole world believes: they all announce it to one, and he does not believe. It was not the day which the Lord had made. Darkness was still on the deep, in the depth of the human heart: darkness was there. May he come, may the head, the source of this day come, and say as one patient, meek, not ang-ered, because a physician: Come, do come, touch this and believe. You said: Unless I shall have touched, unless I shall have placed my finger, I shall not believe. Come, touch, put your finger here, and don't be unbelieving, but faithful. Come, put your finger. I knew your wounds; for you I kept my scars.

Now, clearly, placing his hand, he makes full his faith. For what is the fullness of faith? That Christ be believed not only man, that Christ be believed not only God, but man and God. That is the very fullness of faith: 'For the Word was made flesh and dwelt among us' (John 1:14). This disciple, therefore, when he touched his Saviour's scars and members offered for his touching, exclaimed: 'My Lord and my God' (John 20:28). He touched the man, he recognized his God: he touched the flesh, he looked upon the Word. 'Because the Word was made flesh and dwelt amongst us.' This Word suffered his flesh to be hung upon the wood: this Word suffered the nails to be fixed in his flesh: this Word suffered that his flesh should be pierced by a lance: this Word suffered his flesh to be placed in the tomb: this Word raised his flesh, exhibiting it to the sight of his disciples to be seen, proferred it to be felt by their hands. They touch, they exclaim: 'My Lord and my God'. This is the day which the Lord has made: for you were once darkness, now however light in the Lord.

St Augustine, *Sermon 258*, nn 2, 3

4 July
Saint Elizabeth of Portugal
OPTIONAL MEMORIAL

Elizabeth was born in 1271 and belonged to the royal house of Aragon. At the age of twelve she was married to the king of Portugal and had two children. The marriage was unhappy and there were endless dynastic quarrels. Elizabeth had recourse to prayer and austerity of life in this situation, and persevered in this way of life in spite of seeming lack of fruit or success. When widowed she distributed all her personal goods to the poor and joined the Third Order Regular of St Francis. She died in 1336 while trying to reconcile her son and grandson who had gone to war with each other.

The reading is from the Decree of Vatican II 'On the Apostolate of the Laity'. The passage is almost a commentary on the life and ideals of St Elizabeth.

They who have this faith live in the hope of what will be revealed to the sons of God and bear in mind the cross and resurrection of the Lord.

In the pilgrimage of this life, hidden with Christ in God and free from enslavement to wealth, they aspire to those riches which remain forever, and generously dedicate their entire selves to spreading God's kingdom and to fashioning and perfecting the sphere of earthly things according to the spirit of Christ. Among the struggles of this life, they find strength in hope, convinced that 'the sufferings of the present time are not worthy to be compared with the glory to come that will be revealed in us' (Rom 8:18).

Impelled by divine charity, they do good to all, especially to those of the household of the faith (cf Gal 6:10), laying aside 'all malice and all deceit and pretence, and envy, and all slander' (1 Pet 2:1), and thereby they draw others to Christ. This charity of God, which 'is poured forth in our hearts by the Holy Spirit who has been given to us' (Rom 5:5), enables the laity to express the true spirit of the beatitudes in their lives. Following Jesus who was poor, they are neither depressed by the lack of temporal goods nor puffed up by their abundance. Imitating Christ who was humble, they have no obsession for empty honours (cf Gal 5:26) but seek to please God rather than the world, ever ready to leave all things for Christ's sake (cf Lk 14:26) and to suffer persecution for justice' sake (cf Mt 5:10). For they remember the words of the Lord, 'If anyone wishes to come after me, let him deny himself, and take up his cross, and follow me' (Mt 16:24). Promoting Christian friendship among themselves, they help one another in any kind of necessity.

The lay person's religious programme of life should take its special quality from their status as a married man or woman and a family person, or as one who is unmarried or widowed, from their state of health, and from their professional and social activity. They should not cease to earnestly develop the qualities and talents bestowed on them in accord with these conditions of life, and they should make use of the gifts which they have received from the Holy Spirit.

Furthermore, the laity who in pursuit of their vocation have become members of one of the associations or institutes approved by the Church are trying faithfully to adopt the special characteristics of the spiritual life which are proper to these as well. They should also hold in high esteem professional skill, family and civic spirit, and the virtues relating to social behaviour, namely, honesty, justice, sincerity, kindness, and courage, without which there can be no true christian life.

Decree on the Apostolate of the Laity, n 4

5 July
Saint Anthony Zaccaria, *priest*
OPTIONAL MEMORIAL

Anthony was a native of Cremona in Lombardy and born in 1502. He first qualified as a medical doctor, then entered the priesthood. Working in the priestly ministry at Milan he found there was much need of reform and evangelization. He founded first a congregation of women religious and then the Clerks Regular of St Paul in 1530. The latter came to be called Barnabites after the church they served.

St Anthony died in 1539.

The spiritual emphases favoured by St Anthony were devotion to the passion of Christ, to the scriptures, especially the writings of St Paul, and to the Blessed Sacrament.

The reading is from a sermon of St Augustine, a sermon which one time was read at the Office of St Anthony.

That which the Lord commands seems hard and burdensome, that 'if any man will come after me, let him deny himself and take up his cross and follow me'; but what he commands is neither hard nor heavy when he gives help for the doing of what he commands. For what the psalmist says is true: Because of the words of your lips I have kept to hard ways. That which is hard as a precept is made easy by love.

We know how great the power of love is. But what is this 'let him deny himself'? Let such put no trust in themselves, knowing that he or she is weak and regarding the words of the prophet: Cursed be the one that puts his trust in men. Let such as these mistrust themselves, not sinking down but cleaving to God.

Where are we to follow the Lord? We know where he has gone: he has risen from the dead and gone up into heaven. We must follow him there. And certainly we must not despair, not because we can do anything, but because he promised. Why then need we despair, since we are the members and he the head? It is good to follow him, but we must see where we are to follow. When the Lord Jesus uttered these words he was not yet risen from the dead: he had not yet suffered. He had still to come to the cross, to shame, to abuse, to scourging, to thorns, to wounds, to insults, to outrage, to death. The way is rough: you hold back, you do not wish to take it. Nevertheless, take it. For who would not wish to attain to glory? To be raised up delights all of us, but the first step to it is humility.

Take up your cross and follow the Lord: and what is the cross which the Lord has told us to carry, that we may follow him the more speedily? What does it mean but the frailty of this flesh of ours? For it is that which crucifies us, until death is swallowed up in victory. Therefore this cross itself must be crucified and pierced with the nails of the fear of God, lest you may not be able to shoulder the burden as long as it is free to struggle; for it is impossible to follow the Lord without carrying it. And how can you follow him if you are not his? For they that are Jesus Christ's, says the apostle, have crucified their flesh with its passions and desires.

St Augustine, *Sermon*

6 July
Saint Maria Goretti, *virgin and martyr*
OPTIONAL MEMORIAL

Maria was born into a poor Italian family at Ancona in 1890. The family moved to Ferriere di Conca in the Roman Campagna. There, when Maria was aged twelve, a local eighteen year old came into the house one day wishing to do her violence. She refused, according to his early testimony, and in anger he stabbed her many times. She died in hospital twenty-four hours later. Her last hours were marked by patient consideration for others and complete forgive-

ness of her assailant. Maria had always been remarkable for goodness and
was no sudden saint. She was canonized by Pope Pius XII in 1950.

The reading is from St Augustine, Treatise on St John.

'If anyone serves me, he must follow me.' What is meant by this 'he
must follow me' but, he must imitate me. For Christ suffered for us,
the apostle Peter says, leaving us an example, that we might follow in
his footsteps (1 Pt 2:21). You have heard what has been said, 'If anyone serves me, he must follow me' — with what consequence and for
what reward or prize? 'And where I am', he says, 'my servant will be
there too'. He must be loved gladly, that the reward for work by
which he is served, is to be with him. For where will one be well off
without him, or, with him, when can one be badly off?

Understand more clearly. 'If anyone serves me, my Father will
honour him.' With what honour, except that he should be with his
Son? For what he said earlier, 'where I am, my servant will be there
too', this he is understood to explain when he says, 'my Father will
honour him'. For what greater honour could the adopted child
receive, than that he should be where the only-begotten is, not made
equal according to the divine nature, but sharing in eternity?

We ought preferably ask, what to serve Christ, the work for which
such a reward is offered, means? They serve Jesus Christ, who do not
seek their own interests, but those of Jesus Christ (cf Phil 2:21). For
this is, 'he must follow me', he must walk in my ways, not his: as it is
written elsewhere, 'whoever says, he abides in him, ought to walk in
the same way in which he walked' (1 Jn 2:6). Christ's follower ought
also, if he or she gives bread to the hungry, act out of mercy not out of
ostentation; seek nothing else by such an act than the good work, the
left hand not knowing what the right is doing. One is a servant of
Christ who not only carries out the corporal works of mercy, but does
all good works on account of Christ, up to that work of great love,
which is to lay down one's life for the other: for this is to lay it down
for Christ. For such work Jesus even deigned to make himself and be
called a servant, when he says, 'Just as the son of man did not come to
be served, but to serve and to lay down his life for many' (Matt 20:28).

When you hear the Lord saying, brethren, 'Where I am my servant
will be there too', it follows that you are not to think only of good

bishops and clergy. You, in your way, are to serve Christ — by living well, by giving alms, by spreading his name and teaching as you can.

For that greatest service, that of suffering, many of your number have offered themselves: many who were not bishops or clergy, but youths and virgins, old with young, many married men and women, many fathers and mothers of families, serving Christ, they even laid down their lives in his witness, and received most glorious crowns from the Father who honoured them.

St Augustine, *Treatise 51 on John,* nn 11, 12, 13

11 July
Saint Benedict, *abbot*
MEMORIAL/IN EUROPE: FEAST

Benedict of Nursia, now Norcia, in central Italy, flourished in the first half of the sixth century. It is generally accepted that he was born about the year 480 and died some time around 550. Our only source for his life is the Second Book of the Dialogues of St Gregory the Great. Some query the authorship of the Dialogues but this is of little consequence, for the outline of Benedict's life makes no attempt to give precise dates, and the language of his Rule, his own surviving writing, is typical of central Italy in the first half of the sixth century.

It is, in fact, the Rule of Benedict which constitutes his greatness, and it was one of the formative documents of Western Europe. It should not be thought that Benedict's own disciples were responsible for the Rule's spread and influence. Monasticism spread and developed under the leadership of others, but gradually, whatever about its origins, came to adopt the Rule of Benedict. What commends the Rule is its wisdom and balance, and, for all that it is not very long, its completeness.

Benedict's traditional day of death was 21 March. Since at least the eighth century a celebration has been held on today's date, either to commemorate the transfer of his relics to Gaul, or to celebrate his patronage.

In 1964 Pope Paul VI declared St Benedict Patron of Europe.

The reading is from Chapter 4 of the Rule entitled, 'Which are the tools of good works'. The text of the chapter was taken by Benedict from an earlier rule, but he made it his own — the monk must first be a Christian!

In the first place to love the Lord God from one's whole heart, with all one's mind, with all one's strength,

then to love one's neighbour as one's very self.
Then, not to kill,
not to commit adultery,
not to steal,
not to covet,
not to give false witness;
to honour all men,
and not to do to another what one would not wish done to oneself.
To practice self renunciation, in order to follow Christ:
to bring one's body under control,
not to set one's mind on pleasures,
to love to do without.
To build up those in need:
to clothe the naked,
to care for the sick,
to bury the dead,
to assist those in any distress,
to comfort the afflicted.
To make oneself a stranger to worldly doings:
to put nothing before the love of Christ,
not to give vent to one's anger,
not to store up an occasion for wrathfulness,
not to nurture deceit in one's heart,
not to offer a treacherous peace,
not to abandon love.
Not to swear, lest it happen one perjures oneself,
to utter truth from one's heart and mouth.
Not to return hurt for hurt,
not to do injury, but to suffer patiently injuries done to oneself;
to love those hostile to oneself:
not to return a curse on those who curse one, but rather to bless them;
to bear with persecution for acting righteously . . .
in Christ's love to pray for those hostile to one:
to make peace before sunset with one with whom one has differed.
And never to despair of God's mercy.

Rule of Benedict, c 4: vv 1-33, 72-74

13 July
Saint Henry
OPTIONAL MEMORIAL

Henry was born in 973, and succeeded his father as Duke of Bavaria in 995. In 1002 he was chosen as emperor, but was only crowned by the pope in 1014. He has been accused of using the Church in his own interests, at least in the early years of his reign, but he certainly developed into a great, good and just ruler, a man of prayer and humble of heart. He did much for the reform of the Church, whether among bishops or monks; his policies — at times rather high-handed — were to be continued by the popes, and this was to lead them into conflict with those who succeeded Henry II as emperors.

Among monks, Henry promoted the reforms of Richard of St Vanne and of Cluny — of whose abbot, St Odilo, he became a close friend.

Henry had no children. We do not know whether this was because he and his wife had renounced the use of marriage, or whether it was simply the disposition of providence.

Henry died in 1024 and was canonized by Eugene III in 1146.

The reading is from St Bernard, book I of his *Five Books on Consideration: Advice to a Pope*. The treatise was, in fact, addressed to Eugene III. The passage is chosen because of its universal relevance.

What is as valuable as consideration which benevolently presumes to take part in an action by anticipating and planning what must be done? This is absolutely necessary. Affairs which have been thought out and planned in advance can be accomplished efficiently, but they can lead to great danger if done haphazardly. I have no doubt that you can recall frequent experiences of this kind in legal affairs, in important business matters, or in any deliberations of significance.

Now, of primary importance is the fact that consideration purifies its source, that is, the mind. Notice also that it controls the emotions, guides actions, corrects excesses, improves behaviour, confers dignity and order on life, and even imparts knowledge of divine and human affairs. It puts an end to confusion, closes gaps, gathers up what has been scattered, roots out secrets, hunts down truth, scrutinizes what seems to be true, and explores lies and deceit. It decides what is to be done and reviews what has been done in order to eliminate from the mind anything deficient or in need of correction. Consideration anticipates adversity when all is going well and when adversity comes, it stands firm. In this it displays both prudence and fortitude.

Since you have just seen that prudence is the mother of fortitude, and that it is not fortitude but temerity to dare something that prudence has not conceived, observe the delightful and harmonious inter-mingling of the virtues and how one depends on the other. Prudence is the mean of desire and necessity, and like a judge it sets definite boundaries for both. For some it provides what is needed, for others it curtails what is excessive. In this way it forms a third virtue called temperance. Consideration judges intemperate both the person who obstinately denies himself necessities and the one who indulges in excess. Thus, temperance is not only the rejection of what is excessive, but also the acceptance of what is necessary. The apostle seems not only to have promoted this idea, but to have originated it, for he teaches us not to provide for the flesh in its desires (Rom 13:4). Indeed, when he says not to provide for the flesh, he moderates excess; when he adds, 'in its desires', he admits necessities. There-fore, it seems to me not altogether absurd to define temperance as a virtue which neither excludes necessity nor exceeds it. As the philos-opher says, 'Nothing in excess.'

St Bernard of Clairvaux, *On Consideration: Advice to a Pope*, Bk I, 8-9

14 July
Saint Camillus de Lellis, *priest*
OPTIONAL MEMORIAL

Camillus was a native of south central Italy who was born in 1550, when his mother was long past the usual age for bearing children. He developed into a very tall young man and would have followed his father in the career of arms. This did not quite work out. Eventually Camillus was converted from a rather empty life and tried to become a Franciscan. Health told against him and he undertook the voluntary care of the sick in the Roman hospital of San Giacomo.

Gradually his vocation became clearer. He gathered some like-minded fel-lows devoted to the nursing of the sick and prisoners, 'The Ministers of the Sick'. They were approved as a congregation in 1586, and raised to the status of an Order in 1591. Camillus and his followers cared not only for the bodies but also for the souls of their patients and Camillus and many of his followers were ordained priest.

Camillus was deeply concerned for hygiene and fresh air, in this being several centuries in advance of his times, and also for the sacramental life, penance, anointing of the sick and Viaticum.

St Philip Neri had been a close friend and adviser to him.

St Camillus died in 1614 in Rome.

The reading is the account of his death given by C.C. Martindale, SJ.

All that Sunday, Camillus seemed alive 'only to pray', which he did continuously, helping himself by that picture of the crucifixion which reminded him of that Precious Blood for the sake of which alone he felt he could ask for his salvation. The night seemed to him intolerably long, though he knew he would not die during it and insisted that only one priest should remain with him, adding: 'This is the last night you will have to do so, because tomorrow evening I shall pass from this life. I do not know if the Fathers are thinking about my burial?' Fr Califano said it had been spoken of, but nothing was decided. 'I say so,' replied the Saint, 'because you will not have longer than tomorrow.'

In the morning he asked what time it was. 'Twelve,' he was told.* 'So late? And you have not thought of celebrating Mass yet? Yet it will be the last that I shall hear.' It was then celebrated: he followed it closely, making special signs during the Creed at the words 'Suffered under Pontius Pilate' and at 'Thence He shall come'. At the Memento for the Living, he said: 'Brothers, help me! Now is the time! Prayer, prayer, that the Lord may save me.' At the elevation, he whispered: 'Lord, Lord, mercy through thy Precious Blood!' and again he said this at the Confiteor before that Communion which was his last before the eternal one.

During the day he sent to ask for prayers but would have no visitors save the Cardinal Protector whom he thanked and then two doctors. To one he said: 'I am very soon expecting the Lord's call.' To the other: 'Hullo, Signor Galliano, a different Doctor is expecting me!' At three in the afternoon, he asked the time. ('Oh how long,' he said, 'is

---

* Hours were reckoned from the evening Ave Maria: the twelfth hour, therefore, in the summer, was 8 am.

today!') He begged that his companions should remain around him, saying psalms and other prayers to which he answered as best he could. His confessor sprinkled him — sparingly — with holy water. 'More water! more holy water!' he murmured. The confessor complied. 'Now that is all right,' said he. He recited the evening Ave Maria 'very well'. After an hour and a quarter, they asked him if he would not take some refreshment. 'In another quarter of an hour,' he said, 'I *shall* be refreshed.' After that quarter of an hour, he did indeed seem supernaturally better. A priest bent over him, and said that since God was desirous of recalling him to himself, he must fix all his hope in Christ crucified and his Precious Blood shed for us — in him in whom is our salvation, life and resurrection — through whom we are saved and are set free. Camillus's eyes showed that he understood so dear a recollection. The Passing Bell was sounded, and all his Brothers came. The penitential psalms (as he had wished) were said, and then the prayers for the dying. He looked once more at the crucifix, and then towards heaven. He spread his arms out crosswise and then died, while they said the liturgical words: 'May the vision of Jesus Christ gentle and joyous appear to thee.' This was about 9.45, on Monday evening July 14, 1614: Camillus was sixty-four years old, two months and twenty days.

C.C. Martindale, SJ, Life of St Camillus, p 150-2

15 July

Saint Bonaventure, *bishop and doctor of the Church*
MEMORIAL

Bonaventure was born in the first quarter of the thirteenth century at Bagnoregio in Tuscany. He entered the Franciscans in 1243 and was sent to study in Paris. He was very successful in his studies and became one of the leading theologians in the university, where he was a contemporary and friend of St Thomas Aquinas. In 1257 he was elected Minister General of his Order, and became virtually its second founder, for it was he who suggested the constitutions which were to determine all future developments.

He was named as archbishop of York but managed to effectively decline the appointment. Some years later though, he was appointed Cardinal Bishop of Albano, and the pope would brook no refusal. He became one of the pope's chief theological advisors and did much of the preparatory work for the Council of Lyons. He died in Lyons in 1274, just at the conclusion of the Council.

St Bonaventure's theology and his writings lean more to the tradition of St Augustine and on spiritual affection than on intellect. As a consequence, some would view him more as a mystic than as a theologian, but this is, perhaps, to misjudge theology.

The reading is from his Breviloquium.

When humankind sinned, it went astray, rejecting the most mighty, wise, and benevolent Principle. As a result, we fell headlong into weakness, ignorance, and malice. From having been spiritual, we became carnal, animal, and sensual. We could no longer imitate divine power, behold divine light, or love divine goodness. The most perfect way for us to be raised out of this misery was for the first Principle to come down to our level, offering himself to us as an accessible object of knowledge, love, and imitation. We, carnal, animal, and sensual, could not know, love, or imitate anything that was not both proportionate and similar to ourselves. So, in order to raise us out of this state, 'the Word was made flesh'; that he might be known and loved and imitated by us who are flesh, and that we, so knowing and loving and imitating God, might be healed of the disease of sin.

Finally, humanity could not be completely healed unless it recovered purity of soul, the friendship of God, and its proper excellence whereby it had been subject to none but God. Since such a thing could not be brought about except by God in 'the nature of a slave', it was fitting that the Word be made flesh.

Humankind could not have recovered its former excellence through any restorer other than God. Had it been a mere creature, we would have been subject to this mere creature, and thus could not have recovered the state of excellence.

Nor could we have recovered the friendship of God except through a fitting mediator, who would be the likeness and the friend of both: God in his divinity, and man in his humanity.

Nor, again, could we have recovered purity of soul if our sin had not been blotted out, which divine justice could not fittingly bring about except after adequate atonement had been made. And because God alone could provide atonement for the whole of humankind, and we alone must provide it, for we had sinned: therefore the best of ways was that humankind be restored by the God-man, born of Adam's race.

Now, since we could not have recovered excellence except through the most excellent restorer, nor friendship except through the most friendly mediator, nor purity of soul except through the most superabundant satisfier; and the most excellent restorer could be none but God, the most friendly mediator, none but a human being, and the most superabundant satisfier, none but him who was both God and a human being: therefore, it was absolutely the most fitting thing for our restoration that the Word become incarnate. For as the human race came into being through the Word Not Made, and as it sinned because it failed to heed the Word Inspired, so it would rise from sin through the Word Made Flesh.

St Bonaventure, *Breviloquium,* part IV, c 1

16 July
Our Lady of Mount Carmel
OPTIONAL MEMORIAL

This Memorial was introduced into the Order of Carmel in the fourteenth century and into the Roman Calendar in 1726. The development of the Memorial was closely linked with devotion to the brown scapular.

The Order of Carmel goes back to a group of Western hermits who, at least in the twelfth century, had settled on Carmel, overlooking the plain of Galilee, in imitation of and inspired by the prophet Elijah (cf 1 Kgs 18:19-46; for Elisha: 2 Kgs 2:25). They grouped themselves around a small chapel dedicated to Our Lady, and this was to be the origin of their devotion. In the thirteenth century the Order of Carmel, as we know it, was formed, and it remained marked with the twin devotion of the early hermits — to Elijah and his solitary prayer, and to Our Lady under the title of Mount Carmel.

The reading is from St Vincent of Lerins, a monk of much earlier times: he expounds Mary's title of Mother of God.

This unity of the person in Christ was formed and completed, not after the birth from the Virgin, but in the very womb of the Virgin. We must therefore take utmost care to be precise in our confession, so as to say that Christ is not merely *one*, but that he always has been *one*. It were, indeed, an intolerable blasphemy to assert that, although you admit his now being one, you contend that he once was not one but two — one after his baptism, but two at the time of his birth.

We cannot escape this enormous sacrilege unless we assert that humanity has been united to divinity through the unity of person, not through the ascension or resurrection or baptism, but within his mother, in her womb, and — even more — in the virginal conception itself. Because of this unity of person, it happens that what is proper to God is ascribed to the man, and what is proper to the flesh is ascribed to God — indifferently and without distinction. Therefore, as it is written in holy scripture: 'He that descended from heaven, the son of man who is in heaven' (Jn 3:13), and 'crucified the Lord of glory' (1 Cor 2:8) on earth. Furthermore, since the body of the Lord was made and created, it is said that the 'Word' of God himself was 'made' (Jn 1:14), his wisdom filled up (Sir 24:35), his knowledge created (Sir 1:4; 24:36). Therefore, also, the prophetic writings refer to his hands and feet as 'pierced' (Ps 21:17). Through this unity of person it also becomes perfectly clear — by reason of a similar mystery — that it is most truly Catholic to believe (and most impious to deny) that the Word of God himself was born from the Virgin even as the flesh of the Word was born from an immaculate mother.

Therefore, may God forbid that anyone should attempt to defraud holy Mary of her privileges of divine grace and her special glory. For by a unique favour of our Lord and God she is confessed to be the most true and most blessed mother of God (theótokos). She is truly the mother of God, not merely in name, as a certain impious heresy claims, because she gave birth to a man who later became God, as we call the mother of priests or bishops such, because she gave birth, not to a priest or a bishop, but to a child who later became one.

Not thus, I say, is holy Mary the mother of God, but rather because, as has already been said, in her sacred womb was accomplished the mystery that, by reason of a certain singular and unique unity of person, even as the Word is flesh in flesh, so the man is God in God.

St Vincent of Lerins, *The Commonitories*, c 15

21 July
Saint Laurence of Brindisi, *priest and doctor of the Church*
OPTIONAL MEMORIAL

Laurence was born, as his name suggests, in Brindisi, in 1559, and entered the Friars Minor Capuchins at the age of sixteen. He proved himself a gifted linguist and developed into a competent scripture scholar, as well as an accomplished preacher. He worked for the Catholic counter-reform in Austria, Bohemia and South Germany with great success until elected to be head of the Capuchins. Another gift he possessed was that of diplomacy and he was used by the Church authorities for many delicate tasks.

He died in 1619 while on a diplomatic mission to the king of Spain, his purpose having been to persuade the king to change his viceroy in Naples.

With all his gifts and in spite of much involvement in affairs he was above all a mystic and a man of prayer.

The reading is taken from St Bonaventure, *The Journey of the Mind to God.*

Corresponding to the six degrees of the soul's ascent to God there are within the soul six kinds of faculties or powers by which we rise from depths to the heights, from external to things internal, from things of time to those of eternity. These are sense, imagination, reason, intellect, intelligence, and the fine point or apex of the soul. These powers we have implanted in us by nature; by sin deformed, they are reformed through grace; and they must be purified by justice, exercised by knowledge, and made perfect by wisdom.

In their primitive constitution human beings were created by God capable of untroubled contemplation, and for that reason were placed by God in a 'garden of delights'. But, turning their backs on the true light in order to pursue the mutable good, they found themselves through their own fault, diminished and removed from their pristine stature. The whole human race, through original sin, was thus afflicted in a twofold manner: the human mind by ignorance and the human body by concupiscence. As a result humanity, blinded and bent down, sits in darkness and sees not the light of heaven, unless it be strengthened against concupiscence by grace with justice, and against ignorance by knowledge with wisdom. All this is done by Jesus Christ, whom God made our wisdom and justice and sanctification and redemption.

He, being the Power and Wisdom of God, the incarnate Word full of grace and truth, is the author of both grace and truth. He it is who infuses the grace of charity which, when it comes 'from a pure heart, and a good conscience and sincere faith' is capable of ordering the whole soul according to the threefold aspect above mentioned. He also taught the knowledge of truth according to the triple mode of theology: by symbolic theology in which he teaches us how we might rightly use sensible things, by theology properly so called wherein we learn the use of things intelligible, and by mystical theology through contact with which we may be raised aloft to things unspeakable.

Those, therefore, who would set out in quest of God must first leave aside such sins as deform nature, and engage in the exercise of the aforesaid powers of the soul. By prayer they may hope for grace which will readjust their powers in harmony; in a holy life they must seek for purifying justice; in meditation they will seek that knowledge which enlightens; in contemplation they will acquire perfecting wisdom. Therefore, just as no one comes to wisdom save through grace, justice, and knowledge, so no one comes to contemplation save by clear-sighted meditation, by a holy life and devout prayer. As grace is the foundation of an upright will, and of a clear-sighted enlightened reason, so we must first pray, then live holy lives, and, thirdly, we must look long and attentively at the manifestations of truth; and so attending, we must rise, step by step until we reach the high mountain where the God of gods is seen in Sion.

St Bonaventure, *The Journey of the Mind to God*, nn 6, 7, 8

22 July
Saint Mary Magdalen
MEMORIAL

Mary, healed by the Lord of seven demons, accompanied him on his preaching journeys (Lk 8:3), and was present on calvary with our Lady (Jn 19:25). Then, according to the Gospel of Mark, it was to her the risen Lord first appeared. This is her day in all the Eastern Rites and in the Roman calendar since the twelfth century. We do not know when or where she died.

The reading is from St Augustine. Augustine, in fact, discusses the Lord's appearing to Mary in several of his sermons.

Christ the Lord first said to the woman: 'Who are you looking for? Why are you weeping?' She, however, supposed him to be the gardener and said to him: 'Sir', by way of honouring him, for, because she wanted a favour, she called him 'Sir'. 'If you have taken him away, she says, tell me where you have put him, and I will go and remove him.' As if she were saying: He is indispensable to me, not to you. O woman, you suppose the dead Christ is indispensable to you: recognize the living One. You seek the dead; alive, however, he is speaking to you. For having died he would have been of no use to us, unless he had risen from the dead. And he who was sought as one dead, shows himself alive.

How does he show himself alive? He called her by her own name: 'Mary'. And straightaway, having heard her own name, she replied: 'Rabbuni'. For the gardener could have said: 'Who are you looking for? Why are you weeping?' Only the Lord could have said: 'Mary'. He addressed her by her name, who called her to heaven. He spoke that name, which he himself had written in his book (cf Apoc 3:5; 21:27), 'Mary'. She, for her part, 'Rabbuni' — which means Master. She had recognized him, by whom she was enlightened that she should do so: he who first was supposed to be the gardener, is seen to be the Christ.

And the Lord said to her, 'Do not cling to me, because I have not yet ascended to my Father.' What does this mean? 'Do not cling to me, because I have not yet ascended to my Father.' If she could not cling to him standing here on earth, could she cling to him sitting in heaven? As if he were saying: Do not cling to me now, cling to me when I shall have ascended to the Father. What does cling then mean except to believe? For by faith, we cling, we hold on, to Christ. And it is better not to cling on with one's hand, but to hold on by faith, than to touch with one's hand, and not hold on by faith. It was not a great thing to hold on to Christ with one's hand. The Jews held on to him when they arrested him; they held on to him when they bound him; they held on to him when they hung him: they held on, and by holding on for an evil purpose, they lost what they held on to! By holding on by faith, O Catholic Church, your faith makes you whole (cf Matt 9:21).

Hold on only by faith — that is, approach with faith, firmly believe! If you suppose Christ to have been but a man, you have held on to him on earth. If you believe Christ to be God, equal to the Father, then you hold on to him when he has ascended to the Father. He therefore has ascended for us, when we understand him rightly. He only once ascended in time, but ascends now every day. Oh! for how many has he not yet ascended, and for how many does he not still lie in the earth! Finally, let us listen to his words, 'I am ascending to my Father and your Father, to my God and your God.' He is his Father because he begot him; his God because he created him. He begot him as his only-begotten Word, created him from the seed of David according to the flesh.

St Augustine, *Sermon 246*, nn 3, 4, 5

23 July
Saint Bridget, *religious*
OPTIONAL MEMORIAL

Bridget, or Birgitta, was born in Sweden in 1303 and was married in 1316. She belonged to a princely family, but her spirit was formed by the Third Order of St Francis which she had joined as a married woman. On her husband's death in 1344 she devoted herself to the ascetic life, preaching peace to the rulers of Europe and striving to persuade the popes to return to Rome.

She developed into a mystic and visionary. In 1350 she went to Rome for the Holy Year and spent the remainder of her life there apart from a penitential pilgrimage to the Holy Land. She founded an Order of Nuns and canons regular, since popularly known as the Bridgettines, but papal approval for them was not forthcoming until after her death.

She died in Rome in 1373 and her body was brought back to Sweden. She was canonized in 1391.

Bridget wrote accounts of her visions in Swedish which were translated, and, perhaps, altered by her chaplains. It would be foolish to attach importance to the details of these visions. We should understand them in the light of the scholastic adage: whatever is received is received according to the measure of the one who receives it. In other words, our knowledge, our perceiving, is limited and qualified by our temperamental disposition and intellectual outlook.

The reading is from the account of a vision she had of the Passion of our Lord.

And now, as I looked at all this cruelty, overwhelmed with grief I saw his sorrowful mother, trembling and half dead, and her sisters and John comforting her, and they stood not far from the cross on its right side. And then a new pain pierced me, and it was as though I was pierced with an exceeding bitter sword. At length she rose, the sorrowful mother, and looked up at her Son, and her sisters held her up, and she stood there like one living dead, pierced with the sword of grief. And when her Son saw her and the other friends standing there weeping, he commended her in a wailing voice to John. And it was plain to be seen from his bearing and to be heard from his voice that his heart was pierced with compassion for his mother with the sharpest dart of grief.

And then his adorable and beautiful eyes seemed half dead, his mouth was open and bleeding, his face pale and perished, his whole body wan and pale and colourless because there was hardly any more blood. And the skin on his virginal body was so fine and thin that the least blow made a blue mark. Sometimes, when the pain became excessive, he tried to straighten himself on the cross. Sometimes the pains passed from the limbs up the heart and gave him terrible pain, thus making his martyrdom longer with intense suffering and exceeding bitterness. It was then, that overwhelmed with His great pain and near to death, he cried in a moaning voice to his Father: 'Oh Father, why hast thou forsaken me?' His lips were pale and his tongue bleeding. His stomach had fallen in and touched his back, as if it were hollow. And then he cried the second time in the greatest agony: 'Oh Father, into thy hands I commend my spirit.' Then he lifted up his head for a moment, but it fell again at once, and so he gave up his spirit.

When his mother saw this she trembled all over with exceeding great anguish, and she would have fallen to the ground if the other women had not held her up. At the same time his hands fell forward a little because of the weight of his body, which was only held up by the nails that fastened the feet. The fingers and hands and arms were stretched out more than before, the shoulders and the back being, as it were, pressed inwards to the cross.

Then the Jews who were standing by shouted to Mary and said: 'Mary, your son is dead!' But others spoke words of scorn. Then from among the multitude one came running full of rage and thrust a spear into his side with such force as if he would thrust it right through his body. And when he drew out the spear much blood flowed from the wound, and the spear and part of the shaft were quite red and streaming with blood. When his mother saw this it made her tremble and moan exceedingly, so that it could be understood that a sword was passing through her soul.

Now when all were gone some of the friends of the Lord took him down from the cross, and his mother took him in her most holy arms and laid him upon her knees. And he was wounded all over and stained entirely with blood. His sorrowful mother dried his whole body and all his wounds with a linen cloth and then they bore him away in great grief and much weeping and laid him in the grave.

St Bridget, 'Vision of the Passion'

25 July
Saint James, *apostle*
FEAST

James, the brother of the apostle John, and son of Zebedee, is known as 'the Greater', to distinguish him from James son of Alphaeus.

He was a fisherman, a townsman of Peter and Andrew; he was among the first four called to follow Jesus, and with Peter and John was one of those closest to their Master. He was put to death by Herod Agrippa I about the year 44, the first of the Twelve to die for Christ (cf Acts 12:2).

James' reputed shrine in Compostella was the centre of a great pilgrimage in the Middle Ages.

The reading is a modern commentary on the passage of the Gospel read at Mass today, in which Jesus gently rebukes a mother's misguided love.

And yet there is a way of participating in Christ, of standing near him. We human beings are called to his right and his left hand. But this participation in Christ means suffering. The chalice which Christ must drink is not filled with the fiery wine of joy or the giddy wine of anger, but with the bitterness of suffering, humiliation, persecution, and defeat. The one who is called to share Christ's table must be ready to drink from this cup. He or she must remember that it is Christ's cup. 'You will drink of my cup', were his words to us. If we drink, suffering will become possible, and the cup will become a cup of grace.

A share in Christ means obedience, too. The Father appoints the places we are to occupy, just as Christ keeps to the Father's will in everything and has no will of his own but to carry out the Father's plan. His disciples are not to act in accordance with private plans and personal ideas, but in readiness to carry out the plan of God. The one who is following his or her own designs runs the danger of not acting within God's plan, and therefore of destroying when he or she ought to build, of harming when he or she ought to do good. Obedience brings order and discipline, shows the right way, guides the stream along the bed in which God will have it run. Self-will means disturbance and cutting across others. Here, too, obedience means sharing in Christ, for it is he who was obedient unto death. He speaks no words of his own, but rather the words of him who sent him. He acts only in the hour which the Father has willed to appoint his hour. He goes only to the men and women to whom the Father sent him. Down to the last details he seeks only to finish the picture that the Father has sketched, to go the way which the Father has ordained. This is the way of Christ into the night of his abandonment and the darkness of death. He was obedient unto death, even the death of the cross.

Sharing in Christ means finally the will to serve. Here the antithesis to the spirit of the world is made clear. The great ones of this world live by the will to power and they crush the weak. They have no will to serve but rather to rule, no will to obey but rather to give commands. It is otherwise with the disciples of Christ: among you the one who would be the first is to be the servant of all. If there is to be a christian ambition it should be the desire to be allowed to serve. This, too, is sharing in Christ, who came not to be served but to serve. He is the greatest, the most powerful of all beings, in the most potent sense, Lord of lords. Yet he took upon himself the form of a servant, he became a child, and entered the service of all humankind. The life of all men and women belonged to him, yet he has laid no claim to it; rather has he given up his own life for others. Instead of demanding tribute he paid tribute.

The new education which we must undergo in Christ's school is no easy one; but if we do not undergo it we are no disciples of his.

R. Gutzwiller, SJ, *Day by Day with St Matthew's Gospel*, pp 238-9

26 July
Saints Joachim and Anne, *parents of the Blessed Virgin Mary*
MEMORIAL

The sources for our knowledge of these two saints are primarily the apocryphal texts of the second century, which are probably to be relied upon, at least for the names of Mary's parents.

Devotion to St Anne was widespread in the East by the sixth century, and in the West by the fifteenth. Her feast was introduced into the Roman calendar only in 1584. In the East from the ninth century, Joachim and Anne were celebrated together, but Roman practice has only followed this in our own century.

The reading is taken from St John Damascene's First Sermon on Mary's taking-up into heaven.

Joachim and Anne were the parents of Mary. Joachim kept as strict a watch over his thoughts as a shepherd over his flock, having them entirely under his control. For the Lord God led him as a sheep, and he wanted for none of the best things.

When I say best, let no one think I mean what is commonly acceptable to the multitude, that upon which greedy minds are fixed, the pleasures of life that can neither endure nor make their possessors better, nor confer real strength. They follow the downward course of human life and cease all in a moment, even if they abounded before.

Far be it from us to cherish these things, nor is this the portion of those who fear God. But the good things which are a matter of desire to those who possess true knowledge, giving pleasure to God and fruit to those who possess them, namely, virtues, will bear fruit in due season, rewarding with eternal life those who have laboured worthily and have persevered in their acquisition as far as possible. The labour goes before, eternal happiness follows.

Joachim ever shepherded his thoughts. In the place of pastures, dwelling by contemplation on the words of sacred scripture, made glad by the restful waters of divine grace, withdrawn from foolishness he walked in the path of justice. And Anne, whose name means grace, was no less a companion in her life than a wife, blessed with all good gifts, though afflicted for a mystical reason with sterility. Grace in very truth remained sterile, not being able to produce fruit in human souls. Therefore, humanity declined from good and degenerated; there was not one of understanding nor one who sought after God. Then his divine goodness, taking pity on the work of his hands, and wishing to save it, put an end to that mystical barrenness, that of holy Anne, I mean, and she gave birth to a child whose equal had never been created and never can be. The end of barrenness proved clearly that the world's sterility would cease and that the withered trunk would be crowned with vigorous and mystical life.

St John Damascene, 'On Mary's Taking-up into Heaven'

29 July
Saint Martha
MEMORIAL

Martha is the sister of Mary and Lazarus. All three were close friends of the Lord. Martha and Mary appear in the Gospel according to Luke (the alternative Gospel offered for today's Mass), and in that of St John on two occasions, the second of which would seem to parallel that of St Luke. In the Eastern tradition all three are commemorated today, and this is also followed in the contemporary Benedictine Calendar.

The reading, taken from St Augustine's 49th Treatise on the Gospel of St John, sets out the faith and trust of St Martha.

'Jesus loved Martha, and her sister Mary and Lazarus.' He weak, they cast down, all beloved: but the healer of the weak, more than that, the raiser of the dead, and consoler of the sorrowful, loved them. 'So when he heard that he was ill, he stayed in that same place for two days.' Then after this, he says to his disciples, 'Let us go once more to Judea'. He had left as a man: but in returning, as it were forgetful of weakness, he showed his power. So Jesus came and found Lazarus had already been in the tomb four days.

Martha said to Jesus: 'If you had been here, my brother would not have died, but I know that, even now, whatever you ask of God, he will grant you.' She did not say, 'But now I ask you to raise my brother'. For how would she know, if rising would be of benefit to her brother? She only said, 'I know that you can; if you want to, you do: whether you will do it, is a matter for your judgement, not my presumption.'

'Jesus said to her, "Your brother will rise again"'. This was ambiguous. For he did not say, 'I raise your brother now', but, 'Your brother will rise again'. Martha said, 'I know he will rise again at the resurrection, on the last day'. Of that resurrection I am sure, I am uncertain about the here and now. 'Jesus said to her, "I am the resurrection".'

You say, My brother will rise again on the last day: such is true. He can rise now through him, through whom he will rise then, because, he says, 'I am the resurrection and the life'. Listen well to what he says! Certainly the whole expectation of those around was that Lazarus, a man four days dead, would be brought back to life. Let us listen, let us rise! How many are there in this gathering whom the weight of habit crushes. Perhaps some hear me to whom it is said, 'Do not get drunk with wine, for that is debauchery': they say, 'We cannot give it up'. Perhaps some hear me who are unclean, stained by licentiousness and shameful acts, to whom it is said, 'Do not act like this lest you perish': and they reply, 'We cannot be broken from our habit'. Lord, raise these up! He is the resurrection because he is life.

'If anyone believes in me, even though he dies he will live, and whoever lives and believes in me, will never die.' What is this? 'If anyone believes in me, even though he dies', as Lazarus has done, 'he will live'? Because he is not the God of the dead but of the living, for all live to him (cf Mt 22:32). Believe, therefore, even though you die, you will live: if you do not believe, however, while you live you are dead! Whence death in the soul? Because faith is not. Whence death in the body? Because there the soul is not. It follows that the soul of your soul is faith. 'If anyone believes in me', he says, 'even though he dies' in the flesh, 'he will live' in his soul, until the flesh rises never afterwards to die. That is to say, 'Whoever believes in me', although he should die, 'will live', 'And whoever lives' in the flesh, 'and believes in me', even though he will die for a time on account of the death of the flesh, 'he will not die forever.'

'"Do you believe this?" She said to him, "Yes, Lord, I believe that you are the Christ of God, the one who has come into the world".' When I believed this, I believed that you are the resurrection, I believed that you are the life. I have believed that anyone who believes in you, even though he dies, will live; and whoever lives and believes in you, will never die.

St Augustine, *Treatise on John 49*, nn 8, 12, 13, 14, 15 (excerpts)

30 July

Saint Peter Chrysologus, *bishop and doctor of the Church*
OPTIONAL MEMORIAL

Peter was born at Imola, about twenty-five miles from Ravenna, in the last quarter of the fourth century. He entered the service of the Church in Ravenna and in or about 424 was chosen to be bishop there. He was an active prelate, one who cared greatly for his people and the true faith. He was famous for his eloquence: Chrysologus is a Greek inspired name meaning 'Golden-worded'. In fact his sermons are short and lay much stress on the sacramental life, particularly on the value of frequent communion. He was on terms of real friendship with Pope St Leo the Great. St Peter died about the year 450.

The reading is from the first part of one of his catechetical sermons, which introduces the Our Father.

Dearly beloved, you have received the faith by hearing; now listen to the formula of the Lord's prayer. Christ taught us to pray briefly. He wishes us to put our petitions forward quickly. Why will he not give himself to those who entreat him, since he gave himself to those who did not ask him. Or what delay in answering will he show who by formulating prayers has thus anticipated his suppliants' desires?

The angels stand in awe at what you are going to hear today. Heaven marvels, earth trembles, flesh does not bear it, hearing does not grasp it, the mind does not penetrate it, all creation cannot sustain it. I do not dare to utter it, yet I cannot remain silent. May God enable you to hear and me to speak.

What is more awesome: that God gives himself to earth, or that he places you in heaven? That he himself enters a union with flesh, or that he causes you to enter into a sharing of the divinity? That he himself accepts death, or that he recovers you from death? That he himself is born into your state of slavery, or that he makes you to be free children of his own? That he takes your poverty upon himself, or that he makes you his heirs, yes, co-heirs of his unique self?

It is indeed more awesome that earth is transformed into a heaven, that man is changed by a deification, and that those whose lot is slavery get the rights of domination. All this is indeed something to fill us with fear. Nevertheless, the present situation has reference not to the one instructing but to the one who gives the command. Therefore, my little children, let us approach where charity summons, love draws, and affection invites us. May our hearts perceive God as our Father! Our voice should proclaim this, our tongue should utter it, our spirit should shout it aloud; and everything that is in us should be in tune with grace, not fear. For, he who has changed from a judge into a Father has wished to be loved, not feared.

'Our Father, who art in heaven.' When you say this, do not understand it to mean that he is not on earth, or that he who encompasses all beings is himself contained in a place. But understand that you, whose Father is in heaven, have a lineage derived from heaven. So act, too, that you become your Father's image by your holy way of life. He who does not darken himself with human vices, but shines with virtues like God's, proves himself a son of God.

'Hallowed be thy name.' We are called by the name of him whose offspring we are. Therefore, let us beg that his name, which is holy in itself and by its very nature, may be treated as holy by us. For, God's name either gets honoured because of our conduct, or blasphemed because of our misdeeds. Hear the apostle's words: 'For the name of God is blasphemed through you among the Gentiles.'

'Thy kingdom come.' Was there ever a time when God did not

reign? Therefore we ask that he who always has reigned himself may now reign in us, that we also may be able to reign in him.

St Peter Chrysologus, *Sermon 67*

31 July

Saint Ignatius of Loyola, *priest*

MEMORIAL

Ignatius was born at Loyola, Biscay, in the north of Spain in 1491, and at first followed a military career. Injured during the siege of Pamplona, he was forced to convalesce, and read the only books available. They happened to be The Life of Christ, and a collection of the Lives of the Saints. This reading was not really in accord with his tastes, but it awoke in him, by God's providence, a spiritual appetite. Ignatius resolved to follow Christ more closely, he consecrated his arms to our Lady of Montserrat and then spent a year in retirement at Manresa. He came to see the need for serious study and set about it in earnest, ending up as a Master of Arts of Paris. He gathered some companions to go as missionaries to the Holy Land, and when this scheme fell through, placed them at the disposal of the Pope. Such were the origins of the Company or Society of Jesus. The Society was approved by Pope Paul III in 1540 and Ignatius was to head the Society until his death in Rome in 1556.

Ignatius was remarkable for his prudence, charity and gentleness, as well as for his zeal for souls and the Church of Christ. Apart from the founding of the Society of Jesus, his most important work was the Book of Spiritual Exercises, which is one of the landmarks in the history of Catholic spirituality.

The reading is taken from the Letter of St Ignatius on Holy Obedience to the Brethren in Portugal. This is a famous letter, and a mere extract from it is given here. To understand St Ignatius correctly, it must be realized that he favoured discussion or consultation as a means of arriving at decisions. Side by side with this was the practice of obedience.

St Bernard speaks as follows of those who take it ill when things are enjoined that seem somewhat hard to them: 'If you begin to grieve at this, to judge your Superior, to murmur in your heart, though outwardly you fulfil what is commanded, yet this is not the virtue of patience, but a cloak of your malice.' And if peace and tranquillity of mind is desired, he certainly shall never arrive unto it, who has within himself the cause of his disquiet and trouble, to wit, the dis-agreeing of his own judgment with the law of obedience.

And therefore, for the maintaining of union, which is the bond of every society, the apostle so earnestly exhorts all to 'think and say the same thing' that, by the agreement of their wills and judgements, they may be mutually comforted and sustained. Now if there must be one and the self-same sentiment between the members and the head, you may easily judge whether it is more just that the head should yield to the members, or the members unto the head. It is plain, then, by what has been said, how necessary is this obedience of the under-standing.

But how perfect obedience is in itself and how pleasing to God we may gather by this: first, because thereby the most excellent and pre-cious part of man is consecrated unto him; secondly, because the obedient man is by this means made a living holocaust most grateful to his Divine Majesty, keeping nothing whatever to himself; lastly, by reason of the great difficulty of the combat, for the obedient man overcomes himself for the love of God, and resists that natural incli-nation which all men have to embrace and follow their own opinion.

Hence, therefore, it follows that obedience, though its proper fruit seems to be to perfect the will, inasmuch as it makes it prompt and ready at the beck of the Superior; yet it must also belong to the under-standing, as we have declared, and bring it to be of the selfsame opin-ion in all things with the Superior, that all the forces of our will and understanding being united, we may fulfil what is commanded with all speed and integrity.

It seems to me, most dear brethren, I hear you say that you no longer doubt of the necessity of this virtue, but that you earnestly desire to know how you may attain to the perfection thereof. To this question I answer with St Leo: 'Nothing is difficult to the humble, and nothing hard unto the meek'; so that if you are not lacking in humility or mildness, God will not be wanting in his goodness, to help you perform that which you have promised him, not only patiently, but also willingly.

St Ignatius of Loyola, Letter on Holy Obedience, 26 March 1553

1 August
Saint Alphonsus Liguori, *bishop and doctor of the Church*
MEMORIAL

Alphonsus was born in Naples just a few years before the end of the seventeenth century and was the eldest of his family. He was unusually precocious, and, although privately educated, presented himself before the University of Naples at the age of sixteen for the degree of doctor of laws. He was awarded the doctorate with acclamation! For eight years after this Alphonsus practised law with great success, but then became more interested in spiritual values. At the age of thirty he was ordained priest on his own patrimony. He devoted himself to the care of the poor, and then, with the encouragement of Bishop Thomas Falcoia of Castellamare, founded in turn the Redemptoristine nuns and the Congregation of the Most Holy Redeemer, the Congregation of missionary priests usually called Redemptorists.

The Neapolitan government at that time was anti-religious and Alphonsus had much trouble with it. In 1762 he was made bishop of the small diocese of Sant' Agata dei Gothi, where he worked hard until allowed to retire in 1775.

St Alphonsus was of great importance in the history of moral theology, revolutionizing confessional practice by his gentleness and moderation. His writings on the spiritual life were also of importance, not least his writings on the Blessed Virgin Mary.

He died in 1787.

The reading is from his 'Glories of Mary', where he is treating of her Assumption.

Having lived detached from the things of this world and united to God alone, Mary did not have a bitter death but a sweet and happy one — a death which united her intimately and eternally to God in heaven.

Secondly, peace of mind makes the death of the just precious. Sins committed during life are the worms that torment and gnaw at the hearts of poor dying mortals. About to appear before the divine tribunal, sinners see themselves surrounded by their crimes which cry out, according to St Bernard: 'We are your works; we will not abandon you!' Mary certainly could not be tormented at death by any remorse of this kind, for she was always pure and always free from the least shadow of actual or original sin. Scripture says of her: 'You are beautiful, my beloved, and there is no blemish in you' (Cant 4:7).

From the moment that she first had the use of her reason, that is, from the first moment of her immaculate conception in the womb of St Anne, Mary began to love God with all her strength. And she continued to do so, advancing more and more in love and perfection throughout her life. All her thoughts, desires, and affections were for God alone. She never uttered a word, made a movement, cast a glance, or drew a breath that was not directed to God and his glory. She never strayed even so much as a step from the love of God and never detached herself from him even for a single moment. It stands to reason then that all the beautiful virtues that she had practiced all her life surrounded her blessed bed at the happy moment of her death. That fearless faith, that loving confidence, that unconquerable patience in the midst of so much suffering, that humility in the midst of so many prerogatives, that modesty, that meekness, that compassion for souls, that zeal for the glory of God, and above all, that perfect love for God and total conformity to his will — all these surrounded Mary at her deathbed and spoke reassuringly: 'We are your works; we will not abandon you. We are all daughters of your beautiful heart. Now that you are leaving this earthly life, we will not abandon you. We will be your eternal companions to honour you in heaven, where by means of us you will reign as Queen of all men and of angels.'

Finally, the assurance of salvation makes death sweet. Death is called a passage or a transition, because by death we pass from a short to an eternal life. The dread of those who die uncertain of their ultimate salvation, as well as those who approach the solemn moment expecting to pass into eternal death, must be very great.

St Alphonsus Liguori, 'The Glories of Mary: Mary's Assumption'

2 August
Saint Eusebius of Vercelli, *bishop*
OPTIONAL MEMORIAL

Eusebius was born in Sardinia about the beginning of the fourth century. As a young man he joined the clergy of Rome, then in 345 he was appointed bishop of Vercelli. He was a staunch opponent of the Arian and Semi-Arian heresies and for his defence of the divinity of Christ was exiled by the Emperor Constantius in 355. His exile brought him to the lands which cradled Christianity, but he was treated with much brutality. In 361 he was enabled to return to Vercelli, where he died ten years later. He had met and was on friendly terms with St Athanasius and St Hilary of Poitiers - both of whom also knew what it was to be exiled for the faith.

St Eusebius was the first bishop we hear of who united the clerical and monastic lives, gathering the clergy of his cathedral church to live in community with him.

The reading is from a letter he wrote while in captivity. In this extract, Eusebius is quoting a letter he wrote to those who were responsible for his custody.

Eusebius, the servant of God, with his fellow servants, who labour with me for the sake of the faith: to the 'jailer' Patrophilus, and his fellows.

Both God and the community know, nor can you deny either now or in the future, with what force and fury I was not only dragged on the ground, but that now and then you carried me lying on my back with bared body from this lodging, which you had given me through your own police appointed for such matters and from which I never went out except in these circumstances. Wherefore I reserve my case for God, that it may receive its end as he shall have ordained. In the meantime know that I have resolved as follows: not to eat bread or drink water until each one of you has professed, not only by word, but also by writing, that you will not prohibit my brothers, who freely suffer along with me these things for the sake of the faith, from offering me the necessary foods from the lodging where they stay, nor rebuke those who shall have deigned to enquire after me.

It would indeed be better to leave this body than to be forced to tell to those who wish to know of this crime which you have committed against the divine and public law.* But lest any of the unbelievers call you cruel in our regard and think we, ignorant of the divine precepts, have rather wished to avoid disorder than to obey God, and therefore take for granted that we have wished this, I again say, that unless you have made this declaration both by word of mouth and in writing,

* The public law mentioned is that of the Roman Empire; Eusebius was entitled to his own attendants.

you will not be holding back from murder.

The almighty God knows; his only-begotten Son, whose birth from him cannot be described, he, God of everlasting power, who for the sake of our salvation assumed perfect manhood, wished to suffer, rose the third day having overcome death, sits at the right hand of the Father, is to come to judge the living and the dead, knows; the Holy Spirit knows, the Catholic Church is witness that I shall not be guilty in my regard, but you, who have willed to forbid my fellow servants to minister the necessities of life.

And if you think you ought to despise this, not as if I were fearful of death but lest after my going forth you should say I wished to die of my own will, and lest you should find some vague suspicion of accusation against us, know that I have summoned the Churches which I am able to reach, with sealed letters, and have summoned God's servants, that on their coming together the whole world might know what the true faith, which is approved by all Catholic bishops, suffers from the Ariomanites, whom it has condemned before.

So I, Eusebius the bishop, have signed this. I adjure you, who should read this letter, by the Father, the Son and the Holy Spirit, that you do not suppress it, but pass it on to others to read.

St Eusebius, *Epistula 2*

4 August
Saint John Vianney, *priest*
MEMORIAL

John Vianney was born in 1786, near Lyons, in France. As a result of the disturbances of the French Revolution, his schooling was very limited. These difficulties were compounded by his own slowness as a learner, and, for this reason, he was not readily accepted for ordination. He was ordained priest, however, in 1815, and in 1817 was appointed to Ars-en-Dombe, where he remained until his death in 1859. By his fervour he first awoke the little town from spiritual slumber, then gradually became known as a confessor. He had a supernatural knowledge of souls and of events and, apart from his apostolate of the confessional, worked numerous healings; healings which he, rather unfortunately, attributed to St Philomena.

His fame spread in his life-time, so much so, that a special eight-day ticket on the railway was issued in Lyons for those wishing to travel to Ars. His life was marked by austerity and prayer, and charity towards all.

The reading is from a homily he preached on the last Sunday of the year.

The world is passing, we are passing with it. Kings, emperors are all going hence. Eternity will receive them; that eternity whence is no return. There is only one thing needful: to save one's poor soul.

Think of the saints; they were not attached to the things of earth, they only thought of the things of heaven. Worldlings, on the contrary, think of nothing but the present.

A good Christian acts like one who goes to a foreign country to amass a fortune. He has no idea of remaining there, but wishes for nothing better than to return home directly his fortune is made. Again, we should do as kings do. When they are likely to be dethroned they send their treasure away beforehand; it awaits them when they go. In like manner a good Christian sends all his good works to await him at the gate of heaven.

The good God has placed us on earth to see how we conduct ourselves, and whether we will love him or no; but nobody can remain here. If we only reflected we should turn our thoughts unceasingly towards heaven, our true fatherland. But we permit ourselves to be diverted from that by the world, its riches and the allurement of material things, and we pay no attention to the only thing with which we should be occupied.

Look at the saints: how they were detached from the world and from matter! With what contempt they regarded it all! A religious having lost his parents, found himself lord of vast possessions. When they brought him the news he asked: 'How long have my parents been dead?' 'Three weeks', was the answer. 'Tell me', said he, 'is a dead man capable of inheritance?' 'Assuredly not.' 'Well then, I cannot inherit from those who have only been dead three weeks, for I have been dead twenty years.' Ah! the saints understood the nothingness, the vanity of this world and the happiness of leaving all things for the sake of heaven.

There are two kinds of misers; the heavenly miser and the earthly one. The miser of earth has no thought beyond the present; he is never rich enough; he amasses, amasses — ever amasses. But when death comes he has nothing. I often say that he is just in the same position as those who lay in too much for the winter; when the next harvest comes they are at a loss what to do with it all, it is only in the way. Similarly when death approaches the goods of this life are nothing but an embarrassment. We can take nothing with us; we must leave it all behind. What would you think of a person who heaped up provisions in the house which would have to be thrown away later because they were spoiling, and who passed by precious stones, gold and diamonds that he could keep, carry with him wherever he went, and would make his fortune? Well, my children, we do the same nevertheless: we attach ourselves to matter, to things which must come to an end, and give no thought to gaining heaven — the only prize worth having.

A good Christian, the miser of heaven, makes but little of the good things of earth; he thinks only of enriching his soul, of acquiring what will satisfy for ever and will endure for all eternity.

Pass from country to country, from kingdom to kingdom, from riches to affluence still greater, from one pleasure to another and you will not find your happiness in them. Earth can no more satisfy an immortal soul than a pinch of flour a starving man.

When the apostles had beheld our Lord ascending into heaven they found earth so poor, so vile and so contemptible without him, that they longed for the torments which should tear them from it and unite them once more to their good Master. The mother of the Machabees, who endured a seven-fold death in the sight of the death of her seven sons, encouraged them with the words: 'Think of heaven!'

Our Lord rewarded the faith of the saints by the sensible vision of heaven. Some there were among them who walked with him in paradise. St Stephen while he was being stoned beheld the heavens open above his head. St Paul was rapt to the third heaven and declared himself unable to give an idea of what he saw there. St Teresa saw into heaven and avowed that all things earthly seemed as nothing by comparison.

But we, alas! we are nought but matter. We crawl the earth and know not how to raise ourselves above it. We are too heavy, too sluggish.

Turn then, my children, to these consoling thoughts. With whom shall we be in heaven? With God who is our Father; with Jesus Christ who is our Brother; with the Blessed Virgin, who is our Mother; with the angels and saints who are our friends.

A king said, regretfully, in his last moments: 'I have now to leave my kingdom for a country in which I know no one!' That is, that he had never thought of the happiness of heaven. We must, then, make to ourselves friends there now, so as to meet them again after death, and we need have no fear that we, like that king, shall know no one.

St John Vianney, 'Sermon on the Last Sunday of the Year'

5 August
The Dedication of the Basilica of Saint Mary Major
OPTIONAL MEMORIAL

Today commemorates the dedication of the Liberian basilica in Rome in honour of our Lady. This basilica had been first built under Pope Liberius in the fourth century. Pope Sixtus III rebuilt it after the Council of Ephesus in 431 had proclaimed Mary as Mother of God, and gave it the title of Saint Mary. It was the first church in the West dedicated to God in her honour.

The reading is from a homily of St Bernard on our Lady.

Blessed Mary! She lacks neither humility nor virginity. And what unique virginity. Motherhood did not stain but honoured it. What extraordinary humility. Fruitful virginity did not tarnish but exalted it. And matchless fruitfulness went hand in hand with both virginity and humility. Which of them is not wonderful? Which is not incomparable? Which is not unique? I should not be at all surprised if, having meditated upon them, you hesitated to say which you find more praiseworthy, whether you think more amazing the fruitfulness in the virgin or the integrity in the mother; nobility in child-bearing or, in spite of such nobility, humility. Possibly it is more excellent to have all three together than to have one of them alone. For there is no doubt that she who was thus thrice blessed was more blessed than if she had received only one of them. And yet, is it so extraordinary that God whom we read and see to be wonderful in his saints (Ps 68:35), should show himself even more wonderful in his mother?

You who are married, then, reverence the integrity of her flesh amid frail flesh. And you, consecrated virgins, admire the virgin's fruitfulness. Let all strive to imitate the humility of the Mother of God. Holy angels, revere the mother of your King, you who worship our humble virgin's child, for he is your King and ours, the restorer of our race, the builder of your city. Angels, allow us men to join with you in singing worthy praise of his highness and his lowliness, he who with you is so sublime and yet with us so humble. To him be honour and glory for evermore. Amen.

St Bernard of Clairvaux, 'Homily on our Lady'

6 August
The Transfiguration of the Lord
FEAST

The mystery of the Lord's transfiguration is presented twice in the Church's year: on this day, in the peace and calm, as it were of the day to day, and on the Second Sunday of Lent, in the build up to the solemn commemoration of Christ's paschal mystery, and in the preparation of the catechumens' sharing in that Pasch through baptism and their first eucharist. Because of the three-fold cycle of Sunday readings it is presented four times in the Glenstal Bible Missal.

The transfiguration is full of mystery but a careful reading of the accounts in Matthew, Mark and Luke will show the writers' clear intention of presenting the glory of Christ as a temporary lifting of the veil — for Christ had not yet died and so had not yet entered into his glory. In all three accounts, the transfiguration follows Christ's foretelling of his coming passion and death, to be followed by his resurrection (Mt 16:21; Mk 8:31; Lk 9:26), and the significance of these future events for his followers.

Christ as man must have benefited by the transfiguration, but his bringing of the three leading apostles with him up the mountain indicates that he intended to strengthen them for the coming apparent triumph of the powers of darkness.

As a reading, a passage from Gregory of Nazianzen's *Third Theological Discourse*, is given. The passage is chosen because of its presentation of the mystery of Christ as a whole — it mentions the transfiguration only in passing —; if we believe in our Catholic faith then we must cling to that mystery.

That I too might be made God so far as he is made Man. He was born — but he had been begotten: he was born of a woman — but she was a virgin. The first is human the second divine. In his human nature he had no father, but also in his divine nature no mother. Both these belong to Godhead. He dwelt in the womb — but he was recognized by the prophet, himself still in the womb, leaping before the Word, for whose sake he came into being. He was wrapped in swaddling clothes — but he took off the swathing bands of the grave by his rising again. He was laid in a manger — but he was glorified by angels, and proclaimed by a star, and worshipped by the Magi.

Why are you offended by that which is presented to your sight; is it perhaps because you will not look at that which is presented to your mind? He was driven into exile into Egypt — but he drove away the Egyptian idols. He had no form nor comeliness in the eyes of the Jews — but to David he is fairer than the children of men. And on the mountain he was bright as the lightning, and became more luminous than the sun, initiating us into the mystery of the future.

He was baptized as man — but he remitted sins as God: not because he needed purificatory rites himself, but that he might sanctify the element of water. He was tempted as man, but he conquered as God; yes, he bids us be of good cheer, for he has overcome the world. He hungered — but he fed thousands; yes, he is the bread that gives life, and that is of heaven. He thirsted — but he cried, If any man thirst, let him come to me and drink. Yes, he promised that fountains should flow from them that believe. He was wearied, but he is the rest of them that are weary and heavy laden. He was heavy with sleep, but he walked lightly over the sea. He rebuked the winds, he made Peter light as he began to sink. He pays tribute, but it is out of a fish; yes, he is the King of those who demanded it.

He is called a Samaritan and a demoniac; but he saves him that came down from Jerusalem and fell among thieves; the demons acknowledge him, and he drives out demons and sinks in the sea legions of foul spirits, and sees the prince of the demons falling like lightning. He is stoned, but is not taken. He prays, but he hears prayer. He weeps, but he causes tears to cease. He asks where Lazarus was laid, for he was man; but he raises Lazarus, for he was God. He is sold, and very cheap, for it is only for thirty pieces of silver; but he redeems the world, and that at a great price, for the price was his own blood.

As a sheep he is led to the slaughter, but he is the Shepherd of Israel, and now of the whole world also. As a lamb he is silent, yet he is the Word, and is proclaimed by the voice of one crying in the wilderness. He is bruised and wounded, but he heals every disease and every infirmity. He is lifted up and nailed to the Tree, but by the Tree of Life he restores us; yes, he saves even the robber crucified with him; yes, he wrapped the visible world in darkness. He is given vinegar to drink mingled with gall. Who? He who turned the water into wine, who is the destroyer of the bitter taste, who is sweetness and altogether desire. He lays down his life, but he has power to take it again; and the veil is rent, for the mysterious doors of heaven are opened; the rocks are cleft, the dead arise. He dies, but he gives life, and by his death destroys death. He is buried but he rises again; he goes down into hell, but he brings up the souls; he ascends to heaven, and shall come again to judge the living and the dead.

St Gregory Nazianzen, 'Theological Discourse 3', nn 19, 20

7 August
Saints Sixtus II, *pope and martyr*, **and companions**, *martyrs*
OPTIONAL MEMORIAL

Pope Sixtus and his four deacon companions suffered in the persecution of Valerian in the year 258. He had become pope in the previous year and was arrested while saying Mass in the catacomb of St Callistus on the sixth of this month and put to death there and then. He was the most celebrated of the Roman pontiffs to die as a martyr and is mentioned in the traditional Roman canon of the Mass. In the Divine Office the reading for today's Memorial is from a letter of St Cyprian of Carthage in which he mentions Sixtus' death.

The reading offered here is from a Sermon of St Augustine on the theme of martyrdom, with specific reference to chapter 10 of the Gospel according to Matthew.

By that gospel call when the Lord says, 'He who loves his soul shall lose it, and he who shall have lost it on my account, shall find it' (Mt

210

10:39; Jn 12:25), the martyrs are roused for battle; and they overcame, because they did not rely on themselves, but on the Lord.

'He who loves his soul, shall lose it.' What is meant can be understood in two ways. If you love it, you lose it. And, on the other hand: Don't love it, lest you lose it. The first way has this meaning: If you love, lose it. If therefore you love it, lose it. Here sow it, and in heaven you will reap it. If the farmer does not lose the wheat in the seed, he does not love it in the harvest.

The other way is as follows: Don't love it, lest you lose it. They seem to love their souls who are afraid to die. If the martyrs had loved their souls in this way, without doubt they would have lost them. For what would it have profited them to hold on to the soul in this life, and to lose it in the future one? What use would it be to hold on to the soul on earth, and lose it in heaven? And what is to hold on to it? To hold on for how long? What you hold on to, passes away from you: if you lose it, you find it in you. See the martyrs hold on to their souls. And how would they have been martyrs, if they had held on all the time? See further, if they had held on, would they have lived to our day? If by denying Christ, they had held on to their souls in this life, would they not have passed from this life some time ago, and indeed, lost their souls? But because they did not deny Christ, they passed from this world to the Father. They sought Christ by confessing; they held on to *him* by dying. For a great gain, therefore, they lost their souls, losing the perishable, meriting a crown: meriting a crown, I say, and holding on to life without end.

Accordingly, what the Lord subsequently added, comes about, rather, has come about, in them: 'And he who shall have lost his soul on my account, shall find it' (Mt 10:37). Who shall have lost it, he says, 'on my account'. There is the whole matter. 'Who shall have lost', not any old how, not for just any reason, but 'on my account'. For they were already called martyrs in prophecy: 'On your account we are put to death all the day long' (Ps 43:22). Wherefore it is not the punishment, but its reason which makes the martyr. When the Lord suffered, the case determined three crosses: criminals fixed there on either side, he in the middle. And, as if the wood was a throne of judgement, he condemned the one who insulted, crowned the one who confessed him. What will he do , when he comes to judge, who, himself judged, could do this? Already then he has divided the crosses. For if the punishment were questioned, Christ was like the thieves. But if one asks the cross, why Christ was crucified, it replies to us: On your account.

Let the martyrs say to him, therefore: we are dead on your account. He on our account, we, however, on his. But he on our account, that he might confer a benefit on us: we for his sake, though not in order to bestow any benefit on him. Accordingly it is advantageous for us under both counts: both what comes out of him, comes to us; and what is done on his account, comes back to us. For he it is about whom the soul which rejoices in the Lord says, 'I said to the Lord: you are my God; for you have no need of my goods' (Ps 15:9). For what is: 'of my goods', except what were given by you? And how could he want for any good, by whom every good thing is given?

St Augustine, Sermon 331, nn 1, 2

7 August, also

Saint Cajetan, *priest*

OPTIONAL MEMORIAL

Cajetan was born in Vicenza in 1480 of a noble family. His father was killed in battle just two years after he was born and his mother cared for the up-bringing of the children. She was obviously a woman of real spiritual strength and this bore particular fruit in Cajetan. He studied ecclesiastical and civil law and when he had obtained his doctorate went to Rome. His intention was to seek priestly ordination but he did not achieve this until he was in his early thirties.

In Rome he had associated himself with some like-minded clerics who were concerned to live lives of prayer and service. On ordination he went back to his own part of Italy and in Vicenza, Verona and Venice helped to organize hospitals and other charitable services for the poor.

On the advice of his confessor, after some years of this activity, he went to Rome again and sought out his former associates. They decided to form a con-gregation of Clerks Regular and their institute, after some hesitation, was approved by a commission of cardinals appointed by the pope. The group came to be called the Theatines. They devoted themselves to fostering the knowledge of the faith (particularly of the Bible), the renewal of sacramental life among priests and people, and the fostering of frequent communion. The congregation spread, at first rather slowly, and did much good for the Church.

St Cajetan died in Naples in 1547.

The reading is from the 'Decree on the Ministry and Life of Priests' of the Second Vatican Council. The passage could almost be a commentary on the life and work of St Cajetan.

The other sacraments, as well as every ministry of the Church and every work of the apostolate, are linked with the holy eucharist and are directed toward it. For the most blessed eucharist contains the Church's entire spiritual wealth, that is, Christ himself, our passover and living bread. Through his very flesh, made vital and vitalizing by the Holy Spirit, he offers life to all people. They are thereby invited and led to offer themselves, their labours, and all created things together with him.

Hence the eucharist shows itself to be the source and the apex of the whole work of preaching the gospel. Those under instruction are introduced by stages to a sharing in the eucharist. The faithful, already marked with the sacred seal of baptism and confirmation, are through the reception of the eucharist fully joined to the Body of Christ.

Thus the eucharistic action is the very heartbeat of the congregation of the faithful over which the priest presides. So priests must instruct them to offer to God the Father the divine victim in the sacrifice of the Mass, and to join to it the offering of their own lives. In the spirit of Christ the shepherd, priests should train them to submit their sins with a contrite heart to the Church in the sacrament of penance. Thus, mindful of the Lord's words: 'Repent, for the kingdom of God is at hand' (Mt 4:17), the people will be drawn ever closer to him each day.

Priests should likewise teach them to participate in the celebrations of the sacred liturgy in such a way that they can rise to sincere prayer during them. They must lead the faithful along to an ever-improved spirit of prayer offered throughout the whole of life according to the graces and needs of each. They must persuade everyone to faithfully discharge the duties of their proper state in life, and bring the saintlier ones to an appropriate exercise of the evangelical counsels. They must show the faithful how to sing to the Lord hymns and spiritual songs in their hearts, always giving thanks to God the Father for all things in the name of our Lord Jesus Christ.

Priests themselves extend to the different hours of the day the praise and thanksgiving of the eucharistic celebration by reciting the Divine Office. Through it they pray to God in the name of the Church on behalf of the whole people entrusted to them and indeed for the whole world.

In the house of prayer the most holy eucharist is celebrated and preserved. There the faithful gather, and find help and comfort through venerating the presence of the Son of God our saviour, offered for us on the sacrificial altar. This house must be well kept and suitable for prayer and sacred functions. There, pastors and the faithful are called to respond with grateful hearts to the gift of him who through his humanity constantly pours divine life into the members of his body.

Let priests take care to cultivate an appropriate knowledge and facility in the liturgy, so that by their own liturgical ministry, the christian communities entrusted to them may ever more adequately give praise to God, the Father and the Son and the Holy Spirit.

Vatican II, Decree on the Ministry and Life of Priests, n 5

8 August
Saint Dominic, *priest*
MEMORIAL

Dominic was a native of Castille, in Spain, and was born in 1170. He entered the service of the Church at an early age. As a canon of the cathedral of Osma he accompanied his bishop on a mission which led them through France and was the occasion of Dominic's first encounter with the Albigensian heresy. Dominic and his bishop wanted to work in Russia, but the pope asked them to preach rather in Toulouse where the Albigensians were numerous. It was this work which led to the founding of the Friars Preachers, not as a sudden process but as something which grew out of a need and a work. The institute was established in 1216.

The characteristics St Dominic chiefly emphasized for his followers were charity, poverty, humility and learning, the preaching of truth and combatting of error.

St Dominic died in 1221. Sisterhoods were also established to aid the friars by their prayers.

St Dominic was canonized in 1234, and, as a reading, an extract from the Bull of Canonization is given here.

While he was still young in years, he bore in his boyish breast the heart of a mature man; choosing a life of continual mortification he sought the Creator of all life; dedicated to God and vowed a Nazarene under the rule of St Augustine, rivalling the zeal of Samuel for holy things, he recalled the holiness of Daniel by the zeal with which he chastened his desires.

Strong as an athlete in the way of right and justice and the path of the saints, never departing from the teachings and the service of the Church militant, subjecting the body to the soul, the senses to reason, in spirit uniting himself to God, he strove to approach him while remaining bound to his neighbour by the cords of a wise compassion. In the presence of this man who trod underfoot carnal pleasures and pierced the stony hearts of sinners, the whole body of heretics were afraid and the saints made joyous.

He grew at once in age and in grace, experienced an ineffable delight in the salvation of souls, devoted himself entirely to God's word, and by its means awoke many thousands to life. Made a preacher and leader to the people of God, he, unaided by man, created the new preaching order and strengthened it unceasingly by evident and authentic miracles, for in addition to his deeds of holiness and his wonderfully beautiful character, that made his life here so resplendent and so famous, even after death he has given back health to the sick, speech to the dumb, sight to the blind, hearing to the deaf, strength to the paralysed — a sure sign of the more perfect beauty of the soul within.

Bound to us by ties of friendship, before we were raised to the Pontificate, his life carried with it in our eyes certain proofs of heroic holiness, so that the miracles of which others have brought us due and solemn witnesses do but confirm what even without them was established. Thus we are convinced as also are our people that through his prayers God may do us mercy and that one who was our friend on earth will still in heaven hold us in no less affection; wherefore by the

advice of our brothers in the episcopate and of all the prelates of our
Court, we have determined to add his name to the number of the
saints, and do hereby order and command you on August 5, the eve,
that is, of the day when, laying down his broken earthly body and
rich in grace he entered into the glory of all the saints, to celebrate his
feast and to cause it to be celebrated with full solemnity to the end
that God, in answer to the prayers of one whose life was here an endless service, may give us grace on earth and in heaven a vision of his
glory.

Pope Gregory IX, 'Bull for the canonization of St Dominic'

10 August
Saint Lawrence, *deacon and martyr*
FEAST

After Saints Peter and Paul, St Lawrence was the most celebrated of the martyrs of the Church of Rome. He was perhaps a deacon of Pope St Sixtus II, and
responsible for the charitable activity of the Church. His cult was not confined
to Italy but spread to many other churches in the West, and with his fame his
legend grew.

The reading offered is taken from a Sermon of St Augustine, preached on
this day. The reference to St Lawrence is less specific than in some of his other
sermons, but the teaching is more general, relating as it does to the Gospel.

You, believers, recognize the grain which fell on the ground, and,
having died, has multiplied. You, believers, I say, recognize this
grain, because it dwells in your own minds. For no Christian doubts
what Christ says of himself. But assuredly, that grain having died
and been multiplied, many grains are scattered on the earth; and
among these is blessed Lawrence, whose sowing we celebrate today.
For we see, rejoice over, are, the abundant crop sprouted up from
those grains scattered all over the world: that is if, by his grace, we
belong to his granary. For not everything in the growing crop
belongs to the granary. To be sure the same useful and nourishing
rain feeds the wheat and chaff. Far be it that both together be stored
in the granary; although both together be nurtured in the field, and

both together be threshed in the same device. Now is the time for choice. Before the winnowing come, there must be separation of characters: as on the threshing floor the grain is set out for cleaning, it is not yet finally separated by the winnowing fork.

'He who loves his life in this world, shall lose it.' The grain of wheat speaks, the grain which fell on the ground, and was put to death that it might be multiplied, speaks: let him be heard, because he does not lie. What he urged, he did: he taught by precept, went ahead by example. Christ did not love his life in this world: he came on this account, that here he might lose it, might lay it down for us, and when he wished he took it up again. But because he was man just as he was God: for Christ is the Word, soul and flesh, true God and true man. But a man without sin, who was taking away the sin of the world. He was then of greater power, so that he could truly say: 'I have power to lay down my life, and I have power to take it up again: no one takes it from me; but I myself put it down from me, and again I take it up.' Since then he were of such power, why did he say: 'Now my soul is troubled'? Why is he disturbed, the man-God of such power, unless because in him is the likeness of our infirmity? 'I have the power of laying down my life, and I have the power of taking it up again.' When you hear this from Christ, he is speaking for himself: when you hear this from Christ, I say, he is speaking for himself. When his soul is disturbed by death drawing near, he is speaking in our person. For the Church would not be his body, unless he himself were in us.

When the Lord said: 'My soul is disturbed', we were in him, we were meant. We are disturbed, but we do not perish. 'Why my soul are you sad, and why do you cast me down?' (Ps 42:5). Do you not wish this miserable life to end? For it is so much the more miserable, the more the miserable is loved: it would be less miserable, if it were not loved! What is the blessed life like, when the miserable life is so loved, only because it is called 'life'?

'Why are you sad my soul, and why do you cast me down?' — You have what you should do. Have you grown weak in yourself? 'Hope in the Lord.' Are you disturbed in yourself? 'Hope in the Lord', who chose you before the making of the world, who predestined you, who called you, who justified you when you were a sinner, who promised you everlasting glorification, who bore an undue death for you, who shed his blood for you, who changed you into himself when he said: 'My soul is disturbed.' You belong to him, and are you afraid? Can the world do anything harmful to you for whom he, through whom the world was made, died? You belong to him, and are you afraid? 'If God is for us, who is against us? He who did not spare his own Son but handed him over for us all; how has he not given us all things with him?' (Rom 8:31-32).

Stand up to upsets, do not give way to love of the world. It titilates, flatters, awaits the favourable moment; it is not to be believed in — hold on to Christ!

St Augustine, *Sermon 305*, nn 1, 2, 4

11 August
Saint Clare, *virgin*
MEMORIAL

Clare was a native of Assisi and slightly younger than St Francis. She desired to give herself to God and in this purpose would seem to have been both inspired and aided by Francis. She sought a feminine expression of the ideal of poverty, and, in accord with the notions of the time, this took on a contemplative and enclosed form. The year was 1212. She, and those who came to join her, were established by Francis and his Friars in San Damiano, and there Clare remained until her death in 1253.

The official Church had great difficulty in finding a canonical niche for the Poor Ladies of Assisi, and Clare had a rather thankless task in trying to maintain her ideal of poverty. Various Rules were made out for the Community at San Damiano and those inspired by them, but Clare would not rest until her own Rule, based on that of St Francis, was approved by the Pope. This was done by Pope Innocent IV on 9 August 1253, so, two days later, St Clare was able to go to her rest in peace.

She was canonized by Pope Alexander IV, in a highly poetic Bull. Among other things he says of her were, 'She was the lofty candlestick of sanctity burning brightly in the tabernacle of the Lord'. 'She was the Princess of the poor, the Duchess of the humble, the Mistress of the chaste, and the Abbess of the penitent'. 'Her life was a teaching and instruction to others.'

St Clare was in fact the great custodian of St Francis' values, although her vocation was purely contemplative.

The reading offered is taken from her third letter to Blessed Agnes of
Prague, who had established a community in Prague inspired by that of San
Damiano. The letter has many reminiscences of the Divine Office used in
those days.

Therefore, dearly beloved, may you 'always rejoice in the Lord' (Phil
4:4). And may neither bitterness nor a cloud of sadness overwhelm
you, O dearly beloved Lady in Christ, joy of the angels and crown of
your sisters!

Place your mind before the mirror of eternity!
Place your soul in the brilliance of glory.
Place your heart in the figure of the divine substance:
And transform your whole being into the image of the Godhead itself
    through contemplation!
So that you too may feel what his friends feel
    as they taste the hidden sweetness
    which God himself has reserved
    from the beginning
    for those who love him.

Since you have cast aside all those things which, in this deceitful and
turbulent world, ensnare their blind lovers, love him totally who
gave himself totally for your love. His beauty the sun and moon
admire, and of his gifts there is no limit in abundance, preciousness,
and magnitude. I am speaking of him who is the Son of the Most
High, whom the Virgin brought to birth and remained a virgin after
his birth. Cling to his most sweet mother who carried a Son whom
the heavens could not contain; and yet she carried him in the little
enclosure of her holy womb and held him on her virginal lap.

    Who would not dread the treacheries of the enemy of mankind,
who, through the arrogance of momentary and deceptive glories,
attempts to reduce to nothing that which is greater than heaven
itself? Indeed, is it not clear that the soul of the faithful person, the
most worthy of all creatures because of the grace of God, is greater
than heaven itself? For the heavens with the rest of creation cannot
contain their Creator. Only the faithful soul is his dwelling place and
throne, and this only through the charity which the wicked do not

have. He who is the Truth has said: 'Whoever loves me will be loved by my Father, and I too shall love him, and we shall come to him and make our dwelling place with him' (Jn 14:21).

Therefore, as the glorious Virgin of virgins carried Christ materially in her body, you, too, by following in his footprints (cf 1 Pet 2:21), especially those of poverty and humility, can, without any doubt, always carry him spiritually in your chaste and virginal body. And you will hold him by whom you and all things are held together (cf Wis 1:7; Col 1:17).

The Third Letter of St Clare to Blessed Agnes of Prague, vv 10-26

13 August
Saints Pontian, *pope,* **and Hippolytus,** *priest, martyrs*
OPTIONAL MEMORIAL

Pontian became bishop of Rome in the year 231. During the persecution of the Emperor Maximinus, he was exiled to Sardinia. He resigned the papacy, so that the Church in Rome could have an active leader, and died in Sardinia as a result of ill-treatment about the year 235. His relics were brought back to Rome in the fourth century.

Pontian's lowliness and gentleness were providential, it would seem, for the priest Hippolytus, also of Rome, and who was likewise exiled. Hippolytus was a distinguished writer and teacher (his language Greek, still in the third century very much used in Rome), who had gone into schism when Callistus was elected pope. In exile he made his peace with the Church, and dying like Pontian as a result of ill-treatment was also venerated as a martyr. His relics, too, were brought back to Rome in the fourth century.

The reading is taken from Hippolytus' *Commentary on the Book of Daniel.*

The garden which had been planted in Eden is the figure, and, after a fashion, the model of the true garden. Let him who loves knowledge learn it here. For from the earthly garden we ought to raise our gaze to the heavenly garden, starting from the figure to understand the spiritual, and, from this limited time, lift up our hopes to eternity, as Moses did, who received from the Lord the order to build a tabernacle 'which had been shown to him on the mountain.' What did he see if not the representation of the heavenly magnificence, in imitation of which the fleshly one, that is 'the tabernacle built of wood 'which would not rot' (Ex 25:10 *Septuagint*), had been laid out. In this one who reflects should discern the spiritual and not merely the earthly in the fleshly.

For Eden is the name of the 'new garden of delight planted in the East' (Gen 2:9), embellished with every kind of good tree: which must be understood of the reunion of the just and of the holy place upon which the Church is built. For the Church is not called 'place', or 'house built upon stone or clay', nor can the Church either be called 'the isolated individual'. For houses are destroyed and men die. What then is the Church? The holy coming together of those who live in justice. Agreement, which is the path of the saints towards the community, this is what the Church is, the spiritual garden of God, planted on Christ, as in the East*, where one sees all kinds of trees: the line of the patriarchs who died in the beginning, the works of the prophets accomplished after the Law was given, the choir of apostles, who had their wisdom from the Word, the choir of martyrs, saved by the blood of Christ, the procession of virgins, made holy by water, the choir of teachers, the order of bishops, priests and levites. All these saints flourish in perfect order in the Church's midst, and cannot fade away. If we gather their fruits, we gain a true view of things, by eating the spiritual and heavenly dishes which come from them.

For the blessed patriarchs passed on to us the orders of God — just like a tree planted in the garden and always producing good fruit — so that we should recognize today the sweet fruit of Christ announced by them, the fruit of life which is given to us.

A river of never failing water flows in this garden. 'Four rivers' flow out from it, watering all the earth. The same is true of the Church: Christ, who is the river, is announced in the whole world by the fourfold gospel. He waters the whole earth and makes holy all who believe in him, according to the word of the prophet: 'Rivers flow from his body' (cf Jn 7:38). In paradise the tree of knowledge and the tree of life were found (Gen 2:9), and today in the Church two

---

* In Greek as in Latin the same word signified 'East' and 'Rising Sun'. Hippolytus spiritually interprets the reference of Gen 2:9 in the light of Luke 1:78 etc. Christ is the Rising Sun in whom the Garden of delights, Eden, the Church, is to be found.

trees are planted, the Law and the Word. For through the Law comes the knowledge of sin (Rom 3:20), but through the Word, life is given and pardon granted for sins.

Long ago, Adam, because he disobeyed God and tasted of the tree of knowledge, was hunted from paradise: drawn from the earth, he returned to the earth. So likewise a believer, who does not keep the commandments is deprived of the Holy Spirit, since he is hunted from the Church: he is no longer God's, but becomes earth once more and goes back to the old man he was.

St Hippolytus, *Commentary on Daniel*, I, xvii

14 August
Saint Maximilian Kolbe, *priest and martyr*
MEMORIAL

Raymond Kolbe was born near Lodz in Poland in 1894. He entered the Conventual Franciscans in Poland and received the name of Maximilian. He made first profession in 1911 and solemn profession in 1914, when he added Mary to his religious name. He studied first in Poland and then in Rome, where, with six companions he established the 'Militia of the Immaculate' in 1917. He was ordained priest in 1918 and returned to Poland in 1919.

He taught first in Cracow and, in spite of ill-health, he continued to foster the Militia, the purpose of which was the service of the Church in the world. In 1927 he established the City of the Immaculate (Niepokalanow) near Warsaw, devoted to the religious life and the apostolate of the press. In 1937 there were 762 religious in this monastic city!

From 1930 to 1936 Fr Kolbe himself was in Japan, where, at Nagasaki, he established another such city or town, Mugenzai no Sono.

In 1939, on the German invasion of Poland, he was arrested by the Nazis but released some months later. He was again arrested in 1941 (he had given shelter to some 2,000 Jews), and on 29 May was sent to Auschwitz, the concentration camp where 4 million people died.

At Auschwitz he offered himself for the death bunker in place of a father of nine children. He survived a fortnight of starvation and his life was finally terminated by a lethal injection on 14 August 1941.

The great devotion of his life had been to Mary Immaculate as Mother and Mediatrix.

The reading is from the homily of Pope John Paul II preached at the Mass for the canonization of St Maximilian on 10 October 1982.

'How can I repay the Lord for his goodness to me? The cup of salvation I will raise, I will call on the Lord's name.' These are words of thankfulness. Death undergone for love, in place of a brother, is Fr Kolbe's heroic act, by which we glorify God at the same time as his saint. For it is from God that the grace of such heroism, the grace of this martyrdom, comes.

Today, then, we glorify the great work of God in the man. Before all of us gathered here, Fr Maximilian Kolbe raises his 'cup of salvation', in which is brought together the sacrifice of his whole life, sealed by his death as a martyr 'for his brother'.

Maximilian prepared himself for this final sacrifice by following Christ from the very first years of his life in Poland. From these early years dates the mysterious dream of the two crowns, one white, one red, between which our saint did not choose: he accepted both. From his youth, in fact, he was possessed of a great love for Christ and the desire for martyrdom. This love and this desire went with him along the way of his Franciscan and priestly vocation for which he prepared himself both in Poland and in Rome. This love and this desire followed him everywhere that he lived out his priestly and Franciscan service in Poland and his missionary service in Japan.

The inspirer of his whole life was Mary Immaculate, to whom he entrusted his love for Christ and his desire for martyrdom. In the mystery of the Immaculate Conception the marvellous and supernatural world of the grace of God offered to man revealed itself to the eyes of his soul. Fr Kolbe's faith and his whole life's work show that he conceived his collaboration with grace as a combat (a 'militia service') under the sign of the Immaculate Conception. The Marian note is particularly significant in the life and holiness of Fr Kolbe. His whole apostolate, in his homeland and on the missions, was marked with this same stamp. At the very centre of this apostolate were the 'towns' especially dedicated to Mary Immaculate in Poland and Japan.

Men looked at what went on in the camp at Auschwitz. Even if it seemed to their eyes that one of their companions died in torture, even if humanly they could consider his 'going from them to be a destruction', in reality they were aware that it was not merely death.

Maximilian is not dead, but he has 'given his life for his brother'. There was in that death, humanly so terrible, all the absolute greatness of the human act and human choice: he, himself, on his very own, had offered himself to death out of love.

And in this human death there was the transparent witness given to Christ: witness given in Christ to the dignity of man, to the sanctity of his life and to the saving power of death, in which is revealed the strength of love. It is precisely on this account that the death of Maximilian Kolbe has become a sign of victory. It was a victory achieved over the whole system of outrage and hatred towards man and towards what is divine in man, a victory like to that which our Lord Jesus Christ achieved on calvary. 'You are my friends, if you do what I command you.'

Pope John Paul II, Homily for the Mass of Canonization of Maximilian Kolbe,
10 October, 1982

15 August
The Assumption of the Blessed Virgin Mary
SOLEMNITY

The doctrine of the Assumption of the Blessed Virgin Mary, body and soul, into heaven, was defined as divinely revealed by Pope Pius XII on 1 November, 1950. The feast, originally entitled 'Dormitio', had been celebrated in Rome on this day since the seventh century. In some parts of the East and in the old Gallican and Celtic Churches the feast of our Lady was celebrated in the middle of January. Like all the doctrines of the faith that of the Assumption was not fully formulated overnight, but over several centuries of discussion, reflection and prayer. It has been celebrated as we understand it, though, for well over a thousand years.

The reading offered is taken from a homily of Amadeus of Lausanne. The direct reference is not to Mary's Assumption, but rather to its origin and source, which is the Resurrection of Christ, her Son.

Amadeus was a monk of Clairvaux who became bishop of Lausanne.

Solomon says there is a time for joy and a time for grief. Grief has departed, the time for joy has come, that true joy which proceeds from Christ's resurrection. For he has risen and he has raised up his mother's soul. She lay as in a narrow tomb of grief while the Lord lay in the sepulchre. As he arose, her spirit lived again and, waking as if from deep slumber, she saw in the morning light the sun of justice (Mal 4:2) and the rays of his rising. She gazed upon the beginning of the rising dawn and the future resurrection of her flesh, coming before time in her son. She feasted her eyes upon the glowing flesh of the risen Lord and in her heart perceived the glory of his godhead, so that within and without, leaving and entering, she enjoyed the pasturage of true and everlasting felicity (cf Jn 10:9). Beside herself, therefore, forgetting self for joy, she clung with all her heart to the Father of spirits and bound fast to God she poured out upon him her whole self and was wholly flooded in the immensity of his love.

Lord, in your strength she rejoiced greatly and she will exult mightily in your saving help. You have granted her her heart's desire and not withheld from her the request of her life, since you have anticipated her with sweet blessings. You have placed on her head a crown of precious stone (Ps 21:1-3). The crown of her head is Christ because, as the wise man says, a wise son is his mother's crown. And who is wiser than he who is the Father's wisdom? It is rightly called a crown of stone because in the new testament Christ is spoken of as the 'stone' (cf Mt 21:42). He was called stone because of his power, precious because of his glory. The psalmist, combining the two, says briefly, 'The Lord of hosts, he is the King of glory' (Ps 24:10). Because he is Lord of hosts, he is therefore a stone. Because he is the King of glory, precious. Truly nothing is stronger than stone, nothing more precious than glory.

Therefore, O blessed one, you possess your joy. Your desire is fulfilled and Christ, your crown, has brought you through grace the sovereignty of heaven, through pity the kingdom of the world, through vengeance the submission of hell. For you, the victor rose from hell, he wore down the gates of brass and broke the bars of iron (Ps 107:16). He occupied hell's fortresses and crushed the dragon's head. He inflicted great slaughter upon his enemies and bound the prince of hell. He slew death and cast into chains the author of death. That author of death was bound with chains of fire.

Amadeus of Lausanne, 'Homily VI in Praise of the Blessed Virgin Mary'

16 August
Saint Stephen of Hungary
OPTIONAL MEMORIAL

Stephen was the fourth Magyar duke to rule Hungary. He was born around the year 970 and was baptized along with his father in or about 985. As ruler he showed himself just and fearless. With papal approval he was crowned first king of Hungary in the year 1001. He built up the Church in his kingdom and was a real lover of the poor for Christ's sake. He completed the foundation of the abbey of Pannonhalma, and from the monks there he chose the first bishops and also the first primate of Hungary, St Astrik; such, at least is the tradition.

Stephen died in 1038 and was canonized in 1083. St Stephen was the creator of Hungary in both the civic and religious sense. He was a great king, and a deeply committed Christian, whatever we may feel today about the union of the cross and sword in his policies and acts.

Stephen's almsgiving was very real: he distributed his alms in person and without any security, and on at least one occasion this nearly cost him his life. It is this which has prompted the choice of reading from Fr Faber's *Growth in Holiness.*

All persons can make much more of their worldly calling than they have done hitherto by putting a supernatural intention into it. They can join confraternities, provided they do not allow themselves to be overloaded with vocal prayers. Most people can give alms; but to turn their alms to the temporal necessities of others into alms to their own spiritual necessities as well, they must give till they feel the giving, till it touches, nips, hurts. Without this, where is the sacrifice?

Many also can themselves give time, talent, and pains to the works of mercy, which their pastors or others set on foot around them. Time and pains are worth as much as money to the objects of your charity: they are worth ten times as much considered as spiritual blessings to yourself. But do not be in a hurry, and do not act without counsel; but allow yourself to be guided to some good work in which you can take an abiding interest, and which will suit your spirits, means, and inclinations.

It is surely an obvious mistake for persons to start on a spiritual course as if they were going to be hermits. It is to confound an interior with a solitary life. Their fight is to be in the world's common ways, and their business with its engrossing and multifarious interests, and their trials are to be in no slight measure from their fellow men and women. They must therefore make allowances and arrangements for all this. It must enter into their calculations. It must influence their decisions.

It is true that at the moment of conversion, as in the state of contemplation, we realize nothing but God and our own soul. It is a blessed gift this singleness of vision, blessed at its own time and in its own place. It is one of our beginnings which is so like our endings. But it is not to be our ordinary or normal state of things.

F.W. Faber, *Growth in Holiness,* pp 56-7

19 August
Saint John Eudes, *priest*
OPTIONAL MEMORIAL

John Eudes was born in Normandy in 1601, and there spent most of his life. He joined the secular clergy and then the Oratory. Deeply concerned for others, he preached throughout Normandy, and, in time of plague, nursed those who were stricken. He founded a convent for the care of prostitutes in 1641, and this developed into the institute of the Sisters of Our Lady of Charity of the Refuge.

St John left the Oratory to found his own Congregation of Jesus and Mary — the Eudists — intended chiefly for the running of seminaries.

He promoted devotion to the hearts of Jesus and Mary, and, in fact instituted the liturgical cult of the Sacred Heart of Jesus at Rouen in 1670. He died in 1680 and was canonized in 1925.

The tone of much of his devotional writings would not appeal to many today, but his works were of great significance in seventeenth and eighteenth century France. The reading is from a letter of direction addressed to an Abbess. Note the positive desire for suffering, in order to be one with Christ.

He is there, guiding and leading you along the paths of his love, and drawing you toward the perfection of love by means of those trials and severities.

He is there, bearing with you through his love all the anguish of mind and body that is yours to bear. Even though you may often be unaware of it, he is nevertheless infallibly present, for if he were absent you would find it impossible to support even the least of the infirmities you are suffering.

He is still there, purifying and sanctifying you and preparing great things for you, provided you on your part, give the co-operation he asks.

He is there for the purpose of filling you completely with love for him, and much more so than you are filled with suffering. I will say even more: not only does he wish to imbue you with his love, but also to transform you entirely into love for him through crosses and sufferings, as his cross and sufferings transformed him into love for us.

He is there, finally, with a most ardent desire to draw you to himself, to perfect and consummate you in himself, along the path of these same sufferings. St Paul says that it was fitting that Jesus Christ should be consummated by suffering. 'For it was appropriate that God . . . should make perfect, through suffering, the leader who would take them to their salvation' (Heb 2:10).

O dignity, O holiness, O admirable excellence of suffering to be used for the honour and consummation of a God, for the perfection of Jesus, God and Man, for the consummation of him who is the consummation and perfection of all things! Great was the humiliation of Jesus, who humbled himself to a state in which he was capable of being perfected and consummated! But immense was the dignity of suffering, chosen and used by him and his eternal Father to achieve this perfection and consummation!

Is it not a great honour for you, Madame, is it not a great favour and should it not be a great comfort to you to be consumed and perfected through suffering, as Jesus was consumed by suffering? Does not Jesus show a rare and singular love for you by using the same means for your fulfilment and consummation as he employed for his own? May Christ crucified be forever blessed, for so giving you a share in the blessings of his cross! I implore him to crucify you completely with him, and to do so through the same love which nailed him to the cross for your sake.

St John Eudes, 'A letter of direction to an Abbess'

20 August
Saint Bernard, *abbot and doctor of the Church*
MEMORIAL

Bernard was born of a good family, in Burgundy, France, in 1090. He was well educated and developed into a lively leader of others. When he decided to enter the 'New Monastery', Citeaux, about the age of twenty-two, he managed to persuade a host of others to follow him. It was a turning point in the history of the monastery, and one of the turning points in the history of western monasticism. This was in 1112. Only three years later, in 1115, Bernard was sent as head of a group of monks to found Clairvaux, and he was to rule that house as abbot until his death in 1153.

In his first years as abbot he went to extremes in the practice of asceticism, but ill health forced him to modify his regime. He lived a genuinely mystical prayer life, was an eloquent preacher, and came to dominate his age as few men have done. Clairvaux under him quite eclipsed Citeaux as a centre of monastic life and renewal, its influence reaching from Ireland to eastern Europe.

Bernard was canonized in 1174. He left many writings on the spiritual and monastic life. The reading offered here is from the opening of one of his earliest writings, *The Steps of Humility*, which is a commentary on chapter seven of the Rule of Benedict.

Christ the Way

It is our Lord himself who tells us of the toil accompanying the journey, and of the reward we shall receive for our efforts. 'I am the way and the truth and the life', he says. The way is humility which leads to truth; humility is what we strive to gain, while truth is the fruit of our achievement. But when Christ says merely that he is the way, how can I be sure, you may ask, that he is really talking about humility? To this my reply is that you should listen to what he says elsewhere in the gospel: 'Learn from me, for I am meek and humble of heart'. Here he is setting himself before us as an example of humility and a model of meekness for us to imitate; and if we follow his example we shall not be walking in the dark, but shall have the light which is life. And what is the light of life if it is not the truth that enlightens every soul born into the world, and shows where true life is to be found? And that is why, when he said 'I am the way and the truth', he added — 'and the life'. It is just as if he had said: I am the way that leads to truth; I am the truth itself, and I promise you life. I myself am the life that I give, 'for eternal life is to know thee, Father in heaven, the one true God, and Jesus Christ whom thou hast sent.' Or else it is just as if you had said: I see that the way is humility, and I long for the reward of truth, but what if the effort required for the journey is so great that I cannot come to the prize for which I yearn? And you will hear the reassuring answer that he is the life, the food to sustain and strengthen you on your journey. It is to those who are lost and do not know the way that he cries, 'I am the Way'; to those who doubt or do not believe, 'I am the truth'; to those who are growing weary as they climb, 'I am the life'. In my opinion, these quotations from the gospel show quite clearly that the reward of humility is the knowledge of truth. But in case you are still unconvinced, listen to this: 'I give thee praise, Father, who art Lord of heaven and earth, that thou hast hidden these things (the secrets of truth) from wise and clever men (which I take to mean the proud) and revealed them to simple folk' — in other words, to the humble. These words should make it quite clear, I think, that the truth, hidden from the proud, is revealed instead to the humble.

And now we can give this definition of humility: humility is the virtue by which one comes to be despicable in one's own eyes through the discovery and knowledge of what one really is. This is the virtue possessed by those whose hearts are set on the pilgrimage as they go from step to step until they reach the very top of the ladder of humility.

St Bernard of Clairvaux, *The Steps of Humility*, c 1

21 August
Saint Pius X, *pope*
MEMORIAL

Joseph Sarto was born in humble circumstances in Venice in 1835. He entered the diocesan clergy, and worked in various pastoral charges, becoming a canon of Treviso. Marked by zeal and charity he was chosen as bishop of Mantua in 1884. So successful was he there, that in 1892 he was made patriarch of

Venice and so cardinal. In 1903 he succeeded Leo XIII as pope. The device or motto he chose, 'to restore all things in Christ', expresses his ideal. He was simple and good, gentle and humble, remarkable for holiness. As pope he was the real father of the modern revival of pastoral liturgy and sacramental practice, the reforms he initiated only coming to completion in the aftermath of the Second Vatican Council.

His condemnation of Modernism is a source of controversy today. Undoubtedly there were innocent victims of the champions of orthodoxy, but there were dangerous tendencies in the cult of being 'up-to-date', dangers and tendencies which did not cease to exist with his death on 20 August, 1914.

St Pius was canonized in 1954.

The reading is from his 'Pastoral Exhortation to the Clergy', marking the fiftieth anniversary of his priestly ordination.

A priest is not one who may be good or bad for himself alone: his mode and habit of living has much consequent effect on the faithful. Where a priest is really good how inestimable the blessing to his people!

Therefore, beloved Sons, We begin the exhortation by urging you to that holiness of life which the dignity to which you are raised demands. Whoever is graced with the priestly office is vested with it not for himself alone, but for others also: 'For every high priest taken from among men is appointed to act for men in their relations with God' (Heb 5:1). And this is Christ's own teaching; for when he wished to illustrate the action of priests he compared them with salt and with light. The priest, then, is the light of the world, the salt of the earth. Everybody knows that he is this above all by teaching christian truth; but who does not know that teaching of this kind is almost worthless if the priest does not confirm by his example that which he delivers by word? His hearers will object, with rude sarcasm indeed, but not undeservedly, 'They profess that they know God, but in their works they deny him' (Tit 1:16); and they will refuse the teaching and take no benefit from the light of the priest. Therefore Christ himself, made the pattern of priests, first taught by deed, then by words: 'Jesus began to do and to teach' (Acts 1:1).

Further, when sanctity is neglected, the priest cannot be the salt of the earth; a thing corrupted and infected cannot contribute to soundness, and when sanctity is wanting there must be corruption. Hence

Christ pressing home the same comparison calls such priests salt that has lost its savour, which 'is good for nothing any more but to be cast out, and to be trodden on by men' (Mt 5:13).

All this is more clearly evident because we fulfil the priestly office not in our own name but in the name of Jesus Christ. 'Let a man account of us,' says the Apostle, 'as the ministers of Christ, and the dispensers of the mysteries of God' (1 Cor 4:1). 'For Christ, therefore, we are ambassadors' (2 Cor 5:20). For this reason Christ has enrolled us not in the number of his servants but of his friends: 'I will not call you servants . . . but I have called you friends: because all things whatsoever I have heard of my Father I have made known to you . . . I have chosen you; and have appointed you, that you should go, and should bring forth fruit' (Jn 15:15, 16).

We priests, therefore, must bear as representatives the person of Christ; we must so discharge the embassy entrusted by him to us, that as far as he wills, so far must we reach. And since to will and not to will the same things is the sure and only sign of firm friendship, we are bound as friends to let this mind be in us which was also in Christ Jesus, who is 'holy, innocent, undefiled' (Heb 7:26). Thus, then, as his ambassadors, we ought to draw the faith of men to his teachings and to his law, by first observing them ourselves; and since as sharers in his power we raise souls from the chains of sin, it is only right that we make every effort to avoid becoming entangled ourselves in those same bonds.

Pius X, *Exhortation to the Catholic Clergy on the Fiftieth Anniversary of his Priesthood,* 4 August, 1908

22 August
The Queenship of Mary
MEMORIAL

This feast was first instituted by Pope Pius XII in 1955, and has since been assigned to today to emphasize the link between Mary's Assumption and her Queenship. Mary has been hailed as Queen from very early times, particularly in the prayer of monks.

The reading is from a homily of Amadaeus of Lausanne (cf 15 August).

The glorious Virgin was, with flesh untouched and tranquil mind, the gentlest of the living: the more lowly and more holy she is than all others, the higher was she raised above all until she was received into heaven by its citizens with every mark of honour. There in the fashion of a queen, she was bidden by the supreme Father to sit down in the kingdom of eternal brightness and on the throne of surpassing glory, first in rank after the Son whom she bore incarnate.

Mighty God, terrible and strong, of unspeakable goodness, you raise and exalt your humble handmaid to the place from which you had long ago driven out your jealous foe, so that humility might triumph, adorned by you with the increase of grace and a glorious crown, while pride, empty and dark, might fall in ruin.

Conspicuous therefore by her unparalleled merit the blessed lady stands before the face of her Creator interceding always for us with her powerful prayer (cf Heb 7:25). Taught by that light to which all things are bare and open, she sees all our dangers, and, our merciful and sweet lady, pities us with motherly affection.

The holy creatures which, as one reads in Ezekiel, are full of eyes before and behind, within and without and round about (Ez 1:18), cannot weigh as can the mother of God the toils of men, their griefs, misfortunes, failures, blindness, weaknesses, deadly perils, the uncertain end of life and every ill of the human race; and, by weighing them, with heaven's help dispense and drive them away. The more she beholds from on high the heart of the mighty king the more profoundly she knows, by the grace of divine pity, how to pity the unhappy and to help the afflicted.

Amadeus of Lausanne, 'Homily VIII in Praise of the Blessed Virgin Mary'

23 August
Saint Rose of Lima, *virgin*
OPTIONAL MEMORIAL

Rose was born in 1586 in Lima in Peru and belonged to a Spanish-American family. She was christened Isabel, but because of her beauty as a child she was always called Rose. She herself disfigured that beauty. Her piety was very much under Dominican influence and she joined the Third Order of St Dominic. She sought to model her life on that of St Catherine of Siena and combined a life of prayer and penance with charitable activity, among other things abandoning her parents' house to live in a small hut in the garden. She died at the age of thirty-one in 1617, and was canonized in 1671 by Pope Clement IX.

St Rose had great devotion to the Rosary of our Lady, which seems in no way to have impeded her rise to mystical prayer! On the other hand some of her penitential practices have a rather morbid quality and one can only wonder over the quality of the spiritual direction she received.

The reading is from John of Landsberg, A Letter from Jesus Christ. The author was a Carthusian of the early 16th century; the English version here used is based on that of Blessed Philip Howard. The chapter is entitled 'Using the gifts of God for others.'

I want you to use my gifts to help other people as best you can. If you can do something they cannot, then the one charity in you all will make many of you with diverse gifts, one body. Whatever this body has in one limb should be used to the benefit of the rest. Every member of my body ought to make one another a sharer in the gifts which every one of them receives, because of the union of the body and the communion of love which exists among them.

So be cheerful in serving your neighbours, glad to bear their burdens, meek to suffer with them, gentle to comfort them, ready to help them and willing to rejoice with them, so that no envy at all, no argument, no copying, no trying to please your own inclinations is found in you, or in your neighbours, but there is perfect love and communication of my gifts one with another, as between the members of one body. You have nothing that is your own. What do you possess that you have not received? You have nothing that is not mine. You have nothing that is given to you alone, that is, you have nothing that is given to you for yourself alone, but everything that you have received is committed to your care to be used entirely for the benefit of the whole body of my Church. Be careful with it, for I shall ask for an account of what you have done with it.

Never think that you are contented and perfectly realized in being with me, but remember that if the physical or spiritual needs of your neighbours call you away from even profound contemplation, you must be ready to forsake your own consolation — the pleasures of devotion. Neglect your own pleasure and run in haste to help your neighbour for my sake. It is perfect love not to seek your own but your neighbour's good. That charity is more acceptable to me and more profitable to you than all the contemplation or devotion you practise on your own.

In addition, always remember that in all your actions, feelings, and things you choose or avoid, I must be your beginning, middle and end, so whatever you do or leave undone is for my sake. You are most acceptable to me when you leave yourself for my sake, because you forsake your own concerns and try to help your neighbours in their need.

John of Landsberg, *A Letter from Jesus Christ*, c 30

24 August
Saint Bartholomew, *apostle*
FEAST

Bartholomew is mentioned in the Synoptic Gospels as one of the Twelve, and is constantly linked with St Philip. In the Gospel according to John the name Bartholomew does not appear, but that of Nathanael. The presumption is that the one person is indicated by the two names. Bartholomew would have been a native of Galilee, and tradition variously claims that he preached the Gospel in Armenia and in India, and finally suffered martyrdom.

The reading is from a sermon by John Henry Newman.

An even, unvaried life is the lot of most men, in spite of occasional troubles or other accidents; and we are apt to despise it, and to get tired of it, and to long to see the world, or, at all events we think such a life affords no great opportunity for religious obedience. To rise up, and go through the same duties, and then to rest again, day after day; to pass week after week, beginning with God's service on Sunday, and then to our worldly tasks: so to continue till year follows year, and we gradually get old — an unvaried life like this is apt to seem unprofitable to us when we dwell upon the thought of it.

Many indeed, there are, who do not think at all, but live in their round of employments without care about God and religion, driven on by the natural course of things in a dull irrational way like the beasts that perish. But when a man begins to feel he has a soul, and a work to do, and a reward to be gained, greater or less, according as he improves the talents committed to him, then he is naturally tempted to be anxious from his very wish to be saved, and he says 'What must I *do* to please God?' And sometimes he is led to think he ought to be useful on a large scale, and goes out of his line of life, that he may be doing something worth doing, as he considers it.

Here we have the history of St Bartholomew and the other apostles to recall us to ourselves, and to assure us that we need not give up our usual manner of life, in order to serve God; that the most humble and quietest station is acceptable to him, if improved duly — nay, affords means for maturing the highest christian character, even that of an apostle. Bartholomew read the scriptures and prayed to God; and thus was trained at length to give up his life for Christ, when he demanded it.

But, further, let us consider the particular praise which our Saviour gives him. 'Behold an Israelite indeed, in whom is no guile!' This is just the character which, through God's grace, they may attain most fully, who live out of the world in the private way I have been describing — which is made least account of by man, and thought to be in the way of success in life, though our Saviour chose it to make head against all the power and wisdom of the world.

David describes his character in the fifteenth psalm; and, taken in all its parts, it is a rare one. He asks, 'Lord, who shall abide in thy tabernacle? Who shall dwell in thy holy hill? He that walketh uprightly, and worketh righteousness, and speaketh the truth in his heart. He that backbiteth not with his tongue, nor doeth evil to his neighbour, nor taketh up a reproach against his neighbour. In whose eyes a vile person is condemned; but he honoureth them that fear the Lord. He that sweareth to his own hurt, and changeth not.'

I say it is difficult and rare virtue, to mean what we say, to love without dissimulation, to think no evil, to bear no grudge, to be free from selfishness, to be innocent and straightforward. This character of mind is something far above the generality of people; and when realized in due measure, one of the surest marks of Christ's elect.

J.H. Newman, *Parochial and Plain Sermons*, II, 27

25 August
Saint Louis
OPTIONAL MEMORIAL

Louis was born in 1214, the son of Louis VIII of France and his wife, Blanche of
Castille. His father died when Louis was twelve years of age and he became
king, although, until he was of age, his mother acted as regent. It was her
upbringing which, in large measure, was responsible for Louis' later goodness. In 1234 he married Margaret of Provence and they had eleven children.
Louis, who had joined the Third Order of Saint Francis, hoped that one or
other of these would enter the religious state, but that was not to be.

As king, Louis was just and firm, as he was devout and charitable, and was
possessed of great integrity of character — his word was his bond. The period
of his reign witnessed a great flowering of French culture, particularly in the
building of the great gothic cathedrals, but also in theology and letters, as can
be judged by the influence of the schools of Paris. In this period the Sorbonne
was founded.

Louis went on two crusades, neither of which was successful. While on the
second of them he died of typhus at Tunisia. Today we should be inclined to
see the crusades as a mistaken ideal, but Louis was moved by a sincere zeal for
the interests of Christianity, as he saw them, and not by self-interest.

The reading is an extract from the Instruction he made out for his daughter
Isabelle, who had, through her marriage, become queen of Navarre. This
instruction he wrote out in his own hand.

Dear daughter, I instruct you to love our Lord God with all your heart
and all your strength: for without such love no one can be worth anything, nor can anything be loved so rightly and profitably. It is the
Lord to whom every creature can say: 'Lord, you are my God, who
have no need of my goods.' It is the Lord who sent his blessed Son to
this earth and handed him over to death to deliver us from the death
of hell.

Dear daughter, if you love him, yours will be the profit. The creature who places the love of their heart anywhere else but in him and
under him is very much misled. Dear daughter, the way in which we
ought to love God, is to love him without measure: he has well
deserved that we love him, for he has loved us first. I would that you
had known well to think on the deeds which the blessed Son of God
performed for your redemption.

Dear daughter, desire greatly to know as to how you may please him, and put great care and industry into the avoiding of matters which you think must displease him. You must have this intention, especially, not to commit mortal sin, come what may, and to suffer rather that your limbs be cut off and your life taken away by a cruel martyrdom, than to deliberately commit mortal sin.

Dear daughter, accustom yourself to frequent confession, and always choose confessors of holy life and adequate learning, by whom you may be instructed concerning those matters which you must avoid, and those things which you must do. And so hold yourself that your confessor and other friends may dare to instruct and correct you withour fear.

Dear daughter, listen gladly to the service of holy Church, and when you are in church avoid mooning about and useless conversations. Say your prayers in peace both of tongue and of thought; and, especially when the body of Jesus Christ is present at Mass, be more at peace and more attentive to prayer and a little time before it.

Dear daughter, listen gladly to talk about God in sermons and private conversations, but avoid private conversation except with those remarkable for goodness and holiness. Freely obtain papal and other indulgences. If you have some uneasiness of heart or other uneasiness, and if it is a matter you can tell, tell it to your confessor or to some other persons whom you think to be loyal and who really ought keep your secret, so that you can bear it more in peace.

Dear daughter, keep your heart well disposed towards the people whom you hear are afflicted in heart or body, and help them willingly with consolation or alms, according as you will be able in a proper manner. Dear daughter, love all good people whether in religion or the world, those of whom you hear it said that they honour and serve God. Love the poor and give them help, and especially those who for love of Our Lord are reduced to poverty.

St Louis, Letter of Instruction to his Daughter, Isabelle

25 August, also
Saint Joseph Calasanz, *priest*
OPTIONAL MEMORIAL

Joseph was born in Aragon, Spain, in 1556, of a well-to-do family. He entered the priesthood when in his thirties and journeyed to Rome in 1592. In Rome he established a congregation of Clerks Regular to run free schools for boys — his Roman school was the first free school there. This congregation were called the Piarists and spread through Italy and into Germany. Success roused contention however, and the then Pope suppressed the institute in 1646.

St Joseph died in 1648 and his work began again after he had died. The contradictions and persecutions he underwent caused him to be ranked with Job for patience.

The reading is taken from the Declaration of the Second Vatican Council on 'Christian Education'.

The Church's involvement in the field of education is demonstrated especially by the Catholic school. No less than other schools does the Catholic school pursue cultural goals and the natural development of youth. But it has several distinctive purposes. It aims to create for the school community an atmosphere enlivened by the gospel spirit of freedom and charity. It aims to help the adolescent in such a way that the development of his own personality will be matched by the growth of that new creation which he became by baptism. It strives to relate all human culture eventually to the news of salvation, so that the light of faith will illumine the knowledge which students gradually gain of the world, of life, and of mankind.

So it is that while the Catholic school fittingly adjusts itself to the circumstances of advancing times, it is educating its students to promote effectively the welfare of the earthly city, and preparing them to serve the advancement of the reign of God. The purpose in view is that by living an exemplary and apostolic life, the Catholic graduate can become, as it were, the saving leaven of the human family.

Therefore, since it can contribute so substantially to fulfilling the mission of God's people, and can further the dialogue between the Church and the family of man, to their mutual benefit, the Catholic school retains its immense importance in the circumstances of our times too. Consequently, this sacred Synod proclaims anew a right already made clear in numerous documents of the Church's teaching authority, namely, the Church's right freely to establish and to run schools of every kind and at every level. At the same time, the Council recalls that the exercise of this right makes a supreme contribution to freedom of conscience, the protection of parental rights, and the progress of culture itself.

But let teachers realize that to the greatest possible extent they determine whether the Catholic school can bring its goals and undertakings to fruition. They should, therefore, be trained with particular care so that they may be enriched with both secular and religious knowledge, appropriately certified, and may be equipped with an educational skill which reflects modern-day findings. Bound by charity to one another and to their students, and penetrated by an apostolic spirit, let them give witness to Christ, the unique Teacher, by their lives as well as by their teachings.

Vatican II, *Declaration on Christian Education*, n 8

27 August
Saint Monica
MEMORIAL

Monica was born of christian parents, in North Africa in 332. She was married to a pagan, Patricius, whom, by her gentleness, she converted to the christian faith. He predeceased her. Her desire was to be buried alongside him, but this was not to be, for she died at Ostia, in Italy, in the year 387.

We know of her through her son, the future St Augustine, who loved her dearly and who finally proved the efficacy of her tears and prayers by becoming a Christian and abandoning his errant ways. Among the most beautiful pages in Augustine's *Confessions* are those relating to her last days and death. The reading given below is excerpted from this part of the *Confessions*.

I closed her eyes, and a great wave of sorrow surged into my heart. It would have overflowed in tears if I had not made a strong effort of will and stemmed the flow, so that the tears dried in my eyes. What a terrible struggle it was to hold them back! As she breathed her last, the boy Adeodatus began to wail aloud and only ceased his cries when we all checked him. I, too, felt that I wanted to cry like a child but a more mature voice within me, the voice of my heart, bade me keep my sobs in check, and I remained silent. For we did not think it right to mark my mother's death with weeping and moaning, because such lamentations are the usual accompaniment of death when it is thought of as a state of misery or as a total extinction. But she had not died in misery nor had she wholly died. Of this we were certain, both because we knew what a holy life she had led and also because our faith was real and we had sure reasons not to doubt it.

What was it, then, that caused me such deep sorrow? It can only have been because the wound was fresh, the wound I had received when our life together, which had been so precious and so dear to me, was suddenly cut off. I found comfort in the memory that as I did what I could for my mother in the last stages of her illness, she had caressed me and said that I was a good son to her. With great emotion she told me that she could not remember ever having heard me speak a single hard or disrespectful word against her. And yet, O God who made us both, how could there be any comparison between the honour which I showed to her and the devoted service she had given me? It was because I was now bereft of all the comfort I had had from her that my soul was wounded and my life seemed shattered, for her life and mine had been as one.

When we had succeeded in quieting Adeodatus, Evodius took up a psaltery and began to sing the psalm *Of mercy and justice my song shall be; a psalm in thy honour, Lord,* and the whole house sang the responses. On hearing what was happening many of our brothers in the faith and many pious women came to us, and while those whose duty it was made arrangements for the funeral, I remained in another room, where I could talk without irreverence, and conversed with friends on matters suitable to the occasion, for they did not think it right to leave me to myself. These words of truth were the salve with which I soothed my pain. You knew, O Lord, how I suffered, but my friends did not, and as they listened intently to my words, they thought that I had no sense of grief.

When the body was carried out for burial, I went and returned without a tear. I did not weep even during the prayers which we recited while the sacrifice of our redemption was offered for my mother and her body rested by the grave before it was laid in the earth, as is the custom there. Yet all that day I was secretly weighed down with grief. With all my heart I begged you to heal my sorrow, but you did not grant my prayer. I believe that this was because you wished to impress upon my memory, if only by this one lesson, how firmly the mind is gripped in the bonds of habit, even when it is nourished on the word of truth.

Then I went to sleep and woke up to find that the rest had brought me some relief from my sorrow.

Then little by little, my old feelings about your handmaid came back to me. I thought of her devoted love for you and the tenderness and patience she had shown to me, like the holy woman that she was. Of all this I found myself suddenly deprived, and it was a comfort to me to weep for her and for myself and to offer my tears to you for her sake and for mine. The tears which I had been holding back streamed down, and I let them flow as freely as they would, making of them a pillow for my heart. On them it rested, for my weeping sounded in your ears alone, not in the ears of men who might have misconstrued it and despised it.

St Augustine, *Confessions*, IX, 12

28 August
Saint Augustine, *bishop and doctor of the Church*
MEMORIAL

Augustine was born in Thagaste in North Africa in 354 and received a good education. Possessed of a brilliant mind, he was also rather wayward in his moral life, though never undutiful in his parents' regard, nor in other obligations. He received baptism at the age of thirty-three from St Ambrose in Milan. His mother's role in his conversion has been recalled on her Memorial (see 27 August above).

After his baptism, Augustine returned to North Africa and lived the ascetic life — it might be better to say 'the life of the evangelical counsels' — with some companions. He was then called to serve in the clergy, and in 395 to be bishop of Hippo, a not very important see. He remained bishop of Hippo until his death in the year 430.

Augustine was one of the most influential of christian saints, particularly in the Western Church. He had one of the keenest and humblest minds ever given to the study and proclamation of the christian mysteries — other bishops objected to his practice of inviting his clergy to preach in his presence! An immense body of his sermons and writings has been preserved: inevitably this work was of an uneven value, but his greatest works are of enduring worth. He was the great doctor of God's grace, which is nothing other than an effective gratuitous love, and whichever way we view it, few people have so understood or expounded the meaning of christian love. Perhaps his exposition of the First Letter of Saint John represents the peak of this.

The reading is taken from his *Confessions,* which are more biographical than his other writings.

So, O Lord, all that I am is laid bare before you. I have declared how it profits me to confess to you. And I make my confession, not in words and sounds made by the tongue alone, but with the voice of my soul and in my thoughts which cry aloud to you. Your ear can hear them. For when I am sinful, if I am displeased with myself, this is a confession that I make to you; and when I am good, if I do not claim the merit for myself, this too is confession. For you, O Lord, 'give your benediction to the just' (Ps 5:12), but first 'you make a just man of the sinner' (Rom 4:5). And so my confession is made both silently in your sight, my God, and aloud as well, because even though my tongue utters no sound, my heart cries to you. For whatever good I may speak to men you have heard it before in my heart, and whatever good you hear in my heart, you have first spoken to me yourself.

Physician of my soul, make me see clearly how it profits me to do this. You have forgiven my past sins and drawn a veil over them, and in this way you have given me happiness in yourself, changing my life by faith and your sacrament. But when others read of those past sins of mine, or hear about them, their hearts are stirred so that they no longer lie listless in despair, crying 'I cannot'. Instead their hearts are roused by the love of your mercy and the joy of your grace, by which each one of us, weak though he be, is made strong, since by it he is made conscious of his own weakness. And the good are glad to hear of the past sins of others who are now free of them. They are glad, not because those sins are evil, but because what was evil is now evil no more.

But what good do they hope will be done if they listen to what I say? Is it that they wish to join with me in thanking you, when they hear how close I have come to you by your grace, and to pray for me, when they hear how far I am set apart from you by the burden of my sins? If this is what they wish, I shall tell them what I am. For no small good is gained, O Lord my God, if many offer you thanks for me and many pray to you for me. Let all who are truly my brothers love in me what they know from your teaching to be worthy of their love, and let them sorrow to find in me what they know from your teaching to be occasion for remorse. This is what I wish my true brothers to feel in their hearts. I do not speak of strangers or of 'alien foes, who make treacherous promises, and lift their hands in perjury' (Ps 143:8). But my true brothers and sisters are those who rejoice for me in their hearts when they find good in me, and grieve for me when they find sin. They are my true brothers and sisters, because whether they see good in me or evil, they love me still. To such as these I shall reveal what I am. Let them breathe a sigh of joy for what is good in me and a sigh of grief for what is bad. The good I do is done by you in me and by your grace.

St Augustine, *Confessions*. X, 2, 3, 4

29 August
The Beheading of John the Baptist
MEMORIAL

The story of the death of St John the Baptist is related in the Gospels. The liturgical origins of the Memorial are perhaps to be traced to Sebaste in Palestine, where St John was commemorated on this day in the fifth century. The reading is taken from St John Chrysostom's Homilies on Saint Matthew's Gospel.

Although Herod was so evil, Herodias was more evil than both despot and girl, for she contrived all these evil doings and the whole business, she who ought especially to have been grateful to the prophet for his concern for her salvation. For her daughter, in obedience to her, acted shamefully, and danced and sought John's murder, and Herod was trapped by her.

See how justly Christ said: Anyone who prefers father or mother to me is not worthy of me. For if she had kept this law, she would not have transgressed so many laws, she would not have perpetrated this foul murder.

For what could be worse than this barbarism? to ask a murder by way of a favour, an evil murder, a murder during a feast, a murder, publicly and without shame. For she did not approach him in private to ask these things, but publicly, all pretence cast away, barefaced, and having the devil to plead with her, she said what she said.

Consider the request itself. Give me, she says, here on a dish, the head of John the Baptist. Do you see her lost to all shame, who has given herself wholly to the devil? Give me here on a dish, because I wish to see that tongue silenced. Yet God permitted it, nor did he send a thunderbolt from on high to burn that brazen face, neither did he order the earth to open and swallow that whole evil banquet: God permitted it so that he might crown the just man to a greater degree and leave great consolation to those who afterwards were to suffer anything unjustly.

Let us, therefore, pay heed, whatever troubles we suffer from evil men, while we live uprightly. For God suffered him, who had lived in the desert, in a leather girdle, in a garment of camel's hair, a prophet, greater than the prophets, than whom no one among those born of women was ever greater, to be killed by an immodest girl and a corrupt harlot: and all this while he was upholding the divine laws. Considering these things therefore, let us bear generously all whatever we suffer!

Herodias, this bloodthirsty and evil woman, took vengeance on him who had caused her grief, just as she desired and fully sated her anger, and God permitted it: although John had said nothing to her, nor had he accused her, but only the man. But her conscience was her keen accuser. Therefore she broke out in greater evils, being afflicted and stung, and in one go she disgraced all, herself, her daughter, her departed husband*, her living paramour, and sought to surpass her former acts. If you are afflicted, she said, because he has committed

---

* Chrysostom understood that Herodias' first husband was dead; in fact he was still alive and Herod had divorced his own wife to take her. Hence John's accusation, and Herodias' wrath.

adultery, I shall make him into a murderer, and the killer of his accuser. Pay heed all you who seek to please your wives more than you ought! Pay heed all you who utter oaths concerning matters which are uncertain, and give others power for your own destruction, and dig a pit for yourselves. In this way Herod perished. For he thought she would ask something in harmony with the banquet, and that the girl, on the occasion of the feast, in the course of the meal, would request something joyful and agreeable, not however the head of a man — and he was caught out!

St John Chrysostom, *Homily 48 on Matthew*

3 September
Saint Gregory the Great, *pope and doctor of the Church*
MEMORIAL

Gregory was a Roman noble, born about the year 540. In his early thirties he was Prefect of the City but about 575 he decided to become a monk. He did not have long to enjoy his monastic seclusion for he was ordained deacon and sent by the then pope on a mission to Constantinople which lasted from 580 to 585. In 590 he himself was elected pope, and ruled so well and wisely in spite of constant ill-health, that he has ever since been regarded as one of the greatest of St Peter's successors.

He undertook the repopulating of Rome by encouraging settlement and commissioned the missions to the Lombards, to Sardinia and to England, using monks for these latter tasks and so vitally influencing monastic history in the Latin West. He can truly be considered the founder of the medieval papacy in that he set a pattern and an ideal of action and government, and he can also be considered as in large measure the founder of the European Middle Ages. His writings were among those most read in the medieval monasteries.

St Gregory died in 604.

The reading is from his Pastoral Rule, a treatise on the office of bishop. The chapter chosen outlines the qualities St Gregory saw necessary for one who should be called to be bishop — qualities which we may presume he himself had, or at least aspired to — and his understanding of the office.

That man, therefore, ought be forced by every means to become an example of how to live, who already lives in a spiritual manner, dying to all the passions of the flesh; who has put behind himself worldly prosperity, is afraid of no adversity, who desires only the goods of the soul; whose body and spirit are in harmony with his purpose and are not a source of hindrance.

A man who is not drawn to desire the goods of others, but gives freely of his own. One who by his tender love is moved more quickly to forgiveness, but is never turned away from the summit of righteousness by forgiving more than is fitting. A man who commits no unlawful deeds, but laments as his own those committed by others. Who, out of heartfelt sympathy is compassionate with others' weakness, and likewise rejoices in the good deeds of his neighbour as in his own spiritual advances. Who so makes himself known as a model for imitation to others in everything he does that among them he shall have no cause to be ashamed, at least concerning matters accomplished. A man who strives so to live that he may be able to water even the parched hearts of his neighbours with the streams of doctrine. One who has already learnt by the use and trial of prayer that he can obtain from God what he requests; to whom it is already specially said, as it were, by the maxim of accomplishment, 'While you are still speaking, I shall say, Here I am' (Is 58:9).

For, if by chance someone were to come to us and try to induce us to intercede for them with some powerful person or other, one who is angered with them, who however is unknown to us, we straightaway reply: We cannot come to plead for you, because we have no familiar acquaintance with him. If therefore one is ashamed to act as an intercessor with someone upon whom he has no claim, with what sort of understanding does one take the position of intercession for the people before God, who is not aware that he is a servant of his grace by the merit of his life? Or how can he seek pardon from God for others, who does not know if God is pleased with himself?

In which connection something else is still more particularly to be feared — that he who is believed to be able to appease anger does not merit it by his own guilt. For we all know quite clearly that when one who displeases is sent to make intercession, the mind of the offended party is moved for the worse. One then who is still bound by earthly desires, ought beware, lest kindling more seriously the anger of the severe judge, while he delights in the place of honour, he be to his subjects the occasion of ruin.

St Gregory the Great, *Pastoral Rule*, I, 10

8 September
The Birthday of the Blessed Virgin Mary
FEAST

This feast was first kept in the East. It was accepted in Rome by the end of the seventh century. There is a possibility that in parts of Western Europe the feast was celebrated earlier.

The reading offered is from Cardinal Newman's *Meditations and Devotions*.

How did Mary become the *Rosa Mystica*, the choice, delicate, perfect flower of God's spiritual creation? It was by being born, nurtured and sheltered in the mystical garden or paradise of God. Scripture makes use of the figure of a garden, when it would speak of heaven and its blessed inhabitants. A garden is a spot of ground set apart for trees and plants, all good, all various, for things that are sweet to the taste or fragrant in scent, or beautiful to look upon, or useful for nourishment; and accordingly in its spiritual sense it means the home of blessed spirits and holy souls dwelling there together, souls with both the flowers and the fruits upon them, which by the careful husbandry of God they have come to bear, flowers and fruits of grace, flowers more beautiful and more fragrant than those of any garden, fruits more delicious and exquisite than can be matured by earthly husbandman.

All that God has made speaks of its Maker; the mountains speak of his eternity; the sun of his immensity, and the winds of his almightiness. In like manner flowers and fruits speak of his sanctity, his love, and his providence; and such as are flowers and fruits, such must be the place where they are found. That is to say, since they are found in a garden, therefore a garden has also excellences which speak of God, because it is their home. For instance, it would be out of place if we found beautiful flowers on the mountain-crag, or rich fruit in the sandy desert. As then by flowers and fruits are meant, in a mystical sense, the gifts and graces of the Holy Ghost, so by a garden is meant mystically a place of spiritual repose, stillness, peace, refreshment, and delight.

Such was the garden in which the mystical rose, the immaculate Mary, was sheltered and nursed to be the mother of the all holy God, from her birth to her espousals to St Joseph, a term of thirteen years. For three years of it she was in the arms of her holy mother, St Anne, and then for ten years she lived in the temple of God. In those blessed gardens, as they may be called, she lived by herself, continually visited by the dew of God's grace, and growing up a more and more heavenly flower, till at the end of that period she was suitable for the inhabitation in her of the Most Holy.

J.H. Newman, 'Rosa Mystica' *Meditations and Devotions*

13 September
Saint John Chrysostom, *bishop and doctor of the Church*
MEMORIAL

John was born in Antioch of Syria about the middle of the fourth century. He became a monk, and then was summoned to serve in the ranks of the clergy of his native city. In 397 he was chosen as Patriarch of Constantinople. His zeal for the truth and the poor caused him to lose imperial favour and he died in exile on 14 September, 407.

St John was a celebrated preacher and exegete, whole-hearted in his commitment to what he believed to be the teaching of Christ, but too much inclined to see matters in extreme shades of black and white. If he were not a misogynist, he was at least excessively fearful of women and their influence. In many ways it is interesting to compare his thoughts and attitudes with those of his close western contemporary St Augustine of Hippo.

The reading is taken from his treatise *On the Priesthood*.

Although the priestly office is discharged upon earth, it ranks among celestial ordinances. And this is natural; for no man, no angel, no archangel, no other created power, but the Comforter himself appointed this order, and persuaded us while still abiding in the flesh to represent the angelic ministry. Wherefore the priest must be as pure as if he were standing in heaven itself, amid those powers. Fearful and awful were the symbols which existed before the ministry of grace; as, for example (cf Ex 28), the bells, the pomegranates, the stones on the breastplate, the stones on the ephod, the mitre, the diadem, the long robe, the golden crown, the Holy of Holies, the deep hush within; but should any one examine the things belonging to the ministry of grace, he will find that, however simple they be, they are yet fearful and awful, and the statement made about the law is true in this matter also: 'Compared with this greater splendour, the thing that used to have such splendour now seems to have none' (2 Cor 3:10).

When you see the Lord sacrificed and lying before you, and the priest standing over the sacrifice and praying, and all who partake reddened with that precious blood, can you think that you are still among men and standing on earth? Are you not straightaway transported to heaven, and, having cast forth from your soul every fleshly thought, do you not with naked soul and pure mind, look around upon the things in heaven?

Oh the marvel! Oh the loving-kindness of God to men! He that sits above with the Father is, at the same time, held in our hands, and suffers himself to be clasped and embraced by those who wish; and all then do this by the eyes. Do you think that this work deserves contempt, or that it is such that any one can be uplifted against it?

Would you also see the magnitude of this sacred office from another marvel? Picture, I pray, before your eyes Elijah and the vast crowd standing round him, and the sacrifice lying on the altar of stones. All the rest are still and hushed in deep silence; the prophet alone is praying. Then of a sudden the flame is flung down from heaven upon the offering (1 Kg 18). This is a wonderful and awful picture. Pass from that scene to what is now performed. You will see things not only wonderful to look upon, but transcending all terror. The priest stands bringing down not fire, but the Holy Spirit; and he offers prayer for a long space, not that a fire may be kindled above and destroy the offering, but that grace may fall on the sacrifice through that prayer and kindle the souls of all, and make them appear brighter than silver refined by fire.

Can any one, not utterly distraught and frenzied, despise this awful rite? Do you not know that no human soul could ever have borne the fire of that sacrifice, but they would all have been brought utterly to nought, had not the help of the grace of God been lavishly bestowed?

St John Chrysostom, *On the Priesthood*, c 4, nn 175-180

14 September
The Triumph of the Cross
FEAST

This feast was first celebrated in Palestine, perhaps in the year 335. It was linked with the consecration of the basilica in Jerusalem. The feast was celebrated in Rome by the end of the seventh century. The theme of our celebration is how Christ made of an instrument of humiliation and death, the instrument of our salvation; in a word, we celebrate the triumph of humble obedience.

The reading is from St Robert Bellarmine's *Commentary on the Psalms.*

'Sing to the Lord a new canticle: because he has done wonderful things. His right hand has wrought for him salvation, and his arm is holy.'

He invites us to praise God for his wonderful works: 'Sing to the Lord a new canticle,' for there is not only new but great and wonderful matter for it, 'because he has done wonderful things'; for he was wonderfully, and in an unheard-of manner, conceived of the Holy Spirit, born of a virgin, committed no sin, justified sinners, made the deaf to hear, and the dumb to speak, nay, even the blind to see, the lame to walk, cured the sick, raised the dead; and, what is the most strange and wonderful of all, showed himself alive within three days after he was buried, took his body up to heaven, sent the Holy Spirit from heaven, and through the agency of poor, humble men, persuaded the prudent and the wise to worship the crucified, to despise the things of the present and to look forward to the things of the future; and, finally, as St Augustine says, conquered the world, not by the sword but by the cross. All this may be referred to the Father, who in the Son, and through the Son, effected all these wonderful things; for the Lord says, 'the Father, who abides in me, he does the works.'

'His right hand has wrought for him salvation, and his arm is holy'. He explains what those wonderful things are, and instances one of them that comprehends the whole. The wonderful thing God did consisted in his having saved the world purely by his own power, without associates, without an army, without arms; he alone cast out

251

the prince of this world, and delivered humankind from his power. Such was the object of all the wonderful things enumerated above; and thus this one thing comprehends all. The expression, 'has wrought for him salvation', may apply to the Son, who saved the world by his own power; and to the Father who, through Christ, his right hand, saved it; but it comes to the same thing; 'and his arm is holy', is merely a repetition of the foregoing; right hand and arm being nearly synonymous, and they signify virtue and power; but the word 'holy' is added, for fear we should suppose carnal, not spiritual, strength is intended; for Christ did not overcome his enemy by the force of arms or by bodily strength but by love and patience, by humility and obedience, by the merits of his most holy life, by his most precious blood spilled for love of us, and not by the spear or the sword. So, says the apostle, 'he humbled himself, becoming obedient unto death, even the death of the cross.' In this way, and this way alone, he obtained a signal victory over a most powerful enemy.

St Robert Bellarmine, *Commentary on the Psalms*, Ps 97 (Vulg.):1

15 September
Our Lady of Sorrows
MEMORIAL

Today's celebration was first introduced by the Servites in 1667 and was adopted into the universal calendar in 1814. Until 1913 it was celebrated on the third Sunday of September. There was an older celebration of Our Lady's Sorrows in Passiontide (Friday in the Fifth Week of Lent), which is no longer observed.

The reading is taken from Pope Paul VI's Exhortation, *Marialis Cultus*.

Mary is, finally, *the virgin presenting offerings*. In the episode of the presentation of Jesus in the Temple (cf Lk 2:22-35), the Church, guided by the Spirit, has detected, over and above the fulfilment of the laws regarding the offering of the firstborn (cf Ex 13:11-16) and the purification of the mother (cf Lev 12:6-8), a mystery of salvation related to the history of salvation. That is, she has noted the continuity of the fundamental offering that the incarnate Word made to the

Father when he entered the world (cf Heb 15:5-7). The Church has seen the universal nature of salvation proclaimed, for Simeon greeting in the child the light to enlighten the peoples and the glory of the people Israel (cf Lk 2:32), recognized in him the Messiah, the Saviour of all. The Church has understood the prophetic reference to the passion of Christ: the fact that Simeon's words, which linked in one prophecy the Son as 'the sign of contradiction' (Lk 2:34) and his mother, whose soul would be pierced by a sword (cf Lk 2:35), came true on Calvary. A mystery of salvation, therefore, that in its various aspects orients the episode of the presentation in the Temple to the salvific event of the cross.

But the Church herself, in particular from the Middle Ages onwards, has detected in the heart of the virgin taking her son to Jerusalem to present him to the Lord (cf Lk 2:22) a desire to make an offering, a desire that exceeds the ordinary meaning of the rite. A witness to this intuition is found in the loving prayer of St Bernard: 'Offer your Son, holy virgin, and present to the Lord the blessed fruit of your womb. Offer for the reconciliation of us all the holy victim which is pleasing to God.'

This union of the mother and the Son in the work of redemption reaches its climax on calvary, where Christ 'offered himself as the perfect sacrifice to God' (Heb 9:14) and where Mary stood by the Cross (cf Jn 19:25), 'suffering grievously with her only-begotten Son. There she united herself with a maternal heart to his sacrifice, and lovingly consented to the immolation of this victim which she herself had brought forth' and also was offering to the eternal Father.

To perpetuate down the centuries the sacrifice of the cross, the divine Saviour instituted the eucharistic sacrifice, the memorial of his death and resurrection, and entrusted it to his spouse the Church, which, especially on Sundays, calls the faithful together to celebrate the passover of the Lord until he comes again. This the Church does in union with the saints in heaven and in particular with the Blessed Virgin, whose burning charity and unshakeable faith she imitates.

Pope Paul VI, Apostolic Exhortation, *Marialis Cultus*, n 20

16 September
Saints Cornelius, *pope,* and Cyprian, *bishop, martyrs*
MEMORIAL

The linking of these two saints goes back to the fourth century in Rome and they are both mentioned in the traditional Roman Canon of the Mass. Cornelius became pope in the year 251, was exiled under the Emperor Gallus and died in exile in Città Vecchia in 253. Cyprian was born in Carthage in North Africa in 210, was a convert to Christianity and was chosen as bishop of Carthage in 249. He died as a martyr in 258. He was one of the great Fathers of the Latin Church in North Africa. Saints Cornelius and Cyprian shared the same difficulties with various dissidents and heretics.

The reading is from the treatise *On the Unity of the Catholic Church* by St Cyprian.

Christ gave us peace, he commanded us to be of one heart and one mind, enjoined on us the incorrupt and inviolate bonds of love and charity: no one who has not maintained brotherly love can put himself forward as a martyr. The apostle Paul teaches this and bears witness when he says: 'And if I should have faith so that I may move mountains, but have not charity, I am nothing: and if I should distribute all my possessions in food, and if I should hand over my body so that I burn, but have not charity, I gain nothing. Charity is patient, charity is kind, charity does not envy, is not puffed-up, is not angered, does not act wrongly, does not think evil, loves all things, believes all things, hopes all things, bears all things, charity will never pass away' (1 Cor 13:2).

Charity, he says, will never pass away. For this charity will be forever in the kingdom, will last to eternity in the unity of the brotherhood holding together. Discord cannot attain to the kingdom of heaven; he who, with unbelieving dissension, violated the love of Christ, cannot reach the reward of Christ, who said: 'this is my commandment, that you love one another, as I have loved you.' He who has not love, has not got God. The saying is of the blessed apostle John, he says, 'God is love, and he who abides in love, abides in God and God abides in him.' They who have not willed to be of one mind in the Church of God, cannot abide with God. They may indeed burn in the flames and be given to fires, or, thrown to beasts, they may lay down their lives, there will not be that crown of faith but the punishment of unbelief, nor will there be for them the glorious outcome of religious virtue, but the ruin of despair. Such a one can be killed, he cannot be crowned. He thus professes himself to be a Christian, just as the devil often imitates Christ. The Lord himself gives advance warning of this saying: 'Many will come in my name saying: I am the Christ, and they will deceive many.' Just as such a one is not Christ, although he deceives in his name, so he cannot be seen as a Christian who does not persist in Christ's gospel and in the truth of faith.

St Cyprian, *On the Unity of the Catholic Church*, c 14

17 September
Saint Robert Bellarmine, *bishop and doctor of the Church*
OPTIONAL MEMORIAL

Robert was an Italian, born in Tuscany in 1542. He became a Jesuit: he was an outstanding student and, after his ordination to the priesthood, became a professor in Rome. He was much involved in the theological controversies which were such a feature of the sixteenth century and showed himself both able and fair-minded. These qualities were admitted even by those opposed to him. He was made a Cardinal in 1599 and in 1602 was sent to Capua as its bishop. St Robert proved himself a zealous pastor but returned to Rome in 1605 and died there in 1621. The last years of his life were mostly devoted to spiritual writings.

The reading offered is from the last of these, *The Art of Dying Well*. (The version is adapted from a contemporary translation by Edward Coffin SJ.)

Let us now speak of the *manner* of bestowing alms, for that is necessary more than any other thing, that we may virtuously live and die most happily. First, it is necessary that we give alms with a most sincere intention of pleasing God and not for seeking popular praise. Christ teaches us this when he says: 'When you give alms do not sound the trumpet and do not let your left hand know what your right is doing.'

Again, our alms is to be given *readily*, and with facility, that it may not seem to be wrung out by entreaty, nor delayed from day to day when it may presently be dispatched. . . . Abraham, the friend of

God, requested the travellers to come to his house, and did not wait to be entreated by them. Neither did Tobias wait until the poor people should come to him, but he himself sought them out.

Thirdly, it is requisite that our alms be given *cheerfully*, and not with grudging. 'In everything you give, says Ecclesiasticus, show a cheerful countenance'; and the apostle: 'Not out of sadness or out of necessity, for our Lord loves a cheerful giver.'

Fourthly, it is necessary that our alms be given with *humility*, in such manner as the giver may know himself to receive more than he gives, of which point St Gregory writes: 'It helps much to check the pride of the giver of alms if when he gives his earthly substance he weighs well the words of the heavenly Master, 'Use money, tainted as it is, to win you friends and thus make sure that when it fails you, they will welcome you into the tents of eternity.' For if by the friendship of the poor we gain the tents of eternity, doubtless we who give are to persuade ourselves that we do rather offer presents to our benefactors than bestow alms on the poor.

Fifthly, it is necessary that we give *abundantly*, according to the proportion or measure of our ability, for this is how Tobias, that famous alms-giver, behaved: 'As you are able, so be pitiful to the poor; if you have much give plentifully; if you have but little, study how to give that little willingly.' The apostle teaches us that alms is to be given as a blessing, not as covetousness. St John Chrysostom adds, not simply to give but to give abundantly is to be called alms, and in the same sermon, that those who desire to be heard by God when they cry, 'Have mercy on me O Lord God according to thy great mercy', must also have mercy on the poor according to their great alms.

Last of all, it is specially required that he who will be saved and die well should diligently search out, either by his own reading and meditation or by other devout and learned men, whether a man may keep superfluous riches without sin, or whether such must not of necessity be given to the poor; and further, which are to be deemed superfluous riches, which necessary; for the case may so stand that limited riches to one man may be superfluous, and great wealth to another may seem necessary.

St Robert Bellarmine, *The Art of Dying Well*

19 September
Saint Januarius, *bishop and martyr*
OPTIONAL MEMORIAL

Januarius was bishop of Benevento and with six companions was martyred at Pozzuoli, Naples, during the persecution of Diocletian in the year 305. His memorial was introduced into the Roman Calendar in 1586.

The liquefaction of the alleged relic of his blood, preserved in the cathedral of Naples, is an acknowledged happening, though as yet unexplained.

The reading is from a sermon of St Augustine.

The blessed apostles, the first sheep of the holy flock, saw the Lord Jesus himself hanging on the cross, they grieved for his dying, they were sorely afraid of him rising, they loved him as Master, and they themselves shed their blood for that which they saw.

Think, brothers, what it was to send men over the whole earth, to preach that a dead man had risen, had ascended to heaven, and for this preaching to suffer all that a raving world inflicted, losses, exiles, chains, tortures, flames, beasts, crosses, deaths. This for I know not what? My brothers, did Peter die for his own glory, or did he preach himself? One died that the Other might be honoured; one is killed that the Other might be worshipped! Would he have done this save from the ardour of love, according to his knowledge of the truth?

They had seen what they related. They did not deny: they preached the dead man, whom they knew to be alive. They knew for what life they despised life: they knew for what happiness they bore with passing unhappiness, for what rewards they despised these losses. With the whole world their faith would not be weighed. They had heard, 'What does it profit one, if one gains the whole world, but suffers the loss of one's soul?' (Mt 16:26). The allurement of the world did not hold back the hastening ones, a passing thing the fleeing ones: the happiness to be left here no matter how strongly or in what fashion it shines forth, not to be borne over to the other life, to be abandoned sometimes here even by the living.

Despise the world, then, Christians. despise the world, despise it! The martyrs despised it, the apostles despised it, he whose Memorial we celebrate today, despised it. You wish to be rich, you wish to be honoured, you wish to be healthy: he despised all that for whose memorial you have come together. What, I pray, do you love so much, which he despised whom you so honour? Whom you would not so honour if he had not despised these things! Why do I find you a lover of those things, the despiser of which you venerate. Certainly you would not venerate him if he were to have loved them! For your part do not love them: for he has not gone in and closed the door in your face. Despise them in your turn and go in after him. The door is open by which you go in: Christ is the entrance. And the door was opened for you when his side was pierced with the spear. Call to mind what flowed out from that opening; and choose by which you can enter. From the side of the Lord hanging and dying on the tree of the cross, water and blood flowed out. In one is your cleansing, in the other your redemption.

There is another life, my brothers: after this life there is another life, believe me. Prepare yourselves for it: despise all present goods. If you have them, do good with them; if you don't, do not burn with longing. Change; transfer in advance: let what you have go there where you are to follow. Hear the advice of your Lord: 'Do not lay up treasure for yourselves on earth, where moth and rust consume, and where thieves break in and steal; but lay up treasure for yourselves in heaven, where the thief does not enter, where the moth does not consume. For where your treasure is, there your heart is also' (Mt 6:19f).

You, the faithful one, hear daily: Lift up your heart; and, as if you heard the contrary, you plunge your heart in the earth. Change. Have you the means? Do good. Have you no means? Do not murmur against God. Hear me, you poor ones: What have you not got, if you have God? Hear me, you rich: What have you got, if you have not God?

St Augustine, *Sermon 311*, nn 2, 3, 15 (in honour of St Cyprian)

20 September
Saints Andrew Kim, *priest,*
Paul Chong Hasang and companions, *martyrs*
MEMORIAL

These are 103 martyrs who suffered in Korea for their faith in Christ in the persecutions of 1839, 1846, 1866 and 1867. They were canonized by Pope John Paul II while he was in Korea on 6 May 1984. Ten of those canonized were French — three bishops (vicars apostolic) and seven priests, all members of the Paris Foreign Mission Society — the remainder were Korean.

Korea was closed to all outside influence during the greater part of the nineteeth century and there was a frenetic mistrust of all things foreign. There were many attempts to get the faith through these physical and psychological barriers and the Church was in fact established in Korea. The reaction led to many deaths at the hands of the royal authorities. Those canonized represent only a fraction of those who actually shed their blood for Christ, and who often remained true though deprived of any priestly ministry.

St Andrew Kim was the first Korean to be ordained priest; he trained in Macao, and suffered death in 1846. His father Ignatius Kim had been martyred in 1839. Paul Chong Hasang was a leading layman among the christian converts. The following reading is from a letter Fr Kim wrote in Latin to Mgr Ferréol, who had been appointed vicar apostolic. It was written on 26 August 1846 while he was in prison. On the following 16 September he was slain for his faith in Christ.

When we reached Seoul we were thrown into the prison of thieves. The people of the court, hearing me speak, said I was a Korean. The following day I appeared before the judges, who asked me what I was. 'I am a Korean,' I answered, 'and I was educated in China.' Interpreters of Chinese were then called that I might speak with them.

In the persecution of 1839 the person who betrayed us declared that three young Koreans had been sent to Macao to study the language of the Europeans, so that it was impossible that I should not be recognized: besides, one of the Christians who was arrested with me had told them that I was their countryman. I confessed to the judges that I was Andrew Kim, one of the three Koreans mentioned, and I related to them all that I had gone through in order to return to my country.

When I had told my story every one exclaimed, 'Poor young man! From his infancy upwards he has been in trouble.' The judges ordered me to conform to the king's orders and to apostatize, but I answered, 'The God who orders me to worship him is above the king, and to deny him is a sin which the king's order cannot justify.' When it was suggested to me to denounce the Christians I objected to them the duties of charity and the commandment of God to love our neighbour. Being asked about religion I spoke to them at length of the existence and unity of God, of the creation and immortality of the soul, of hell, of the necessity of worshipping our Creator, and of the falsehood of the religions of the heathen.

When I had finished speaking the judges answered: 'Your religion is good, but ours is so also, and therefore we practise it.' 'If such is your opinion,' I replied, 'you ought to leave us alone and live at peace with us. But instead of that you persecute us, and treat us worse than the greatest criminals: you confess that our religion is good, and you attack us as if its teaching was abominable.' They laughed loudly at my reply, and handed to me the letters and papers they had taken. The judges read the two that were written in Chinese; they only contained salutations to friends. They then told me to translate the European letters, but I only explained to them what was of no consequence to the Mission.

St Andrew Kim, *Letter to Mgr Ferréol*

21 September
Saint Matthew, *apostle and evangelist*
FEAST

Matthew is traditionally identified with Levi, son of Alphaeus. He was a customs officer before being called by Jesus to follow him. The earliest ecclesiastical writers credit him with the authorship of the first Gospel, and state that he wrote in Aramaic before leaving Judaea. Tradition relates that he preached the gospel in the lands east of the Persian Gulf and there suffered martyrdom.

The reading is from a sermon by John Henry Newman.

In order that we might be delivered from the bondage of corruption,

Christ has expressly told us that the necessaries of life shall never fail his faithful follower, any more than the meal and oil the widow-woman of Sarepta; one that while he is bound to labour for his family, he need not be engrossed by his toil — that while he is busy, his heart may be at leisure for his Lord. 'Be not anxious, saying, what shall we eat? or what shall we drink? or wherewithal shall we be clothed? For after all these things do the Gentiles seek; for your heavenly Father knoweth that ye have need of all these things. But seek ye first the kingdom of God and his righteousness; and all these things shall be added unto you' (Mt 6:31-33).

Here is revealed to us at once our privilege and our duty, the christian portion of having engagements of this world without pursuing objects. And in accordance with our divine teacher are the words of the apostle, 'We brought nothing into this world, and it is certain we can carry nothing out; and having food and raiment, let us therewith be content.' There is no excuse then for that absorbing pursuit of wealth, which many men indulge in as if a virtue, and expatiate upon as if a science. 'After all these things do the Gentiles seek!' Consider how different is the rule of life left us by the apostles. 'I speak this for your own profit,' says St Paul, 'that ye may attend upon the Lord, without distraction.' 'This I say, brethren, the time is short; it remaineth, that both they that have wives be as though they had none, and they that weep as though they wept not, and they that rejoice as though they rejoiced not, and they that buy as though they possessed not, and they that use this world as not abusing it, for the fashion of this world passeth away' (1 Cor 7:29-31, 35). 'Be anxious for nothing; but in everything, by prayer and supplication with thanksgiving, let your requests be made known to God' (Phil 4:6). And St Peter, 'Casting all your anxiety upon him, for he careth for you' (1 Pet 5:7).

I have now given the main reason why the pursuit of gain, whether in a large or small way, is prejudicial to our spiritual interests, that it fixes the mind upon an object of this world; yet others remain behind. Money is a sort of creation, and gives the acquirer, even more than the possessor, an imagination of his own power; and tends to make him idolize self. Again, what we have hardly won, we are unwilling to part with; so that a man who has himself made his wealth will commonly be penurious, or at least will not part with it except in exchange for what will reflect credit upon himself, or increase his importance. Even when his conduct is most disinterested and amiable (as in spending for the comfort of those who depend upon him), still this indulgence of self, of pride and worldliness, insinuates itself.

J.H. Newman, *Parochial and Plain Sermons*, II, 28 (St Matthew)

26 September
Saints Cosmas and Damian, *martyrs*
OPTIONAL MEMORIAL

These two martyrs were formerly commemorated on the twenty-seventh of this month. They were, apparently, Syrian martyrs, whose legend makes them out to have been medical doctors, who enjoyed a wide and popular cultus in the early Church. Pope Felix IV (525-530) dedicated a basilica in their honour in the Roman forum, and they are mentioned together in the traditional Roman Canon of the Mass.

The reading is taken from a sermon of St Augustine.

All people whosoever, of no matter what kind they be, wish to be happy. There is no one, no matter what manner of life is chosen, who does not desire a happy life. What then, my brothers and sisters, what is the happy life, which all wish and not all have? Let us seek then. . . .

If it be said to someone: Do you want to live? Is it ever understood as if it were said: Do you want to be a soldier? For to that question, which is: Do you want to be a soldier? some would say to me: I want to; and perhaps many: I don't want to. If, however, I should say: Do you want to live? I think there is no one who would say: I don't want to. For all have it implanted by nature to want to live, not want to die. Again, if I should say: Do you want to be healthy? I think there is no one who would say: I don't want to; for no one wants to suffer pain. Health is even precious to the rich, surely the only thing to the poor; for what use is opulence to the rich if health is absent, which is the patrimony of the poor? The rich would gladly change his silver bed for the poor man's canvas, if his sickness could go along with the bed! See, in these two, the opinion of all is at one — life and health. When then a man is alive and well, does he seek nothing more? If he be wise, perhaps he ought seek nothing more. For where life and health are perfect, if more is sought, what will it be but evil desire?

What is the situation, my brothers and sisters? When I asked you if you wanted to live, all replied that you wanted to live; if you wanted to be healthy, all replied that you wanted to be healthy. But it is no life at all if it be feared that health and life may end! For that is not always to live, but always to fear. If always to fear, then always to be tormented. If everlasting torment, where is eternal life? We certainly hold that only eternal life is happy; indeed, that life only is happy: because if not eternal and if not with lasting abundance, beyond doubt it is neither happy nor life.

If therefore you seek the supreme good, that is, life, be good, that you may reach the good. 'If you wish to enter into life, keep the commandments.' When then we shall have reached life (on what account should I add, eternal? on what account should I add, happy?), Life only, because *that* is life which is both eternal and happy. When we shall have attained life, it will be certain for us that we will always dwell in it. For if we should be there, and should be uncertain whether we should always be there, there also will be fear. And if fear will be there, there will be torment, not of the flesh, but, what is worse, of the heart. Where there is torment, however, what kind of happiness can there be? Therefore it will be certain for us, because we shall always be in that life, and we shall not have been able to limit it: because we shall be in his kingdom of which it is said: 'And his kingdom shall have no end' (Lk 1:33), and since Wisdom pointed out the glory of the saints of God, whose death is precious in his sight, saying: 'and their Lord will reign for ever' (Wis 3:8). We then shall be in a great and everlasting kingdom: a kingdom, on this account great and everlasting, because it is just.

St Augustine, *Sermon 306*, nn (3), 4, 7

27 September
Saint Vincent de Paul, *priest*
MEMORIAL

Vincent was a Gascon, a native of South West France, born about the beginning of the last quarter of the sixteenth century. In search of a career he entered the secular clergy and was ordained priest. He moved to Paris in the exercise of his ministry and there came under the influence of Pierre de Berulle, with a consequent deepening of his life of prayer and religious practice. As his own prayer and love of God developed he became more and more aware of the needs of others, both spiritual and physical. He did much for the prisoners sentenced to the galleys, and promoted active, concerned charity among the faithful by the founding of confraternities of charity among men and women. These were to be the inspiration for the present-day Society of St Vincent de Paul, but out of them in St Vincent's own day, with St Louise de Marillac, he developed the Daughters of Charity for work among the poor and the sick.

Another need he recognized was the religious poverty of the peasants, and this led to his founding the Congregation of the Mission, for preaching in the countryside and the formation of the clergy. In his own lifetime St Vincent sent his priests to Ireland, which in the seventeenth century was hardly an easy mission.

St Vincent died in Paris in 1660.

As a reading I offer an account he himself gave of one of his converts in 1659. There is no mention in the account of himself, but it tells us much about the religious standards he set and the values he inculcated — in God alone is my strength, he alone is my love.

I knew a gentleman of Bresse, of the name of de Rougemont — I have related this once before — who had been a great fighter of duels; he was a big man, and well proportioned, who, on behalf of others who had a difference with someone or on his own account to settle his personal quarrels, frequently had occasion to call out his adversary for a duel. He himself told me of it and it is scarcely credible how many men he had fought, wounded and killed. At length God touched his heart so effectually that he entered into himself, and realizing the precarious state of his soul he resolved to change his life, which indeed he did.

After this conversion, when he had given proof of his sincerity and made some progress, he asked his Lordship of Lyons to allow him to have the Blessed Sacrament reserved in his private chapel that he might honour Our Lord there and nourish his piety which was outstanding and well known to all. This aroused in me one day the desire to visit him at his house. He told me of his devotions and, among other things, of his detachment from creatures. 'I am certain,' he said, 'that if I am attached to nothing, I shall belong to God, who is my only desire; and for that reason I consider whether the friendship of this nobleman, of that relation or neighbour is an obstacle, whether it is love of myself which impedes my progress, or my goods or vanity which hold me back, and when I see that something distracts me from my sovereign good I pray, I cut, I slash and so I rid myself of that possession. That is my method of devotion.'

I always remember that he told me particularly that one day when he was travelling, as was his practice he was thinking of God and he examined himself to discover if since the time he had given up all, anything still remained to which he was attached; he went over his affairs, his possessions, his connexions, his reputation, his exalted position, the little amusements of the human heart; he turned it all over and at length his thoughts alighted on his sword. 'What do I carry it for?' he thought, and then, 'How could I do without it? What, give up this beloved sword which has so often served me well and which, under God, has preserved me from so many dangers! If I were attacked I should be lost without it. Yet, I might be involved in a quarrel and with a sword at my side should not have the strength to avoid using it and should thus offend God. My God, what shall I do? Can my heart still cleave to this instrument of my shame and sin? This sword alone stands in my way; no longer will I be so cowardly as to wear it!' At this moment he was riding past a boulder. He dismounted from his horse, took his sword and struck it hard against the stone several times. At length the sword broke in pieces and he proceeded on his way. He told me that this act of detachment, this breaking of the iron chain which held him in thrall, gave him such great freedom that, although it was against the inclinations of his heart, for he loved this sword, never afterwards had he the least affection for the perishable things of earth; he clung now to nothing save to God alone.

St Vincent de Paul, Conference of 16 May, 1659

28 September
Saint Wenceslaus, *martyr*
OPTIONAL MEMORIAL

Wenceslaus was born about 905 in Bohemia and was brought up in a very christian atmosphere and spirit by his grandmother. He became Prince of Bohemia while still in his teens and devoted himself to the general uplifting of his people in both the religious and social sense. There were those who resented his rule — among them it seems, his own mother — and in consequence he was slain, on this day, in 929, by his own brother, Boleslaus, and a conspiracy of non-Christians. He was immediately declared a martyr and is venerated as patron saint of Bohemia and so of Czecho-Slovakia. Interestingly, Boleslaus, who succeeded him, was also responsible for his being enshrined. Such are the contradictions of history!

The reading is from an anonymous Life and Passion of Wenceslaus dating from the first half of the thirteenth century; written, therefore, just three centuries after the event. It is difficult for us to assess its accuracy, but the picture it presents of the christian ruler is not without significance.

He was indeed faithful and wise, truthful in speech, just in judgement, prudent in counsel, outstanding in goodness, most renowned in the uprightness of his ways; he rendered with care due service as one devoted to God. He was most instant in prayer, knowing that it was written 'Pray without ceasing' (1 Thess 5:17); he was girded with spiritual arms against the various devices of his seen and unseen enemies, energetic in battle, joyful in adversities, sober in success, resolute against the proud, a companion to the meek and humble, noble in his strength, but more noble in his faith and action. As regards the emperor he fought with the spirit of bravery, as regards Christ with the innocence of devotion, and in warfare, not forgetful of the precept of the Gospel, he rendered to God what are God's, and returned what belonged to Caesar to Caesar (Mt 22:21).

Further, such and so great were the humility and virtue of patience which shone forth in him that he would no more be thought a nobly born duke or an energetic soldier, but rather a most humble monk, according as it is written: 'The greater you are, humble yourself in all things' (Sir 3:20). He wholly abounded with sentiments of mercy; extremely compassionate towards those in misery and want, he was the honour of the clergy, the consoler of the afflicted, the joy of the poor, the father of orphans, the defender of widows, the visitor of prisoners, the liberator of captives, and the pious consoler of all in need. For in the heart of the blessed man, there burned the glorious fire of charity and incomparable compassionate love.

Moreover, lest any of the Christians be evilly punished by calumny, he destroyed all the prisons throughout the divisions of his duchy, he cut down the gallows, and reduced all kinds of torment to nothing. When indeed any man, caught in criminal vice, was brought to the judgement of the holy man, he used to be dismissed, corrected sometimes with fatherly words, at other times with motherly chiding, warned by the holy man that he make satisfaction by suitable penance for his sins. He never gave sentence of death in anyone's regard, or gave his assent to the giving of such sentence. If, however, he was unable to free a man from sentence of death because of the great guilt of his crimes, or on account of the insistence of his nobles and the accustomed justice of the land, he begged from the judges and nobles on his behalf, that space of time be afforded him for the doing of penance and making confession. And, if he could not help the guilty one in this way, the most pious duke, moved with compassion and overflowing with copious tears, would rise from his throne and leave the place of council, lest he should see the blood of his neighbour condemned to death. Nevertheless, sending messengers to the judges, he used to enjoin that one or more days' or nights' stay of execution be granted; and, approaching him secretly during the nights, consoled him with persuasive words, and gave him money, that he might buy himself off. For he always kept in mind the saying of the Lord when he said, 'Be merciful and do not judge, so that you be not judged, and do not condemn and you will not be condemned' (Lk 6:36, 37).

The Life and Passion of Wenceslaus, nn 9, 10

29 September
Saints Michael, Gabriel and Raphael, *archangels*
FEAST

The liturgical cult of the angels is first known in the East in the fifth century; that of St Michael had spread to the West by the sixth. The angels had, however, been a very conscious part of Christian tradition from earliest times: Christians and angels were considered as intimately associated in the worship of God.

Today's celebration was originally the anniversary of the dedication of the basilica of St Michael on the Via Salaria in Rome.

The reading is taken from John Henry Newman's *Parochial and Plain Sermons*. The references he makes are to the liturgy of the Church of England. The whole sermon should be read fully to understand his thought but, in brief, his teaching is that the angels are responsible for the ordering and governing of the whole natural order.

When then we walk abroad, and 'meditate in the field at the eventide,' how much has every herb and flower in it to surprise and overwhelm us! For, even did we know as much about them as the wisest of men, yet there are those around us, though unseen, to whom our greatest knowledge is as ignorance; and, when we converse on subjects of nature scientifically, repeating the names of plants and earths, and describing their properties, we should do so religiously, as in the hearing of the great servants of God, with the sort of diffidence which we always feel when speaking before the learned and wise of our own mortal race, as poor beginners in intellectual knowledge, as well as in moral attainments.

Now I can conceive persons saying all this is fanciful; but if it appears so, it is only because we are not accustomed to such thoughts. Surely we are not told in scripture about the angels for nothing, but for practical purposes; nor can I conceive a use of our knowledge more practical than to make it connect the sight of this world with the thought of another. Nor one more consolatory; for surely it is a great comfort to reflect that, wherever we go, we have those about us who are ministering to all the heirs of salvation, though we see them not. Nor one more easily to be understood and felt by all men; for we know that at one time the doctrine of angels was received even too readily. And if any one would argue hence against it as dangerous, let him recollect the great principle of our Church, that the abuse of a thing does not supersede the use of it; and let him explain, if he can, St Paul's exhorting Timothy not only as 'before God and Christ,' but before 'the elect angels' also. Hence, in the Communion Service, our Church teaches us to join our praises with that of 'angels and archangels, and all the company of heaven'; and the early Christians even hoped that they waited on the Church's seasons of worship, and glorified God with her. Nor are these thoughts without their direct influence on our faith in God and his Son; for the more we can enlarge our view of the next world, the better. When we survey almighty God surrounded by his holy angels, his thousand thousands of ministering Spirits, and ten thousand times ten thousand standing before him, the idea of his awful majesty rises before us more powerfully and impressively. We begin to see how little we are, how altogether mean and worthless in ourselves, and how high he is, and fearful. The very lowest of his angels is indefinitely above us in this our present state; how high then must be the Lord of angels! The very seraphim hide their faces before his glory, while they praise him; how shame-faced then should sinners be, when they come into his presence!

J.H. Newman, Parochial and Plain Sermons, II, 29

30 September
Saint Jerome, priest and doctor of the Church
MEMORIAL

Jerome was born in Strido, near Aquileia, in Italy, about the year 340. His background was christian, but only as a young man did he awake to the value of Christianity: he was baptized in Rome, where he had studied. He was a gifted linguist and had received a very good education, so that he was fluent in both Latin and Greek. When aged about thirty he went to Syria to undertake the monastic life. His monastic wanderings brought him to Antioch, where he was ordained priest, then to Constantinople, lastly to Rome, where he lectured in the ascetic life and biblical studies, gathering quite a clientele of cultured christian ladies.

He became secretary to Pope Damasus and was commissioned by him to produce a reliable Latin version of the New Testament. On the death of Damasus he went to Bethlehem, and established a Latin monastery there. He devoted himself to study and set about producing a worthy Latin translation of the Old Testament from the Hebrew, which he had mastered. In this work he was supported by Paula, a wealthy widow who had followed him from Rome and established a convent for women in the same neighbourhood.

St Jerome was very learned and a great scholar, but he was something of a fire-eater and could be most wounding. Although admired for his learning he made many enemies. Yet he was a sincere lover of Christ and of the christian faith and has since his death, which took place in 420, been venerated as a saint.

His great legacy to posterity was his scriptural work, his translations and his commentaries on the books of the bible.

As a reading, an extract of his Letter 52 is given. This was addressed to one Nepotian who had joined the clergy of Altinum where his uncle was bishop. The whole letter is a treatise on the duties of the clergy, and, in its day aroused quite a lot of resentment. No one could quarrel with the extract given.

Read the divine scriptures constantly; never, indeed, let the sacred volume be out of your hand. Learn what you have to teach. Hold fast the faithful word you have been taught so that you may be able by sound doctrine to give instruction and confute those who contradict it. Continue in what you have learned and have firmly believed, knowing from whom you learned it; and be ready always to give an answer to anyone who asks you for an account of the faith and hope that is in you. Do not let your deeds belie your words; lest when you speak in church someone may mentally reply 'Why do you not practice what you profess? Here is a lover of dainties turned censor! His stomach is full and he reads us a homily on fasting. As well might a robber accuse others of greed.' In a priest of Christ, mouth, mind and hand should be one.

Be obedient to your bishop and welcome him as the parent of your soul. Sons love their fathers and slaves fear their masters. 'If I am a father,' he says, 'where is my honour? And if I am a master, where is my fear?' In your case the bishop combines in himself many titles to your respect. He is at once a monk, a prelate, and an uncle who has before now instructed you in all holy things.

This also I say, that the bishops should know themselves to be priests not lords. Let them render to the clergy the honour which is their due that the clergy may offer to them the respect which belongs to bishops. There is a witty saying of the orator Domitius which is here to the point: 'Why am I to recognize you as leader of the Senate when you will not recognize my rights as a private member?' We should realize that a bishop and his priests are like Aaron and his sons. As there is but one Lord and one Temple; so also there should be but one ministry. Let us ever bear in mind the charge which the apostle Peter gives to priests: 'Tend the flock of God that is in your charge, exercising the oversight not by constraint but willingly as God would have you; not for shameful gain but readily; not as domineering over those in your charge but being examples to the flock,' and that gladly; so that 'when the chief Shepherd is manifested you will obtain the unfading crown of glory.'

St Jerome, *Letter 52, 7*

1 October
Saint Teresa of the Child Jesus, *virgin*
MEMORIAL

Marie-Françoise-Thérèse Martin was born in Lisieux in France in 1873. She entered Carmel in 1888 when aged only fifteen. Her health prevented her observing the fasts prescribed by the rule, but she followed the life in all other details until her final sickness and death in 1897, when aged only twenty-four. Outwardly her life was undistinguished but she pioneered in the Church of the nineteenth century the 'little way' — fidelity in small things, trust and complete self-surrender to God. She had wanted to go on the missions but her health made this impossible, her apostolate was to be by offering up her day to day life for the mission of the Church.

She was canonized in 1925 and declared one of the patrons of the Church's missionary apostolate.

The reading is from her autobiography, a work undertaken at the request of her elder sister, Pauline, who was prioress of the convent. (The emphases on words and the suspended sentences are St Thérèse's own. My only addition to the text is the date [1890].)

At last my longed for wedding day arrived, it was a cloudless day, but on its eve a storm rose up within me such as I had never experienced. Not a single doubt about my vocation having crossed my mind up to then, I had to know this trial. That evening, while making the stations of the cross after Matins*, my vocation seemed to me a *dream*, a mere fancy. . . . I found the Carmelite life fine indeed, but the devil gave me the *certain conviction* that it was not made for me, and that I should be deceiving my superiors by going forward along a way to which I had not been called. My darkness was so great that I only saw and understood one thing: I did not have a *vocation*. . . . Dear me! How describe my anguish of mind? It seemed to me (an absurdity which shows that this temptation came from the devil), that if I told my fears to my novice-mistress, she would go and prevent my taking my vows; however, I did wish to do the will of the good God and to return to the world rather than remain in Carmel by doing my own: so I took my novice-mistress aside, and, *full of confusion*, told her of my state of mind. . . . Happily she saw more clearly than I did, and completely reassured me; moreover the act of humility which I had performed had succeeded in putting to flight the devil, who thought perhaps, that I was not going to dare to admit to the temptation. As soon as I had finished speaking, my doubts vanished; however, in order to make my act of humility more complete, I further wished to disclose my strange temptation to Mother Prioress, who confined herself to laughing at me.

The morning of the 8 September [1890], I felt myself *flooded* by a river of *peace*, and it was in this peace *'surpassing all understanding'*, that I made my vows. My union with Jesus took place not in the midst of thunderbolts and lightning, that is extraordinary graces, but in the midst of a *gentle breeze*, like that which our Father Saint Elijah heard on the mountain. . . . There was no limit to the graces I asked on that day! I really felt myself the queen, and so I made use of my title to deliver captives, to obtain the favours of the King for his ungrateful subjects, then I wished to free all the souls in purgatory and to convert sinners. I prayed a lot for my *mother*, my dear sisters, . . . for all the family, but above all for my little father, so tried and so holy. . . . I offered myself to Jesus so that he might perfectly accomplish his *will* in me without creatures ever blocking his way. . . .

Manuscrits Autobiographiques, Office central de Lisieux, 1957

* Matins, has now been replaced by the Office of Readings. It was very frequently 'anticipated', that is said on the previous evening, in this case on the evening of 7 September.

2 October
The Guardian Angels
MEMORIAL

This Memorial had been celebrated, in several local calendars at least, in the sixteenth century but was introduced into the Roman calendar in 1615. The Gospel read at today's Mass has served to sustain belief in the guardian angels through the centuries, though thought about them and devotion to them has varied. The reading offered is taken from Newman's *Dream of Gerontius*. This is not because the guardian angels belong to the realm of poetic fancy (see 29 September), but because of the way in which the writer expresses their role in our lives.

Angel
My work is done,
My task is o'er,
And so I come,
Taking it home,
For the crown is won.
Alleluia,
For evermore.

My Father gave
In charge to me
This child of earth
E'en from its birth,
To serve and save,
Alleluia,
And saved is he.

This child of clay
To me was given,
To rear and train
By sorrow and pain
In the narrow way,
Alleluia,
From earth to heaven.

Soul
It is a member of that family

Of wondrous beings, who, ere the worlds were made,
Millions of ages back, have stood around
The throne of God; he never has known sin;
But through those cycles all but infinite,
Has had a strong and pure celestial life,
And bore to gaze on the unveil'd face of God,
And drank from the eternal Fount of truth,
And served him with a keen ecstatic love.
Hark! he begins again.

Angel
O Lord, how wonderful in depth and height,
But most in man, how wonderful thou art!
With what a love, what soft persuasive might
Victorious o'er the stubborn fleshly heart,
Thy tale complete of saints thou dost provide,
To fill the throne which angels lost through pride!

He lay a grovelling babe upon the ground,
Polluted in the blood of his first sire,
With his whole essence shattered and unsound,
And coiled around his heart a demon dire,
Which was not of his nature, but had skill
To bind and form his opening mind to ill.

Then was I sent from heaven to set right
The balance in his soul of truth and sin,
And I have waged a long relentless fight,
Resolved that death-environed spirit to win,
Which from its fallen state, when all was lost,
Had been repurchased at so dread a cost.

O what a shifting parti-coloured scene
Of hope and fear, of triumph and dismay,
Of recklessness and penitence, has been
The history of that dreary, life-long fray!
And O the grace to nerve him, and to lead,
How patient, prompt, and lavish at his need!

O man, strange composite of heaven and earth!
Majesty dwarfed to baseness! fragrant flower
Running to poisonous seed! and seeming worth
Cloking corruption! weakness mastering power!
Who never art so near to crime and shame,
As when thou hast achieved some deed of name;

How should ethereal natures comprehend
A thing made up of spirit and of clay,
Were we not tasked to nurse it and to tend,
Linked one to one throughout its mortal day?
More than the Seraph in his height of place,
The Angel-guardian knows and loves the ransomed race.

> J.H. Newman, *The Dream of Gerontius*, lines 236-302

4 October
Saint Francis of Assisi
MEMORIAL

Francis was born in 1181 in Umbria and grew up, in circumstances of wealth and comfort, into a rather irresponsible and pleasure-loving young man. Experience as a prisoner of war and then of illness caused him to reappraise his values and life itself. He was led by grace to abandon all things for love of Christ. Francis was neither theologian nor practical man but a visionary and prophetic figure deeply consumed with love of Christ, and particularly of Christ as poor and bereft. Thus he came to found a congregation of God's poormen, a congregation which developed into the Order of Friars Minor. With St Clare he also established a female form of his new way.

Before the end of his life he had resigned the headship of his friars, many of whom did not really appreciate his ideal. Francis, however, should be seen more as an inspirer than as a law-giver — though this is not to write off his Rule. He died in 1226 and was canonized two years after his death.

The reading is taken from his Letter to the Order. He himself was not a priest which makes the emphasis in the extract given on the eucharist and worthiness all the more striking. The concluding, and very beautiful, prayer is also given.

Listen, sons of the Lord and my brothers, 'pay attention to my words'

(Acts 2:14). 'Incline the ear' (Is 55:3) of your heart and obey the voice of the Son of God. Observe his commands with your whole heart and fulfil his counsels with a perfect mind. 'Give praise to him since he is good' (Ps 135:1) and 'exalt him by your deeds' (Tob 13:6), for he has sent you into the entire world for this reason (cf Tob 13:4): that in word and deed you may give witness to his voice and bring everyone to know that there is 'no one who is all-powerful' except him (Tob 13:4). Persevere in discipline and holy obedience (Heb 12:7) and with a firm and good purpose fulfil what you have promised to him. The Lord God offers himself to us as to his children (Heb 12:7).

Therefore, kissing your feet and with all that love of which I am capable, I implore all of you brothers to show all possible reverence and honour to the most holy body and blood of our Lord Jesus Christ in whom that which is in the heavens and on the earth is brought to peace and is reconciled to the all-powerful God (cf Col 1:20).

In the Lord I also beg all my brothers who are priests, or who will be or who wish to be priests of the Most High, that, whenever they wish to celebrate Mass, being pure, they offer the true sacrifice of the most holy body and blood of our Lord Jesus Christ purely. Let them do this with reverence and with a holy and pure intention, not for any mundane reason or out of fear or out of love of some person, as if they were pleasing people (cf Eph 6:6; Col 3:22). But let every wish be directed to God inasmuch as grace will help them, desiring thereby to please only the most high Lord since he alone does these things as he pleases. Therefore as he himself says: 'Do this in memory of me' (Lk 22:19; 1 Cor 11:24); if anyone acts otherwise, he becomes Judas the traitor and 'is guilty of the Body and Blood of the Lord' (cf 1 Cor 11:27).

Remember, my brothers who are priests, what is written of the law of Moses: that whoever committed a transgression against even the externals died without mercy by a decree of the Lord (cf Heb 10:28). How much greater and more severe will be the punishment for the person 'who tramples on the Son of God, and who treats the blood of the Covenant which sanctified him as if it were not holy, and who insults the Spirit of grace' (Heb 10:29)? For a person despises, defiles, and tramples on the Lamb of God when, as the apostle says, 'he does not recognize' (1 Cor 11:29) and discern the holy bread of Christ from other foods or actions or eats it unworthily or indeed, even if he were worthy, eats it unthinkingly or without the proper dispositions, since the Lord says through the prophet: 'Cursed is that person' who performs the work of God fraudulently (cf Jer 48:10). And he will surely condemn priests who do not wish to take this to heart saying: 'I will curse your blessing' (Mal 2:2).

Prayer
Almighty, eternal, just, and merciful God,
grant us in our misery the grace
to do for you alone
what we know you want us to do,
and always
to desire what pleases you.

Thus,
inwardly cleansed,
interiorly enlightened,
and inflamed by the fire of the Holy Spirit,
may we be able to follow
in the footprints of your beloved Son,
our Lord Jesus Christ.

And,
by your grace alone,
may we make our way to you,
Most High,
Who live and rule
in perfect Trinity and simple Unity,
and are glorified
God all-powerful
forever and ever.
Amen.

St Francis of Assisi, *Letter to the Order*, nn 5-20, 50-52

6 October
Saint Bruno, *priest*
OPTIONAL MEMORIAL

Bruno was born at Cologne, Germany, in the first half of the eleventh century but made an ecclesiastical career for himself at Rheims in France, where he came to be rector of the cathedral school. By the quality of his lectures he won for himself lasting friends and admirers. After eighteen years of this life however, Bruno felt drawn to live a simple monastic life. He and some companions received the permission and encouragement of bishop Hugh of Grenoble and the abbot of Chaise-Dieu to establish themselves at La Chartreuse in 1084. Their eremitical ideal, though given western expression, looked back to the eastern deserts for its inspiration, and ideal.

Some six years after the foundation Bruno was summoned to Rome by Pope Urban II, a former pupil, who wished to use his virtues in his programme of Church reform. Eventually Bruno prevailed on him to release him from the papal service to found another monastery. This was La Torre in Calabria and there Bruno died in 1101. St Bruno was never formally canonized.

As a reading, I offer part of a Meditation by Guigo II, ninth prior of La Chartreuse, on being alone.

'Woe to the lonely one' when you alone, my good Jesus, are not with him or her. How many in a crowd are alone because you are not with them? Be always with me, so that I may never be alone! I am in no one's company, and yet I am not alone. I myself am a crowd. My wild beasts are with me, those whom I have nourished in my heart from my childhood. There they have made their lairs which they love so much that even in my loneliness they will not leave me. How often have I protested to them: 'Go away from me, wicked ones, so that I may search out the commandments of my God.' It is as though frogs were croaking in my entrails, as if Egypt's plague of flies were blinding my eyes.

Let one sit alone, the scripture says; and indeed, unless one sits and rests, one will not be alone. So it is good to be humbled, Lord, and to bear your burden. By carrying your burden the proud learn meekness. And you say to those who take up your burden: 'Learn from me, for I am meek and humble of heart.' The one who is mounted on pride does not know how to sit still. But your throne is humility and peace. And now I see that no one can be at peace until they have become humble. Humility and peace: how good it is for a man or woman to be humbled so that they can attain to peace. Then indeed will one sit alone and be silent. The one who is not alone cannot be silent. And the one who is not silent cannot hear you when you speak to him or her.

The scripture says: 'the words of the wise are as a goad' to those who listen to them in silence. Let all my world be silent in your presence, Lord, so that I may hear what the Lord God may say in my heart. Your words are so softly spoken that no one can hear them except in a deep silence. But to hear them lifts the one who sits alone and in silence completely above his or her natural powers, because the one who humbles himself will be lifted up. The one who sits alone and listens will be raised above himself. But where? This surely does not mean a lifting up of the body? No: It means of the heart. But how can one's heart be above one's self? It can because one forgets one's self, does not love one's self, thinks nothing of one's self. Of what then does one think? Of that which is above one, one's highest good, one's God. And the more one sees and loves God, the more one sees and loves one's self.

Guigo II, *The Ladder of Monks and Twelve Meditations,* Meditation 1

7 October
Our Lady of the Rosary
MEMORIAL

This Memorial was first instituted as Our Lady of Victory, following the battle of Lepanto in 1571. In 1573 the title was changed to that of the Rosary. It was extended to the universal Church in 1716. Up to the time of St Pius X it was celebrated on the first Sunday of the month, and October is still considered as in a special way devoted to the Rosary.

The Dominicans played a large part in spreading the devotion of the rosary, but there are no real grounds for crediting St Dominic with its invention. The reading is an extract from the Address of Pope John Paul II, given at Knock as a homily at Mass, in which he mentions how we should pray the rosary.

By entrusting yourselves to Mary, you receive Christ. In Mary, 'the

Word was made flesh'; in her the Son of God became man, so that all of us might know how great our human dignity is. Standing on this hallowed ground, we look up to the Mother of God and say 'Blessed are you among women, and blessed is the fruit of your womb'.

The present time is an important moment in the history of the universal Church, and, in particular, of the Church in Ireland. So many things have changed. But the task of renewal in Christ is never finished. Every generation, with its own mentality and characteristics, is like a new continent to be won for Christ. The Church must constantly look for new ways that will enable her to understand more profoundly and to carry out with renewed vigour the mission received from her Founder. In this arduous task, like so many times before when the Church was faced with a new challenge, we turn to Mary, the Mother of God and the Seat of Wisdom, trusting that she will show us again the way to her Son.

Mary was truly united with Jesus. Not many of her own words have been preserved in the gospels; but those that have been recorded refer us again to her Son and to his word. At Cana in Galilee, she turned from her Son to the servants and said: 'Do whatever he tells you' (Jn 2:5). This same message she still speaks to us today.

'Do whatever he tells you'. What Jesus tells us — through his life and by his word — has been preserved for us in the gospels, and in the letters of the apostles and of St Paul and transmitted to us by the Church. We must make ourselves familiar with his words. We do this by listening to the readings from sacred scripture in the liturgy of the word, which introduce us to the eucharistic sacrifice; by reading the scriptures on our own, in the family, or together with friends; by reflecting on what the Lord tells us when we recite the rosary and combine our devotion to the Mother of God with prayerful meditation on the mysteries of her Son's life. Whenever we have questions, whenever we are burdened, whenever we are faced with the choices that our faith imposes on us, the word of the Lord will comfort and guide us.

Christ has not left his followers without guidance in the task of understanding and living the gospel. Before returning to his Father, he promised to send his Holy Spirit to the Church: 'But the Counsellor, the Holy Spirit whom the Father will send in my name, he will teach you all things, and bring to your remembrance all I have said to you' (Jn 14:26).

This same Spirit guides the successors of the apostles, your bishops, united with the bishop of Rome, to whom it was entrusted to preserve the faith and to 'preach the gospel to the whole creation' (Mk 16:14). Listen to their voices, for they bring you to the word of the Lord.

'Do whatever he tells you'. So many different voices assail the Christian in today's wonderful but complicated and demanding world. So many false voices are heard that conflict with the word of the Lord. They are the voices that tell you that truth is less important than personal gain; that comfort, wealth and pleasure are the true aims of life; that the refusal of new life is better than generosity of spirit and the taking up of responsibility; that justice must be achieved but without any personal involvement by the Christian; that violence can be a means to a good end; that unity can be built without giving up hate.

> Pope John Paul II, Homily given at the Shrine of Our Lady
> at Knock, 30 September, 1979

9 October

Saints Denis, *bishop and martyr,* **and companions,** *martyrs*
OPTIONAL MEMORIAL

The death of these martyrs for Christ is mentioned in the early Martyrologies. It would seem that St Denis was sent to preach in Gaul, and suffered martyrdom about the year 251 with his companions.

The church of his burial became one of the great shrines of France, and many of France's kings were buried there. Benedictine monks served the church for many centuries and it would appear that it was they, in the tenth century, who invented and certainly spread the ridiculous legend which identified St Denis with Dionysius (Denis) the Areopogite of Acts 17:34.

The reading offered is taken from a Sermon by Pope St Leo the Great, on the Macchabees.

It is useless to recall the sufferings of the martyrs just to give pleasure to your ears. Knowledge puffs up, unless obedience builds up; things heard are a burden unless they are accepted for imitation. It is not because the persecutor and executioner have laid off, because all the powers of state now serve God, that for Christians sufferings are lacking which they may overcome. 'My child', he says, 'undertaking the service of God, persevere in justice and fear, and prepare your soul for trial' (Sir 2:1); and the apostle says: 'All who wish to live piously for Christ, suffer persecution for righteousness' sake' (2 Tim 3:12 & Mt 5:10).

You then who think that persecution has died down and there is no struggle for you with our enemies, search the intimate hidden place of your heart, and as a careful examiner enter into all the windings of your soul; and see if no opposed forces attack you, if no tyrant wants to dominate in the fortress of your mind. Make no peace with avarice, and despise the growth of evil gains. Refuse any pact with pride, and fear more to be received in honour than to be walked on in lowliness! Distance yourself from anger, let not the passion for vengeance excite the torment of envy. Renounce the desire for pleasure, turn away from impurity, reject luxury, fly iniquity, resist falsehood; and, when you have seen that you have a battle on many fronts, then, like the martyrs, seek a manifold victory. For as often as we die to sins, just so often does sin die in us; and 'precious in the sight of the Lord' is even this 'death of his saints' (Ps 115:15) when one is slain to the world, not by the destruction of bodily life, but by the end of vices.

If, therefore, dearly beloved, you do not mismate yourselves with unbelievers (cf 2 Cor 6:14), if you cease to be sinners, and give way to no temptations to fleshly desires, you lawfully celebrate this solemn day.

Therefore, my dearest brothers and sisters, receive what you see with your eyes, and bear them in your minds for the furtherance of your spiritual growth, and may each of you so use the dwelling built by previous generations, that he may remember the temple of God established within himself! Let him add nothing depraved to his structure, nothing weak; but by agreeing with the living and chosen stones, may he grow, through an indissoluble living bond, into the unity of the Lord's body: and this by the help of the Corner Stone itself, our God and Lord, Jesus Christ, who with the Father and the Holy Spirit lives and reigns for ever and ever. Amen.

St Leo the Great, *Sermon 97,* nn 2, 3 & 4

9 October, also
Saint John Leonardi, *priest*
OPTIONAL MEMORIAL

John Leonardi was a native of Tuscany and born about the year 1541. He was first a pharmacist but then opted to become a priest and devoted himself to teaching christian doctrine to children. In 1574 he founded the Order of the Clerks Regular of the Mother of God. He later formed a body of priests for the spreading of the faith, and this was developed later by the popes into what became the Congregation for the Propagation of the Faith. He did much to foster the renewal of religious life in Italy.

St John died in 1609.

The reading is from Charles de Foucauld and deals with vocation — a theme not unrelated to the Gospel which can be read at today's Mass.

God speaks through the Catholic Church, teaching mankind those things which all men must do and be. And the Church tells us not only what God commands and counsels in general, but also what he requires from each one of us in particular. She invites us all to perfection, and makes known to everyone the kind of life to which one is called by God, that is, one's *vocation* or calling.

God calls all the souls he has created to love him with their whole being, here and hereafter, which means that he calls all of them to holiness, to perfection, to a close following of him and obedience to his will. But he does not ask all souls to show their love by the same works, to climb to heaven by the same ladder, to achieve goodness in the same way of life. What sort of work, then, must *I* do? Which is *my* road to heaven? In what kind of life am *I* to sanctify myself? Apart from the universal calling of all of us to perfect love, to holiness, to the following of Jesus, and obedience to his will in everything, however small, a calling at the last to heaven, what is the particular and special vocation that he puts before me and you and each one of us? It is a most important question, and a question that each of us must ask ourselves when we reach the age at which we must prepare for what we are going to do in the world.

This question: 'What kind of life am I going to undertake?' is the question of *vocation*. And it has got to be answered rightly. For if it is answered rightly and we take the way to which God calls us we shall be living obediently to him, we shall be strengthened by his help, and so we shall come to heaven. But if, on the contrary, the question is answered wrongly, then we shall be living in disobedience to God; we shall not be on the road that he has mapped out for us, we shall be without the helps that he has prepared for that road, and it will be very difficult to get to heaven. This shows how extremely important it is not to make a mistake in this matter of vocation: if we allow ourselves to be deceived about it we shall be in the state of disobeying God.

There is therefore a very grave duty for each one of us when we reach a certain age to take the most careful trouble to find out what vocation we have to follow. This vocation is God's call to undertake such-and-such a sort of holy life in preference to all others, his urgent call to each individual soul to sanctify itself in this particular way. There can never be any question of *choosing* a vocation: the word 'choice' is excluded by the word 'vocation', which means 'calling', a call from God.

Charles de Foucauld, *Sermons in the Sahara*, Sermon 19

14 October
Saint Callistus I, *pope and martyr*
OPTIONAL MEMORIAL

Callistus had been a slave who, though capable, had rather disgraced himself in early life. He was reinstated in the christian community and, under Pope St Zephyrinus, was made a deacon and placed in charge of the burial ground now known as San Callisto. He succeeded St Zephyrinus as pope and died, it would seem as a result of mob action against the Christians, in 222.

His pontificate was remarkable for the storm raised over various practical pastoral rulings he made. These chiefly concerned a studied moderation in the administration of penance and absolution and the permitting of marriage among Christians contrary to the rulings of civil law, e.g., between a male slave and a woman who was a Roman citizen. Hippolytus, the future saint and martyr went into schism over these questions.

The reading is taken from the Address of St Cyprian to Demetrianus. The purpose of the Address was apologetic — Demetrianus was the Roman official governing Proconsular Africa. I have chosen it because of its emphasis on the mercy as well as on the justice of God, and on Christian-Pagan relations.

Firmness of hope and steadfastness of faith are esteemed among us and, amidst the very ruins of this decaying world, our minds are uplifted and our courage is unmoved. Then our patience is always joyous and our soul is ever composed about its God, as through the prophet the Holy Spirit speaks and encourages, confirming with a heavenly voice the steadfastness of our hope and faith. 'The fig tree', he says, 'will not bear fruit and there will be no shoots on the vines. The growth of the olive will deceive and the fields will yield no food. The sheep will stray away from their feed and there will be no cattle in the stalls. I, however, shall exult in the Lord, I shall rejoice in God, my salvation' (Hab 3:17f). He asserts that the man of God and a worshipper of God, supported by the truth of hope and founded on the stability of faith, is not disturbed by the troubles of this world and generation. Although the vine may fail and plants are dying from drought, what is this to Christians, what to the servants of God whom paradise calls, whom every grace and the abundance of the heavenly kingdom awaits? They always exult in the Lord and are glad and rejoice in their God, and bear bravely the evils and contradictions of the world, while they look to future goods and prosperity. For, from common earthly birth, we are created and born anew by the Spirit, nor do we now live for the world but for God: only when we shall have come to God shall we lay hold of God's gifts and promises. And, nevertheless, we always ask and pour out prayers for the keeping off of our enemies and the petitioning of rain, and for either the removing or moderating of adversities; and by day and by night we continually and earnestly pray, propitiating and appeasing God for your peace and salvation.*

* 'Salvation' translates *salus*, which in secular language has the meaning of 'well-being'.

Be mindful, therefore, while there is time, of the true and eternal salvation and, because the end of the world is at hand, turn your minds to God in the fear of God. Nor let this useless and empty dominion among the just and meek in this world delight you, when even in a field the darnel and wild oats dominate among the standing crops. Nor let you say that evils occur because your gods are not worshipped by us; know rather, that this is the wrath of God, this his judgement, so that he who does not understand by his favours, at least may be brought to understand by his afflictions.

Seek God even this late, because God, forewarning us through the prophet already long ago, exhorts and says: 'Seek God and your soul will live' (Amos 5:6). Know God even this late, because Christ, who is coming, admonishes and teaches saying: 'But this is eternal life that they may know you the one and true God and Jesus Christ whom you have sent' (Jn 17:3). Believe him who by no means deceives. Believe him who foretold all these things were to be. Believe him who will give the reward of eternal life to believers. Believe him who will inflict eternal punishments in the fires of hell on unbelievers!

St Cyprian, Ad Demetrianum, nn 20, 23

15 October
Saint Teresa of Avila, virgin and doctor of the Church
MEMORIAL

Teresa was born in Avila, Spain, in 1515, and died in 1582. Of the many great women given by God to his Church she should surely be considered as among the greatest. This does not mean that she was always great or always a saint! A somewhat spoiled young woman she entered the Carmelites when aged eighteen and was hardly remarkable for her prayer-life. Then, when aged about thirty, and after ten years of religious profession, grace finally won through. Teresa resolved to give herself seriously to prayer and the life of perfection. This was in 1555. As she advanced in prayer she also felt called to restore the primitive rule. This was not easily realized, but she did succeed in founding a Carmel in Avila when she was aged about forty, and before she died, some sixteen such Carmels had been established in Spain. She also inspired the reform of the Carmelite friars. Both nuns and friars are referred to as Discalced Carmelites.

St Teresa wrote some major and still influential and inspiring works on the life of prayer and its flowering in the mystical life. Besides these, many of her letters have been preserved, and one of these is offered as a reading. It was addressed to Fr Gracián, a friar of the Discalced Carmelites and her closest confidant. It is not directly on a spiritual theme but does bring the woman before us.

Jesus be with your Paternity [Fr Gracián]. You will realize now how troublesome the regulations are which have been made by Father Fray Juan de Jesús. As I see it, he is going over the same ground as your Paternity's Constitutions: I cannot imagine why. What my nuns are afraid of is that we shall get some tiresome superiors who will lay heavy and excessive burdens on them. That will lead us nowhere. It is a strange thing that Visitors think they have not carried out their duties properly unless they have made new regulations. If the fathers are to have no recreation on days when they receive holy communion, are those who say Mass daily never to get any recreation at all? And, on the other hand, if this rule is not to be kept by priests, why should the other poor friars have to keep it?

The Father himself writes to me, saying that all this severity was necessary because that particular house had never previously had a visitation. That may be so. In certain details he was right to act as he did. But even reading the regulations made me tired. So what would it be if one had to keep them? Believe me, our Rule will not stand additions from tiresome people like that: it is quite hard enough to keep as it is.

Salazar [Fr Gaspar de Salazar] is going to Granada: he has been sent for by the archbishop, who is a great friend of his. The archbishop is very anxious to have one of our convents founded there. I should not mind that at all, for the foundation could be made even without my going. But I should like to have Cyril's [Fr Gracián's] approval first, for I am not sure if Visitors can give licences to found houses for women as well as for men. Of course, we should have to see that the Franciscans do not forestall us as they have done at Burgos.

I must tell you that Santelmo [Fr Olea] is extremely angry with me about that nun, who has now left. But I could not in conscience have done otherwise than reject her, and neither could your Paternity. Everything possible in the matter has been done, and, as it is a thing which concerns the will of God, the world may come to an end before I do otherwise. It has not caused me the least distress, nor need it cause your Paternity any. May we never prosper if we act against the will of our Good. I assure your Paternity that, even had the girl been one of my Paul's [Fr Gracián's] sisters — and I cannot speak more strongly than that — I would not have acted differently. Santelmo has simply refused to listen to reason. He is annoyed with me because I believe my nuns tell the truth. He has got the idea that the Prioress dislikes the girl and thinks they are making a case against her. He has now arranged for her to enter a convent at Talavera, with some others who are going there from Madrid: that is why he sent for her.

May God deliver us from dependence upon creatures. May he grant us to see what we ought to do and to be dependent on none but himself. Santelmo says I have done this because I no longer need him and they have told him a great tale about this being a trick of mine. But you will realize that I never needed him more than when we were discussing the rejection of this postulant: they have quite misunderstood me. May the Lord grant me to learn how I may always do his will. Amen.

Today is the nineteenth of November.

Your Paternity's unworthy servant and subject,

Teresa of Jesus

St Teresa of Avila, *A Letter to P. Gracián*, November 19, 1576

16 October
Saint Hedwig, *religious*
OPTIONAL MEMORIAL

Hedwig [Jadwiga] was born in Bavaria towards the beginning of the last quarter of the twelfth century and as a very young girl was placed in a nunnery for her upbringing, an arrangement which was to influence her whole life. At the age of twelve she was married to Henry, the future Duke of Silesia, who was aged only eighteen. They ultimately had seven children, some of whom caused Hedwig anything but joy. She lived a life of great simplicity, abnega-

tion and renunciation, coupled with an active charity for the less fortunate.
Her husband shared her ideals.

When Henry died she entered the Cistercian nunnery at Trebnitz, which
had been founded by Henry and herself, and where one of her daughters was
abbess.

St Hedwig died in 1243 and was canonized in 1267.

As a reading a text from Guerric of Igny is offered, an extract from a sermon
preached to his monks on St John the Baptist.

It is thus written: When he saw that he could not overcome him, he
touched the nerve of his thigh and it immediately withered. And do
you not see yourself do battle with an angel, rather with God himself,
when daily he resists your over-hasty desires? You wash yourself
with snow waters, as it were, that you may be clean in heart and
body, and he himself plunges you in uncleannesses. You say: I shall
be made wise, and he retires further from you. You cry to him, and he
does not hear you; you wish to approach him, and he repels you. You
decide on something, and its contrary comes your way; and, almost
in all things, in the 'harshness of his hands', he is against you.

O self-disguising mercy, you present yourself as harshness! With
what kindness you fight against those for whom you fight! For
although you hide these matters in your heart, nevertheless I know
that you love those loving you, and the manifoldness of your sweetness is boundless which you hide for those fearing you.

Do not therefore despair, happy soul which has begun to contend
with God; act continually; he indeed loves to suffer violence from
you, desires to be overcome by you. For when he is angered and
stretches his hand to strike, he seeks, as he himself acknowledges, a
man like Moses who resists him; and if he does not find such, he com-
plains and says: There is no one who rises up and holds me. For if his
anger is implacable and his sentence unbending, Jeremiah, who had
tried to resist, will weep and say: 'You were stronger and prevailed.'

But far be it, brothers, who demand what is pleasing to him, far be
it that he be strong against you, who wished to be weak unto death
for you. He was pierced through with so many wounds, crucified in
his whole body: whence, I ask, can the strength come to him to resist
that charity, which led him, as it were overcome and captive, through
all kinds of infirmities, even unto death, and to death on the cross?

Now love is not as strong as death, but stronger than death, since by virtue of love the strength of God is made weak unto death, and nevertheless God's weakness is found stronger than even the most strong, whose death has proved to be your death, O death!

May you be armed then with the power of love, whoever you are, you pious invader who seek to snatch the kingdom of heaven; and you may be free from care because you will easily overcome the king of heaven himself. For if any difficulty or hardship seems to be opposed to you, do not be pusillanimous, but understand with what intent he does that; namely, so that by that very opposition he may sharpen your spirit — as the nature of the great-hearted and brave is apt to be — that he may exercise your forces, test your constancy, multiply your victories, and increase your crowns.

Guerric of Igny, *Sermon 2 on St John the Baptist*

16 October, also
Saint Margaret Mary Alacoque, *virgin*
OPTIONAL MEMORIAL

Margaret Mary was born in Burgundy in 1647 into a well-to-do family. Her father died when she was very small, and she had an unhappy childhood. She was, anyway, a strange child, possessing an almost morbid religious sense. In 1671 she entered the Visitation Convent of Paray-le-Moniale. She was already well-advanced in the way of prayer, but humanly was quite a puzzle to her superiors. She and they persevered, however — in this the influence of Blessed Claude de la Colombière SJ, her confessor, was of critical importance.

In 1673 she had the first of her revelations concerning devotion to the Sacred Heart of Jesus, and these continued into 1675. There had been devotion to the Sacred Heart in the Middle Ages but Margarert Mary was God's chosen instrument in reviving it in the post-Tridentine Church. The message of God's mercy and love was particularly relevant in a France threatened by a rigid Jansenism. Though the primary message given to us through St Margaret Mary was of God's love and mercy and the confidence one should have in it, there was another aspect, that of reparation for sin, which played a large part and an increasingly important one in her own life. The penances she inflicted on herself are quite frightening. In all these she was guided by apparitions; such, at least, was her belief.

She died in 1690.

As a reading I offer a letter she wrote to one of her spiritual directors, a Jesuit Father (but not Blessed Colombière).

It's quite beyond me to set on record the whole story of this lovely devotion as I know it. I've no way of disclosing to all the world the treasures of grace stored in the Sacred Heart of Jesus. What can I do to reveal his purpose — the prodigal outpouring of grace on those who practise this devotion! I entreat you, reverend Father: leave no means untried of instilling it in every heart. In ways beyond question, Jesus has shown me that he means to establish this important devotion everywhere, and so recruit untold loyal servants, perfect friends and truly grateful children — all this, chiefly through the Fathers of the Society of Jesus.

The Sacred Heart is a treasure-house of graces and blessings past all counting. I know of no other devotion in the whole range of the spiritual life which affords the same guarantee of lifting souls in a very short time to the peak of perfection and allowing them to relish the sweetness of serving Jesus Christ. Indeed, I'd even make it a principle: given the knowledge that our Lord finds this such a welcome devotion, there isn't a single Christian — striking merely the tiniest sparks of love — who wouldn't begin it immediately.

Do your very utmost to get religious to adopt it. They will find it so helpful, they won't need to look any further for ways of reviving their first fervour, or of restoring lax communities to strict observance, or of bringing the most exemplary religious to the very summit of perfection.

My divine Master has informed me that those who labour for the salvation of souls will acquire the art of touching the hardest hearts, and see their work crowned with success, if they have a tender devotion to the Sacred Heart and use their influence to encourage and establish it everywhere.

Lay people, too, will find in this devotion all the help they need: peace in their families, rest amid their toils, the blessing of heaven on all their ventures, comfort in time of trouble. There, in the Sacred Heart, they will find a home and shelter all their life long — but, above all, at the hour of death. A lifetime of tender and true devotion to the Sacred Heart of our Saviour and our Judge ensures the blessing of a happy death!

Lastly, it's quite evident that there's no one in the whole wide world but would receive every help from heaven in all circumstances, provided he has a truly grateful love for Jesus — the essence of devotion to the Sacred Heart.

St Margaret Mary Alacoque, 'A letter to one of her spiritual directors', 1689

17 October
Saint Ignatius of Antioch, *bishop and martyr*
MEMORIAL

According to tradition, and it is reasonable, Ignatius was a disciple of the apostles. Of him we know both little and much. Little with regard to the external details of his life, save that he was bishop of Antioch, and, about the year 107, died a martyr in Rome. Much, because in the course of his journey to Rome as a prisoner, he wrote a series of letters which are among the greatest treasures of the early Church. They are letters which reveal a man completely given to the love and service of Christ, in himself, and in his body, the Church.

The reading offered below is from *The Letter to the Philadelphians.* It expresses two of the saint's great themes: union, centred on one's bishop, and salvation in Christ.

I am thankful to say that, where you are concerned, my conscience is clear. Nobody can be bold enough to claim that I have ever been oppressive to a single one of you in any matter, great or small. I can only pray that none of those I spoke to may ever find the words I said rising up in evidence against him.

It is true that some people did once take it into their heads to impose upon me, in my unspiritual capacity. My spiritual self, however, no man can impose upon; for that comes from God, and its origin and its destination are alike known to it, and it can bring hidden things to light. Thus, at the time I was with you, I cried out, speaking with a loud voice — the very voice of God — 'Be loyal to your bishop and clergy and deacons'. Some who were there, suspected me of saying this because I already knew of certain dissensions among you; but He whose prisoner I am will bear me witness that no such information had ever reached me from human lips. No; that was the preaching of the Spirit itself, telling you never to act in independence of the bishop, to keep your bodies as a temple of God, to cherish unity and shun divisions, and to be imitators of Jesus Christ as he was of his Father.

As for me, I did my part as one dedicated to the cause of unity; for where disunion and bad blood exist, God can never be dwelling. That is why the Lord offers forgiveness to all who repent, if their repentance brings them back into unity with God and with the bishop's council of clergy. I have the fullest confidence in the grace of Jesus Christ, that he will cast loose every chain that binds you; and I appeal to you not to let your actions be prompted by any party spirit, but rather by the teaching of Christ.

Certain people declared in my hearing, 'Unless I can find a thing in our ancient records, I refuse to believe it in the Gospel'; and when I assured them that it is indeed in the ancient scriptures, they retorted, 'That has got to be proved'. But for my part, my records are Jesus Christ; for me, the sacrosanct records are his cross and death and resurrection, and the faith that comes through him. And it is by these, and by the help of your prayers, that I am hoping to be justified.

The priests of old, I admit, were estimable men; but our own high priest is greater, for he has been entrusted with the holy of holies, and to him alone are the secret things of God committed. He is the doorway to the Father, and it is by him that Abraham and Isaac and Jacob and the prophets go in, no less than the apostles and the whole Church; for all these have their part in God's unity. Nevertheless, the Gospel has a distinction all its own, in the advent of our Saviour Jesus Christ, and his passion and resurrection. We are fond of the prophets, and they did indeed point forward to him in their preaching; yet it is the Gospel that sets the coping-stone on man's immortality. It is in all these different elements together that goodness resides, if you have a loving faith.

St Ignatius of Antioch, *The Epistle to the Philadelphians*, nn 6-9

18 October
Saint Luke, *evangelist*
FEAST

The feast of St Luke is celebrated today in both East and West. It is generally believed that he did not die as a martyr. He was either a very hellenized Jew or a Greek-speaking gentile who came to Christianity through Judaism. He was traditionally believed to be a physician, perhaps the 'beloved physician' mentioned by St Paul. He certainly was closely associated with Paul, and possibly passed himself off as his slave, which was the usual condition of a physician in the Greco-Roman world.

Luke was the author of the Gospel which bears his name and of the Acts of the Apostles.

The reading is taken from St Ambrose's *Commentary on the Gospel according to Luke.*

'It seemed good to me', Luke says. It may be that what Luke states seemed good to himself, seemed good not only to him! For not only by the will of man did it seem good, but as it pleased him who, he says, speaks in me — Christ (cf 2 Cor 13:3) who brings it about that that which is good for us, may also *seem* good; for he calls one on whom he has pity. On this account, one who follows Christ can reply, when asked why he wanted to be a Christian, 'It seemed good to me'. When he says this, he does not deny 'it seemed good to God', for the 'will of men is made ready beforehand by God'. For it is a grace of God that God is honoured by his saint. Accordingly, many wanted to write a gospel, but only four were accepted, who merited the divine grace.

'It seemed good', he says, 'to me also, having followed all things in order closely'. That his book of the gospel is longer than the others, no one would doubt. On this account he claims for himself not matters which are false but which are true. Accordingly he earned a testimonial for diligence even from the apostle Paul. For Paul praises Luke in this way: 'whose praise', he says, 'is in the gospel throughout all the churches'. And he is indeed praiseworthy, who deserved to be praised by such a teacher of the nations.

Therefore, he says, that he had 'followed' not a *few* things, but '*all* things', and to one who had followed all things, it seemed good to write not everything, but drawing on everything. He did not write everything, but he did follow all things, for, if all the things which Jesus did were written down, it is said, I think the world itself would be too small (Jn 21:25). For you will note that he deliberately passes over matters which are written by others, so that a varied grace might shine out of the Gospel, and each of the books stand out with its own particular wonders of mysteries and deeds.

Then the Gospel is written for Theophilus: this means, for him whom God loves. If you love God, it is written for you; if it is written for you, accept the evangelist's gift. Guard carefully the token of your friend in the depths of your soul, watch over the good deposited there by the Holy Spirit, who is given to us, consider it frequently, examine it more often. Faith is the first duty owed to a token, careful attention follows faith, lest the moth or rust destroy the tokens entrusted to you; for what is entrusted to you, can be destroyed. The gospel is a good token, but see that in your mind neither moth nor rust destroy it. The moth destroys if what you have read well, you believe badly.

St Ambrose, *Commentary on St Luke's Gospel*, I, 10-12

19 October

Saints John de Brebeuf and Isaac Jogues, *priests and martyrs,* and companions, *martyrs*
OPTIONAL MEMORIAL

These were eight missionaries, members of the Society of Jesus, who preached the gospel among the Indians of North America and were slain by them in the seventeenth century. St Isaac died on 18 October 1647 and St John was slain on 16 March 1648, both of them undergoing the most fearful torments. The others were also slain by the Huron and Iroquois Indians. The killing of the Jesuit fathers was partly the result of tribal conflict among the Indians, but also of superstition. Many of their Indian converts were also slain for the faith.

The reading given in the Divine Office is from the spiritual diaries of St John de Brebeuf; the reading offered here is a Letter from St Isaac Jogues.

Alas, my dearest Father, when shall I begin at length to serve him and to love him whose love for us has been without any beginning? When shall I begin to give myself entirely to him who has given himself wholly to me and without reserve? Although I am the most miserable of creatures, and though I have made poor use of the graces which Our Lord has bestowed upon me in this country and have responded to these so wretchedly, nevertheless, I do not despair in my soul; for I see that he takes care to offer me new opportunities through which I may die to myself and by which I may unite myself to him inseparably. Because of these opportunities, he may make me worthier.

Some Iroquois have come for the purpose of obtaining the liberty of some people of their nation, and to treat of peace in the name of the whole country. They brought gifts for the Governor, according to their custom. That peace has already been established, to the great joy of the French. It will last as long as pleases the will of God. It seemed necessary, to maintain the peace, and unobtrusively to see what might be done in the matter of instructing the Iroquois, to send some one of our Fathers there. I have reason to believe that I shall be employed there, for I have some knowledge of the language of that nation and country. You well understand what need I have of the powerful aid of your prayers as a protection for me living among those barbarians.

It will be required that I shall live among them without any freedom to pray, without Mass* and the sacraments. It will happen that I shall be held responsible for all that may chance to occur between the French, the Iroquois, the Hurons and Algonquins, all of whom have subscribed to this treaty, if any difficulty arises, a thing not unlikely to happen. But what of that? My confidence is placed in God who does not need our help for accomplishing his designs. Our single endeavour should be to give ourselves to the work and to be faithful to him, and not to spoil his work by our short-comings.

I trust that you will beg this favour for me from God; after such great slothfulness in his service, I may at length begin to serve him more diligently. And so, if I shall be employed in this mission, my heart tells me: '*Ibo et non redibo* — I shall go, but I shall not return.' In

---

*The reference to doing without Mass relates to the Indians' fear of witchcraft, which was how they interpreted such private prayer.

very truth, it will be well for me, it will be a happiness for me, if God will be pleased to complete the sacrifice there where he began it, if the little blood which I shed there in that land will be accepted by him as a pledge that I would willingly shed all the blood which I bear in all the veins of my body and of my heart. In conclusion, that Iroquois people 'is the spouse of blood to me; this people have I espoused to me by my blood.' Our good Master who gained this people for himself by his own blood, may open to it the door of the Gospel, if it pleases him, and not only to this nation but to the four other nations allied and neighbouring to them. Farewell, my dear Father, and beg God that he may join me with himself, never to be separated from him.

Isaac Jogues, SJ

St Isaac Jogues, Letter written about 1646 to an unnamed Jesuit friend in France

19 October, also
Saint Paul of the Cross, *priest*
OPTIONAL MEMORIAL

Paul was born in the town of Ovada in Liguria, north Italy, in January 1694. His father ran a small business which was not very prosperous, and Paul had to help with running it until he reached his mid-twenties. From his mother he derived his great devotion to the passion of Christ. In 1713 he made a general confession, in the course of which he came to believe he was called to the service of God. It was only in 1720, though, that he was free from family obligations and fully able to follow this call. His spiritual guide at this time was Bishop Gattinara of Alessandria. He clothed Paul in a black tunic and encouraged him to make a forty days' retreat. During this time Paul wrote the Rule for his future Congregation, which we know as the Passionists.

His ideal was marked by poverty and penance and the preaching of God's love as manifested in the passion of Christ. His first follower was his brother, John Baptist. After some initial reverses they obtained verbal permission from the pope to form a community in 1725. Initially they worked in a hospital in Rome but their qualities were soon recognized and they were ordained priests. Shortly after this Paul established his first 'Retreat' well north of Rome. The church there was blessed in 1737, and in 1741 Pope Benedict XIV gave formal approbation to the Rule. Eleven other Retreats or monasteries were founded by Paul, including St John and Paul in Rome. He also founded the Passionist Nuns and a Confraternity for lay people.

St Paul was a visionary, endowed with gifts of prophecy and healing, as well a spirit of penance. He died in Rome on 18 October 1775.

As a reading I offer an excerpt from a letter of direction he wrote to Lucy Berlini, in 1751. He began the letter by talking of his crosses and fears for himself. He continues:

My blessed daughter, know now that prayer is more perfect when it is made in the essence of the soul — when the soul prays in the Spirit of God. This is a most profound language, but when God wants to, he can make even stones speak. Allow then this great Good, this immense Good to repose in your spirit. This is a reciprocal rest: God in you, you in God. Oh, what a sweet work! What a divine work!

God nourishes himself (I speak in this way because I don't know how else to put it) — God nourishes himself on your spirit and your spirit nourishes itself on the spirit of God. Christ is my food and I am his. You can't be mistaken in this divine work because it is a work of faith and love.

If I were speaking to you face to face, I would be able to explain myself better, but sometimes it's best to remain silent about these sacred things. Lucy, listen — act justly: remain in your horrible nothingness which is capable of bringing to birth every possible evil. Leave God his part because everything good is his.

I don't want your examination of conscience to be anything other than what you are doing. To give a quick glance over the mighty deeds of mercy which God does in you, a glance over the gifts God has shared with you and which you know have been marred by the foulness of your own imperfections. Then return quickly to him who has given the gifts to you; but return with a humble and contrite heart so that he may purify your imperfections in the fire of his love. Since it is God who puts his treasures into your stench-filled mire, return them to him so that they might be cleansed. And, you are to do this in the twinkling of an eye. In this way, the soul is prepared in pure truth for even greater graces.

Lucy, my daughter in Christ, God wants you to be a saint; he wants you to be holy. So be humble of heart, persevering in the prayer God gives you as I mentioned above, and never omit holy communion.

I want you to enter even more deeply into that holy desert, into that divine solitude within you, in the very essence of your soul, and there you will be reborn in the divine Word to a new life of love. God rests in you: God fills you and you are all in God. God is transforming you completely in his love. How I am lost for words and ideas!

St Paul of the Cross, *Letter to Lucy Berlini*, 1751

23 October
Saint John of Capistrano, *priest*
OPTIONAL MEMORIAL

John was born at Capistrano in Italy in 1386. He studied law first and for a time held the office of judge; then decided to enter religion. He joined the Franciscans in 1416 and was ordained priest in 1420. He aided St Bernardine of Siena in preaching and in establishing the Observantine friars, a reform within the Friars Minor.

He was elected several times as vicar general of the Observants. Then he went on various papal missions to Bohemia and Hungary, largely to preach against the Hussite heresy. Then in 1453 the Turks overran Constantinople and invaded Europe. The reaction in Europe was one of alarm but it was left to John to raise an army. As it turned out he had also to lead it into battle, not with a sword, be it said, but bearing a cross in his hands while riding on horseback. The Christian army was victorious, and the Turkish threat faded. This was in 1456.

St John died that same year as a result of the plague.

Today we should hardly approve of his warlike activities, but. . .!

The reading is from a letter he wrote to the friars of the Observance in favour of study.

The priest cannot dispense holiness if he does not possess it himself. The Church needs the power of the keys. Is no science necessary for the proper use of those keys? Is knowledge not counted among the seven gifts of the Holy Spirit? O ignorance, thou foolish and blind mother of all errors, who has now beguiled thee? How can a person know if he does not learn? How can he learn without teachers? O stupid and idle gossip of the ignorant! An enemy of nature is the one who despises knowledge: the longing for knowledge lies within human nature. Therefore the person that despises knowledge sins against human nature. To neglect the gifts of the Holy Spirit is to despise the Spirit who gives those gifts. Beware, dearest ones, lest you fall under the curse which says: 'Wisdom will not enter into a malicious soul, nor dwell in a body subject to sins.' Do you consider it more useful to spend your time in complaints and criticism, in idle conversations, in faultfinding, than to spend it in the attainment of knowledge?

You prophesy a repetition of the same failure that met my plan of reform. Was it wrong that I laboured with all my power for the reform of the whole Order? If only I could see that reform reached before I depart from this world! I wish for nothing but your progress, your prosperity and honour. Forgive me, please, that I am planning to lift you higher. Or are you, without study, able to have a clear idea of faith, hope, and charity, prudence, fortitude, temperance and the other virtues? Of the gifts, of the corporal and spiritual works of mercy; of the difference of sins, their degrees and species? Must you not deal with these things? How do you expect to justify your ignorance? How shall your light shine before men if you yourselves are obscurantists, hiding in the general darkness? Together with your followers you will fall into the ditch.

Do you not believe that the Lord will demand an account of your ignorance? The lips of the priest shall keep knowledge, and they shall seek the law at his mouth: because he is the angel of the Lord of hosts (Mal 2:7). But angel, messenger, he will not be if he does not announce the truth; and the truth is not made known by one who does not know it; and one cannot know it unless he learns it; and he cannot learn it without a teacher. And you flee from teachers and still feel satisfied. The crafty devil will test your ignorance as he once did Eve's.

Let no one claim the example of St Francis. Only to a very few, and by miracle, was knowledge granted without studies. Did not Anthony of Padua, with St Francis' permission, spend five uninterrupted years in study? The danger lies not in knowledge, but in the abuse of knowledge.

St John of Capistrano, *Letter on Study to the Friars of the Observance*

24 October
Saint Anthony Claret, *bishop*
OPTIONAL MEMORIAL

Anthony was born in Spain in 1807, his family background being Catalan and working-class. He was ordained as a secular priest on 13 June, 1835. After some years of diocesan work he tried his vocation as a member of the Society of Jesus but had to leave on account of ill-health. Returning to Spain he became a very successful popular preacher, though his uncompromising spirituality made him some enemies. In 1849 he founded an institute of missionary priests, usually known as the Claretian Fathers.

In 1849 he was made archbishop of Santiago in Cuba and worked there for six years with great pastoral care and solicitude, his zeal bearing great fruit in the bettering of christian standards among his flock, but also serving to rouse the slave-owners against him. In1857 he was called back to Spain as confessor to Queen Isabella and was careful to resign his see of Santiago. When the queen was driven from Spain in 1868 he accompanied her into exile in France.

He attended the First Vatican Council in 1870 and died that same year in the Cistercian abbey of Fontfroide.

St Anthony was not an original thinker, but a man of great fervour of life and prayer, deeply concerned for the good of souls.

The reading, taken from the decree of the Second Vatican Council on the Office of Bishops, might be a commentary on his work in Cuba.

Bishops should dedicate themselves to their apostolic office as witnesses of Christ before all peoples. Not only should they look after those who already follow the Prince of Pastors, but they should also devote themselves wholeheartedly to those who have strayed in any way from the path of truth or who are ignorant of the gospel of Christ and his saving mercy. Their ultimate goal as bishops is that all may walk 'in all goodness and justice and truth' (Eph 5:9).

In fulfilling their duty to sanctify, bishops should be mindful that they have been taken from among the people and appointed their representatives before God in order to offer gifts and sacrifices for sins. Bishops enjoy the fullness of the sacrament of orders, and all priests as well as deacons are dependent upon them in the exercise of authority. For the 'presbyters' are prudent fellow workers of the episcopal order and are themselves consecrated as true priests of the new testament, just as deacons are ordained for service and minister to the people of God in communion with the bishop and his presbytery. Therefore bishops are the principal dispensers of the mysteries of God, just as they are the governors, promoters, and guardians of the entire liturgical life in the church committed to them.

Hence, they should constantly exert themselves to have the faithful know and live the paschal mystery more deeply through the eucharist and thus become a firmly knit body in the solidarity of Christ's love. 'Intent upon prayer and the ministry of the word' (Acts 6:4), they should devote their labour to this end, that all those committed to their care may be of one mind in prayer and through the reception of the sacraments may grow in grace and be faithful witnesses to the Lord.

As those who lead others to perfection, bishops should be diligent in fostering holiness among their clerics, religious, and laity according to the special vocation of each. They should also be mindful of their obligation to give an example of holiness through charity, humility, and simplicity of life. Let them so hallow the churches entrusted to them that the true image of Christ's universal Church may shine forth fully in them. For that reason they should foster priestly and religious vocations as much as possible, and take a special interest in missionary vocations.

Vatican II, *Decree on the Bishop's Pastoral Office in the Church*, nn 11, 15

28 October
Saints Simon and Jude, *apostles*
FEAST

In the Gospel read at today's Mass we learn of Simon known as 'the Zealot', perhaps because of his early history, perhaps because of some incident, but the title does serve to distinguish him from 'Simon, whom he (Christ) called Peter'. It is hard to establish where he laboured after the dispersal from Jerusalem.

Jude, or Thaddeus, is called 'son of James', to distinguish him from 'the Iscariot'. He may have been a relation of James, son of Alphaeus. Like St Simon we cannot establish where he later exercised his ministry.

The reading is from St Ambrose's *Commentary on the Gospel according to Luke*.

He spent, he says, the night in praying to God. An example is given to
you, a pattern prescribed, which you ought to follow. For what ought
you to do for your salvation, when Christ spent the night for you in
prayer? What is it fitting for you to do when you would undertake
some duty of piety, when Christ, about to send the apostles, first
prayed, and prayed on his own? Nor is he ever found anywhere, if I
am not mistaken, to have prayed with his apostles: everywhere he
petitions alone; for human desires do not understand the divine plan,
nor can anyone be a sharer in the inner things with Christ. Do you
wish to know how far he prayed for me, not for himself?

He called, he says, his disciples, and chose twelve from them,
whom he appointed sowers of the faith, to spread the help of human
salvation through the whole earth. Note at the same time the heavenly plan: he did not choose wise folk, nor rich ones, nor noble ones,
but fishermen and publicans, whom he would direct, lest they seem
to have drawn some to his grace by the authority of power and nobility, lest by prudence they had brought them over, lest by riches they
had redeemed them; so that the account of the truth might prevail,
not the attractiveness of human argument.

And Judas is chosen, not through imprudence, but through providence. How great is truth, which not even an enemy minister
weakens! How great is the character of the Lord, who wished to put
his judgement in peril in our eyes rather than his love! For he had
taken on the weakness of our humanity and therefore did not reject
these aspects of human weakness. He wished to be abandoned, he
wished to be betrayed, he wished to be handed over by his apostle, so
that you — deserted by a companion, betrayed by a companion, may
bear calmly that your judgement erred, your doing of good has
perished.

And he went down, he says, with them and stood in a level place.
Pay heed carefully to all, both how he goes up with the apostles and
comes down to the crowds; for how would the crowd see Christ, save
in the lowly? He is not followed to the heights, it does not go up to
sublime things. Then when he comes down, he finds the infirm; for
the infirm cannot be on the heights. Thus Matthew also teaches that
the weak were healed on the lower levels; for first each was healed,
so that, litle by little, with the development of the virtues, he could go

up the mountain. And on this account he heals each on the lower slopes, this means, he recalls from wantonness, he turns away the harm of blindness; he comes down to our wounds, that by a certain use and access to what is his he might make us to be sharers in heavenly things.

And he indeed healed these, but he left them there on the lower slopes. As you have read, 'Seeing the crowd, however, he went up the mountain, and when he had sat down, his disciples went up to him. . . .'

St Ambrose, *Commentary on St Luke's Gospel*, V, 43-46

1 November
All Saints
SOLEMNITY

The celebration of All Saints began in the eastern Church, though not on this day. The choice of today for the solemnity may have been influenced by the celtic festival of the Samhna, which contained elements of a harvest feast. It is certain that the earliest mention of All Saints in the west is in the Felire of Oengus, an old Irish martyrology, and then we find it referred to in the writings of the Anglo-Saxons.

Whatever may be its origins, we now celebrate, in common with the whole western Church, the triumph of God in his Saints.

The reading is taken from a sermon of John Henry Newman.

So many were the wonderful works which our Saviour did on earth, that not even the world itself could have contained the books recording them. Nor have his marvels been less since he ascended on high: those works of higher grace and more abiding fruit, wrought in the souls of men, from the first hour till now — the captives of his power, the ransomed heirs of his kingdom, whom he has called by his Spirit working in due season, and led on from strength to strength till they appear before his face in Zion.

Surely not even the world itself could contain the records of his love, the history of those many saints, that 'cloud of witnesses', whom we today celebrate, his purchased possession in every age!

We crowd these all up into one day; we mingle together in the brief remembrance of an hour all the choicest deeds, the holiest lives, the noblest labours, the most precious sufferings, which the sun ever saw. Even the least of those saints were the contemplation of many days — even the names of them, if read in our Service, would outrun many settings and risings of the light — even one passage in the life of one of them were more than sufficient for a long discourse.

'Who can count the dust of Jacob, and the number of the fourth part of Israel?' (Num 23:10). Martyrs and confessors, rulers and doctors of the Church, devoted ministers and religious brethren, kings of the earth and all people, princes and judges of the earth, young men and maidens, old men and children, the first fruits of all ranks, ages, and callings, gathered each in his own time into the paradise of God. This is the blessed company which today meets the Christian pilgrim in the Services of the Church. We are like Jacob, when, on his journey homewards, he was encouraged by a heavenly vision. 'Jacob went on his way, and the angels of God met him; and when Jacob saw them, he said, This is God's host: and he called the name of that place Mahanaim' (Gen 32:1, 2).

J.H. Newman, *Parochial and Plain Sermons*, II, 32

2 November
The Commemoration of All the Faithful Departed

This commemoration was first instituted by St Odilo, abbot of Cluny, and spread with the Cluniac movement before being taken into the universal calendar. That our prayers could help those faithful departed who had not immediately entered into the glory of the Lord was already a belief of late Judaism and is a consistent tenet of the Christian tradition.

The reading is taken from a sermon of St Augustine, On the resurrection of the Dead. It may be felt that Augustine here is somewhat unfeeling with regard to the bereaved. The passage given above, for St Monica, 27 August, and taken from Augustine's *Confessions*, serves to show another side to his thought. The passage below is about the resurrection and is deeper than it seems.

You are saddened concerning your buried dearest one, because you have not immediately heard their voice. He was alive, he is dead: she ate, now she eats no more; he was feeling, now he does not feel; she is not present to the joys and gladness of the living. . . .

Would you bewail the seed, when you ploughed? If indeed, there were someone so unversed in affairs and ignorant of even proximately future matters, who when the seed is brought into the field, and put in the ground, and buried in the broken soil would bewail the wheat, because they remembered the summer, and would think to themselves, saying: This corn, which now has been buried, with how much labour was it not stored in the barn, having been harvested, brought in, thrashed, winnowed? We saw its splendour, and gave thanks; now it is taken from our eyes; I see the ground ploughed up, the corn, though, I do not see, either in the barn or here.

They would plaintively bewail the corn as if it were dead and buried; they would weep abundantly, looking on the fields and the earth, not, however, seeing the harvest. . . .

And what would they who knew have said to them if it happened that they lamented because they knew nothing of these matters? Do not be sad. What we have buried is surely no longer in the barn, it is not in our hands: we shall come to this field and it will delight you to see the beauty of the standing corn, where now you weep the bareness of the ploughing. . . .

But the harvests are wont to be seen each year: the one last harvest of humankind, however, will rise at the end of the world. It cannot now be shown to the eyes: but there is proof given concerning the one chief grain. The Lord himself says: 'If the grain should remain as it is, and not be put to death, it will remain alone', speaking of his own being put to death, for there is a multiple future resurrection of believers in him. The precedent is given concerning a single grain, but a precedent of such kind in which all were to believe, who wished to be grains.

Although, indeed, if we were not deaf, the whole of creation tells of resurrection: from which we ought to infer what God is about to do with regard to humankind once for all at the end, since we see so many similar things every day. The resurrection of Christians will be once for all, the sleeping and waking of animals is a daily affair. To sleep is like to death: to wake, like to rising. From what takes place daily, believe what is once for all in the future. The moon in every month is born, waxes, is full, wanes, wholly declines, is renewed. What happens in the moon through the months, that once for all in the whole of time in the resurrection. Just as that daily happens in sleepers, so in the moon for each month. Where do the leafy branches of the trees go to and come from, to what secret places do they go, from what secret places do they come? It is winter, surely the trees, now like parched places, grow green in the spring time. Has it happened now for the first time, or was it not so last year? Indeed, and it was so last year! The year is snatched away by autumn into winter, it comes back through spring into summer. The year therefore comes back in time, and shall men, made in the image of God, when they die, perish?

St Augustine, *Sermon 361*, nn 9, 10 (extracts)

3 November
Saint Martin de Porres, *religious*
OPTIONAL MEMORIAL

Martin was born in Lima in Peru in the year 1579, the son of a Spanish father and an Indian mother. He studied to become a medical assistant, but then entered the Dominicans, opting to be a Lay Brother. As a Dominican he dispensed medical aid to the poor of Lima. He is also well-known for his concern for dumb animals.

He lived a humble and austere life, which was sustained by his fervent practice of prayer and a lively devotion towards the Blessed Eucharist.

St Martin died in 1639 and was canonized in 1962.

The reading is from an address of Pope John XXIII, preached the day after the canonization of St Martin.

In the life of Brother Martin there were three loves; the crucified Jesus, our Lady of the Rosary, and St Dominic. Three passions burned in his heart; charity, particularly with regard to the poor and the sick, the most rigorous penance, which he regarded as 'the price of love', and the humility which fed these virtues. Allow us to dwell particularly on this last, humility, and to contemplate it in Brother Martin's transparent soul.

Humility brings the vision that one has of oneself within the true limits marked out by human reason. It brings to its perfection the gift of the fear of God, by which the Christian, aware that the sovereign good and its authentic greatness are found only in God, offers him a unique and supreme respect, and avoids sin, the only evil which can separate the soul from him. This is the key to the practical wisdom which governs the life of those who are prudent and discreet. 'The fear of God is the school of wisdom' we are told in the holy book (cf Prov 15:33).

Martin de Porres was the angel of Lima. The novices turned to him in their difficulties, the most important of the Fathers sought advice from him. He reconciled households, healed the most refractory diseases, brought enmities to an end, resolved theological disputes and gave his decisive opinion on the most difficult of matters. What an abundance of wisdom, balance and goodness was found in his heart! He was not a learned man, but he possessed that true knowledge which ennobles the spirit, the 'inner light in the heart' which God gives to those who fear him, that 'light of discernment' of which St Catherine of Siena speaks (Letter 213). In his soul there reigned the holy fear of God, the foundation of all upbringing, of true spiritual progress, and, in the last analysis, of civilization itself. 'The fear of God is the beginning of wisdom' (Ps 110:10).

When we see him raised to the honours of the altar, we admire Martin de Porres with the delight of one who gazes upon a magnificent panorama from the top of a mountain. But it must not be forgotten that humility is the way which leads to these heights: 'Humility goes before glory' (Prov 15:33). The higher the building, the deeper must be the foundations. 'Before it is raised, the building must go down: before putting on the roof, the foundations must be dug' (St Augustine). Martin teaches us the same lesson. . . .

May the light of his life guide all people on the path of christian social justice and of universal love without distinction of colour or race.

Pope John XXIII, Homily on St Martin de Porres, 3 June 1962

4 November
Saint Charles Borromeo, *bishop*
MEMORIAL

Charles was born in 1538 of an Italian noble family. He entered the service of the Church early and was advanced with a speed which was the fruit not of recognition for his virtue, but of the most shameless nepotism on the part of his uncle, Pope Pius IV. So it was that in 1559, at the age of twenty-one Charles was made a cardinal and archbishop of Milan. He, however, was of tender conscience, and serious to the point of gravity, and made good use of the benefices and offices bestowed on him. He played a leading role in the later stages of the Council of Trent, and drafted its famous Catechism.

From 1566 he was able to devote his full attention to the diocese of Milan and its suffragan sees. He set about a thorough reform of his diocese, providing for the formation of the clergy, the education of children, the care of the sick, devoting himself to the latter in the great plague of 1576.

He died in 1584, worn out by his labours at the early age of forty-six, and was looked upon by his people as a second Ambrose. He was certainly one of the really great bishops of the sixteenth century.

The reading offered is from Cardinal Manning, an extract from a sermon entitled 'The Good Shepherd'.

Traits of St Charles Borromeo's tenderness are to be found throughout his life. They are not isolated acts, but the texture of his character. They describe not his condescension — a word that implies assumed superiority — but the profound humility which he chose for his legend and manifested in his person. In his dealings with the poor, they never felt his greatness. His presence was no burden; and his acts of humility had such a delicate grace and such a sensitive forbearance, that the lowest were at ease with him. It was the gentleness and the attraction of the Great Shepherd of the sheep; for the Sacred Heart burned and beat in his, and made him the rest and solace of his flock. And yet this tenderness had in it no mere softness, no weak emotions, or effeminate sensibility: it was a firm and truthful sympathy; the genuine fellow-feeling of a soul conformed to the sacred humanity of Jesus in its vast and profound compassion.

It might, however, be thought that in a life of such unresting toil and ceaseless occupation, there could have been no time for prayer, no love for the interior spirit of devotion; and yet whole hours he spent upon his knees before the tabernacle or the Exposition in the Duomo, or in the crypt of San Sepolcro, or in the cells of the Capuchins and of the Barnabites. Long hours of the morning, before business began, were spent in mental prayer. He would do nothing until he had celebrated the holy Mass. It seems incredible how he could have found the time; but the use and order of his day was so minute and so exact, that he seemed never to be in haste, and to have leisure for every duty.

It may be said, that his whole life was prayer; for all his works were begun and ended in the presence of God. They did not distract him from union with his Lord; but were so penetrated with the intention and spirit of devotion that every several action had the nature of prayer. We read that when present in the choir, he was sometimes so rapt in union with God, that the master of ceremonies had need to rouse him to recite the office.

H.E. Manning, *Sermons on Ecclesiastical Subjects*, vol I, p 328-9

9 November
The Dedication of the Lateran Basilica
FEAST

This is the dedication of the cathedral church of Rome, the basilica of the Most Holy Saviour, commonly called St John Lateran. The palace of the Laterani was part of the dowry of Fausta, the emperor Constantine's second wife. The emperor gave it to the bishop of Rome as his official residence, which it remained until the Avignon period.

The basilica built beside the palace came to be called St John Lateran from the titulars of the two monasteries which served its choir in the early medieval period, one being St John the Baptist, the other St John the Divine.

The reading, On the Lordship of Christ, is taken from St Cyril of Jerusalem.

It is written in the gospel according to Matthew, 'But I tell you, hereafter you will see the Son of man seated at the right hand of Power': in accordance with which the apostle Peter also writes, 'through the resurrection of Jesus Christ, who has gone into heaven and is at the right hand of God.' And the apostle Paul, writing to the

Romans, says, 'It is Christ Jesus, who died, yes, who was raised from the dead, who is at the right hand of God.' And he speaks as follows, when addressing the Ephesians, 'according to the working of his great might, which he accomplished in Christ when he raised him from the dead, and made him sit at his right hand.' And he taught the Colossians in this way, 'If then you have been raised with Christ, seek the things that are above, where Christ is, seated at the right hand of God.' And in the letter to the Hebrews he says, 'When he had made purification for sins, he sat down at the right hand of the Majesty on high.' And again, 'But to what angel has he ever said, "Sit at my right hand, till I make thy enemies a stool for thy feet"?' And another time, 'But when "Christ" had offered for all time a single sacrifice for sins, he sat down at the right hand of God, then to wait until his enemies should be made a stool for his feet.' And, once more, 'looking to Jesus the pioneer and perfecter of our faith, who for the joy that was set before him endured the cross, despising the shame, and is seated at the right hand of the throne of God.'

And though there are many other texts concerning the Only-begotten being seated at God's right hand, yet let these suffice us for the present; with a repetition of my comment that it was not after his being present in the flesh that he obtained the dignity of this seat; no, for even before all ages, the only-begotten Son of God, our Lord Jesus Christ, always possesses the throne on the right hand of the Father.

Now, may he himself, the God of all, who is Father of the Christ, and our Lord Jesus Christ, who came down, and ascended, and sits together with the Father, watch over your souls; may he keep your hope in him who rose again unshaken and unchanged; may he raise you together with him from your dead sins to his heavenly gift; may he count you worthy to be 'caught up in the clouds, to meet the Lord in the air', in his proper time. And, until that time of his glorious second coming does arrive, may he write all your names in the book of the Living, and, having written them, may he never blot them out, (for the names of many who fall away, are blotted out). And may he grant to all of you belief in him who rose again, and watchfulness for him who is gone up, and is to come again, who is seated on high and is here present together with us, seeing how each holds himself and the steadfastness of his faith. For do not think that because he is now

absent in the flesh, he is absent therefore also in the Spirit. He is here
present in the midst of us, listening to what is said of him, and seeing
your innermost thoughts, and testing our minds and our hearts; he
who is ready to present all of you in the Holy Spirit to the Father, and
to say, 'Here am I, and the children God has given me': to him be
glory for ever. Amen.

St Cyril of Jerusalem, *Catechetical Lectures*, n XIV

10 November
Saint Leo the Great, *pope and doctor of the Church*
MEMORIAL

Leo, a Tuscan by birth, entered the service of the Roman Church as a young
man. By the year 430 he was already an influence in the Church and was in
contact with the learned Gallo-Romans who were the main thinkers of the
Latin Church outside North Africa — John Cassian, Prosper of Aquitaine and
Palladius, to name three of the most outstanding.

In 440 he was elected pope. He is of importance in the history of dogma
above all for his 'Tome', on the doctrine of the Incarnation, which he sent to
Flavian of Constantinople, and which was acclaimed at the Council of Chalcedon in 451, an acclamation which included an acknowledgement of the primacy of Peter. Leo firmly held that, as the see of Peter, his see held the chief
place (principatus) in and over the whole church.

His thought was strongly sacramental, so that the mysteries of Christ are
efficacious in the lives of all the faithful through their sharing in the sacraments with faith and love. His teaching and the expression of that teaching in
his sermons had a lasting influence on the liturgy of the Church of Rome.

He is the first of the popes of whom we have extensive collections of his sermons and letters.

The reading is taken from one of his letters written in 453 to the monks of
Palestine, urging them to abandon the teaching of Eutyches and to accept the
Catholic faith. The opening sentence of the excerpt given refers to the heresies
of Nestorius, Eutyches, Apollinaris, Manichaeus and Marcion which Leo had
just outlined as 'iniquitous lies'.

As these iniquitous lies were once rejected by the catholic Faith, and
such men's blasphemies condemned by the unanimous votes of the

blessed Fathers throughout the world, whoever these are that are so blinded to the light of truth as to deny the presence of human, that is our, nature in the Word of God from the time of the Incarnation, they must show on what ground they claim the name of Christian, and in what way they harmonize with the true Gospel, if the child-bearing of the blessed Virgin produced either the flesh without the Godhead or the Godhead without the flesh. For as it cannot be denied that 'the Word became flesh and dwelt in us', so it cannot be denied that 'God was in Christ, reconciling the world to himself'. But what reconciliation can there be, whereby God might be propitiated for the human race, unless the mediator between God and man took up the cause of all?

And in what way could he properly fulfil his mediation, unless he who in the form of God was equal to the Father, were a sharer of our nature also in the form of a slave: so that the one new Man might effect a renewal of the old, and the bond of death fastened on us by one man's wrong-doing might be loosened by the death of the one Man who alone owed nothing to death.

For the pouring out of the blood of the righteous on behalf of the unrighteous was so powerful in its effect, so rich a ransom that, if the whole body of us prisoners only believed in their Redeemer, not one would be held in the tyrant's bonds: since as the apostle says, 'where sin abounded, grace also did much more abound.' And since we, who were born under the imputation of sin, have received the power of a new birth unto righteousness, the gift of liberty has become stronger than the debt of slavery.

What hope then do they who deny the reality of the human person in our Saviour's body, leave for themselves in the efficacy of this mystery? Let them say by what sacrifice they have been reconciled, by what blood-shedding brought back. Who is he 'who gave himself for us an offering and a victim to God, or what sacrifice was ever more hallowed than that which the true high priest placed upon the altar of the cross by the immolation of his own flesh? For although in the sight of the Lord the death of many of his saints has been precious, yet no innocent's death was the propitiation of the world. The righteous have received, not given, crowns: and from the endurance of the faithful there has arisen examples of patience, not the gift of justification. For their deaths affected themselves alone, and no one has paid off another's debt by his own death: one alone among the sons of men, our Lord Jesus Christ, stands out as one in whom all are crucified, all dead, all buried, all raised again. Of them he himself said: 'when I am lifted from the earth, I will draw all things to myself'.

St Leo the Great, *Letter 124*, nn 3, 4

11 November
Saint Martin of Tours, *bishop*
MEMORIAL

Martin was born about the year 335 in Upper Pannonia, in present day Hungary, the son of an officer in the Roman army. His family were pagans, but when they moved to Italy and while at Pavia, Martin, though aged only ten, enrolled himself as a catechumen. He was conscripted at the age of fifteen and while stationed at Amiens, following on an act of charity, he had the famous vision or dream which changed the whole course of his life. He received baptism at Amiens and, on leaving the army at the age of twenty, he joined St Hilary of Poitiers. By Hilary he was ordained deacon. In 360 Hilary gave him some land, since called Ligugé, where Martin planned to live the solitary life. Others came to join him, however, and so a community was formed.

He was made bishop of Tours in about 371 and became, in effect, the apostle of rural Gaul. He never lost his love for the monastic life, and established the monastery at Tours which was later called Marmoutier. What Anthony was to Egypt, Martin was to Gaul, and the whole of western Europe — the father of monks. He died in the year 397.

The reading is taken from the life of Martin by Sulpitius Severus. Sulpitius Severus was a friend and admirer of Martin towards the end of the latter's life.

Martin as Bishop of Tours

And now having entered on the episcopal office, it is beyond my power fully to set forth how Martin distinguished himself in the discharge of his duties. For he remained with the utmost constancy, the same as he had been before. There was the same humility in his heart, and the same homeliness in his garments. He kept up the position of a bishop properly, full of both dignity and courtesy, yet in such a way as not to lay aside the objects and virtues of a monk.

Accordingly he made use, for some time, of the cell connected with the church; but afterwards, when he felt it impossible to tolerate the disturbance caused by the numbers of those visiting it, he established a monastery for himself about two miles outside the city. This spot was so secret and retired that he enjoyed in it the solitude of a hermit. For on one side it was surrounded by a precipitous rock of a lofty mountain, while the river Loire had shut in the rest of the plain by a bay extending back for a little distance; and the place could be approached only by one, and that through a very narrow passage. Here, then, he possessed a cell constructed of wood. Many also of the brethren had, in the same manner, fashioned retreats for themselves but most of them had formed these out of the rock of the overhanging mountain, hollowed into caves.

There were altogether eighty disciples who were being disciplined after the example of the saintly master. No one there had anything which was called his own; all things were possessed in common. It was not allowed either to buy or to sell anything, as is the custom among most monks. No art was practiced there, except that of transcribers, and even this was assigned to the brethren of younger years, while the elders spent their time in prayer. Rarely did any one of them go beyond the cell, unless when they assembled at the place of prayer. They all took their food together, after the hour of fasting was passed. No one used wine, except when illness compelled them to do so. Most of them were clothed in garments of camels' hair. Any dress approaching to softness was there deemed criminal, and this must be thought the more remarkable, because many among them were such as are deemed of noble rank. These, though far differently brought up, had forced themselves down to this degree of humility and patient endurance, and we have seen numbers of these afterwards made bishops. For what city or church would there be that would not desire to have its priests from among those in the monastery of Martin?

Sulpitius Severus, *Life of St Martin of Tours*, c 10

12 November
Saint Josaphat, *bishop and martyr*
MEMORIAL

St Josaphat, who was christened John, was born in the Ukraine about the year 1580. There was a strong re-union movement among the Christians there at the time, and this as well as the troubled political situation led to much dissension. John was deeply in love with the Eastern liturgy and Church Slavonic but became convinced of the rightness of the Uniate position, seeing that this involved no surrender of the traditions of his own Church. He joined the Catholic party and then became a monk at Vilna. His ability and his conviction were such that he soon came to be seen as one of the leaders of the cause of re-union and was made bishop of Polotz in 1617. He worked hard at the renewal of his diocese, reforming clergy and monasteries, fostering the liturgy.

There were many different factions in the Church there at the time and much violence, among those who opposed Josaphat there were Catholics as well as Orthodox. He was murdered by his enemies during a pastoral visit to Vitebsk in 1623. This was largely the result of a particular clerical agitator's campaign against him. The shock of the murder did much to promote the Uniate cause, and the conversion of the agitator himself.

St Josaphat was canonized in the last century.

As a reading I offer something from the tradition of the spirituality of the Eastern Church, a short passage from *The Way of a Pilgrim* on the Jesus Prayer.

He taught me about the excellence and greatness of the Jesus Prayer in this way. 'Even the very form of the Jesus Prayer ,' he said, 'shows what a great prayer it is. It is made up of two parts. In the first, i.e., "Lord Jesus Christ, Son of God", it leads our thoughts to the life of Jesus Christ, or, as the holy Fathers put it, it is the whole Gospel in brief. In the second part, "Have mercy on me, a sinner", it faces us with the story of our own helplessness and sinfulness. And it is to be noted that the desire and petition of a poor, sinful, humble soul could not be put into words more wise, more clear cut, more exact than these — "have mercy on me". No other form of words would be as satisfying and full as this. For instance, if one said, "Forgive me, put away my sins, cleanse my transgressions, blot out my offences", all that would express one petition only — asking to be set free from punishment, the fear of a faint-hearted and listless soul. But to say "Have mercy on me" means not only the desire for pardon arising from fear, but is the sincere cry of filial love, which puts its hope in the mercy of God and humbly acknowledges it is too weak to break its own will and to keep a watchful guard over itself. It is a cry for mercy — that is, for grace — which will show itself in the gift of strength from God, to enable us to resist temptation and overcome our sinful inclinations. It is like a penniless debtor asking his kindly creditor not only to forgive him the debt but also to pity his extreme poverty and to give him alms — that is what these profound words "have mercy on me" express. It is like saying: "Gracious Lord, forgive me my sins and help me to put myself right; arouse in my soul a strong impulse to follow thy bidding. Bestow thy grace in forgiving my actual sins and in turning my heedless mind, will and heart to thee alone".'

The Way of a Pilgrim, c 5, pp 155-6

15 November

Saint Albert the Great, *bishop and doctor of the Church*
OPTIONAL MEMORIAL

Albert was born in Swabia (in present-day Germany), about the beginning of the thirteenth century. As a student he went to Padua and, while there, entered the Dominicans. As a Dominican he became a teacher of theology, spending most of his time in Germany, although he also taught in Paris for a few years. He was appointed bishop of Ratisbon in 1260 but resigned after only two years to spend most of his remaining years in the Dominican 'studium generale' at Cologne. He was one of the pioneers in the use of Aristotle in the elaboration of christian theology, though he was eclipsed in this by a former student, St Thomas Aquinas. His work as a natural historian in geography, botany and animal study was especially well-founded.

St Albert died in 1280.

As a reading I offer a text from his Commentary on Matthew's Gospel treating of the passage suggested for today's Mass. In translating I have filled the text out somewhat for ease of reading and have omitted one biblical reference.

On Matthew 13:52

At the end of his discourse Christ does two things: he seeks understanding of what he has said from the disciples (who are under obligation to be his vicars), knowing that those set over others have need of understanding; then, having obtained understanding, he teaches in what fullness they ought set this forth. . . . 'He said to them: Therefore every scribe instructed in the kingdom of heaven is like to a man, head of a household, who brings forth from his treasure new and old.' This is the second part of his conclusion, and in it he touches on three matters — the name, duty and quality of the one who teaches; then, whom they should teach; and whom they should imitate.

Concerning the first of these matters he says: 'Therefore every scribe', as treating of all who perform this duty; then 'scribe', as one who inscribes the will of God on the hearts of their hearers and has it inscribed on their own; 'instructed', however, he says, for an inner quality, for one not well-versed ought not teach! As touching on these points, consider Wisdom 3:9 'Who trusts in him, will understand the truth, and the faithful will abide with him in love'; then Wisdom 6:2-3 'Hear, O kings and understand . . . Give ear, you who hold in check the multitudes.' And, further, Matthew 23:34 'I send you wise men and scribes.'

'In the kingdom of heaven': this, now, is where the scribe ought to abound: for just as Christ himself, the scribe ought to teach the justice, the power and the joy of the kingdom of heaven (cf Mt 4:17). He adds, then, whom the scribe ought to imitate, saying: 'He is like to a man head of a household.' The head of the household is the Son of man himself (cf Mt 20:1; Lk 14:21), as St Paul says in 1 Corinthians 11:1 'Be you imitators of me, as I am of Christ.'

'Who brings forth from his treasure': this means from the fullness of his heart, as we read earlier, in 12:35 'A good man brings forth good from his good treasure'. 'New and old': the things brought forth are new on account of their worth, old, however, on account of their purpose, for these reasons the scribe brings them forward. There are, however, new things appropriate to the new in spirit, those, namely, to whom it is given to know the mystery of the kingdom of God (Mk 4:11). The old, however, are still appropriate for the instructing of the old by bodily comparisons. So we read in the Song of Songs 7:13 'All the fruits, new and old, I have kept for you, my beloved', and in Leviticus 26:10 'You shall eat the oldest of the old, and throw out the old, the new having come.' .

Alternatively, it can be said, that the new are those which belong to the new order, the old, however, those which belong to ancient times. The former are brought forth, so that the hearers may be invited to them, the latter disparaged, that the hearers may fly them. In this sense we find Colossians 3:9, 10 'Stripping yourselves of the old man with his deeds, and putting on the new, him who is renewed unto knowledge, according to the image of him who created him.' Ephesians 4:22, 23 'You must lay aside the old man, who is corrupted according to the desire of error. And be renewed in the spirit of your mind: And put on the new man who according to God is created in justice and holiness of truth.'

St Albert the Great, 'On Matthew's Gospel'

16 November
Saint Margaret of Scotland
OPTIONAL MEMORIAL

Margaret was probably born in Hungary, around the year 1045, but she had English blood in her veins. At the time of the Norman invasion, she with her mother and sister were living in England, and they took refuge in the Scottish court for safety. In 1070 she was married to the king, Malcolm III. She proved herself a model christian queen and did much to promote the Gregorian reform in Scotland. One of her daughters married Henry I of England and has passed to history as 'Good Queen Maud'.

St Margaret died in 1093 and she was buried in the church of the Holy Trinity at Dunfermline which she had founded.

As a reading I offer an excerpt from her Life, written by Theodoric, monk of Durham, who was her confessor, in which he describes her death.

When she had finished talking of necessary matters, she began speaking in the following way to me again. Farewell, she said, I shall not last long after this in this life: you, however, will live for no little time after me. There are two things then I ask of you; one, that for as long as you live you will be mindful of my soul in your Masses and prayers; the other, that you take care of my sons and daughters, give them your love, especially teach them to fear and love God; and that you never cease from teaching them. And when you shall have seen

319

anyone of them raised to the height of earthly dignity, you approach them especially as his father and at the same time their master: namely by warning, and, when the matter demands it, reproving, lest on account of a momentary honour they might be puffed up with pride, lest they should offend God through avarice, lest through prosperity on this earth, they neglect the happiness of eternal life. These are, she said, what I ask you to promise that you will do then with care, in the presence of God, who is present to us now as a third party.

The account of Margaret's death he had from her chaplain:
The fourth day before her death, when the king was on a campaign, a great distance from her, she became sadder than usual and said this to us who were sitting with her: Today such an evil has occurred for the kingdom of the Scots as perhaps has not happened for many ages back. We indeed hearing these things, accepted her sayings carelessly in truth then, but on a messenger coming after a few days, we understood that the king had been killed on the very day the queen had said these things. She had indeed, as it were aware of future events, strongly urged him not to go anywhere with the army; but, I know not for what cause, it came about that he did not then heed her warnings.

When therefore the fourth day after the killing of the king was come, she entered the oratory to hear Mass, her illness having lessened a little; and there took care to fortify herself with the most holy viaticum of the Lord's body and blood for her going forth which was already close.

Having been made strong by this saving partaking of Christ she lay prostrate, her former sufferings becoming immediately more acute, and by her increasing anguish she was impelled more forcibly to her death. . . . Her face had already grown pale in death, when she ordered me and other ministers of the holy altar with me, to stand by her and, singing psalms, commend her soul to Christ. . . .

Her going forth was with such tranquillity, with such quiet that there ought be no doubt that that soul had passed over to the region of eternal quiet and peace. And what was wonderful, in such a way after death red colour suffused with radiance flooded her face, which had grown wholly pale after the manner of the dying, that she could have been believed not dead but asleep.

Theodoric, *Life of St Margaret of Scotland*, c 4, nn 27, 29, 30, 32

16 November, also
Saint Gertrude, *virgin*
OPTIONAL MEMORIAL

Gertrude was born in 1256 and given to the convent of Helfta in Thuringia at the age of five. The convent followed the Rule of Benedict with an observance modelled on that of Citeaux, though not belonging to the latter Order. Gertrude was a gifted child and received a good education. She possessed considerable charm as well, and managed to 'get away' with a rather careless approach to her duties until recalled by a vision when aged about twenty-six. She subsequently lived a quiet life in her convent continually deepening her prayer-life and her love of God. She studied the scriptures and the Fathers deeply, among the latter especially the writings of Saints Augustine, Gregory the Great and Bernard. Of the so-called *Revelations of Saint Gertrude* only the second book is actually by her, but the *Spiritual Exercises* are hers.

She was one of the leading exponents of the medieval devotion to the Sacred Heart and advocated frequent Communion, which would suggest some Cluniac influence in the traditions of Helfta.

St Gertrude died in 1302, and is styled 'the Great' to distinguish her from others who bear the same name.

The reading is taken from the Fifth of her Exercises.

O Love, O God, who have created me, in your love recreate me. O Love who have redeemed me, fill up and redeem for yourself in me whatever part of your love has fallen into neglect within me. O Love, O God, who, to make me yours, in the blood of your Christ have purchased me, in your truth sanctify me. O Love, O God, who have adopted me as a daughter, after your own heart fashion and foster me. O Love, who as yours and not another's have chosen me, grant that I may cleave to you with my whole being. O Love, O God, who have first loved me, grant that with my whole heart, and with my whole soul, and with my whole strength, I may love you.

O Love, O God almighty, in your love confirm me. O Love most wise, give me wisdom in the love of you. O Love most sweet, give me sweetness in the taste of you. O Love most dear, grant that I may live for you alone. O Love most faithful, in all my tribulations comfort and succour me. O Love who are ever with me, work all my works in me. O Love most victorious, grant that I may persevere to the end in you.

O Love most cherished, who have never forsaken me, to you I commend my spirit. In the hour of my death receive me to yourself, calling me to you with your own voice and saying: 'This day you shall be with me; come forth now from your exile unto the solemn *Morrow* of that eternity which shall never fade! There you shall find me, Jesus, the true *Today* of the divine glory, who am the beginning and the end of every created being. In this immutability never again shall you know a *Morrow*; but in me, the true *Today*, you shall have an eternal *Today*, that as I live, you also shall live in me, Jesus, your God and your Lover, in the transports of happiness without end!' Let all the powers, all the thoughts, and all the affections of my body and soul say: 'Amen!'

St Gertrude, Exercises, V

17 November
Saint Elizabeth of Hungary, *religious*
MEMORIAL

Elizabeth was born in 1207, the daughter of the King of Hungary, and married at the age of fourteen to Ludwig of Thuringia. Her married life was ideally happy but many of the nobles of Thuringia resented Elizabeth's truly evangelical concern for the poor, and her husband's indulgence of her! Their chance came when Ludwig set out to join the Crusade and died. This was in 1227 and Elizabeth was barely twenty. Her brother-in-law drove her from her home — he was regent for her son — and she was forced to live in exile. She took the habit of the Third Order of St Francis and died in 1231 at the age of twenty-four.

She was remarkable for her prayer, her deeds of charity, her spirit of penance, and of great gentleness, in spite of much ill-treatment. Conrad of Marburg, her spiritual director towards the end of her life, out of a misguided zeal, treated her with what can only be described as brutality. Brutality can make brutes or saints. Elizabeth was one of the saints.

The reading offered is from a homily on her given by Fr Delp, S.J. When he wrote this homily Fr Delp was already perhaps a marked man, but was to die in a Nazi concentration camp in great holiness. He spoke against the background of Nazi tyranny, but we may ask ourselves if Nazism was the only tyranny.

Here is the first message Elizabeth brings us: a message about the true meaning of rulership. Elizabeth was a princess. Generally speaking, our temptations tend to stem not so much from what we are not, as from what we are. The temptations of the unimportant and the weak usually lie not in aspirations to greatness, but rather in the danger of being suffocated by mediocrity and cowardice; and the temptations of the great and the mighty also involve power. Elizabeth gave power a threefold blessing and revealed a threefold meaning of rulership.

This is the first blessing: She linked power with law. When Elizabeth came to the Wartburg, that castle that has played such a fateful role in the life of our country, forces held sway there as in all other regions of Germany; gathered around the lord of the castle were robber barons from the surrounding countryside, who consumed and squandered what they had extorted from the people. And then history tells us of the quiet transformation that originated with this woman's heartbreak, like a fire started by a spark: how she refused dishes from the banquet table that she knew had been prepared from stolen food; how she profoundly changed her husband, so that he was able to overcome force with law and came to understand that as the wielder of highest power, he himself must serve the law and use force only to guarantee that law for his subjects. That was the first realization that Elizabeth brought to the Wartburg: Man needs laws that no prince and no strong man may encroach upon without sullying his own power and indelibly staining his position, his dignity and his crown.

The second blessing that Elizabeth imparted to power is this: She revealed that service is the very meaning of power. Because of her quiet influence, a new spirit pervaded her husband's chanceries and their official decrees. The land became profoundly healed, because its master, who held power and responsibility, understood this: Power is given, not so that men may lord it over others but so that it may bring benefits and blessings to all.

And St Elizabeth gave yet another blessing to power: She placed the might of her lord and husband at the service of an even greater Lord, the King of kings, from whom all true sovereignty takes its meaning and without whom power becomes an arrogant rebellion, a caricature, an empty charade. In the eyes of the world, it was this very act on Elizabeth's part that wrecked her life, for her husband, in his eagerness to serve the Lord, took the cross and died as a crusader. Outwardly, her good fortune died with her lord and husband. But within her there burst open a whole new world, a great world blazing with the light of God, and in place of her former glory, there came an answer from heaven: her true importance was, and always it is it which makes every creature important — the privilege of worshipping and serving the honour and glory of God. When power no longer has behind it the splendour and brilliance of the ultimate sovereign, it is a drab thing, devoid of dignity and worth, and its reign extends only as far as the terror it inspires. The minute this kind of power can no longer sustain itself by physical compulsion, it is forgotten and abandoned. The true meaning of earthly rule: that was Elizabeth's first message to our people.

This woman brought a second message to our people and our land: a message about the true meaning of love. Elizabeth was a wife and mother. She was not the kind of saint we have become accustomed to from paintings, altar statues and pious legends, a figure without blood, passion or life. Hear her desperate cries when she learned of her husband's death: 'Dead! He is dead? Then for me the whole world is dead!' This woman loved as deeply as anyone has ever loved, and with the death of her love, light and song went out of her life and the stars became dim. It was precisely in this consecrated love, so genuine, so human, that the great secret lay. What a change she brought to Wartburg! When she arrived, it was little more than a nest of robbers; and when she left it, driven out and forgotten, the countryside had enjoyed many years of peace and well-being. The starting-point of this change was the true, holy, quiet love of a wife and mother. If you think about it, you realize that the transformation of the world, what man will become, what he will do with his life, is brought about least of all by official programs and announcements and other great undertakings. It comes about in the quiet home of all life, the family. It comes whenever people understand that the true meaning of love is not the will to dominate, to exploit and to possess; but that it lies in service, generosity, sacrifice, willingness to change and a desire that others be blessed and brought close to God. When our countrymen have learned once more the lesson of the Wartburg, so that they can emerge from the quiet and solitude of their homes touched and renewed by true love, a love that sanctifies us and helps us find the way to heaven, then our land and our people will be blessed, and we will have the strength to face whatever lies ahead.

Alfred Delp SJ, homily on Elizabeth of Hungary.

18 November
The Dedication of the Basilicas of Saints
Peter and Paul, *apostles*
OPTIONAL MEMORIAL

The Vatican Basilica of St Peter was originally built by the emperor Constantine about the year 330 on the traditional site of St Peter's martyrdom. The dedication ceremony was performed by Pope St Silvester. The present Basilica was begun in 1506 and consecrated in 1626.

The Basilica of St Paul on the Ostian Way at the traditional site of the apostle's burial was also originally built by Constantine. This proved too small and was replaced towards the end of the fourth century under the emperor Theodosius I. That building, repaired several times, lasted until a tragic fire of 1823. Smaller than St Peter's it was still large and was very beautiful. The present Basilica was built on the plan of the old and consecrated in 1854. In honouring the dedication of their Basilicas we honour the memory of the two apostles.

The reading offered is taken from the treatise of St Cyprian of Carthage on the Unity of the Catholic Church. The theme is unity — in love, in peace, in a living faith; unity not just among ourselves but between ourselves and the first followers of Christ.

God is one and Christ is one and his Church one, and the faith one, and the people one, joined by the bond of mutual agreement into the firm unity of a body. What is one cannot be rent assunder, nor the one body be divided by the rupture of its structure, in vain is it destroyed by the tearing apart of its sundered inner parts. Whatever departs from the womb of the Church, is unable to live and breathe on its own, it loses the very essence of salvation.

The Holy Spirit warns us and says: 'Who is the man who desires life and wants to see really good days? Keep your tongue from evil and your lips from speaking deceitfully. Turn away from evil and do good. Seek peace and pursue it.' The son of peace ought to seek and pursue peace; he, who knows and loves the bond of charity, ought to check his tongue from the evil of dissension. The Lord, already close to his Passion, added to his divine commandments and saving instruction when he said: 'Peace I leave to you, my peace I give you.' He gave this inheritance to us, he assured us of all the gifts and the rewards of his promise for the keeping of peace. If we are the heirs of Christ, let us remain in the peace of Christ: if we are sons of God, we ought to be peaceable. 'Blessed are the peaceable', he says, 'because they will be called sons of God.' The sons of God ought to be peaceable, meek of heart, simple in speech, united in love, faithfully holding together by the bonds of agreement.

Of old, under the apostles, agreement of this kind existed: in this way, the new believing people, keeping the commandments of God, maintained their charity. The scripture demonstrates this which says: 'The multitude moreover of them who believed acted with one soul and mind'. And again: 'and all were persevering with one mind in prayer with the women and Mary who had been the mother of Jesus, and with his brothers.' And therefore they prayed with efficacious prayers, therefore they could obtain with confidence whatever they sought from the mercy of God.

In us, however, the bond of agreement is so lessened that the liberality of charitable activity is weakened. Then they sold houses and properties, and heaping up treasure for themselves in heaven, they offered the proceeds to the apostles to be distributed for the use of those in need. But now we do not give even a tenth part of our possessions and, while the Lord orders to sell, we rather buy and become richer! In this way the vigour of the faith has withered away in us, the strength of believers in this way has grown faint. And, on this account, the Lord, looking upon our times, says in his gospel: 'When the Son of man comes, do you think he will find faith on earth?' We are seeing come about what he foretold. There is no faith — in the fear of God, in the law of justice, in love, in the works of mercy. No one thinks of the terror of future events, no one considers the day of the Lord and the anger of God and the coming punishments for unbelievers and moreover the eternal torments laid down for unbelievers.

Let us, therefore, rouse ourselves up as best we can, my dearly beloved. Let our light shine and gleam in good works, that Christ may bring us to the very light of eternal glory from this night of the world. Let us look to the sudden coming of the Lord, always watchful and careful, that when he knocks, our faith may be wakeful, in such a way as to receive the reward of watchfulness from the Lord. If these commandments are kept, if these warnings and precepts are heeded, we cannot be overwhelmed, like those who sleep, by the deceiving one, the devil — we shall reign, as watchful servants, with Christ, the absolute ruler.

St Cyprian, *On the Unity of the Catholic Church*, nn 23-7 (excerpts)

21 November
The Presentation of the Blessed Virgin Mary
MEMORIAL

The belief that Mary was presented to be brought up in the Temple in Jerusalem goes back at least to the second century. In the East this presentation was celebrated liturgically from the seventh century, and soon afterwards was celebrated in Anglo-Saxon England. In the fourteenth century it was adopted by the papal court and was inserted into the universal calendar by Pope Sixtus V.

The sense of the celebration is not alone that Mary belonged wholly to God but that, as the daughter of Zion, she fulfilled the destiny of God's people Israel.

The reading is from a sermon of St John Damascene.

O truly divine wonder! O mystery transcending all nature and understanding! O marvellous virginity! What, O holy Mother and

Virgin, is this great mystery accomplished in you? 'Blessed art thou amongst women, and blessed is the fruit of thy womb.' You are blessed from generation to generation, you who alone are worthy of being blessed. Behold all generations shall call you blessed as you have said. The daughters of Jerusalem (I mean, of the Church) saw you. Queens have blessed you, that is, the spirits of the just, and they shall praise you for ever. You are the royal throne which angels surround, seeing upon it their very King and Lord, You are a spiritual Eden, holier and more divine than Eden of old.

That Eden was the abode of the mortal Adam, whilst the Lord himself came from heaven to dwell in you. The ark foreshadowed you who have kept the seed of the new world. You brought forth Christ, the salvation of the world, who destroyed sin and its angry waves. The burning bush was a figure of you, and the tablets of the law, and the ark of the testament. The golden urn and candelabra, the table and the flowering rod of Aaron were significant types of you.

From you the splendour of the Godhead arose, the eternal word of the Father, the most sweet and heavenly manna, the sacred name above every name, the light which was from the beginning. The heavenly bread of life, the fruit without seed, took flesh of you. Did not that flame foreshadow you with its burning fire an image of the divine fire within you?

St John Damascene, 'Sermon on the Crowning of Our Lady'

22 November
Saint Cecilia, *virgin and martyr*
MEMORIAL

It would seem that there was a lady Cecilia who, sometime in the first centuries of Church history, gave her house to the Church in Rome, and, subsequently, her name was attached to the church built on the site. A late legend made her out to be a martyr, and, later still, perhaps through a misunderstanding of that legend, she came to be considered the patron of musicians.

Her Memorial has been left in the calendar (it has been celebrated on this day since the sixth century), out of consideration for popular devotion. Historians were naturally disappointed with the decision, but, while their reserves are well-founded, no one has, as yet, come up with an explanation for the appearance of her cult which has found general acceptance.

The reading offered is from an Oration delivered by St Gregory Nazianzen in 373. The passage used refers to the time of judgement and so is in harmony with the spirit of the liturgical time as well as referring to the gospel passage suggested for the Mass of the Memorial.

God has confined life and action to this world, and to the future the scrutiny of what has been done.

What shall we do in the day of visitation, with which one of the prophets terrifies me, whenever it may be, when God will reason with us, and oppose us, and set before us those bitter accusers, our sins, comparing our wrongdoings with our benefits, and striking thought with thought, and scrutinising action with action, and calling us to account for the image which has been blurred and spoilt by wickedness, till at last he leads us away self-convicted and self-condemned, no longer able to say that we are being unjustly treated — a thought which is able even here sometimes to console in their condemnation those who are suffering.

But then what advocate shall we have? What pretext? What false excuse? What plausible artifice? What device contrary to the truth will impose upon the court, and rob it of its right judgement, which places in the balance for us all, our entire life, action, word, and thought, and weighs against the evil that which is better, until that which preponderates wins the day, and the decision is given in favour of the main tendency; after which there is no appeal, no higher court, no defence on the ground of subsequent conduct, no oil obtained from the wise virgins, or from them that sell, for the lamps going out, no repentance of the rich man or woman wasting away in the flame and begging for repentance for their friends, no statute of limitations; but only that final and fearful judgement-seat, more just even than fearful (or rather more fearful because it is also just) when the thrones are set and the Ancient of days takes his seat, and the books are opened, and the fiery stream comes forth, and the light before him, and the darkness prepared.

Then it will be that they that have done good shall go into the resurrection of life, now hid in Christ and to be manifested hereafter with him, and they that have done evil, into the resurrection of judgment, to which they who have not believed have been condemned already by the word which judges them. Some will be welcomed by the unspeakable light and the vision of the holy and royal Trinity, which now shines upon them with greater brilliance and purity and unites itself wholly to the whole soul, in which solely and beyond all else I take it that the kingdom of heaven consists. The others among other torments, but above and before them all must endure the being outcast from God, and the shame of conscience which has no limit.

St Gregory Nazianzen, 'On his Father's Silence', *Oration XVI*

23 November
Saint Clement I, *pope and martyr*
OPTIONAL MEMORIAL

Clement was bishop of Rome and pope towards the end of the first century. It has been suggested that he was the Clement mentioned in Philippians 4:3, but we may well hesitate. The name suggests a freedman of the imperial household, though this again is uncertain. While the account of his martyrdom is late and untrustworthy, we can, however, be reasonably sure he did die a martyr, for such was the constant tradition.

He wrote a remarkable letter to the Church at Corinth, a letter which in the first centuries of the Church was received almost as scripture; and some thirteen excerpts from it are used in the Divine Office. It was written about the 95 AD. Its main purpose was to encourage the Corinthian Christians to live in peace among themselves.

The reading is the epilogue of this letter.

Of what is due to our holy religion, and of the more useful aids to virtue for those who desire to advance in godliness and righteousness, we have now written enough to you, my brothers and sisters. Belief, repentance, true christian love, self-discipline, discretion, perseverance — we have touched on these in all their aspects. We have reminded you of your duty to earn in all holiness the approval of almighty God by a life of rectitude, truthfulness, and patient resignation, and to live amicably and without malice together, in peace and charity and unfailing consideration for others. This is how our forefathers won approval by the humility of their bearing towards God, their Father and Creator, and towards all their fellow-men. And we have been the more encouraged to lay these things before you, inasmuch as we knew we were addressing persons of faith and good repute, who have spent careful study on the maxims of the divine teaching.

In view of the shining examples that have been set before us, then, it is a moral duty for us to bow the head and take our seat on the stool of submission; so that these fruitless differences may be composed, and our rightful destiny fulfilled without occasion for reproach. So you will afford us great joy and happiness if you will lay to heart what we have written through the Holy Spirit, and will respond to the appeal for peace and harmony which we have made in this letter, by putting an end once and for all to the rancours of an impious rivalry. We have sent envoys of trustworthiness and discretion to you, whose lives here among us have been irreproachable from youth to age; and they shall be witnesses between ourselves and you. Our purpose in so doing is to let you see that our whole concern has been, and still is, for the speedy restoration of peace among you.

In conclusion, may the all-seeing God, the ruler of spirits and Lord of all flesh, who has chosen the Lord Jesus Christ, and through him ourselves, to be a people for his possession, grant to every soul that is called by his glorious and holy name such faith and fear, such peace and patience, such forbearance, self-restraint, purity and sobriety, that they may be pleasing to his name; through our high priest and protector Jesus Christ, by whom be glory, majesty, might and honour to him both now and for ever, world without end. Amen.

St Clement of Rome, *Letter to the Corinthians,* nn 62-4

23 November, also
Saint Columban, *abbot*
OPTIONAL MEMORIAL

Columban was a native of the Province of Leinster, in Ireland, and was born about the middle of the sixth century. He became a monk in the north of the country and joined the community of Bangor, one of the most austere and learned of Irish monasteries. When aged about forty he set out from Ireland, as an exile for Christ, with some twelve companions. The group established themselves first at Annegray in Burgundy, then at Luxeuil and finally at Fontaine. At these three sites many Gaulish disciples gathered round them. Columban paid little heed to the susceptibilities of the Gaulish bishops and was eventually forced to leave Burgundy when the royal and episcopal authorities combined against him. After a trek through present day Switzerland, he finally settled at Bobbio in north Italy, where he established a thriving community.

Columban and his local disciples established monasticism as a vital force in north-west Europe; indeed, it would not be unfair to say that he was one of the founding fathers of medieval Europe. He was a man of great holiness, deeply committed to the love of Christ, and very well-versed in Latin letters. More austere than many of his fellow Irishmen he yet had a gentle side to his character and could command great loyalty to his person and leadership. His greatest defect was not (and is not) untypical of the Irish — a wholly exaggerated esteem for Irish values and the Irish way of doing things. Nonetheless he should certainly be seen as one of the greatest of the Irish Saints.

Columban died at Bobbio in 615.

The reading is taken from one of his Instructions or Sermons.

Thus let us eat the same our Lord Jesus Christ as bread, let us drink him as the fountain, who calls himself the living bread, who gives life to this world, as it were to be taken by us, and who likewise shows himself as the fountain when he says, let him that is thirsty come to me and drink; of which fountain the prophet also says, Since with you is the fountain of life.

Observe whence that fountain flows; for it flows from that place whence also the bread came down; since he is the same who is bread and fountain, the only Son, our God Christ the Lord, for whom we should ever hunger. For though we eat him in loving, though we feast on him in desiring, let us still as hungering desire him. Likewise as the fountain, let us ever drink of him with overflow of love, let us ever drink of him with fulness of longing, and let us be gladdened by some pleasure of his loveliness. For the Lord is lovely and pleasant; though we eat and drink of him, yet let us ever hunger and thirst, since our food and drink can never be consumed and drained entire; for though he is eaten he is not consumed, though he is drunk he is

not lessened, since our bread is eternal, and our fountain is perennial, our fountain is sweet. Wherefore the prophet says, Go you who
are thirsty to the fountain; for that is the fountain of the thirsting, not
of the surfeiting, and thus he calls to himself the hungry and the
thirsty who have never enough of drinking, but the more they quaff,
so much the more they thirst.

Justly, my brethren, the fountain of wisdom, the Word of God on
high, is to be desired by us, sought after and ever loved, in whom are
hid, according to the apostle's saying, all the treasures of wisdom
and knowledge, of which he calls them that thirst to drink deeply. If
you thirst, drink the fountain of life; if you hunger, eat the bread of
life. Blessed are they who hunger for this bread and thirst for this
fountain; for ever eating and drinking they still long to eat and drink.
For that is lovely to excess which is ever eaten and drunk, and ever
hungered and thirsted after, ever tasted and ever desired; wherefore
the prophet king David says, Taste and see how lovely, how pleasant
is the Lord. Therefore, my brethren, let us follow this calling, with
which we are called to the fountain of life by the Life who is the fountain, not only the fountain of living water, but also of eternal life, the
fountain of light, yes, and the fount of glory; for from him come all
these things, wisdom and life and light eternal. The author of life is
the fountain of life, the creator of light, the fount of glory; and thus,
spurning the things that are seen, making a passage through the
world, let us seek the fount of glory, the fountain of life, the fountain
of living water, like intelligent and most wise fishes,* that there we
may drink the living water which springs up to eternal life.

St Columbanus, *Instruction* 13, 1 (part), 2

*'fishes' — perhaps an allusion to the theme of the fish as a symbol of Christ, but more
probably the reference is to the 153 fish of John 21:11.

30 November
Saint Andrew, *apostle*
FEAST

Andrew was one of the first four disciples called by Jesus. According to the synoptic tradition he was a fisherman in partnership with his brother Simon Peter and the brothers James and John. According to John's Gospel, on the other hand, all four were in fact disciples of John the Baptist when Jesus first summoned them. The two traditions are not, however, irreconcilable. Andrew is mentioned in various passages in the gospels.

After Pentecost he is believed to have preached in Scythia and traditionally was martyred at Patras in Achaia on this day. Today, in fact, is his day in the tradition of East and West and can be taken as fairly certain.

The fables linking him with the founding of the see of Constantinople, with the conversion of Scotland and of Russia can be safely discounted.

The reading is from a sermon by Newman commenting on John's account of the calling of the brothers Andrew and Peter (Jn 1:35-4).

Who taught the doctors and saints of the Church, who, in their day, or in after times, have been the most illustrious expounders of the precepts of right and wrong, and, by word and deed, are the guides of our conduct? Did almighty Wisdom speak to them through the operation of their own minds, or rather, did it not subject them to instructors unknown to fame, wiser perhaps even than themselves? Andrew followed John the Baptist, while Simon remained at his nets. Andrew first recognized the Messiah among the inhabitants of despised Nazareth; and he brought his brother to him. Yet to Andrew Christ spoke no word of commendation which has been allowed to continue on record; whereas to Simon, even on his first coming, he gave the honourable name by which he is now designated, and afterwards put him forward as the typical foundation of his Church.

Nothing indeed can hence be inferred, one way or the other, concerning the relative excellence of the two brothers; so far only appears that, in the providential course of events, the one was the secret beginner, and the other the public instrument, of a great divine work. St Paul, again, was honoured with the distinction of a miraculous conversion, and was called to be the chief agent of the propagation of the Gospel among the heathen; yet to Ananias, an otherwise unknown saint, dwelling at Damascus, was committed the high office of conveying the gifts of pardon and the Holy Ghost to the apostle of the Gentiles.

Providence thus acts daily. The early life of all men is private; it is as children, generally, that their characters are formed to good or

evil; and those who form them to good, their truest and chief benefactors, are unknown to the world. It has been remarked, that some
of the most eminent Christians have been blessed with religious
mothers, and have in after life referred their own graces to the instru-
mentality of their teaching. Augustine has preserved to the Church
the history of his mother Monica; but in the case of others, even the
name is denied to us of our great benefactress, whosoever she was,
and sometimes, doubtless, the circumstance of her service altogether.

J.H. Newman, *Parochial and Plain Sermons*, II, 1

3 December
Saint Francis Xavier, *priest*
MEMORIAL

Francis was born in 1506 in Navarre in Spain. He studied arts in Paris, qualifying as a master of arts, and then took up the teaching of philosophy in the university. So it was that he met St Ignatius when the latter came to Paris, and
joined himself to him to become one of the first Jesuits. It was resolved that he
commit himself to the evangelizing of the pagans in the Far East. He was
ordained priest in Venice and then sailed for the East Indies in 1541.

He landed in Goa in 1542 and worked among the Portuguese settlers and
the native Indian peoples until 1545, when he went to the Malay peninsula.

He returned to India in 1548, reorganized the mission there and sailed to
Japan, where he landed in 1549. He returned to Goa in 1552, and then set out
for China, only to die on the island port of Shang-chuen at the mouth of the
Canton river, in that same year. He had been only ten years in the East, but he
made good and lasting converts, and is venerated as one of the patrons of the
missions.

St Francis was canonized in 1622. He was an inspiration to all who followed
him as missionaries: a man meek, humble and charitable, but not lacking in
firmness. He made himself all things to all men, in order to bring all to Christ.
The letter he wrote to a brother Jesuit, older in years but younger by profession, and just before leaving for China, expresses all these values. I offer it
here as a reading.

Right badly have you carried out the instructions I gave you as to your conduct in San Thomé, and it is clear to see how little remains to you of the spirit of our blessed Father Ignatius. It was very wrong of you to go to the Vicar* with your lists of claims and complaints. You must always act according to your headstrong nature, and the result is that you undo with one hand whatever good you may have achieved with the other. Be it known to you that I do not like your way of acting nor its results. If the Vicar behaved as he should not have done, he was hardly likely to be converted by your reprehensions, especially when delivered in your fashion, with little prudence. You are so accustomed to do as you like that wherever you happen to be you give scandal by your way of acting and betray your brusque character. Please God, you will some day do penance for these imprudences. For the love of our Lord I beg you to control yourself and to let the future amend the past. You would not be so irascible if you paid more attention to God, your conscience, and the love of your neighbour. Take it from me that at the hour of death you will see the truth of what I say. I do beseech you in the name of our blessed Father Ignatius that, in the few days remaining to you, you turn over a new leaf and become a patient, gentle, humble man. . . . By your love and obedience to Father Ignatius, I entreat you to go to the Vicar and beg his pardon on your knees for the past. Kiss his hand, though it would console me more if you kissed his feet, and promise him never to withstand him in anything again. Believe me, you will be glad to have done this when you come to die. I have the fullest confidence in God our Lord that when he sees your humility and it becomes known to the people, all the merit lost to you in his service and in your work for souls, will be restored and credited to you once more.

Your error, and that of others also, was to imagine that without deep humility you could get people to do what you required of them, merely because you were a member of the Society. You neglected to build on the foundation of those virtues through which God gave and gives our Father Ignatius so much authority with all men. I beg you above all things to avoid open discord with the Vicar, the clergy, the captains and others holding office in your parts even when you

---

* San Thomé is now Mylapore. The Vicar was a Portuguese secular priest.

see them misbehaving. If there is anything you can remedy in a genial, inoffensive way, remedy it, but do not risk everything by coming to a quarrel when you could save everything with humility and meekness.

O Cyprian, if you only guessed the love with which I write these things to you, you would have me in your mind day and night, and you might perhaps even weep remembering my great love for you. If it were possible in this life to see into the hearts of men, believe me, my brother Cyprian, you would be clearly seen in mine. Entirely yours, without my being able ever to forget you. Francisco.

St Francis Xavier, *Letter to Cyprian, a fellow Jesuit,* early 1552

4 December
Saint John Damascene, *priest and doctor of the Church*
OPTIONAL MEMORIAL

John was a native of Damascus and was born into a christian family in the second half of the seventh century. He received a good education and as an adult was first an officer at the court of the Khalif at Damascus. He then decided to become a monk and joined the community of Mar Sabas near Bethlehem, where he was, as well, ordained priest. He was a great champion of the orthodox faith and in Byzantine tradition can be seen as the last of the Fathers and the first of the scholastics — scholasticism appeared earlier in the Greek Church than in the Latin. He wrote in defence of the use of ikons and also on the Virgin Mary, as well as a comprehensive outline of the faith.

St John died about the middle of the eighth century.

As a reading an extract is given from his Second Sermon on the Dormition of our Blessed Lady. In the West we speak of the Assumption, but we are celebrating the same mystery. The sermon abounds in imagery, but a prevailing one is of Mary as the Ark of the Covenant.

Taking flesh of the sacred Virgin, the Word of God is born without man, remaining himself perfect God, and becoming perfect man, perfect God in his flesh, and perfect man in his Godhead. Thus, recognizing God's mother in this Virgin, we celebrate her falling asleep, not proclaiming her as God — far be from us these heathen fables — since we are announcing her death, but recognizing her as the mother of the incarnate God.

O people of Christ, let us acclaim her today in sacred song, acknowledge our own good fortune and proclaim it. Let us honour her in nocturnal vigil; let us delight in her purity of soul and body, for she next to God surpasses all in purity. It is natural for similar things to glory in each other. Let us show our love for her by compassion and kindness towards the poor. For if mercy is the best worship of God, who will refuse to show his mother devotion in the same way?

She opened to us the unspeakable abyss of God's love for us. Through her the old enmity against the Creator is destroyed. Through her our reconciliation with him is strengthened, peace and grace are given to us, men are the companions of angels, and we, who were in dishonour, are made the children of God. From her we have plucked the fruit of life. From her we have received the seed of immortality. She is the channel of all our goods. In her God was man and man was God. What more marvellous or more blessed? I approach the subject in fear and trembling. With Mary, the prophetess, O youthful souls, let us sound our musical instruments, mortifying our members on earth, for this is spiritual music. Let our souls rejoice in the Ark of God, and the walls of Jericho will yield, I mean the fortresses of the enemy. Let us dance in spirit with David; to-day the Ark of God is at rest. With Gabriel, the great archangel, let us exclaim, 'Hail, full of grace, the Lord is with thee. Hail, inexhaustible ocean of grace. Hail, sole refuge in grief. Hail, cure of hearts. Hail, through whom death is expelled and life is installed.'

St John Damascene, Sermon 2 'On Crowning our Lady'

6 December
Saint Nicholas of Myra, *bishop*
OPTIONAL MEMORIAL

Nicholas was bishop of Myra in Lycia, now Turkey, in the fourth century and came to enjoy an immense cultus, first in the East and later in the West. So popular was he in the early Middle Ages that he was chosen as joint patron of Russia with St Andrew.

In 1087 the citizens of Bari seized his relics from Myra, which was then under Muslim control, and enshrined them in their own city. Bari subsequently became a great centre of pilgrimage. Nicholas is venerated particularly as the patron of sailors and of children: in the English-speaking world, through American influence, he still plays a partial and impoverished part of this latter role as Santa Claus (derived from the Dutch Sint Klaas).

As a reading I offer part of St Anselm's Prayer to St Nicholas, which serves as an indication of how wide and significant veneration for him had become.

Good Lord, thank you.
Truly you have sought out your lost one in the abyss,
and brought out him
whom you had driven there in fear because of his sin.
By the merits of St Nicholas, your beloved,
lead out from the abyss of sin
your lost one whom you have sought and found.
Do not lose your servant whom you have sought and found
in the abyss of hell, where no one is found.
I hear, Lord, that you order me to come forth,
but I cannot get out,
miserably bound and weighed down with so great a weight.

But, St Nicholas, why do I pray to God by your merits,
when you are in his presence and can do this better?
I pray you, sir, through his name,
do not turn away from one
whom he has already looked upon,
however much his accused slave he may be.
I ask you to plead for me in the presence of God,
I do not ask you to defend me, but to pray for me.
Before his face I cannot defend my sins;
I show them, not to excuse but to accuse.
I am the accused; I am under him,
and before him I am myself my accuser.
He who made me does not accuse me.
Alone I was sufficient for sinning,
alone I will be sufficient for accusing.
If he is judge to pass sentence on his accused,
he is also Lord, to protect his servant,
Creator to watch over his handiwork,

and God, to save him who believes in him
and is his baptized.
For how will he judge that sinner to deserve condemnation,
who knows his wretched sins and is penitent?
Or how can he damn a sinner as an adversary,
when he grieves over his sin,
and flees to his friend as an intercessor?

God, in you have I trusted,
St Nicholas, to you I entrust my prayers,
upon you both I cast my care,
even on you I throw my soul.
This is what you exact from me,
you by your commands, you by your counsels.
Receive him who throws himself upon you both,
have him who is prostrate before you.
Keep me when I sleep, help me in whatever I do,
inspire me in whatever I think,
you, Lord, by your grace,
you, Nicholas, by your intercession;
you for the merits of your so loved confessor,
you according to the name of your and my Creator,
'who is blessed for evermore'.   Amen.

St Anselm, 'Prayer to St Nicholas'

7 December
Saint Ambrose, *bishop and doctor of the Church*
MEMORIAL

Ambrose was born in Trier sometime around the year 340. His family
belonged to the Roman aristocracy, and in Rome he was reared and educated.
The Roman Empire was still a reality and the education he received was excellent; he specialized in the study of law and was a master of both Latin and
Greek. He was appointed governor of Liguria and Aemilia, and as governor
had occasion to intervene in a dispute over the election of the bishop of Milan.
He was, himself, only a catechumen. The result of his intervention was that he

was chosen as bishop. He regarded this as irregular but was prevailed on to accept. He was baptized and ordained. His judgement of the situation always remained that emotion had triumphed over the canons. History would judge it as a case when the saying *vox populi, vox dei* — the call of the people is the call of God — was vindicated in the event.

Ambrose's theological achievement was remarkable; he really mastered the teaching of the faith, and as bishop he was zealous, orthodox, loving and firm — even with the emperors, with whom he was on terms of intimate personal friendship. Such an achievement would have been impossible without a deep personal commitment to and love for Christ. Ambrose's writings are important in the history of western mysticism, and, just as it was he who received the future St Augustine into the Church, so it was his preaching, under grace, which largely decided Augustine to receive baptism.

St Ambrose died in the year 397.

I offer as a reading an excerpt from his work, *The Sacrament of the Incarnation of our Lord.* It must be remarked that it is difficult to render his Latin into English, for it is not always easy for us to grasp the reference and the overtone. The second sentence in the following extract is a case in point. However, the overall sense is clear, the message plain: Christ's humanity was whole and real.

Could Jesus Christ our Lord, who saved others from the hazardous condition of the flesh have feared lest he himself also be overcome by the domination of this flesh?

Yet, as they wish it, he did fear the snares of this flesh. Then he ought to have declined the assumption of flesh, lest he be dragged to the hazardous condition of sin. But how could he have feared the hazardous condition of sin, who had come to remit sin? And so, when he took on the flesh of man, it follows that he took on the perfection and fullness of the Incarnation, for there is nothing imperfect in Christ. So he took on flesh, that he might raise it up again; he took on a soul, but he took on and received a perfect soul, rational and human.

For who can deny that he received a soul, when he himself says: 'I lay down my life for my sheep,' and again, 'Therefore does the Father love me, because I lay down my life, that I may take it up again.' After this mention of the death and resurrection of the Lord, he then adds: 'No man takes it away from me: but I lay it down of myself, and I have power to lay it down: and I have power to take it up again.' He lays

down, then, the same as he has taken up. 'He has taken up', I say, for
the very Word of God was not made living in his flesh in the place of
our soul, but just as he has taken up our flesh, so too he has taken up
our perfect soul by the assumption of human nature. He has
assumed, I say, the soul that he might bless it with the sacrament of
his incarnation; he has taken up my disposition of mind to amend it.

But what need was there to take up flesh without a soul, since,
surely, insensible flesh and an irrational soul is neither responsible
for sin nor worthy of reward? So he has taken up for us that which in
us was in greater danger. Moreover, what does it profit me, if he has
not redeemed me entirely? But he has redeemed me entirely, who
says: 'Are you angry at me, because I have healed the whole man on
the sabbath day?' He has redeemed me entirely, because the faithful
one rises again into the perfect man not in part, but entirely.

St Ambrose, *The Sacrament of the Incarnation of our Lord,* nn (64), 65-68

8 December

The Immaculate Conception of the Blessed Virgin Mary
SOLEMNITY

Before the definition of the doctrine in 1854 this celebration was known as the
Conception of the Blessed Virgin, and earlier still, in the East, as the Concep-
tion of Saint Anne. It was celebrated first in Palestine and then spread
through the East and into Italy. From pre-Norman England, where it had been
introduced, it spread to Normandy and so across the more northern parts of
Europe. It was largely propagated by monks and celebrated in monasteries.
Through the Middle Ages it was favoured and defended by the Franciscans.
I offer a reading from Karl Rahner which puts in context what we celebrate.

The Immaculate Conception means that Mary possessed grace from
the beginning. What does it signify, though, to say that someone has
sanctifying grace? This dry technical term of theology makes it sound
as though some *thing* were meant. Yet ultimately sanctifying grace
and its possession do not signify any *thing*, not even merely some
sublime, mysterious condition of our souls, lying beyond the world
of our personal experience and only believed in a remote, theoretical

way. Sanctifying grace, fundamentally, means God himself, his communications to created spirits, the gift which is God himself. Grace is light, love, receptive access of a human being's life as a spiritual person to the infinite expanses of the Godhead. Grace means freedom, strength, a pledge of eternal life, the predominant influence of the Holy Spirit in the depths of the soul, adoptive sonship and an eternal inheritance.

Mary does not differ from us because she possessed these gifts. It is her possession of them from the beginning, and incomparably, that is the sole difference between her and us. As for the content of this gift, its nature and intrinsic meaning, the eternal Father could not intend anything for the mother of his incarnate Son, without intending it for us too, and giving it to us in the sacrament of justification. For us too he eternally intended this saving grace from the beginning, in his eternity, even though it was only effected in us after the beginning of our earthly, temporal life, in order that it might be plain that it is all his grace, that nothing in our salvation belongs to us of ourselves. God has eternally kept his eternal love in readiness for us too, so that in the moment that we call our baptism, he may come into the depths of our heart. For we too are redeemed, saved, marked with God's indelible seal. We too have been made the holy temple of God. In us too the triune God dwells. We too are anointed, hallowed, filled with the light and life of God. We too have been sent by him, from this beginning, into our life, that we too may carry the light of faith and the flame of love through this world's darkness, to the place where we belong, in his eternal radiance, his eternity.

Karl Rahner, *Mary Mother of the Lord*, pp 48-9

11 December
Saint Damasus I, *pope*
OPTIONAL MEMORIAL

Damasus was born in Rome early in the fourth century. His father was a priest of the Roman Church and is said to have been of Spanish descent. Damasus followed his father in the service of the Church and in 366 was chosen as pope. He had to endure the opposition of a certain faction, vocal, and violent also, for twelve years. He summoned various synods to counter heresy, particularly the heresy of Arianism, but Donatism was also a problem.

Damasus was an energetic pontiff and pastor, a keen supporter of the ideal of Christian asceticism among men and women, and an enlightened promoter of scriptural studies. He consistently encouraged St Jerome and ultimately commissioned the Vulgate translation from him. He gave much attention to the veneration of the martyrs, built the basilica of St Lawrence in Damaso, and composed epitaphs for the tombs of other martyrs.

St Damasus died in the year 384.

As a reading I give the opening paragraphs of a letter to him from St Jerome. It was written from Syria and the reference in the second last sentence is to the rival claimants to the see of Antioch. Though St Damasus was to become a close friend, in fact St Jerome's reverence is for the occupant of the see of Peter.

Since the East, shattered as it is by the long-standing feuds subsisting between the peoples, is bit by bit tearing into shreds the seamless tunic of the Lord, 'woven from the top throughout', since the foxes are destroying the vineyard of Christ, and since among the broken cisterns that hold no water it is hard to discover 'the sealed fountain' and 'the garden inclosed', I think it my duty to consult the chair of Peter, and to turn to a church whose faith has been praised by Paul. I appeal for spiritual food to the church whence I have received the garb of Christ. The wide space of sea and land that lies between us cannot deter me from searching for 'the pearl of great price'. 'Wheresoever the body is, there will the eagles be gathered together.' Evil children have squandered their patrimony; you alone keep your heritage intact. The fruitful soil of Rome, when it receives the pure seed of the Lord, bears fruit a hundredfold; but here the seed corn is choked in the furrows and nothing grows but darnel or oats. In the West the sun of righteousness is even now rising; in the East, Lucifer, who fell from heaven, has once more set his throne above the stars. 'You are the light of the world', 'you are the salt of the earth', you are 'vessels of gold and of silver'. Here are vessels of wood or of earth, which wait for the rod of iron and eternal fire.

Yet, though your greatness terrifies me, your kindness attracts me. From the priest I demand the safe-keeping of the victim, from the shepherd the protection due to the sheep. Away with all that is overweening; let the state of Roman majesty withdraw. My words are spoken to the successor of the fisherman, to the disciple of the cross. As I follow no leader but Christ, so I communicate with none but your blessedness, that is with the chair of Peter. For this, I know, is the rock on which the church is built! This is the house where alone the paschal lamb can be rightly eaten. This is the ark of Noah, and he who is not found in it shall perish when the flood prevails. But since by reason of my sins I have betaken myself to this desert which lies between Syria and the uncivilized waste, I cannot, owing to the great distance between us, always ask of your sanctity the holy thing of the Lord. Consequently I here follow the Egyptian confessors who share your faith, and anchor my frail craft under the shadow of their great argosies. I know nothing of Vitalis; I reject Meletius; I have nothing to do with Paulinus. He that gathers not with you scatters; he that is not of Christ is of Antichrist.

St Jerome, 'Letter to Damasus', letter XV

12 December
Saint Jane Frances de Chantal, *religious*
OPTIONAL MEMORIAL

Jane Frances was born at Dijon in France in 1572. As a young woman she married and had six children, but then in 1601, she was widowed as the result of a shooting accident. At first she gave way to depression, but overcame that and sought instead to live a more spiritual life. She had always been pious. In 1604 she met St Francis de Sales and placed herself under his direction.

In 1610 she founded the first convent of the Visitation at Annecy. By the time she died in 1641 sixty-four further convents had been founded.

St Jane Frances was purified by sufferings in her affections and in her faith. St Vincent de Paul rated her among the holiest souls he had met.

As a reading, a letter from St Jane Frances to St Francis de Sales is offered. This is the first of her letters to St Francis to be preserved. It was written in 1617. It concerns her prayer-life: she had obviously attained a high form of prayer.

I have many things to tell you, my unique Father, but I know not where they are, so overwhelmed and distracted is my poor mind with a thousand worries. I no longer feel that abandonment and sweet confidence (which I used to have in prayer), nor can I make any acts of those virtues, although it seems to me they are more solid and firm than ever. In its superior part, my soul is in a state of very simple union. It does not bring about this union itself; for when, on certain occasions, it wishes to make acts of union, it feels a difficulty in doing so. It clearly sees that it cannot unite itself, but can only remain united. It has no inclination to change this state for any other. It neither thinks nor acts, if I except the consciousness of desire, formed almost imperceptibly that God may do with it and with all creatures, in all things, whatever he shall please. It would wish to do nothing but this for the morning exercise, at holy Mass, in preparation for holy communion, and in thanksgiving for all benefits; in a word, for everything. It wishes only to remain in this most simple unity of mind with God, without looking elsewhere, and whilst in this state to say sometimes vocally an *Our Father* for the whole world, for individuals, and for itself, without, however, diverting its attention or thinking for whom or for what it prays.

Frequently, according to occasions, necessity, or inclination, which last comes without being sought, my soul flows into this union. With regard to this manner of prayer, I believe indeed that it suffices for everything; nevertheless, my unique Father, I am very often assailed by fears on this head, and I force myself (which I find very difficult) to make acts of union, adoration, the exercise of the morning, of Mass, and of thanksgiving. If I do wrong in this, please do tell me. Tell me, also, whether this simple union suffices, whether it will satisfy God for all the acts I have just mentioned, which are of obligation for us; nay, even, if it will suffice during spiritual aridity when the soul has no perception or consciousness of such union, except in its very highest point. I do not ask you for a long answer on the subject. In a dozen words you can tell me all that, repeating my question if you choose, and assuring me that this simple union will suffice for everything; then I shall, with God's help, be faithful to make no more acts.

St Jane Frances de Chantal, 'Letter to Francis de Sales', 1617

13 December
Saint Lucy, *virgin and martyr*
MEMORIAL

Lucy suffered for her faith in Christ about the year 304 at Syracuse in Sicily. In the fourth and fifth centuries devotion to her was spread through both East and West and legend smothered the real person. During the Middle Ages her aid was invoked for eye-trouble: this was due in part to her name, which is related to 'light', and partly to her legend, where she is said to have plucked out her own eyes.

The reading below I have taken from Guerric of Igny, a sermon on St Benedict, in which he treats of faith. Whatever about our faith, the faith and love of St Lucy did not fail!

I indeed know that the earth is full with the confession of faith; but nevertheless I hear the prophet lamenting because faith has perished from the earth! For do you think that if the son of Man were to come now, he would find faith upon the earth? Would he reckon faith this feigned faith of the neglectful and careless, compared to which he condemned more lightly the blindness of the unbelieving, compared with which he judges better the belief of the demons? 'The demons believe and tremble'; men believe and do not tremble. The demons respect him whom they believe; men, while they neither fear nor respect him whom they believe, are judged more seriously for their contempt.

Let us not be mistaken, my brothers and sisters, by the general term 'faith', as if faith of any kind ought to be reckoned unto justice; but let us bear in mind the kind of faith 'the teacher of the nations in faith and truth' defined, by which God is to be pleased, saying: 'faith is the substance of things to be hoped for, the proof of things which do not appear.' This is the faith which works by love, so that by the conscience being persuaded of Christ's merits, hope is born of faith; and faith is supposed as the foundation laid down, upon which may be built the eternal goods which are to be hoped for. Without this particular faith it is impossible to please God, and with it it is impossible not to please God. 'Your eyes, O Lord, look upon my faith', he said, 'who continually stood in your sight through faith.' The reciprocal influence is altogether justly and certainly deservedly due, so that your eyes, Lord, should regard faith faithfully saying: you understand faith, because 'my eyes are always on the Lord.'

We, brethren, however, if we be as if without faith and place God behind our backs, so that neglecting fear of him we look rather upon vanities, on what account do we think we shall be looked upon? Indeed, we shall be looked upon, but with what expression of countenance? 'The countenance of the Lord on those who do evil'; but how angered, how terrible, how unbearable, will then at length be known, when they who hate him flee from before his face!

And where will they flee from before your face, Lord, except into the outer darknesses, into that chaos and abyss of fire and heat? For then they will say 'to the mountains: fall upon us, and to the hills: cover us', judging it a lesser thing to be swallowed up by the depth of hell than to bear the face of an angered God. For 'then indeed the just will stand in great assurance'; then faith, which now stands in the sight of God, concerned to perceive his will, will stand assured to see his glory.

Watch, brothers, stand firm in the faith. One whom faith fills with fear cannot doze off through carelessness; one whom faith grounds in hope cannot waver for want of trust. However, 'Let everything you do be done in love', that gentleness be joined to faith, so of each of you it may be said: 'the Lord made him holy in his faith and gentleness'. May he, the Holy of Holies, grant this, who lives and reigns for ever and ever. Amen.

Guerric of Igny, *Sermon 4 on St Benedict*

14 December

Saint John of the Cross, *priest and doctor of the Church*
MEMORIAL

John was born at Fontiveros in old Castille in 1542, and studied at a poor school and then with the Jesuits. He entered the Carmelites at Medina del Campo and was ordained priest in 1567. He felt drawn to a more contemplative life and thought of becoming a Carthusian, but then he met St Theresa. Under her inspiration he thus became one of the first friars of the reform in the monastery of Duruelo. His subsequent life was marked by much suffering, first at the hands of the friars of the common Observance, but then at those of the Discalced.

He died in 1591. He was one of the greatest mystics given to the Church and his writings are not only classics of spirituality but also of Spanish literature.

The reading is an excerpt from his *Ascent of Mount Carmel*.

The father of a family has on his table many and different kinds of food, some of which are better than others. A child is asking him for a certain dish, not the best, but the first that meets its eye, and it asks for this dish because it would rather eat of it than any other; and as the father sees that, even if he gives it the better kind of food, it will not take it but will have that which it asks for, since that alone pleases it, he gives it that, regretfully, lest it should take no food at all and be miserable. In just this way, we observe, did God treat the children of Israel when they asked him for a king: he gave them one, but unwillingly, because it was not good for them. And thus he said to Samuel: *Audi vocem populi in omnibus quae loquuntur tibi: non enim te abjecerunt, sed me.* Which signifies: Hearken unto the voice of this people and grant them the king whom they ask of thee, for they have not rejected thee but Me, that I should not reign over them (1 Sam 8:7). In this same way God condescends to certain souls, and grants them that which is not best for them, because they will not or cannot walk by any other road. And thus certain souls attain to tenderness and sweetness of spirit or sense; and God grants them this because they are unable to partake of the stronger and more solid food of the trials of the cross of his Son, which he would prefer them to take, rather than aught else.

I consider, however, that the desire to know things by supernatural means is much worse than the desire for other spiritual favours pertaining to the senses; for I cannot see how the soul that desires them can fail to commit, at least, venial sin, however good may be its aims, and however far advanced it may be on the road to perfection; and if anyone should bid the soul desire them, and consent to it, he sins likewise. For there is no necessity for any of these things, since the soul has its natural reason and the doctrine and law of the Gospel, which are quite sufficient for its guidance, and there is no difficulty or necessity that cannot be solved and remedied by these means, which are very pleasing to God and of great profit to souls; and such great use, in fact, must we make of our reason and of Gospel doctrine that, if certain things be told to us supernaturally, whether at our desire or no, we must receive only that which is in clear conformity with reason and Gospel law. And then we must receive it, not because it is revelation, but because it is reason, and not allow ourselves to be influenced by the fact that it has been revealed. Indeed, it is well in such a case to look at that reason and examine it very much more closely than if there had been no revelation concerning it; inasmuch as the devil utters many things that are true, and that will come to pass, and that are in conformity with reason, in order that he may deceive.

Wherefore, in all our needs, trials and difficulties, there remains to us no better and surer means than prayer and hope that God will provide for us, by such means as he wills.

St John of the Cross, *Ascent of Mount Carmel*, Book 2, c 21, nn 3, 4, (5)

21 December

Saint Peter Canisius, *priest and doctor of the Church*
OPTIONAL MEMORIAL

Peter (whose family name has been Latinized), was born in Nijmegen in Holland in 1521. As a student he attended a retreat preached by St Peter Favre and decided to enter the Society of Jesus. He was ordained priest in 1546. As a Jesuit he worked, for the most part, in what was the Holy Roman Empire — South Germany, Austria, Bohemia and Switzerland. He died in Fribourg, Switzerland, in 1597.

His energy and achievement were quite incredible, so that he is considered, and with reason, the second apostle of Germany. Much of his work was to counteract Lutheranism, and this he did not only by direct pastoral action but chiefly by fostering an educated Catholic laity, particularly at second and third level. His earliest publications were in the area of patrology, but when he had entered more fully into pastoral activity he wrote his most famous book, a catechism. This met with immediate success, and was translated into many European languages in his lifetime.

As a man he was gentle, courteous and moderate and had no great belief in controversy.

The reading is taken from his Confessions. We must work to acquire humility, but God's opening of our inward eye alone causes us to really *experience* how little we are. When God does this it is not a source of discouragement but the starting point of a new and fuller commitment of our whole being to him. The St John quoted is St John the Baptist — 'I am not' (see Jn 1:20-23).

I thank you from the bottom of my heart, O my God most pitiful, my creator, my Saviour, my protector, my life, my refuge, my salvation, every day and moment that I sail at random on this stormy sea of human life, and am so strangely impelled in various ways to good and evil that I often know not what wind it is which frets me, whither my ship is borne, where I stand, or how I ought to set my course.

That also was my experience at Ancona when I came thither in June of the year 1568 with the Cardinal of Augsburg. For, while I was examining my conscience in the cathedral, you opened the eyes of my mind, O Light Eternal, and mercifully illumined him who lay in darkness, so that he should know himself, abase his mind in the truth, and learn in a new way to be submissive to you and serve you, O holy Lord God, the complete and only good of every creature.

This light which you poured into my soul was of such sort that I might learn, both then and ever after, to put all my intentions and actions on a true and solid foundation. I understood from you that the foundation is knowledge of self and of one's own vileness and nothingness, so that looking upon myself I should see how in the realm of goodness, I am nothing, know nothing, wish nothing, do nothing, possess nothing, for in you alone is the beginning, middle, and end of all good, and in you alone ought every rational creature to place his good always.

You taught me, O perfect Master, the foulness of much that is in me, for I had neglected and little considered the foundation of my own nothingness and nakedness in the eyes of your Majesty. I looked upon and appraised myself and my deeds with human eyes, and cried not with St John, 'I am not'.

Oh would that you might increase in me your grace to walk with the Magi in this new light, and to regard myself in all my ways as I truly am and not as I seem to be; so that I may be able to say from my heart, *Abyssus abyssum invocat* (an abyss calls on the Abyss), the abyss I mean, of my nothingness . . . ever calling to the abyss of your infinite majesty, power and perfection.

I confess my sin, O most loving Father, in that I did not refer to you the gifts which I received from you, but oftentimes took credit to myself for them or gladly allowed others to praise me on their account, neither saying nor doing in the spirit of him who cried: *Non nobis, Domine, non nobis, sed nomini tuo da gloriam* (Not to us, O Lord, not to us, but to your name give the glory). But now I am resolved with your help . . . to look upon myself with new eyes and to walk, as I ought, in humility and simplicity of heart.

St Peter Canisius SJ, 'Confessions'

23 December
Saint John of Kanty, *priest*
OPTIONAL MEMORIAL

John was born in Kanty in Polish Silesia in 1390. He became a priest in the diocese of Cracow and subsequently taught in the university there as either a lecturer or a professor in the faculty of theology. He ended his life as parish priest of Olkusz. He was remarkable not only for his learning and for his teaching and preaching of the faith, but also for the simplicity, charity and austerity of his life. He died on Christmas Eve night in 1473 and was canonized in 1767. His standing and reputation in the university of Cracow were such that for many years after his death all graduate doctors wore his academic gown for their conferring.

As a reading an excerpt from Newman's discourse on the bearing of theology on other branches of knowledge is given.

By theology, I simply mean the science of God, or the truths we know about God put into system; just as we have a science of the stars and call it astronomy, or of the crust of the earth, and call it geology.

For instance, I mean, for this is the main point, that, as in the human frame there is a living principle, acting upon it and through it by means of volition, so, behind the veil of the visible universe, there is an invisible, intelligent Being acting on and through it, as and when he will. Further, I mean that this invisible agent is in no sense a soul of the world, after the analogy of human nature, but, on the contrary, is absolutely distinct from the world, as being its creator, upholder, governor, and sovereign Lord.

Here we are at once brought into the circle of doctrines which the idea of God embodies. I mean then by the supreme being, one who is simply self-dependent, and the only being who is such; moreover, that he is without beginning or eternal, and the only eternal; that in consequence he has lived a whole eternity by himself; and hence that he is all-sufficient, sufficient for his own blessedness, and all-blessed, and ever-blessed. Further, I mean a being, who, having these prerogatives, has the supreme good, or rather is the Supreme Good, or has all the attributes of good in infinite intenseness; all wisdom, all truth, all justice, all love, all holiness, all beautifulness; who is omnipotent, omniscient, omnipresent; ineffably one, absolutely perfect; and such, that what we do not know and cannot even imagine of him, is far more wonderful than what we do and can. I mean one who is sovereign over his own will and actions, though always according to the eternal rule of right and wrong, which is himself. I mean, moreover, that he created all things out of nothing, and preserves them every moment, and could destroy them as easily as he made them; and that, in consequence, he is separated from them by an abyss, and is incommunicable in all his attributes. And further, he has stamped upon all things, in the hour of their creation, their respective natures, and has given them their work and mission and their length of days, greater or less, in their appointed place. I mean, too, that he is ever present with his works, one by one, and confronts everything he has made by his particular and most loving providence, and manifests himself to each according to its needs; and has on rational beings imprinted the moral law, and given them power to obey it, imposing on them the duty of worship and service, searching and scanning them through and through with his omniscient eye, and putting before them a present trial and a judgement to come.

Such is what theology teaches, about God, a doctrine, as the very idea of its subject-matter presupposes, so mysterious as in its fulness to lie beyond any system, and to seem in parts even to be irreconcilable with itself, the imagination being unable to embrace what the reason determines. It teaches of a Being infinite, yet personal; all-blessed, yet ever operative; absolutely separate from the creature, yet in every part of the creation at every moment; above all things, yet under everything.

J.H. Newman, 'Bearing of Theology on other Branches of Knowledge', *On the Scope and Nature of University Education*, pp 53-5

26 December
Saint Stephen, *martyr*
FEAST

This feast goes back to the fourth century at least. The name Stephen is Greek and he must have been a Jew of the diaspora who had settled in Jerusalem. He is the first named among the seven chosen to minister to the Greek-speaking Christians in Jerusalem at the very dawn of church history.

He is the first recorded martyr of the New Testament, the very first fruit, as it were, of Christ's coming among us, the 'crown of victory' (the meaning of the name) of the Infant King.

The reading is taken from Newman's sermon On Martyrdom, preached on this day.

Christ had said to his apostles, 'Satan hath desired to have you, that he may sift you as wheat.' Consider what is meant by sifting, which is a continued agitation, a shaking about, to the early discipline inflicted on the Church. No mere sudden stroke came upon it; but it was solicited day by day, in all its members, by every argument of hope and fear, by threats and inducements, to desert Christ. This was the lot of the martyrs. Death, their final suffering, was but the consummation of a life of anticipated death.

Consider how distressing anxiety is; how irritating and wearing it is to be in constant excitement, with the duty of maintaining calmness and steadiness in the midst of it; and how especially inviting any prospect of tranquillity would appear in such circumstances; and then we shall have some notion of a Christian's condition, under a persecuting heathen government. I put aside for the present the peculiar reproach and contempt which was the lot of the primitive

Church, and their actual privations. Let us merely consider them as *harassed*, shaken as wheat in a sieve.

Under such circumstances, the stoutest hearts are in danger of failing. They could steel themselves against certain definite sufferings, or prepare themselves to meet one expected crisis; but they yield to the incessant annoyance which the apprehension of persecution, and the importunity of friends inflict on them. They sigh for peace; they gradually come to believe that the world is not so wrong as some men say it is, and that it is possible to be over-strict and over-nice. They learn to temporize and to be double-minded. First one falls, then another; and such instances come as an additional argument for concession to those that remain firm as yet, who of course feel dispirited, lonely, and begin to doubt the correctness of their own judgement; while, on the other hand, those who have fallen, in self-defence become their tempters.

Thus the Church is sifted, the cowardly falling off, the faithful continuing firm, though in dejection and perplexity. Among these latter are the martyrs; not accidental victims, taken at random, but the picked and choice ones, the elect remnant, a sacrifice well pleasing to God, because a costly gift, the finest wheat flour of the Church: men who have been warned what to expect from their profession, and have had many opportunities of relinquishing it, but have 'borne and had patience, and for Christ's name sake have laboured, and have not fainted.' Such was St Stephen, not entrapped into a confession and slain (as it were) in ambuscade, but boldly confronting his persecutors, and, in spite of circumstances that foreboded death, awaiting their fury.

J.H. Newman, 'On Martyrdom', *Parochial and Plain Sermons II*, 4

27 December
Saint John, *apostle and evangelist*
FEAST

John, son of Zebedee, brother of James (with whom, as with Peter, he appears in all the gospel accounts as amongst the closest of the apostles to Christ), is celebrated today as author of the Fourth Gospel, of the Apocalypse and the

three Letters which bear his name. There are critical problems in connection
with this identification, particularly with regard to the Apocalypse, but it does
represent the consensus of tradition. According to that same tradition St John
died at Ephesus in advanced old age.

The celebrating of his feast today reflects an ancient but not a universal tradition.

The reading is taken from Newman, *Parochial and Plain Sermons,* a sermon
preached on this feast. The whole series of these sermons dates from Newman's ministry as an Anglican, and not every point or observation in all of
them would he have repeated as a Catholic. The sermon the present extract is
drawn from, however, should be read in its entirety.

'Beloved, let us love one another, for love is of God. If we love one
another, God dwelleth in us, and his love is perfected in us. God is
love, and he that dwelleth in love dwelleth in God, and God in him.'
Now did he begin with some vast effort at loving on a large scale?
Nay, he had the unspeakable privilege of being the *friend of Christ.*
Thus he was taught to love others; first his affection was concen-
trated, then it was expanded. Next he had the solemn and comfort-
able charge of tending our Lord's mother, the blessed Virgin, after
his departure. Do we not here discern the secret sources of his special
love of the brethren? Could he, who first was favoured with his Saviour's affection, then trusted with a son's office towards his mother,
could he be other than a memorial and pattern (as far as man can be),
of love, deep, contemplative, fervent, unruffled, unbounded?

Further, that love of friends and relations, which nature pre-
scribes, is also of use to the Christian, in giving form and direction to
his love of mankind at large, and making it intelligent and discrimi-
nating. A man who would fain begin by a general love of all men
necessarily puts them all on a level, and, instead of being cautious,
prudent, and sympathizing in his benevolence, is hasty and rude;
does harm, perhaps, when he means to do good, discourages the virtuous and well-meaning, and wounds the feelings of the gentle. Men
of ambitious and ardent minds, for example, desirous of doing good
on a large scale, are especially exposed to the temptation of sacrific-
ing individual to general good in their plans of charity. Ill-instructed
men, who have strong abstract notions about the necessity of showing generosity and candour towards opponents, often forget to take

any thought of those who are associated with themselves; and commence their (so-called) liberal treatment of their enemies by an unkind desertion of their friends. This can hardly be the case, when men cultivate the private charities, as an introduction to more enlarged ones. By laying a foundation of social amiableness, we insensibly learn to observe a due harmony and order in our charity; we learn that all men are not on a level; that the interests of truth and holiness must be religiously observed; and that the Church has claims on us before the world.

J.H. Newman, 'Love of Relations and Friends',
Parochial and Plain Sermons, II, 5

28 December
The Holy Innocents, *martyrs*
FEAST

In the Eastern Church these are called the Holy Infants and are the male children recorded as slain by Herod in the gospel according to St Matthew, as read in today's Mass. The meaning of St Matthew's account is to stress Jesus as the 'new Israel', persecuted and forced to flee (a theme which appears in the Haggadah), and the 'new Moses' marvellously saved from the general slaughter of the Hebrew children. Some scholars, accordingly, would be quite happy to discount the historicity of the actual event, as against tradition which has accepted it. The massacre, which would not have been very extensive, however, would have been quite in accord with what is known of Herod's character and actions.

The reading is taken from a sermon by Newman, which he preached on this feast.

The longer we live in the world, and the further removed we are from the feelings and remembrances of childhood (and especially if removed from the sight of children), the more reason we have to recollect our Lord's impressive action and word, when he called a little child unto him, and set him in the midst of his disciples, and said, 'Verily I say unto you, except ye be converted, and become as little children, ye shall not enter into the kingdom of heaven. Whosoever, therefore, shall humble himself as this little child, the same is greatest in the kingdom of heaven.' And in order to remind us of this our Saviour's judgement, the Church, like a careful teacher, calls us back year by year upon this day from the bustle and fever of the world. She takes advantage of the Massacre of the Innocents recorded in St Matthew's Gospel, to bring before us a truth which else we might think little of; to sober our wishes and hopes of this world, our high ambitious thoughts, or our anxious fears, jealousies, and cares, by the picture of the purity, peace, and contentment which are the characteristics of little children.

And, independently of the benefit thus accruing to us, it is surely right and meet thus to celebrate the death of the Holy Innocents: for it was a blessed one. To be brought near to Christ, and to suffer for Christ, is surely an unspeakable privilege; to suffer anyhow, even unconsciously. The little children whom he took up in his arms, were not conscious of his loving condescension; but was it no privilege when he blessed them? Surely this massacre had in it the nature of a Sacrament; it was a pledge of the love of the Son of God towards those who were included in it. All who came near him, more or less suffered by approaching him, just as if earthly pain and trouble went out of him, as some precious virtue for the good of their souls — and these infants in the number.

Surely his very presence was a Sacrament; every motion, look, and word of his conveying grace to those who would receive it: and much more was fellowship with him. And hence in ancient times such barbarous murders or martyrdoms were considered as a kind of baptism, a baptism of blood, with a sacramental charm in it, which stood in the place of the appointed laver of regeneration. Let us then take these little children as in some sense martyrs, and see what instruction we may gain from the pattern of their innocence.

J.H. Newman, 'The Mind of Little Children',
Parochial and Plain Sermons, II, 6

29 December
Saint Thomas à Becket, *bishop and martyr*
OPTIONAL MEMORIAL

Thomas was born in London about the year 1118 and received a good education, finishing his studies in Paris. As a young man he subsequently joined the household of Archbishop Theobald of Canterbury. He studied canon law at Auxerre and Bologna, was ordained deacon and in 1154 was appointed archdeacon of Canterbury. He had all the characteristics of a careerist, little sign of being a man of God. He was exceptionally capable, however, and was chosen by King Henry II to be his Lord Chancellor. He served the king very well, and Henry, thinking him a fitting tool, had him appointed archbishop of Canterbury. This was confirmed in 1162.

Thomas must have long had qualms about the kind of life he had been living, for he now became a churchman in earnest, and lived in great personal austerity. More than that, he devoted his immense energy and capacity to the interests of the Church as he conceived them and was on a collision course with the king from the outset. Eventually he was forced into exile. The quarrel was patched up, and Thomas was finally allowed to return to England. He was hardly back four weeks when he was slain by four knights in his cathedral. He was canonized three years later.

In a fundamental principle, from the ecclesiastical point of view, Thomas clearly had right on his side, but the clash between himself and the king would hardly have had such a dramatic outcome were not both men strong and determined characters. For all that, Thomas did die for his conscience and the Church.

The reading is taken from a letter of his to the English bishops, and, quite clearly, Thomas was aware that the course he was on was a dangerous one. It will be noted that the greater part of the extract is made up of arguments addressed to the king, who (Thomas knew well) would get to know of the letter. It is an example of the strategy of the indirect approach!

May my lord, therefore, hear the petition of his liegeman, the advice of his bishop, the exhortation of his father, that God may do good by him and increase his days and years, and those of his sons, for a long time. May he allow the Church to enjoy the peace and freedom under him, as under the most christian king, the Roman Church to exercise its right and freedom in his land, a freedom it ought have and has in other kingdoms. May he restore to the Church of Canterbury, and to us, its rights and liberties and everything taken from it, with all peace and our safety, so that we may serve God freely and quietly under him and that he himself be bound to avail of our allegiance as it should be pleasing to him, having respect to the honour of God and of the Roman Church, and our order.

These are the kingly dignities, the most excellent laws which the most christian king is bound to seek and observe; by which the Church ought to rejoice and flourish under him. These are the laws, acknowledging the divine law, not taking from it. He becomes an enemy of God, whoso does not observe them, 'For the law of the Lord is unstained, converting souls.' For concerning his laws the Lord says: 'Keep my laws'; and the prophet: 'Woe to those who establish evil laws, and writing have written injustices, so that they may oppress the poor in judgement, and do violence to the cause of the lowly ones of the people of God.'

Let not my Lord, then, be ashamed to come back to his heart, to be humble in sorrow of heart and the meekness of lowliness before God, to make satisfaction to him and to his Church for the injuries inflicted. For God does not despise the contrite and lowly heart, but embraces it more sincerely. Thus the holy David, who when he sinned, humbled himself before God, sought mercy and obtained forgiveness. So, too, the king of Niniveh, and the whole city, when the severity of destruction was threatened on it, because he humbled himself before God in ash and sackcloth merited to ward off the censure of vengeance, the sentence having been changed, by contrition of heart and compunction of tears.

We do not write these things to you, brothers, that we may abash your faces, but that our letters having been read and understood, you may be strong, and may will to exercise the necessary duties of your office more bravely and effectively. For the rest I wish you always to do better, so that peace may be quicker with us, and greater freedom for the Church. Pray for us, that our faith fail not in this tribulation, and that we may be able to say fearlessly with the apostle, that neither death, nor life, nor the angels, nor any other creature be able to separate us from the love of God; which has subjected us to tribulation, until he come who is to come. May he perform for us his mercy, and lead us into the land of promise, the land flowing with milk and honey, which he will give only to those who love him.

Farewell, all of you, in the Lord; we beg that the whole English Church always and more earnestly pray for us.

Thomas à Becket, the conclusion of Ep 223

31 December
Saint Sylvester I, *pope*
OPTIONAL MEMORIAL

Sylvester was the first pope to be elected after the Edict of Milan — the edict which granted the christian religion recognition and freedom — and was to rule the Church of Rome for almost twenty-one years. The first great christian basilicas were built during his pontificate by the emperor and various patricians. The heresy of Arius and the schism of Donatus appeared to trouble the Church also in his time, and Rome became the great rallying ground for orthodoxy. He died in the year 335 and was buried first at Santa Priscilla. His remains were transferred to San Silvestro in Capite in the year 761.

The reading is taken from Henri de Lubac, SJ, *The Splendour of the Church.*

The Roman Church is the object *par excellence* of accusations of tyranny; she is even sometimes — absurdly — put on a parallel with the various systems of political absolutism. And she is also the primary object of the objections of many Christians, who nevertheless recognize the necessity of a visible authority. Conversely, it is primarily of her that Catholics think when they call the Church their mother. In common with tradition, they consider her as 'root and mother of the Catholic Church', as 'the mother and mistress of all the Churches', as 'mother and mistress of all the faithful of Christ'. Catholics consider her head as 'the head of the episcopate' and 'the father of the Christian people', 'the master of the whole household of Christ' as St Ignatius Loyola puts it. For them, the see of Rome is the 'Holy See', the 'Apostolic See' *par excellence.* They know that Peter was given the charge of not only the lambs but the sheep as well; that Christ himself prayed that the faith of Peter might not fail, and that he gave Peter the keys of the kingdom of heaven and the command to confirm his brethren. They realize that Peter personifies the whole Church, and that just as each bishop is the bridegroom of his own particular Church, so Peter, the bishop of Rome, may be said to be the bridegroom of the universal Church, the whole of which has in him its visible foundation.

As against a frequently lodged objection (based on a misunderstanding), Catholics will, of course, be equally clear that this visible foundation in no way prejudices that unique Foundation which is Christ, any more than the visible chief shepherd puts into eclipse the Good Shepherd, since here there is no question of duplication, the very name 'Peter' having been chosen by Christ to express this identity of submission, which is in itself the fruit of faith. Believing as they do that the Church has received the promise of perpetuity and victory over death, and holding that it was she who was in Christ's mind in that scene on the road to Caesarea, they will naturally grasp the consequence that as long as the Church goes on building herself up and subsisting in her visible state — that is to say, as long as this world lasts — she cannot be without a visible foundation for her building. Peter was not given his office simply in order to relinquish it almost at once; he was given it to hand on after him. 'In his successors — the bishops of the See of Rome, which was founded by him and consecrated by his blood — he lives, presides and judges perpetually.'

H. de Lubac, *The Splendour of the Church*, pp 198-200

Saints of the National Calendars
of England, Ireland, Scotland and Wales

13 January
Saint Kentigern, *bishop*
In Scotland: MEMORIAL

Kentigern, or Mungo, is venerated as the patron of Glasgow and Strathclyde. He is reputed to have died in 603 and so would have been a sixth century figure. It is difficult to determine the details of his life, and they are much discussed and disputed. Traditionally he was said to have preached to the Britons of Strathclyde, and to have been consecrated as their bishop. Driven from the area for a time, he would have preached, according to some, in northwest England and in Wales.

The oldest Life we have of him dates from fully six centuries after this period. The reading given is from the Life by Jocelyn of Furness, and describes the last moments of the saint. The images and terms are drawn from scripture and are rather stereotyped, but this is true of almost all medieval Lives. In the translation I have omitted one detail, which was that towards the end of his days St Kentigern kept his jaw from falling open by means of a cloth wrapped round his head.

Worn out by exceeding old age, the blessed Kentigern began sensing by his frequent falls that the destruction of his earthly dwelling-place was at hand, yet the foundation of his faith set upon a rock continued to comfort his soul. By this faith he was confident that he had a dwelling, not made by hands, prepared in heaven after the dissolution of this earthly habitation. He, beloved of God and men, being aware then that the hour was drawing near for his passing from this world to the Father of lights, fortified himself with the sacred anointing — effective of the remission of sins — and with the life-giving sacraments of the Lord's Body and Blood, so that the ancient serpent, lying in wait for his heel, would be unable to sink-in a poisoned fang and inflict a lethal wound, but would depart confounded with his head crushed.

Just so, by the Lord's crushing satan quickly in this way under his feet lest his holy soul be confounded when in his going forth from Egypt he be caught speaking to his enemies at the gate; from this time on, as a most excellent watchman, waiting he waited on the Lord, who had saved him from the storm of this world. The proximate landing on the shore in the port of a certain inner quiet furthermore consoled him by peaceful navigation after so many perils and risks at sea; in a safe and secure place in the region of his desires he had cast an anchor bound to hope, an anchor, namely, reaching into the places behind the veil, where the precursor, the Lord Jesus Christ, entered for him.

And Jesus was preparing for him the only means of going out from the tents of Cedar, and entrance into the land of the living, so that, a most excellent athlete, as it were, he might receive the crown of glory and the diadem of the kingdom, which does not decay, from the hand of the supernal king in that city of hosts, namely, the heavenly Jerusalem.

Then, as far as his strength allowed, he reminded his disciples, gathered together before him, about the following of our holy religion, about the preservation of mutual love and peace, of the grace of hospitality, of application to prayer and reading. And above all, also of the avoiding of every kind of evil simoniacal depravity, and of fleeing all communion with and company of heretics and schismatics. He reminded them of the decrees of the holy fathers, and especially of the unwavering keeping of the ordinances and customs of holy Church, the mother of all.

Then he gave to each, humbled before him on bended knees, as was fitting, the kiss of peace; and, having lifted up his hand as he best was able, he blessed them. And, making his last farewell, entrusting them all to the tutelage of the Blessed Trinity and the protection of the holy mother of God, he composed himself on his noble bed of stone. . . .

Jocelyn of Furness, *Life of St Kentigern*, c 42

1 February

Saint Brigid, *virgin*

In Ireland: FEAST

Brigid died at Kildare, the double monastery which she had founded, about
the year 525. Her legend abounds in miraculous happenings most of which
tend to show her charity, her compassion, and her sense of justice. She was
affectionately and rather extravagantly known in earlier times as 'Mary of the
Gael'. Some confusion existed between St Brigid and the Celtic goddess Brig,
particularly in connection with the fire-cult linked with this day in pagan tradition. We do not know the precise explanation for this, but tradition died
hard in ancient Ireland.

    The Life of Brigid was written by Cogitosus in the seventh century, but as a
reading I offer an extract from another Irish writing of the seventh century —
one which has no connection with Brigid but which illustrates that there were
other preoccupations in the early Irish Church — *The Marvels of Sacred Scripture* by the Irish Augustine.

The Lord Jesus went out to baptism, in truth, not because he, who
had no guilt of his own or of original sin, needed the sacrament and
washing of baptism, but in order that he might purify the waters,
which, although God had not cursed them at the sin of Adam, had
been infected by the curse of the land by which they were contained.
And in order that no one should neglect the sacrament of baptism,
seeing that he who was without sin entered the waters of baptism;
and that no one should think it not worth their while to be baptised
by an inferior since the Lord sought to be purged in the waters of
baptism by his servant; and so that he might hide himself from the
devil (until the temptation was accomplished), who saw him, as if
needing baptism, wash away his sins by the waters among sinners.

    He saw indeed the Holy Spirit coming down upon him in baptism
and heard the voice of the Father confessing him to be his Son, and
saw heaven open before him: not that before his baptism the Son of
God did not have all these things but that he might show what the
sacrament of baptism is worth. For he did not then begin to receive
the Spirit who is believed to have the same substance with the Holy
Spirit. Nor did the Father then first profess that he was his Son to
whom he said: 'From the womb before the day-star I begot thee',

365

namely before the whole angel creation, which often has the title of day-star in the scriptures. Nor had the bridal chamber of the heavens then begun to open to him who said: 'Heaven is my seat, the earth however the footstool of my feet.' But the Holy Trinity on this account gathered together all these things that each one of us might know what a gift we received in the mystery of holy baptism. For then everyone cleansed from the stains of their sins receives the Holy Spirit, and begins as a child by the grace of adoption to be acknowledged by God the Father, and then one understands that the gate of heaven is open to him or her and that one is a citizen of the heavenly fatherland as the fellow of the holy angels.

The Irish Augustine, *De mirabilibus sacrae scripturae*, III, 5

1 March
Saint David, *bishop*
Patron of Wales
In Wales: SOLEMNITY
In England: FEAST

David, or Dewi, died about the year 589. He founded a monastery at Mynyw, in Latin, Menevia, in the west of Pembrokeshire, and is venerated as the first bishop of those parts. The life led by his monks was very austere, so much so, that his contemporary, St Gildas, made the rather acid comment, that they were more ascetics than Christians. Otherwise the earliest references to him are in Irish liturgical sources and traditionally he had some link with the Order of Mass followed in Ireland.

Materials bearing on his life are rather scant. As a reading the English version of a medieval Latin sequence is given.

David, star of heavenly splendour,
latter covenant's defender,
glitters o'er Britannia;
by his holy conversation,
by the true faith's conservation,
He adorns Menevia.

As the harbinger was naméd

by the angel, so proclaiméd
was he e'er his natal day;
hart and honey, water flowing,
mystic signs of fame foreshowing,
Christ's devoted thrall portray.

He, the Britons' champion fearless,
of the Welsh the teacher peerless,
takes the heavenly freemen's part;
now the Sage, the city quitting,
seeks the vale's retreat befitting
men of humbleness of heart.

Dewi Sant his sons acclaim him!
From his birth the people name him
Dewi Ddyfrwr — 'Waterman';
halt and maimed and blind he healeth,
Satan in confusion reeleth
at the Christian psalmist's ban.

Whilst a treatise he was writing,
God, this man of law requiting,
gilds the letters of the tome;
holy David, be our pleader,
as thy namesake, be our leader,
our Goliath overcome!

Athelstan Riley

10 March
Saint John Ogilvie, *priest and martyr*
In Scotland: FEAST

John was born at Drum, near Keith, in 1580, and his family was old and important in Scotland. He was brought up in Calvinism. He was sent to France for further education and there was received into the Catholic Church by Father Cornelius a Lapide. He then entered the Society of Jesus and was ordained priest in 1613. That same year he went back to Scotland and worked for two years in Edinburgh and Glasgow bringing back many to the ancient faith. He was soon betrayed, however, and was hanged in Glasgow in the year 1615.

He was canonized in 1976. The reading is taken from the homily of Pope Paul VI pronounced at his canonization.

The life of a saint, looked at with loving understanding, suffices to reveal much about the kingdom of God. As with every saint close attention to him enables one to see through him Christ, who is his and whom he reveals in what is always a personal and original way. The life-story of the saint we celebrate today allows us to perceive many, very many things of immense interest. First the historical setting, characterized by the crisis of the various expressions of the protestant reform, Lutheran, Anglican, Calvinist and Presbyterian, counteracted by the immense and not vain efforts of the Council of Trent and the intense rebirth of Catholic life, a setting racked by wars, by religious struggle and also by decadence. Our saint cannot be understood outside that violent spiritual storm.

What was the cause of John Ogilvie's martyrdom? It is easy to discover: we would say the faith. But the faith is a world: what point of the faith, what truth of the faith was the keynote of the struggle of his martyrdom? The call authorized by Christ, to announce the faith: 'You will be my witnesses', witnesses, heralds, martyrs. 'Go and teach', 'who hears you, hears me', says Jesus. The teaching Church, the faith taught by an authority, both preceding the very book which documents that authority; we should say today, authentic ecclesiology, which from the Reformation on, has become the very centre of the controversies which disturb the religious unity founded by Christ.

Having discovered this central and sorrow-laden point of the witness of John Ogilvie, we shall go no further in our discourse; here it is enough to note that the holiness of our champion is marked by his testimony of devotion to the Church's magisterium and of faith in the Mass, an act of worship which celebrates the Word of God and truly makes that Word present. But we do not wish to make this tribute an occasion for polemics. We wish rather to express our supreme hope that his martyrdom help to confirm our faith in the Church's magisterium and in the sacramental and sacrificial marvel of the Eucharist. To express the hope that around these supreme truths witnessed to by the new saint may converge the steps, the hearts, of those who then, at the time of his martyrdom, condemned him as a traitor to the loyalty due to the civil power of his country, while he was nothing other than the champion of the autonomy of the religious power, according to the eternal saying of Christ the Lord: 'Render to Caesar what is Caesar's, and to God what is God's.'

Thus it is that, with calm understanding of the dramas of past history and with a favourable indication of a happier one in the future, we can today attribute to the glory of our martyr, with so many others who suffered for the same cause, the merit of having heroically contributed by his sacrifice to claim for society religious freedom, such as Vatican II has set out in its declaration on Religious Freedom: no one ought to be constrained, no one ought to be impeded in the matter of religious profession, while for all there exists the serious moral obligation to seek and follow the truth, especially religious truth.

On this account the saint venerated by us, far from being a symbol of civil or religious difference, will soften the unhappy memory of violence or of the abuse of authority in the interest of religion, and will help all of us to resolve the divisions relating to our respective creeds into sentiments of mutual respect, of calm research into and faithful adherence to the Truth in order to recover that longed-for unity of faith and love, which Christ taught us was the supreme expression of his gospel.

Pope Paul VI, 'Homily on the Occasion of St John Ogilvie's Canonization', 17 October, 1976

17 March
Saint Patrick, *bishop*
Patron of Ireland
In Ireland and Australia: SOLEMNITY
In England, Wales and Scotland: FEAST

See 17 March, General Calendar.

21 April
Saint Anselm, *bishop and doctor of the Church*
In England: MEMORIAL

See 21 April, General Calendar.

23 April
Saint George, *martyr*
Patron of England
In England and Wales: FEAST

See 23 April, General Calendar.

4 May
The Beatified Martyrs of England and Wales
In England: FEAST
In Wales: MEMORIAL

These are some one hundred and sixty martyrs for the faith from the sixteenth and seventeenth centuries who have been beatified but not yet canonized. Their witness is a glory of the Church in England.

The reading is from a Sermon by Mgr Ronald Knox on the English Martyrs in May 1924.

We see around us a proportion of our fellow countrymen, we dare not ask how large a proportion, who are practically out of contact with any sort of Christianity. Not only do they doubt or cold-shoulder the claims of christian doctrine, but they are losing even their hold on christian morality. All that vital legislation of almighty God which protects the sanctity of marriage and family life is simply thrown aside as old-fashioned by the world at large; and what of those, even, who call themselves Christians? Those professedly christian bodies, which might at least have fought by our side for sanctities such as these, debate the law of God as an open question, and decide to adopt it with a minority report! And is the battle finished?

There is, it is no use denying it, an urgency about this daily contact with a half-pagan world which threatens the faith of Catholics and tempts them to lose hope. In the labour of that mental strife, it is from the shrines of the martyrs, from the hiding-places where they lurked and the gibbets where they suffered, that the voice of comfort still hails English Catholics, and bids them fight on. Do we look few and lonely, when we protest at the laxity of our countrymen over the marriage law? Not fewer, not more lonely, than the martyrs who protested against the divorce of Henry VIII. Do we look weak and ill-equipped against the propaganda of our enemies and our rivals? Not weaker, not worse-equipped, than the little stream of missionaries that stole into England, year by year, in the days of the persecution. If we doubt, if we hesitate, how shall we bear comparison with these Old Contemptibles of the Catholic Religion?

We have, St Paul tells us, a great cloud of witnesses standing over us — witnesses, that is, martyrs: it is all the same word. And he tells us to run through patience to the prize that is set before us; he thinks of us, then, as competitors in some race, and of the martyrs as spectators who are watching us, looking down from heaven. And are they content with watching? Do they simply look on, and wonder which side will win? Is that the common attitude of spectators, when they watch an athletic contest? That is not my memory of the days, nearer thirty years ago than I care to think, when I used to watch football matches at the Aston Villa ground. My memory is rather of a small boy, wearing a claret-and-light-blue favour, who stood up on the seat and booed the referee. They are witnesses of our race, these martyrs of ours, but something more than witnesses, partisans who can cheer us to victory with the breath of their applause. For the applause of the saints is that prayer which goes up day and night before the throne of God: 'How long, O Lord, holy and true, dost thou not judge and avenge our blood upon them that dwell on the earth?' And that prayer must be heard, in his own time.

Ronald Knox, 'On the English Martyrs', *Occasional Sermons*, pp 107-8

24 May
Our Lady Help of Christians
Patroness of Australia
In Australia: SOLEMNITY

Our Lady Help of Christians was chosen at the First Provincial Synod of Sydney in 1844 as the Patroness of Australia. In her maternal love Mary cares for those who have become the children of God through baptism in their way through this valley of tears.

As a reading a ninth century hymn to Mary is given.

AVE MARIS STELLA

Mary — 'Star of Ocean' —
Chosen as God's Mother,
Virgin yet remaining —
Very gate of heaven.

Humble Maid of Zion
Use the angel's greeting —
Our salvation founding;
Eva's harm undoing.

Loose the chains that bind us
Ask for all God's favours —
Sight for eyes unseeing,
Evil from us driving.

Show you are a Mother,
He will hear you praying,
Who made man for our sake,
In your womb was carried.

Virgin of all virgins,
In whom is no evil,
Make us pure and holy,
Have our sins forgiven.

Guide us to right living —
Help us as we journey,

So that seeing Jesus
We find rest in heaven.

Prais'd be God our Father,
Who in Christ has saved us —
Born of you, O Mary,
Through the Holy Spirit.

tr. Gerard MacGinty, OSB

25 May
Saint Bede the Venerable, *priest and doctor of the Church*
In England: MEMORIAL

See 25 May, General Calendar.

27 May
Saint Augustine of Canterbury, *bishop*
In England: FEAST

See 27 May, General Calendar.

9 June
Saint Columba (Colmcille), *abbot*
Secondary Patron of Ireland
In Ireland: FEAST
In Scotland: MEMORIAL

Columba was born in County Donegal in the first half of the sixth century, and was of very noble birth. He became a monk at Clonard, then studied at Glasnevin, now a suburb of Dublin, and returned from Glasnevin to found his monastery at Derry — the remnant of the Irish name which meant 'The Oakwood of Colmcille' — at that time Ireland being covered with oakwoods. Other foundations followed in Ireland, notably at Durrow in present-day Offaly. Between 560 and 570 he left Ireland and founded a monastery on the island now known as Iona. There he was to die in 597. Columba was gentle either by nature or grace but could be fearless in the cause of right.

For a generation or two the monastic tradition from Iona was dominant in North Britain, and much of Scotland was evangelized or re-evangelized by its monks, as well as the territories further south.

The reading is taken from the Life of Columba by Adomnan, a later abbot of Iona.

Columba's last days, and death

While the rites of the Mass were celebrated on a Lord's-day according to custom, the venerable man lifted up his eyes, and suddenly his face was seen to flush with a ruddy glow; for, as it is written, 'The countenance glows when the heart is glad'; and in fact at the same moment he alone saw an angel of the Lord hovering above, within the walls of the oratory itself; and because the calm and lovely sight of holy angels fills the hearts of the elect with joy and exultation, this was the cause of the sudden gladness that filled the blessed man.

When those that were present there asked about this, the cause of the gladness inspired in him, the saint, gazing upward, gave them this reply: 'Wonderful and incomparable is the fineness of angelic nature! See, an angel of the Lord, sent to recover a deposit dear to God, looking down upon us within the church and blessing us, has returned through the roof-courses of the church, leaving no trace of that departure.'

At the end of the same week, that is, on the Sabbath Day, the venerable man himself and his devoted attendant Diormit, went to bless the nearest barn. After entering it, and blessing it and two heaps of grain that were there in store, the saint spoke thus, and rendering thanks said: 'I greatly congratulate my family of monks, because in this year also, if I have to depart from you to any place, you will have enough bread for the year'. Then he said: 'This day is called in the sacred books "Sabbath", which is interpreted "rest". And truly this day is for me a Sabbath, because it is the last day for me of this laborious life. In it after my toilsome labours I keep Sabbath; and at midnight of this following venerated Lord's-day, in the language of the scriptures I shall go the way of the fathers. For now my Lord Jesus Christ deigns to invite me. To him I shall depart, I say, when he invites me, in the middle of this night. For so it has been revealed to me by the Lord himself.' The attendant hearing these sad words

374

began to weep bitterly, and the saint tried to comfort him, as well as he could.

He returned to the monastery, and sat in the hut, writing a psalter. And when he came to that verse of the 33rd psalm where it is written, 'But they that seek the Lord shall not want for anything that is good', he said: 'Here, at the end of the page, I must stop. Let Baithene write what follows.'

When his spirit had left the tabernacle of the body, his face continued to be ruddy, and in a wonderful degree gladdened by the vision of angels, so much that it seemed like the face not of a dead man, but of a living sleeper.

This was the end of our memorable patron's life; these were the beginnings of his rewards. Being, in the language of the scriptures, added to the fathers as a sharer in eternal triumphs, united to the apostles and prophets, and joined to the number of the thousands of white-robed saints who have washed their robes in the blood of the Lamb, he attends the Lamb his leader; a virgin unstained, free from every flaw, by the grace of our Lord Jesus Christ himself, who has, with the Father, honour, power, praise, glory, and everlasting dominion, in the unity of the Holy Spirit, through all the ages of the ages. Amen.

Adomnan, *Life of St Columba*, III, 23

20 June
Saint Alban, *protomartyr of Britain*
In England: MEMORIAL

Saints Alban, Julius and Aaron, *protomartyrs*
In Wales: MEMORIAL

Alban would have died probably in the third century. He was beheaded at Verulamium, subsequently named St Alban's. We have abundant fourth century evidence for his martyrdom and the veneration paid to his memory but our first details are contained in the writings of Gildas, though St Bede is a more accessible source. Gildas also mentions Julius and Aaron, who were citizens of Caeleon, and he is followed by Bede, but neither writer gives us any details about them.

The reading is taken from the *Meditation on Christ Crucified* by the Monk of Farne. This is a fourteenth century English writing, long after St Alban, but the passage treats of the question — what can we render to Christ for all he has done for us. St Alban, and all martyrs, have certainly given him their hearts and all their lives too. The reading is appropriate to St Alban, who died as the result of his charity in shielding a priest of Christ and then giving himself up for him.

'There the love of the members for their head will be perfect and without measure, such as it cannot be here. For there will be ineffable joy in the unspeakable delight of divine fruition, unsurpassable longing, unimaginable sweetness, all-embracing knowledge, power which can do all things, satiety which knows no distaste, security which has no fear. It is for these and other such like things that I suffered.'

What then, Lord, of the law, the prophets, the gospel, in all of which we are bidden to do so many and such great things in order to see thee? Answer me yet, I beg you, Lord, this one question: what do you desire us to give you in return for the sufferings you have endured for us? Speak, Lord, for your servants listen, ready to receive the engrafted word which is able to save their souls. 'If you desire to know this plainly, call your husband, that you may understand aright. Let him who has ears to hear, hear what Christ says now to the churches.

'Behold the inheritance of the Lord and reward of the son is the fruit of the womb. It is this that I desire above all things, nor is there anything among men which I so long for.' Good Jesus, what is this that you desire so ardently and claim as your special reward? Does not every man, every womb, every fruit belong to you, and in short are not all things yours both visible and invisible? What is this fruit of the womb that you so eagerly demand? Something desirable and inestimably precious is here implied, which, because we are as yet without understanding, is hidden from our eyes, until the declaration of your words give understanding to little ones. O kind and lovable Lord Jesus, tell us plainly what you mean by the fruit of the womb.

You answer: 'In all your house there is nothing that I so covet as your heart; not that fleshy object but its love. This is the fruit that I desire, which is more precious to me than all riches, and nothing that is desirable can be compared with it. There is nothing more precious within you, and therefore it may with reason be called the fruit of the womb. It is for this that I ask, it is this that I prize beyond all other offerings; to dwell within it is my delight, and I suffered for you solely that you might give it to me.'

Good Jesus, I grant what you ask, and wish to give you what you desire; but you will never have my heart, unless you first give me yourself, partly because I will not hand over my treasure except in exchange for something better, and partly because without you I can do nothing.

The Monk of Farne, Meditation on Christ Crucified, cc 16-17

22 June

Saints John Fisher, bishop, and Thomas More, martyrs

In England: FEAST
In Wales: MEMORIAL

See 22 June, General Calendar.

1 July

Saint Oliver Plunkett, bishop and martyr

In Ireland: FEAST

Oliver belonged to an old Pale family and was born in the first half of the seventeenth century. His life ambition was to become a priest and he was ordained in Rome in 1654. In Rome he taught theology for twelve years, then, in 1669, he was nominated archbishop of Armagh. On coming back to Ireland he was first fairly free to work among his people, and did an immense amount to raise christian standards and observance. The political situation became less and less favourable and Oliver's difficulties were compounded by a group of mal-contents, a rather unsavoury group of renegade priests and friars.

In 1679 he was indicted on perjured evidence, and brought to London in 1680 because no Irish jury would condemn him. He was executed at Tyburn in 1681, and was the last Catholic to suffer there.

During his time in prison he formed a close spiritual relationship with an English fellow prisoner, a Benedictine monk, Dom Maurus Corker. The reading is from a lengthy letter the latter wrote the day after St Oliver's martyrdom.

Concerning the manner and state of his prayer he seemed most devoted to pathetic sentences taken out of holy Scripture, the Divine Office and missal, which he made me procure for him three months before he died, upon these sentences he let his soul dilate itself in love following herein the sweet impulse and dictate of the Holy Spirit, and reading his prayer wrote rather in heart than in his book according to that of the Apostle.

'The Spirit comes to the aid of our weakness; when we do not know what prayer to offer, to pray as we ought, the Spirit himself intercedes for us, with groans beyond all utterance: and God, who can read our hearts, knows well what the Spirit's intent is; for indeed it is according to the mind of God that he makes intercession for the saints.'

And 'The influence of his anointing lives on in you, so that you have no need of teaching.' For this reason I suppose it was, that when with great humility he sent me his last speech to correct, he also wrote me word, he would not at the place of execution make use of any other set form or method of prayer than the *Pater Noster, Ave Maria, Credo, Miserere, In manus tuas Domine,* etc. And for the rest he would breathe forth his soul in such prayer and ejaculations as God Almighty should inspire him withal.

He continually endeavoured to improve and advance himself in the purity of divine love and by consequence also in contrition for his sins past, of his deficiency in both which this humble soul complained to me as the only thing that troubled him. Indeed the more we love, the more we desire it, and the more we desire it the more we love, so that desire increaseth our love, and love our desire. And if we may measure this happy martyr's love by the rule of our Saviour, 'This is the greatest love a man can show, that he should lay down his life for his friends,' we shall find him perfect in love. For in him was fulfilled that saying of the Canticles, *love is strong as death* (Cant 8:6).

This love it was which extinguished in him all fear of death, 'Love has no room for fear' says the apostle 'and indeed, love drives out fear when it is perfect love'. A lover feareth not but rejoices at the approach of his beloved; hence the joy of our holy martyr seemed still to increase together with his danger and was fully accomplished by an assurance of death. The very night before he died being now as it were at heart's ease he went to bed at eleven of the clock and slept quietly and soundly till four in the morning, at which time his man who lay in the room awakened him; so little concern had he upon his spirits, or rather so much had the loveliness of the end beautified the horror of the passage to it. 'Not that I could take these present sufferings as the measure of that glory which is to be revealed in us.' He further likewise received an exceeding comfort (as well he might) in that divine pledge of present love and future glory, viz. the most holy sacrament and sacrifice of the altar. The happiness of which by God's blessing and the private assistance of his man he enjoyed daily, for a whole week together, and even that very morning whereon he died.

Dom Maurus Corker, A Letter Concerning the Death of Oliver Plunkett,
2 July 1681

26 August
Saint Ninian, bishop
In Scotland: MEMORIAL

Ninian is an extremely hazy figure. It would seem that he spanned the fourth and fifth centuries, and is said to have died in the year 432, although if some early Irish sources are to be relied on, his dates would be a generation or two later. Traditionally he built a church and a monastery, called 'Candida Casa' (the White Cottage), at Whithorn in Galloway. He and his disciples are said to have preached the gospel in Scotland, south east of the Highlands. These traditions are probably well founded.

The reading is from Aelred of Rievaulx's Life of Saint Ninian. Many centuries separated the two saints and, although Aelred states that his work is based on an earlier 'barbarously' written Life, there is little concrete evidence of this. The account here given concerns the death of Ninian and it contains litle more than pious generalities expressed, originally, in elegant medieval Latin which we, inevitably, find contrived. In the translation I have tried to retain some of the cadences of the original.

On the death of Ninian

Marvellously resplendent with these, and other marvels of the same kind, and mighty with the virtues that count most, the most blessed Ninian, after a successful journey, arrived at the day of his being called forth. That day, for the blessed man, was a day of rejoicing and gladness, but, for the people over whom he presided, it was a day of distress and misery. He, to whom the heavens were opening, exulted, the people, who were being deprived of such a father, grieved. He, for whom an everlasting crown was being got ready, rejoiced; the people, whose everlasting salvation was still at risk, were made sad. Indeed, love was qualifying his joy, since it seemed a serious matter to abandon them, yet intolerable to be separated any longer from Christ. But Christ was comforting the soul which hesitated. Rise up, he says, my beloved, rise up my dove, and come. Yes! Rise up, he says, my beloved, rise up my dove, rise up by understanding, set out by desire, come by love. This call well suited, as a friend of the bridegroom, that most blessed man, to whom the heavenly bridegroom had entrusted his bride; to whom he had revealed his secrets, and opened his treasures. Rightly is that soul called beloved, as it holds fast wholly out of love with no trace of fear. My love, he says, my dove. Truly a dove! a dove taught to lament, which did not know the gall of bitterness, wept with those who wept, was weak with the weak, was disturbed with those made to fall! Rise up, set out, my beloved, my dove, and come; for winter now is passed, gone away has the heavy rain and departed. Then indeed, O blessed man! the winter has passed when you merited to contemplate with fortunate eye your heavenly fatherland, a land which the Sun of justice enlightens with the light of his glory, which love reddens, which the marvellous harmony of things, as it were the temperateness of spring, regulates with a seasonal concord too great for words. . . .

So the blessed Ninian, made perfect in life, seasoned in age, passed happily from this world. He is borne to heaven by accompanying angelic spirits to receive his eternal reward. Where, beyond all doubt, joined to the choir of apostles, added to the ranks of the martyrs, set among the multitudes of confessors, furnished even

with the flowers of the virgins, he does not cease to aid those who
hope in him, those who cry to him, those who praise him. . . . At his
most holy tomb the sick are healed, the lepers cleansed, the impious
put in fear, the blind given light: by all of which the faith of believers
is strengthened to the praise and glory of our Lord Jesus Christ!

Vita Niniani, c 11

26 August, also
Blessed Dominic of the Mother of God, *priest*
In England: OPTIONAL MEMORIAL

Dominic Barberi was born near Viterbo in Italy in 1792. In 1814 he joined the
Passionists and received the added patronage of the Mother of God. As he
developed in the religious and spiritual life he felt himself called to work for
the reconciliation and conversion of England. This was not something which
he could set his hand to overnight, but he did prepare himself very carefully
by studying the English religious scene and Anglican positions. He eventually
arrived in England in 1841 and within eight years had established four houses
of his Congregation. He preached up and down England and brought many to
the faith. It was he who received the future Cardinal Newman into the
Church.

Newman was an admirer of his, but attributed his conversion more to the
influence of Dr Russell of Maynooth. Blessed Dominic did, though, play a
major role in the movement to Rome in the 1840's and not least by a very significant article he wrote in the French Review 'Univers'. He died at Reading on
27 August, 1849. The reading is from the homily preached by Pope Paul VI on
the occasion of Blessed Dominic's Beatification in 1963. Another part of the
same homily is used in the Divine Office for today.

One of the purposes which inspires the Church to accord to any one
of its members such a solemn exaltation, which we now call beatification, is to make known a particular and victorious son of hers, and
to propose him to the veneration of the faithful, either as a privileged
soul, in whom the action of grace has been deeper and more manifest, or as an example, in whom the strength of virtue has been more
vigorous and instructive.

This means that the Church confers on one of its sons a public and official honour, which from one aspect resounds to the glory of God, from another reflects on itself, for our common edification, just as a lamp, lit in honour of the divinity, also lights up the assembly of the faithful gathered for prayer. And this time such a bright reflection shines on us almost by surprise, because, apart from the confreres of the new Beatus, and a small section of devout and studious people, Fr Dominic was not very well known among us. He was not a popular figure. This beatification then, comes to cast light on a person of great merit, and not only on one account.

We come to know in this way that Fr Dominic is worth remembering as a scholastic writer of some good studies in theology and philosophy: his study of papal infallibility, for example, anticipated with sure insight into the doctrine, the definition which so many years later the First Vatican Council was to proclaim. We discover that Fr Dominic was a fecund author of books on asceticism and mysticism, among them his own autobiography, the greater part of which remain in manuscript: writings which perhaps are not always satisfying with regard to our literary standards, but always of significance for the worthy illustration of religious life in the last century, and still of value for the enriching of thought and of the experience of the history of spirituality, being the fruit of wide and deep study, of prolonged reflection and inner elaboration.

This profile of the man of sacred letters will certainly make the profile of the man of action and of prayer more interesting for all of us. We must know that Fr Dominic was a great master of ascetic discipline, a tireless preacher, an apostle and an apologist fully abreast of the patterns of thought contemporary with himself, aware also of old and new ideas, and of dangerous errors; and that he gave himself to a correspondence with men of ideas and of action in a much wider circle than his religious house or its neighbourhood. Action then entered his life: positions of authority in his religious congregation, journeys, foundations. He dedicated himself to the Passion of Christ and to devotion to the Mother of Sorrows.

> Pope Paul VI, 'Homily on the Occasion of the Beatification of
> Blessed Dominic Barberi', 27 October 1963

3 September
Saint Gregory the Great, *pope and doctor of the Church*
Apostle of the English
In England: FEAST

See 3 September, General Calendar.

24 September
Our Lady of Ransom
In England: MEMORIAL

This celebration is of Spanish origin and was linked with the recovery of captives from the Muslims. It was introduced into England in the last century, with the active encouragement of Pope Leo XIII, with the idea of recovering the Dowry of Mary.

The reading is a prayer of St Anselm to Mary.

Well does the world know, nor can we sinners ever forget it; well, O Lady, do we know who was that Son of man who came to seek and to save that which was lost; nor do we forget that if he was the Son of man, it was because he was your Son. Will you then, O Lady and the Mother of my hope, will you forget that truth which was so mercifully revealed to the world, so gladly published, and so lovingly received? That good Son of man came to save what was lost, and came without being asked; and will his mother despise that lost one even when she is asked? That good Son of man came to call the sinner to repentance; and will his good mother despise the sinner even when the sinner repents? That good God, I say — that meek and lowly man, that merciful Son of God, that compassionate Son of man — came to seek the sinner wandering far away; and will you, his good mother and powerful mother of God, will you repel the wanderer when he returns and prays?

As the Son of God is the bliss of the saints, so is your Son the salvation of sinners. There is no hope of pardon but in him who was conceived of you; no justification but in him who was borne by you; no salvation but in him who was born of you. Therefore, O Lady, you are the mother of him who pardons and of those who are pardoned — of him who justifies and of those who are justified — of him who saves and of those who are saved. O blessed confidence! O safe refuge! The mother of God is our mother; the mother of him in whom alone we hope and whom alone we fear is our mother; the mother of him who alone can save or destroy is our mother.

St Anselm, 'Prayer to Mary'

13 October
Saint Edward the Confessor, *king*
In England: MEMORIAL

Edward was the last Saxon king of England and came to the throne in 1042. He was not a failure as a king but was not strong in the sense of his Norman successors and England was a disturbed land during most of his reign, as it had been for decades past. He was deeply concerned for the poor and a great benefactor of the Church. He died on 5 January, 1066.

Today is the anniversary of his enshrining in Westminster Abbey in 1268. The Abbey had been rebuilt by him as part commutation for a vow to go on pilgrimage to the Holy Land.

The reading is taken from the Sermons of Mgr Ronald Knox: part of the same sermon is used in the Divine Office for today, but that given here has a more direct message for us.

Our divine Lord, quoting from the psalms of David, has assured us that the meek shall possess the earth. Does that mean that meekness is one of those qualities which will gain men a brighter crown in the heavenly kingdom that is to come? It does, of course, but does it mean nothing more? Certainly in this, as in any other age of history, it does not seem as if it is the meek who carry off the world's prizes; go where you will, the advertisements of the mind-training systems and the correspondence colleges will cry out to you that life is a stern battle, that success is for the ambitious, and that the weakest goes to the wall. There is no room, it would seem, for the saintly albinos. Does Christianity, then, simply preach the survival of the unfittest, by promising us in heaven a reversal of all human values and a revision of all human judgments? And must it always be, in this world, the Godwins and the Harolds and the Williams who have the best time, make the best use of their opportunities?

The land of a certain rich man brought forth plenty of fruits. And he thought within himself, saying: 'What shall I do, because I have no room here to bestow my fruits?' And he said: 'This will I do; I will pull down my barns, and will build greater and into them I will gather all things that are grown to me and my goods. And I will say to my soul: "Soul, you have many good things laid up for many years: take your rest, eat, drink, make good cheer".' But God said to him: 'You fool, this night do they require your soul of you. And whose shall those things be which you have provided?' So is he that layeth up treasure for himself and is not rich towards God.

In that telling, almost bitter parable, our divine Lord has shown us the fallacy of the successful life, not only from the point of view of the next world, but even in this. If the rich fool had not died then, do you think he would really have carried out his resolution of retiring from business? Not he. He would have gone on, as he had already gone on all those years, wearing himself out in the pursuit of a visionary contentment which he continually promised himself, yet could never rest to enjoy. A record harvest? Why, then, he must build yet greater barns. And when the barns were built, he would have extended his farming operations so as to have more fruits to fill them with. He was a fool, because he became the slave of his own ambitions. Mind you, we are not told that he was wicked. We are not told that, like Dives, he neglected the poor, and went like Dives into the place of torment. No, we are only told that he was a fool; that his life was a wasted one. No doubt but his funeral sermon and his obituary notices called him a successful man; a pioneer of agriculture, and one who had revolutionized the old type of barn. But in the stillness of the night in which God spoke to him, he knew that he was a failure.

R.A. Knox, *Occasional Sermons*, pp 26-27

25 October
The Forty Martyrs of England and Wales
In England: FEAST

The Six Welsh Martyrs and Companions, *martyrs*
In Wales: FEAST

These are some seven laymen and women, thirteen secular priests and twenty religious who were canonized by Pope Paul VI in 1970. They are representative of the many faithful souls who gave their lives for their Catholic convictions in the course of the sixteenth and seventeenth centuries.

As a reading a poem of one of their number St Robert Southwell is given here. It is entitled *Of the Blessed Sacrament of the Aulter,* and the Real Presence in the Sacrament was one of the doctrines for which the martyrs died.

Of the Blessed Sacrament of the Aulter

The angells' eyes, whome veyles cannot deceive,
Might best disclose that best they do descerne;
Men must with sounde and silent faith receive
More then they can by sence or reason lerne;
God's poure our proofes, His workes our witt exceede,
The doer's might is reason of His deede.

A body is endew'd with ghostly rightes;
And Nature's worke from Nature's law is free;
In heavenly sunne lye hidd eternall lightes,
Lightes cleere and neere, yet them no eye can see;
Dedd formes a never-dyinge life do shroude;
A boundlesse sea lyes in a little cloude.

The God of hoastes in slender hoste doth dwell,
Yea, God and man with all to ether dewe,
That God that rules the heavens and rifled hell,
That man whose death did us to life renewe:
That God and man that is the angells' blisse,
In forme of bredd and wyne our nurture is.

Whole may His body be in smallest breadd,
Whole in the whole, yea whole in every crumme;

With which be one or be tenn thowsand fedd,
All to ech one, to all but one doth cumme;
And though ech one as much as all receive,
Not one too much, nor all too little have.

One soule in man is all in everye part;
One face at once in many mirrhors shynes;
One fearefull noyse doth make a thowsand start;
One eye at once of countlesse thinges defynes;
If proofes of one in many, Nature frame,
God may in straunger sort performe the same.

God present is at once in everye place,
Yett God in every place is ever one;
So may there be by giftes of ghostly grace,
One man in many roomes, yett filling none
Sith angells may effects of bodyes shewe,
God angells' giftes on bodyes may bestowe.

St Robert Southwell, *Of the Blessed Sacrament of the Aulter*

6 November
All Saints of Ireland
In Ireland: FEAST

This globular feast was instituted by indult of Pope Benedict XV. It includes all the Saints who were revered in Ireland before the Reformation, and who are far too many to be named.

The reading given is from a pastoral letter from the archbishops and bishops of Ireland, St Patrick's Day 1980.

'Tradition' is a basic Christian term.
It means 'handing on';
'handing on the faith'.
In the Church today and always,
it means exactly the same thing
as it meant in the Bible from the beginning:
it means the handing on of faith

from father and mother
to son and daughter,
to grandson and granddaughter.
The link across the generations
must never be broken.
No 'generation gap' must ever be allowed to break
the continuity in the handing on of the faith,
If ever one generation is lost to the Faith,
it is difficult and rare
for the next generation to return once more
to the faith of their grandparents.
The believing and praying hands
must be kept linked across the generations,
and the link must not be broken.

You parents must choose.
You can either be a 'hander on'
or you can be a deserter and betrayer.
Parents either hand on faith to their children
or they hand on unbelief.
They can't just take a neutral stance
and leave the child 'to decide for himself or herself'
when he or she grows up.
Such a parent has already taken a decision
for the child;
and that decision is that religion
isn't really important.

Handing on the faith is like a relay race,
in which one team hands on the torch or baton
to the team taking over from it.
If the torch is once allowed to fall,
if the baton is once dropped and lost,
each succeeding team, however hard it tries,
will have great difficulty
in reaching the finishing tape.

It is not so much a question

of handing on a set of truths or facts.
It is more a matter
of keeping hands linked
with the young faithful who will follow us.
It is a matter of training and forming
the next 'relay team' of young believers.

We must remember that
before there were any schools,
the faith was handed on by the family.

If we have the precious gift of faith today,
this is because the parents and families
of the past
knew it was their primary duty as Catholics,
to teach the faith to their children.

Pastoral Letter from the Archbishops and Bishops of Ireland,
March 17, 1980, 'Handing on the Faith in the Home', n 5

16 November
Saint Margaret
Secondary Patron Saint of Scotland
In Scotland: FEAST

See 16 November, General Calendar.

30 November
Saint Andrew, *apostle*
Principal Patron of Scotland
In Scotland: SOLEMNITY

See 30 November, General Calendar.

29 December
Saint Thomas of Canterbury, *bishop and martyr*
In England: FEAST

See 29 December, General Calendar.

INDEX OF AUTHORS AND SOURCES OF READINGS

The publishers acknowledge with thanks permission to reproduce copyright texts listed in this index.

The readings have been chosen from existing published sources or prepared for this edition. Classic English texts, such as those of Newman, are given as originally printed, but otherwise the vocabulary and grammatical forms of older texts have been adapted to contemporary usage, as well as universalized, where feasible. Texts which are translations have been revised in a similar sense, and this particularly because the primary purpose of this book is spiritual usefulness and not scientific exactitude. Care has, however, been taken not to falsify the thought of the original writer.

In this index:

(a) after an entry indicates that some *a*lterations have been in the vocabulary or divisions of the text.

(r) indicates a more extensive *r*evision or *r*ewriting of the original.

(e) indicates a version done for this edition.

*after a date indicates that the reading is to be found in the National Calendar of Saints at the end of the volume.